THE FATHERS
OF THE CHURCH

A NEW TRANSLATION

VOLUME 143

THE FATHERS OF THE CHURCH

A NEW TRANSLATION

MORALIA ET ASCETICA ARMENIACA

THE OFT-REPEATED DISCOURSES

Translated by

ABRAHAM TERIAN

Armenian Title

YAČAXAPATUM ČAṘK'

THE CATHOLIC UNIVERSITY OF AMERICA PRESS

Washington, D.C.

The Scripture quotation marked as NIV on page 205 is taken from the
Holy Bible, New International Version®, NIV®. Copyright © 1973, 1978, 1984,
2011 by Biblica, Inc.™ Used by permission of Zondervan. All rights reserved
worldwide. www.zondervan.com. The "NIV" and "New International Version"
are trademarks registered in the United States Patent and Trademark Office
by Biblica, Inc.™

Library of Congress Cataloging-in-Publication Data
Names: Terian, Abraham, 1942– translator.
Title: Moralia et ascetica armeniaca : the oft-repeated discourses :
Yačaxapatum čaṙkʻ / translated by Abraham Terian.
Other titles: Hachakhapatum. English. | Oft-repeated discourses :
Yačaxapatum čaṙkʻ
Description: Washington : The Catholic University of America Press, 2021. |
Includes bibliographical references and index.
Identifiers: LCCN 2021038265 | ISBN 9780813234793 (cloth) |
ISBN 9780813234809 (ebook)
Subjects: LCSH: Sermons, Armenian—Translations into English. |
Armenian Church—History.
Classification: LCC BX126.6 .G6813 2021 | DDC 248.8/94—dc23
LC record available at https://lccn.loc.gov/2021038265

To my daughter Sonia

CONTENTS

CONTENTS

APPENDICES

INDICES

TRANSCRIPTION OF ARMENIAN

Hübschmann-Meillet-Benveniste System

Ա	Բ	Գ	Դ	Ե	Զ	Է	Ը	Թ	Ժ
ա	բ	գ	դ	ե	զ	է	ը	թ	ժ
a	**b**	**g**	**d**	**e**	**z**	**ē**	**ě**	**t'**	**ž**

Ի	Լ	Խ	Ծ	Կ	Հ	Ձ	Ղ	Ճ	Մ
ի	լ	խ	ծ	կ	հ	ձ	ղ	ճ	մ
i	**l**	**x**	**c**	**k**	**h**	**j**	**ł**	**č**	**m**

Յ	Ն	Շ	Ո	Չ	Պ	Ջ	Ռ	Ս	Վ
յ	ն	շ	ո	չ	պ	ջ	ռ	ս	վ
y	**n**	**š**	**o**	**č'**	**p**	**ǰ**	**ṙ**	**s**	**v**

Տ	Ր	Ց	Ւ	Փ	Ք	Օ	Ֆ	ՈՒ	ԵՒ
տ	ր	ց	ւ	փ	ք	օ	ֆ	ու	և / ու
t	**r**	**c'**	**w**	**p'**	**k'**	**o**	**f**	**u**	**ew**

ABBREVIATIONS

ANF	Ante-Nicene Fathers
AVANT	AVANT: Treasures of the Armenian Christian Tradition
BAR	*Biblical Archaeology Review*
BM	*Banber Matenadarani*
BSOAS	*Bulletin of the School of Oriental and African Studies*
CCSG	Corpus Christianorum: Series Graeca
CSCO	Corpus Scriptorum Christianorum Orientalium
CSS	Cistercian Studies Series
CWS	The Classics of Western Spirituality
DOP	*Dumbarton Oaks Papers*
ECTT	Eastern Christian Texts in Translation
EncMon	*Encyclopedia of Monasticism* (see Johnston and Renkin)
FC	The Fathers of the Church
GECS	Gorgias Eastern Christianity Studies
HA	*Handēs Amsōreay* (*Handes Amsorya*)
HATS	Harvard Armenian Texts and Studies
HR	*History of Religions*
HUAS	Hebrew University Armenian Studies
IJAIS	*The International Journal of Ancient Iranian Studies*
JCSSS	*Journal of the Canadian Society for Syriac Studies*
LASBF	*Liber Annuus Studii Biblici Franciscani*
LCL	The Loeb Classical Library
LEC	Library of Early Christianity

LR	Basil of Caesarea, *Long Rules*
LXX	Septuagint
MH	Matenagirkʻ Hayocʻ (Armenian Classical Authors)
Mus	*Le Muséon: Revue d'études orientales*
NBHL	*Nor baṙgirkʻ haykazean lezui* (see Awedikʻian et al.)
NPNF[1-2]	*Nicene and Post-Nicene Fathers* (1st and 2nd series)
OC	*Oriens Christianus*
OCA	Orientalia Christiana Analecta
OECS	Oxford Early Christian Studies
OECT	Oxford Early Christian Texts
ParOr	*Parole de l'Orient*
PBH	*Patma-banasirakan handes*
PG	Patrologia Graeca
PGL	*A Patristic Greek Lexicon* (see Lampe)
PL	Patrologia Latina
PO	Patrologia Orientalis
PPS	Popular Patristics Series
REArm	*Revue des études arméniennes*
REG	*Revue des études grecques*
RHE	*Revue d'histoire ecclésiastique*
ROC	*Revue de l'Orient chrétien*
RSR	*Recherches de science religieuse*
SC	Sources chrétiennes
SISOT	Sophia Institute Studies in Orthodox Theology
SNTR	*St. Nersess Theological Review*
SR	Basil of Caesarea, *Short Rules*
ST	Studi et Testi
TCH	Transformation of the Classical Heritage
TSEC	Texts and Studies in Eastern Christianity
TU	Texte und Untersuchungen

BIBLIOGRAPHY

Editions of the *Yačaxapatum*

Girk' or koč'i Yačaxapatum, Asac'[ea]l S. Hōrn meroy eranelwoyn Grigori Lusaworč'in ... (*Book Which Is Called Yačaxapatum, spoken by our Father the Blessed St. Gregory the Illuminator ...*). Constantinople: Tparan Astuacatur Kostandnupolsec'u, 1737; repr. Calcutta: Tparan Awet Jĕnt'lumeani, 1813; Constantinople: Gorcaran Abraham Amirayi, 1824.

Srboy Hōrn Meroy Grigori Lusaworč'i Yačaxapatum Čaŕk' ew Ałot'k' (*Oft-Repeated Discourses and a Prayer of Our Holy Father Gregory the Illuminator*). Venice: S. Łazar, 1838, 1954.

Srboy Hōrn Meroy Eranelwoyn Grigori Lusaworč'i Yačaxapatum Čaŕk' Lusawork' (*Oft-Repeated [and] Enlightened Discourses of Our Blessed Father Gregory the Illuminator*). Edited by Aršak Tēr Mik'elian. Vałaršapat / Ējmiacin: Mother See of Holy Ējmiacin, 1894.

"*Yačaxapatum čaŕk'.*" Pages 7–137 in MH 1: E. Dar (Armenian Classical Authors 1: Fifth Cent.). Edited by Hakob K'eōsēian. Armenian Library of the Calouste Gulbenkian Foundation. Antelias: Armenian Catholicosate of Cilicia, 2003.

Translations of the *Yačaxapatum*

Reden und Lehren des hl. Gregorius des Erleuchters, Patriarch von Armenien. Translated by Johann M. Schmid. Regensburg: Druck & Verlag von G. J. Manz, 1872.

"Ausgewählte Reden aus dem *Hatschachapatum* vom hl. Mesrop." Pages 1:237–318 in *Ausgewählte Schriften der armenischen Kirchenväter.* Edited by Simon Weber. 2 vols. Bibliothek der Kirchenväter, Series 1, 57–58. Munich: Verlag Josef Kösel & Friedrich Pustet, 1927 (incl. Disc. 1–2, 4–6, 14–15, numbered 1–7, with an introduction by Weber).

"S. Grigor Lusaworč'i «Yačaxapatumĕ»" (E. Armenian). Translated by Mesrop Aramian and Seta Stambōlc'ian. Ganjasar 4 (1993): 134–64 (Disc. 1–2, 16, and 19).

S. Grigor Lusaworič'. Yačaxapatum čaŕer (E. Armenian). Translated by Vazgēn Hambarjumian. Tehran: Armenian Prelacy, 2003.

Yačaxapatum. S. Mesrop Maštoc' (E. Armenian). Translated by Movsēs A. Načarian. Aleppo: Tp. Arewelk', 2005.

Primary Sources

Aelius Aristides. *Xōsk' srboyn Aristideay Imastasiri At'enac'woy / Sancti Aristides Philosophi Atheniensis sermones duo.* Edited and translated by Félix A. P. Dupanloup. Venice: Patres Mechitaristae, 1878. Reprinted in *Analecta Sacra, Tom. IV: Patres Antenicaeni.* Edited and translated by Joannes Baptista Pitra. Paris: Ex Publico Galliarum Typographeo, 1883.

Agathangelos. *Patmut'iwn Hayoc'.* MH 2:1295–1424, 1647–1735. *Agathangelos: History of the Armenians.* Translated by Robert W. Thomson. Albany, NY: State University of New York Press, 1976 (Armenian text included).

―――. *The Lives of Saint Gregory. The Armenian, Greek, Arabic, and Syriac Versions of the "History" Attributed to Agathangelos.* Translated by Robert W. Thomson. Ann Arbor, MI: Caravan, 2010.

Aphrahat. *Demonstrationes. The Demonstrations of Aphrahat, the Persian Sage.* Translated by Adam Lehto. GECS 27. Piscataway, NJ: Gorgias Press, 2010.

―――. *Srboy Hōrn meroy Yakobay Mcbnay Episkoposi Čařk'. Sancti Patris Nostri Jacobi Episcopi Nisibeni Sermones (sic).* Edited by Niccolò M. Antonelli. Rome: Typiis Sacrae Congregationis de Propaganda Fide, 1756.

―――. *La version arménienne des œuvres d'Aphraate le Syrien.* Edited and translated by Guy Lafontaine. CSCO 382–383, 405–406, 423–424. Leuven: Sécretariat du CSCO, 1977–1980.

Apophthegmata Patrum (see *Vark' Haranc'*).

Athenagoras. *Legatio pro Christianis.* PG 6:889–972.

Basil of Caesarea. *Regulae.* In *Ascetical Works.* Translated by M. Monica Wagner. FC 9. Washington, DC: The Catholic University of America Press, 1950. Armenian version with Italian translation: *Basilio di Cesarea: Il libro delle domande (Le regole).* Edited and translated by Gabriella Uluhogian. CSCO 536–537, Scriptores Armeniaci 19–20. Leuven: Peeters, 1993.

―――. *Adversus iratos* (Hom. 10). PG 31:353–372. Translated by Wagner. In *Ascetical Works,* 447–61. (See above.)

―――. *Epistulae.* In *Letters. Vol. I (1–185).* Translated by Agnes Clare Way. FC 13. Washington, DC: The Catholic University of America Press, 1951.

―――. *Homiliae in hexaemeron.* Syriac version: *The Syriac Version of the Hexaemeron by Basil of Caesarea.* Edited by Robert W. Thomson. CSCO 511, Scriptores Syri 223. Leuven: Peeters, 1995. Armenian version: *Barseł Kesarac'i: Yatags vec'aw-reay arařč'ut'ean.* Edited by Kim Muradyan. Erevan: Haykakan SSH GA Hra-tarakč'ut'yun, 1984.

―――. *De humilitate* (Hom. 20). PG 31:525–540. Translated by Wagner. In *Ascetical Works,* 475–86. (See above.)

―――. *De jejunio* (Hom. 1–2). PG 31:163–184, 185–198. Armenian version: *S. Barseł Kesarac'i: Girk' Pahoc'.* Edited by Kim Muradyan. Ekełec'akan Matenagrut'yun 2. Ējmiacin: Mayr At'oř, 2008.

―――. *Quaestiones fratrum (Small Asketikon).* Syriac version: *Questions of the Brothers: Syriac Text and English Translation.* Edited and translated by Anna M. Silvas. TSEC 3. Leiden: Brill, 2014.

―――. *De Spiritu Sancto.* PG 32:68–217.

The Book of Steps: The Syriac Liber Graduum. Translated by Robert A. Kitchen and Martien F. G. Parmentier. CSS 196. Kalamazoo, MI: Cistercian Publications; Edinburgh: Alban, 2004.

Cyril of Alexandria. *Commentarius in Johannem.* PG 73–74.

Cyril of Jerusalem. *Catecheses. The Works of Saint Cyril of Jerusalem.* Translated by Leo P. McCauley and Anthony A. Stephenson. FC 61, 64. Washington, DC: The Catholic University of America Press, 1969–1970.

Cyril of Scythopolis. *Vitae. Cyril of Scythopolis: Lives of the Monks of Palestine.* Translated by Richard M. Price. CSS 114. Kalamazoo, MI: Cistercian Publications, 1991.

———. *Kyrillos von Skythopolis, Leben des Euthymius.* Edited by Eduard Schwartz. TU 49.2. Leipzig: Hinrichs, 1939.

Eusebius of Caesarea. *Praeparatio evangelica.* Edited and translated by Edwin H. Gifford. *De evangelica praeparatione.* 4 vols. Oxford: E Typographeo academico Novi Eboraci: H. Frowde, 1903.

Evagrius of Pontus: The Greek Ascetic Corpus (Chapters on Prayer). Translated by Robert E. Sinkewicz. OECS. Oxford: Oxford University Press, 2003.

Eznik of Kołb. *Ełc ałandoc' (Refutation of the Sects [De Deo]).* MH 1:433–512. *A Treatise on God Written in Armenian by Eznik of Kołb.* Translated by Monica J. Blanchard and Robin Darling Young. ECTT 2. Leuven: Peeters, 1998.

The Gospel of Nicodemus: The Descent of Christ into Hell. Pages 94–165 in *The Apocryphal New Testament.* Translated by M(ontague) R(hodes) James. Oxford: Clarendon Press, 1924.

Gregory of Narek. *Matean ołbergut'ean (Book of Penitential Prayers).* MH 12:49–605. Edited by P. M. Khach'atryan and A. A. Ghazinyan. Erevan: Haykakan SSH GA Hratarakč'ut'yun, 1985. *Speaking with God from the Depths of the Heart: The Armenian Prayer Book of St. Gregory of Narek.* Translated by Thomas J. Samuelian. 2nd ed. Erevan: Vem Press, 2001. *From the Depths of the Heart: Annotated Translation of the Prayers of St. Gregory of Narek.* Translated by Abraham Terian. Collegeville, MN: Liturgical Press, 2021.

Gregory Nazianzen. *Orationes.* PG 35–36.

Gregory of Nyssa. *De beatitudinibus.* PG 44:1193–1301.

———. *De virginitate.* PG 46:317–416.

Hermes Trismegistus. *Hermetica (Asclepius). Hermès en Haute-Égypte.* Edited and translated by Jean-Pierre Mahé. 2 vols. Quebec: Presses de l'Université Laval, 1978–1982.

Hippolytus. *De Fide.* Edited and translated by Gérard Garitte. "Le traité géorgien 'Sur la Foi' attribué à Hippolyte." *Mus* 78 (1965): 119–72.

Ignatius of Antioch. *Epistle to the Ephesians.* Pages 87–95 in *The Apostolic Fathers.* Translated by Francis X. Glimm, Joseph M.-F. Marique, and Gerald G. Walsh. FC 1. Washington, DC: The Catholic University of America Press, 1947.

Infancy Gospel. *The Armenian Gospel of the Infancy.* Translated by Abraham Terian. Oxford: Oxford University Press, 2008.

Irenaeus. *Adversus haereses. Irénée de Lyon: Contre les hérésies,* Livres I–V. Edited and translated by Adelin Rousseau et al. SC 100.1–2, 152, 153, 210, 211, 263, 264, 293, 294. Paris: Éditions du Cerf, 1965–1982.

———. *Epideixis tou apostolikou kērygmatos. Irénée de Lyon: Démonstration de la prédication apostolique.* Edited and translated by Adelin Rousseau. SC 406. Paris: Éditions du Cerf, 1995. Translated (from Armenian) by John Behr. *St. Irenaeus of Lyon: On the Apostolic Preaching.* PPS 17. Crestwood, NY: St. Vladimir's Seminary Press, 1997.

John IV of Jerusalem. *Epistula.* Edited by Karapet Tēr-Mkrtč'ian, "Erusałēmi Yovhannēs episkoposi t'ułt'ĕ." ("The 'Letter' of John Bishop of Jerusalem"). *Ararat* 29 (1896): 252–56; intro., 214–15. Translated (Lat.) by Aristaces Vardanian. "Des Johannes von Jerusalem Brief an den albanischen Katholikos Abas." *OC* n.s. 2 (1912): 64–77. Edited and translated by Abraham Terian. In "Monastic Turmoil in Sixth-Century Jerusalem and the South Caucasus: The Letter of Patriarch John iv to Catholicos Abas of the Caucasian Albanians." *DOP* 74 (2020): 9–39.

John Chrysostom. *Homiliae in Matthaeum. The Homilies of S. John Chrysostom, Archbishop of Constantinople, on the Gospel of St. Matthew.* Translated by George Prevost. 3 vols. Library of Fathers of the Holy Catholic Church 11, 15, 34. Oxford: J. H. Parker, 1843–1851.

John of Ephesus. *Lives of the Eastern Saints.* Edited and translated by E[rnest] W. Brooks. Patrologia Orientalis 17 (1–307), 18 (513–698), 19 (151–285). Paris: Firmin-Didot, 1923–1926.

Josephus, Flavius. *The Works of Josephus.* Translated by William Whiston. New updated ed. Peabody, MA: Hendrickson Publishers, 1987.

Justin Martyr. *Apologiae. Justin, Philosopher and Martyr: Apologies.* Edited and translated by Denis Minns and Paul Parvis. OECT. Oxford and New York: Oxford University Press, 2009.

Kanonagirk' Hayoc' (Canon Law of the Armenians). Edited by Vazgen Hakobyan. 2 vols. Erevan: Haykakan SSH GA Hratarakč'ut'yun, 1964–1971.

Knik' hawatoy (Seal of Faith). MH 4:51–311. Edited by Karapet Tēr-Mkrtč'ian. Ējmiacin: Mother See Press, 1914; repr. Antelias: The Armenian Catholicosate of Cilicia, 1998; repr. under the title *Le Sceau de la Foi.* Bibliothèque arménienne de la Fondation Calouste Gulbenkian. Leuven: Peeters, 1974.

Komitas Catholicos (see *Knik' hawatoy*).

Koriwn. *Vark' Maštoc'i.* MH 1:229–257. Edited by Manuk Abełyan. Erevan: Haypethrat, 1941. *Koriwn: The Life of Mashtots.* Translated by Bedros Norehad. New York: AGBU, 1965. Translated by Abraham Terian. In *The Life of Mashtots' by His Disciple Koriwn: Translated from the Classical Armenian with Introduction and Commentary.* OECT. Oxford: Oxford University Press (forthcoming).

Łazar P'arpec'i. *Patmut'iwn Hayoc' ew T'ułt'.* MH 2:2201–2375; *Letter,* 2377–2394. *The History of Łazar P'arpec'i.* Translated by Robert W. Thomson. Scholars Press Occasional Papers and Proceedings: Columbia University Program in Armenian Studies / Suren D. Fesjian Academic Publications 4. Atlanta: Scholars Press, 1991.

Macarius I of Jerusalem. *Epistula. T'ułt' Makaray Erusałemi. Macarius of Jerusalem: Letter to the Armenians, AD 335.* Edited and translated by Abraham Terian. AVANT 4. Crestwood, NY: St. Vladimir's Seminary Press, 2008.

Maštoc' (jeřnadruteanc') (Euchologion [mega]). Translated by Frederick C. Conybeare and Arthur J. Maclean. Pages 140–60 in *Rituale Armenorum, Being the Administration of the Sacraments and the Breviary Rites of the Armenian Church ... and the East*

Syrian Epiphany Rites. Oxford: Clarendon, 1905; repr. Hildesheim: Georg Olms, 2004.

Matenagirk' Hayoc' (MH / Armenian Classical Authors). Gen. ed. Zaven Yegavian. Armenian Library of the Calouste Gulbenkian Foundation. Antelias: Armenian Catholicosate of Cilicia, 2003–.

Maximus the Confessor. *Liber asceticus.* PG 90:912–956. CCSG 40 (ed. Van Deun).

———. *Quaestiones et dubia.* PG 90:785–856. CCSG 10 (ed. Declerck).

P'awstos Buzand / *Buzandaran Patmut'iwnk'.* MH 1:277–417. *The Epic Histories Attributed to P'awstos Buzand (Buzandaran Patmut'iwnk').* Translated by Nina G. Garsoïan. HATS 8. Cambridge, MA: Harvard University Press, 1989.

Philo of Alexandria. *Philo of Alexandria: The Contemplative Life, The Giants, and Selections.* Translated by David Winston. CWS. New York: Paulist Press, 1981.

———. *Philon d'Alexandrie: De Providentia.* Translated by Mireille Hadas-Lebel. Les œuvres de Philon d'Alexandrie 35. Paris: Éditions du Cerf, 1973.

Pseudo-Athanasius. *De Trinitate. Pseudo-Atanasio: Dialoghi IV e V sulla santa Trinità: Testo greco con traduzione italiana, versione latina e armena.* Edited and translated by Alessandro Capone. CSCO 634, Subsidia 125. Leuven: Peeters, 2011.

Pseudo-Dionysius Areopagita. *De caelesti hierarchia. De ecclesiastica hierarchia.* In *Pseudo-Dionysius: The Complete Works.* Translated by Colm Luibheid. CWS. New York: Paulist Press, 1987. Armenian version: *The Armenian Version of the Works Attributed to Dionysius the Areopagite.* Edited and translated by Robert W. Thomson. CSCO 488–489, Scriptores Armeniaci 17–18. Leuven: Peeters, 1987.

Pseudo-Macarius. *Homiliae spirituales.* In *Pseudo-Macarius: The Fifty Spiritual Homilies and the Great Letter.* Translated by George A. Maloney. CWS. New York: Paulist Press, 1992.

Step'anos Siwnec'i. *Meknut'iwn Žamakargut'ean (Commentary on the Daily Office).* MH 6:458–477. Edited and translated by M. Daniel Findikyan. *Commentary on the Armenian Daily Office by Bishop Step'anos Siwnec'i (d. 735): Critical Edition and Translation with Textual and Liturgical Analysis.* OCA 270. Rome: Pontificio Istituto Orientale, 2004.

Stobaeus. *Ioannis Stobaei Anthologium.* Edited by Curt Wachsmuth and Otto Hense. 5 vols. Berlin: Weidmann, 1884–1912; repr. 1974.

Teaching of St. Gregory (see *Vardapetut'iwn Srboyn Grigori*).

Tertullian. *Opera omnia.* PL 1–2.

Theodoret of Cyrrhus. *Historia religiosa.* PG 82:1283–1496. *A History of the Monks of Syria by Theodoret of Cyrrhus.* Translated by Richard M. Price. CSS 88. Kalamazoo: Cistercian Press, 1985.

———. *De sancta et vivifica Trinitate.* PG 75:1147–1189 (wrongly ascribed to Cyril of Alexandria).

Vardapetut'iwn Srboyn Grigori. MH 2:1425–1646. *The Teaching of St. Gregory.* Translated by Robert W. Thomson. Rev. ed. AVANT 1. New Rochelle: St. Nersess Armenian Seminary, 2001.

Vark' Haranc' (Apophthegmata patrum). Armenian version: *Vark' Srboc' Haranc'.* Edited by Nersēs Sargisian. Matenagrut'iwn Naxneac'. 2 vols. Venice: S. Łazar, 1855. *Paterica armeniaca a P. P. Mechitaristis edita (1855) nunc latine reddita I.* Edited by

Louis Leloir. CSCO 353, Subsidia 42. Leuven: Secrétariat du CSCO, 1974. Translated (E. Arm.) by Shahé Ananyan, Siranuš Grigoryan, and Vałaršak Tʻangamyan. Ējmiacin: Mayr Atʻoṙ, 2016.

Yovhan Mayragomecʻi. *Verlucutʻiwn Katʻotikē Eketecʻwoy ew or i nma yawrineal kargacʻ* (*Analysis of the Universal Church and of the Orders Therein*). MH 4:349–354. Translated by Abraham Terian. In "A Discourse on the Church by Yovhan Mayragomecʻi." Pages 225–41 in *Armenia between Byzantium and the Orient: Celebrating the Memory of Karen Yuzbashyan (1927–2009)*. Edited by Bernard Outtier, Cornelia B. Horn, Basil Lourié, and Alexey Ostrovsky. TSEC 16. Leiden: Brill, 2020.

Secondary Sources

Adontz, Nikoghayos. *Armenia in the Period of Justinian*. Edited and translated by Nina G. Garsoïan. Lisbon: Calouste Gulbenkian Foundation, 1970.

———. "Le Questionnaire de Saint Grégoire l'Illuminateur et ses rapports avec Eznik." *ROC* 25 [n.s. 5] (1925–1926): 309–57.

Aleanakʻian, Edward. "Hnagir *'Yačaxaptuam'* (*sic*) mě" ("An Old-Script *Yačaxapatum*"). Pages 463–66 in *Amēnun Tarecʻoycʻē: 21rd Tari* (*Almanack for All: 21st Year*). Edited by Tʻēodik (Tēodoros Lapʻčʻinčian). Paris: Imprimerie Massis, 1927.

Amadouni, Garabed. "Armeno (monachesimo)." In *Dizionario degli Istituti di perfezione*, 1:879–899. Edited by Giancarlo Rocca and Guerrino Pelliccia. 10 vols. Rome: Edizioni Paoline, 1974–2003.

———, ed. *Disciplina Armena: Testi vari di diritto canonico secolo IV–XVII*, Codificazione canonica orientale, fonti; ser. 1, fasc. 7. Vatican: Tipografia poliglotta vaticana, 1932.

———. "Le rôle historique des hiéromoins arméniens." Pages 279–305 in *Il monachesimo orientale: Atti del Convegno di studi orientale che sull predetto tema si tenne a Roma: sotto la direzione del Pontificio Istituto orientale, nei giorni 9, 10, 11 e 12 aprile 1958 allocuzione di S.S. Pio XII*. Edited by Irénée Hausherr et al. OCA 153. Rome: Pontificium Institutum Orientalium Studiorum, 1958.

Arevshatyan, Sen. "Maštocʻ et les débuts de la patristique arménienne." Pages 309–24 in *From Byzantium to Iran: Armenian Studies in Honour of Nina G. Garsoïan*. Edited by Jean-Pierre Mahé and Robert W. Thomson. Scholars Press Occasional Papers and Proceedings 8 / Columbia University Program in Armenian Studies–Suren D. Fesjian Academic Publications 5. Atlanta: Scholars Press, 1997.

Aune, David E. *The New Testament in Its Literary Environment*. LEC 8. Philadelphia: Westminster Press, 1987.

Awedikʻian, Gabriēl et al., eds. *Nor Baṙgirkʻ Haykazean Lezui* (*New Dictionary of the Armenian Language*). 2 vols. Venice: S. Łazar, 1836–1837; repr. Erevan: University of Erevan, 1979–1981.

Bauernfeind, Otto. "*Aretē*." In *Theological Dictionary of the New Testament* [*Theologisches Wörterbuch zum Neuen Testament*] 1:457–461. Edited by Gerhard Kittel. Translated by Geoffrey W. Bromiley. 10 vols. Grand Rapids, MI: Eerdmans, 1964–1976.

Beeley, Christopher A. *Gregory of Nazianzus on the Trinity and the Knowledge of God: In*

Your Light We Shall See Light. Oxford Studies in Historical Theology. Oxford: Oxford University Press, 2008.

Binns, John. *Ascetics and Ambassadors of Christ: The Monasteries of Palestine, 314–631.* OECS. Oxford: Clarendon Press; New York: Oxford University Press, 1994.

Bousset, Wilhelm. *Apophthegmata: Studien zur Geschichte des ältesten Mönchtums.* Tübingen: Mohr, 1923.

Brock, Sebastian P. "Radical Renunciation: The Idea of *msarrqûtâ.*" Pages 22–133 in *To Train His Soul in Books: Syriac Asceticism in Early Christianity (Festschrift for Sidney H. Griffith).* Edited by Robin Darling Young and Monica J. Blanchard. CUA Studies in Early Christianity. Washington, DC: The Catholic University of America Press, 2011.

Cadenhead, Raphael A. *The Body and Desire: Gregory of Nyssa's Ascetical Theology.* Christianity in Late Antiquity 4. Oakland, CA: University of California Press, 2018.

Calzolari, Valentina. "Philosophical Literature in Ancient and Medieval Armenia." Pages 349–76 in *Armenian Philology in the Modern Era: From Manuscript to Digital Text.* Edited by Valentina Calzolari. Leiden and Boston: Brill, 2014.

Caner, Daniel. *Wandering, Begging Monks: Spiritual Authority and the Promotion of Monasticism in Late Antiquity.* TCH 33. Berkeley: University of California Press, 2002.

Copleston, Frederick C. *A History of Philosophy, Vol. I: Greece and Rome.* Westminster, MD: Newman Press, 1962.

Drobner, Hubertus R., and Albert Vicciano, eds. *Gregory of Nyssa, Homilies on the Beatitudes: An English Version with Commentary and Supporting Studies: Proceedings of the Eighth International Colloquium on Gregory of Nyssa, Paderborn, 14–18 September 1998.* Supplements to Vigiliae Christianae 52. Leiden: Brill, 2000.

Droge, Arthur J., and James D. Tabor. *A Noble Death: Suicide and Martyrdom among Christians and Jews in Antiquity.* San Francisco: Harper, 1992.

Durian, Ełišē. *Patmut'iwn Hay Matenagrut'ean (History of Armenian Literature).* Durian Matenadaran 2. Ambołj Erker Ełišē Patriark' Duriani 1. Jerusalem: St. James Press, 1933.

Ebersole, Gary L. "The Function of Ritual Weeping Revisited: Affective Expression and Moral Discourse." *HR* 39 (2000): 211–46.

Eganyan, Ō(nnik) et al., eds. *Mayr c'uc'ak hayerēn jeṙagrac' Maštoc'i anvan matenadarani (General Catalogue of Armenian Manuscripts of the Maštoc' Matenadaran).* Multivolume series, ongoing. Erevan: "Nairi" Hratarakč'ut'iwn, 1984–.

Elm, Susanna. *'Virgins of God': The Making of Asceticism in Late Antiquity.* Oxford Classical Monographs. Oxford and New York: Oxford University Press, 1994.

Fedwick, Paul J. "The Translations of the Works of Basil before 1400." In *Basil of Caesarea: Christian, Humanist, Ascetic. A Sixteen-hundredth Anniversary Symposium* 2:439–512. Part One: *Vita, Opera, Doctrina;* Part Two: *The Tradition.* Edited by Paul J. Fedwick. 2 vols. Toronto: Pontifical Institute of Medieval Studies, 1981.

Finlan, Stephen, and Vladimir Kharlamov, eds. *Theōsis: Deification in Christian Theology.* Princeton Theological Monograph Series. Eugene, OR: Pickwick Publications, 2006.

Flussin, Bernard. "Palestinian Hagiography and the Reception of the Council of

Chalcedon." Pages 261–80 in *Languages and Cultures of Eastern Christianity: Greek.* Translated by Emily Corran. Edited by Scott Fitzgerald Johnson. The Worlds of Eastern Christianity, 300–1500, vol. 6. Farnham, UK: Ashgate Variorum, 2015; New York: Routledge, 2016. Translation of "L'hagiographie palestinienne et la réception du concile de Chalcédoine." Pages 25–47 in *Leimôn: Studies Presented to Lennart Rydén on His Sixty-Fifth Birthday.* Edited by Jan Olof Rosenqvist. Studia Byzantina Upsaliensia. Uppsala: University of Uppsala, 1996.

Froidevaux, Léon-Marie. "Les Questions et Réponses sur la Sainte Trinité attribuées à Hippolyte, évêque de Bostra." *RSR* 50 (1962): 32–73.

Garitte, Gérard. "Une nouvelle source du 'De fide' géorgien attribué à Hippolyte," *RHE* 43 (1968): 835–43.

Garsoïan, Nina G. *L'Église arménienne et le grand schisme d'Orient.* CSCO 574, Subsidia 100. Leuven: Peeters, 1999.

———. "Introduction to the Problem of Early Armenian Monasticism." *REArm* 30 (2005–2007): 177–236.

———. *Studies on the Formation of Christian Armenia.* Variorum Collected Studies Series CS959. Farnham: Ashgate / Variorum, 2010.

———. "Le témoignage d'Anastas Vardapet sur les monastères arméniens de Jérusalem à la fin du VIe siècle." Pages 257–67 in *Mélanges Gilbert Dagron.* Edited by Vincent Déroche et al. Travaux et mémoires 14. Paris: Association des Amis du Centre d'Histoire et Civilisation de Byzance, 2002.

van Ginkel, Jan J. *John of Ephesus. A Monophysite Historian in Sixth-century Byzantium.* Groningen: Rijksuniversiteit Groningen, 1995.

Golitzin, Alexander, with the collaboration of Bogdan G. Bucur. *Mystagogy: A Monastic Reading of Dionysius Areopagita: 1 Cor 3:16, John 14:21–23.* Edited by Bogdan G. Bucur. CSS 250. Collegeville, MN: Cistercian Publications, 2013.

Grabbe, Lester L. *Etymology in Early Jewish Interpretation: The Hebrew Names in Philo.* Brown Judaic Studies 115. Atlanta: Scholars Press, 1988.

Gribomont, Jean. *Histoire du texte des Ascétiques de S. Basile.* Bibliothèque du Muséon 32. Leuven: Publications universitaires, 1953.

Hac'uni, Vardan. "Erb šaradruac en *Yač̣axapatum Čařk*'" ("When were the *Yač̣axapatum Discourses* Composed?"). *Bazmavep* 88 (1930): 401–6.

Harvey, Susan Ashbrook. *Asceticism and Society in Crisis: John of Ephesus and The Lives of the Eastern Saints.* TCH 18. Berkeley: University of California Press, 1990.

———. *Scenting Salvation: Ancient Christianity and the Olfactory Imagination.* TCH 42. Berkeley: University of California Press, 2006.

Hausherr, Irénée. *Penthos: The Doctrine of Compunction in the Christian East.* Translated by Anselm Hufstader. CSS 53. Kalamazoo, MI: Cistercian Publications, 1982.

van Henten, Jan Willem, and Joseph Verheyden, eds. *Early Christian Ethics in Interaction with Jewish and Greco-Roman Contexts.* Studies in Theology and Religion 17. Leiden: Brill, 2013.

Hirschfeld, Yizhar. "Euthymius and His Monastery in the Judean Desert." *LASBF* 43 (1993): 339–71, Plates 19–24.

———. "Spirituality in the Desert: Judean Wilderness Monasteries." *BAR* 21.5 (1995): 28–37, 70.

Johnston, William M., and Claire Renkin, eds. *Encyclopedia of Monasticism*. Chicago and London: Fitzroy Dearborn, 2000.

Kertsch, Manfred. *Bildersprache bei Gregor von Nazianz: Ein Beitrag zur spätantiken Rhetorik und Popularphilosophie*. Grazer theologische Studien 2. Graz: Eigenverl. des Inst. f. Ökumenische Theologie u. Patrologie an d. Univ. Graz, 1978.

Khach'ikyan, Levon. "Grigor Part'evin veragruac 'Harc'umě', orpes hay matenagrut'yan eraxayrik'" ("Le 'Questionnaire' attribué a Grégoire le Parthe, prémices de l'écriture arménienne"). *BM* 7 (1964): 301–30.

———. "Otaralezu hay grakanut'iwně č'orrord darum" ("Foreign-language Armenian Literature in the Fourth Century"). *PBH* (1973): 3:27–51.

K'iparian, Kiwregh. "'Yač'axapatum' čaṙeru heḷinaki harc'ě" ("The *Yač'axapatum* Discourses' Authorship Question"). *Bazmavep* 120 (1962): 237–42.

Laird, Martin S. *Gregory of Nyssa and the Grasp of Faith: Union, Knowledge, and Divine Presence*. OECS. Oxford and New York: Oxford University Press, 2004.

Lampe, Geoffrey W. H. *A Patristic Greek Lexicon*. Oxford: Oxford University Press, 1968.

Lang, David M. Review of *Geschichte der kirchlichen georgischen Literatur, auf Grund des ersten Bandes der georgischen Literaturgeschichte von K. Kekelidze*, by Michael Tarchnišvili and Julius Assfalg. *BSOAS* 19.1 (1957): 179–81.

Lutz, Cora E. *Musonius Rufus: "The Roman Socrates."* Yale Classical Studies 10. New Haven: Yale University Press, 1947.

Maksoudian, Krikor H. "Introduction." Pages vii–xxxii in *Koriwn: Vark' Maštoc'i*. Classical Armenian Text Reprint Series. Delmar, NY: Caravan Books, 1985.

Malherbe, Abraham J., ed. *The Cynic Epistles: A Study Edition*. SBL Sources for Biblical Study 12. Missoula: Scholars Press, 1977.

———. *Moral Exhortation: A Greco-Roman Sourcebook*. LEC 4. Philadelphia: The Westminster Press, 1986.

Malxasianc', Step'an. *Hayerēn Bac'atrakan Baṙaran (Armenian Explanatory Dictionary)*. 4 vols. Erevan: Petakan Hratarakč'ut'iwn, 1944–1945.

Maspero, Giulio. "Anthropology." Pages 38–39 in *The Brill Dictionary of Gregory of Nyssa*. Edited by Lucas Francisco Mateo-Seco and Giulio Maspero. Translated by Seth Cherney. Leiden and Boston: Brill, 2010.

Mathews, Edward G., Jr. "Early Armenian and Syrian Contact: Reflections on Koriwn's *Life of Maštoc'*." *SNTR* 7 (2002): 5–27.

———. "The Early Armenian Hermit: Further Reflections on the Syriac Sources." *SNTR* 10 (2005): 141–67.

———. "Syriac into Armenian: The Translations and Their Translators." *JCSSS* 10 (2010): 20–44.

McCullough, William S. *A Short History of Syriac Christianity to the Rise of Islam*. Scholars Press General Series 4. Chico, CA: Scholars Press, 1980.

McGuckin, John A. "Embodying the New Society: The Byzantine Christian Instinct of Philanthropy." Pages 50–71 in *Philanthropy and Social Compassion in Eastern Orthodox Tradition: Papers of the Sophia Institute Academic Conference, New York, Dec. 2009*. Edited by Matthew J. Pereira. SISOT 2. New York: Theotokos Press / Sophia Institute, 2010.

Menze, Volker L. *Justinian and the Making of the Syrian Orthodox Church*. OECS. Oxford and New York: Oxford University Press, 2008.

Minassian, Martiros. "Grigor Partʻewi kam S. Maštocʻi veragruac 'Harcʻumě' ew Eznik Kołbacʻi" ("Le 'Questionnaire' attribué à Grégoire l'Illuminateur ou à Mesrop Machtotz n'est pas une source d'Eznik"). *HA* 85 (1971): 355–70, 463–82; 86 (1972): 73–94, 199–212, 347–54, 439–62; 87 (1973): 51–60.

———. "Kanovn srboyn Grigori Partʻewi dardzeal hartsʻumn ew patasxanikʻ nora" ("Le 'Questionnaire' de Saint Grégoire l'Illuminateur"). *Bazmavep* 139 (1981): 57–72.

Morison, E(rnest) F. *St. Basil and His Rule: A Study in Early Monasticism*. The Saint Deinol's Series 3. London and New York: H. Frowde, 1912.

Muradyan, Gohar. *Grecisms in Ancient Armenian*. HUAS 13. Leuven: Peeters, 2011.

Muradyan, Kim. *Grigor Nazianzacʻin hay matenagrutʻyan mēǰ* (*Gregory of Nazianz in Armenian Writings*). Erevan: Haykakan SSH GA Hratarakčʻutʻyun, 1983.

Mušełyan, Albert V. "Koriwn tʻe Agatʻangełos: Bnagreri kʻnnutʻyun nor tesankyunicʻ" ("Koriwn or Agathangelos? Textual Analysis from a New Perspective"). *Lraber* (1996/2): 49–64.

North, Helen F. "Canons and Hierarchies of the Cardinal Virtues in Greek and Latin Literature." Pages 165–83 in *The Classical Tradition: Literary and Historical Studies in Honor of Harry Caplan*. Edited by Luitpold Wallach. Ithaca: Cornell University Press, 1966.

Outtier, Bernard. "The Church Fathers in Armenia and the Armenian Fathers." Pages 295–302 in *Armenian Philology in the Modern Era: From Manuscript to Digital Text*. Edited by Valentina Calzolari with the collaboration of Michael E. Stone. Handbook of Oriental Studies. Section 8. Uralic & Central Asian Studies 23/1 = History of Armenian Studies 1. Leiden and Boston: Brill, 2014.

Paramelle, Joseph, and Jean-Pierre Mahé. "Nouveaux parallèles grecs aux *Définitions* hermétiques arméniennes." *REArm* 22 (1990–91): 115–34.

———. "Extraits hermétiques inédits dans un manuscrit d'Oxford." *REG* 104 (1991): 109–39.

Pingree, David. "Classical and Byzantine Astrology in Sassanian Persia." *DOP* 43 (1989): 227–39.

(Połarian) Covakan, N(orayr). "*Yačaxapatum* (1215): J̌eṙ. S.Y. Tʻ. 94." *Sion* 35 (1961): 74–75.

Rackham, H., trans. Aristotle. *Nicomachean Ethics*. Loeb Classical Library 73. Cambridge, MA: Harvard University Press, 1926.

Ramelli, Ilaria. "Embryo." Pages 256–57 in *The Brill Dictionary of Gregory of Nyssa*. Edited by Lucas Francisco Mateo-Seco and Giulio Maspero. Translated by Seth Cherney. Leiden and Boston: Brill, 2010.

Rapp, Claudia. *Holy Bishops in Late Antiquity: The Nature of Christian Leadership in an Age of Transition*. TCH 37. Berkeley: University of California Press, 2005.

Redgate, Anne E. *The Armenians*. The Peoples of Europe. Oxford: Blackwell, 1998.

Rousseau, Philip. *Basil of Caesarea*. TCH 20. Berkeley: University of California Press, 1994.

Rubenson, Samuel. "Asceticism: Christian Perspectives." Pages 92–94 in *EncMon*.

Edited by William M. Johnston and Claire Renkin. Chicago and London: Fitzroy Dearborn, 2000.

Ruether, Rosemary R. *Gregory of Nazianzus: Rhetor and Philosopher.* Oxford: Clarendon Press, 1969.

Russell, James R. *Zoroastrianism in Armenia.* Harvard Iranian Series 5. Cambridge, MA: Harvard University Press, 1987.

Russell, Jeffrey Burton. *Satan: The Early Christian Tradition.* Ithaca and London: Cornell University Press, 1981.

Sargisian, Barseł. *Agatʻangełos ew iwr bazmadarean gałtnikʻn. Kʻnnadatutʻiwn (Agathangelos and His Enigmas of Many Centuries: A Critical Study).* Venice: S. Łazar, 1890.

Silvas, Anna M. "The Syriac Translator of Basil's Small Asketikon: Translation Techniques and Personal Identity." *ParOr* 40 (2015): 404–15.

Srapyan, A(rmenuhi) N. "'Yačaxapatum' čařeri hełinaki harcʻē" ("The 'Yačaxapatum' Discourses' Authorship Question"). *Haykakan SSŘ Gitutʻyunneri Akademiayi Tełekagir: Hasarakakan Gitutʻyunner* 5 (1962): 25–38.

Stone, Michael E. "The Armenian Questions of St. Gregory: A Text Descended from *4 Ezra:* Edition of Recension I." *Mus* 131 (2018): 141–72.

Taft, Robert F. *The Liturgy of the Hours in East and West: The Origins of the Divine Office and its Meaning for Today.* 2nd rev. ed. Collegeville, MN: Liturgical Press, 1993.

Tamrazyan, Hračʻya. "Stełcagorc anhati ew arvesti tesutʻyan xndirnerē Mesrop Maštocʻi 'Yačaxapatum čařerum'" ("Matters of Artistic Individuality and Art-Perception in the 'Yačaxapatum' Discourses" of Mesrop Maštocʻ"). *BM* 19 (2012): 9–20.

Tarchnišvili, Michael, and Julius Assfalg. *Geschichte der kirchlichen georgischen Literatur, auf Grund des ersten Bandes der georgischen Literaturgeschichte von K. Kekelidze.* ST 185. Vatican: Biblioteca Apostolica Vaticana, 1955.

Tēr-Minasian, Ervand. *Die Beziehungen der Armenischen Kirche zu den Syrischen bis zum ende des 6. Jahr-hunderts.* Leipzig: A. Pries, 1904.

———. *Hayocʻ Eketecʻu yaraberutʻiwnnerē Asorwocʻ eketecʻineri het (The Relations of the Armenian Church with the Syrian Churches).* Ējmiacin: Tparan Mayr Atʻořoy, 1908.

Tēr-Mkrtčʻian, Karapet. "Yovhan Mandakuni ew Yovhan Mayragomecʻi." *Šołakatʻ hayagitakan taregirkʻ* (1913): 84–136.

Ter-Petrosyan, Levon H. *Daser Hay Eketecʻakan Matenagrutʻyunicʻ (E Dar) (Lessons from Armenian Ecclesiastical Bibliography [5th Century]).* Sočʻi: Armenian Diocese of Nor Naxijewan and Russia, 1993.

———. "Grigor Lusaworčʻi *Vardapetutʻyan* asorakan ałbyurnerē" ("The Syriac Sources of Gregory the Illuminator's *Teaching*"). *BM* 15 (1986): 95–109.

———. *Hay hin tʻargmanakan grakanutʻiwn / Ancient Armenian Translations.* Translated by Nubar Kupelian (W. Armenian) and Krikor Maksoudian (Eng.). A Publication of the Krikor and Clara Zohrab Information Center. New York: St. Vartan Press, 1992.

Tēr Pōłosian, Petros. "S. Parseł Kesaracʻi ew ir grutʻiwnnerē hayerēn tʻargmanutʻeamb" ("S. Basil of Caesarea and His Works in Armenian Translation"). *HA* 82 (1968): 385–418; 83 (1969): 129–58, 257–92, 385–98.

Terian, Abraham. "A Compounded Interpolation in Koriwn's *Life of Maštocʻ.*"

Pages 617–22 in *Mélanges Jean-Pierre Mahé*. Edited by Aram Mardirossian, Agnès Ouzounian, and Constantin Zuckerman. Travaux et mémoires 18. Paris: Centre d'Histoire et Civilisation de Byzance, 2014.

———. "A Discourse on the Church by Yovhan Mayragomecʻi." Pages 225–41 in *Armenia between Byzantium and the Orient: Celebrating the Memory of Karen Yuzbashyan (1927–2009)*. Edited by Bernard Outtier, Cornelia B. Horn, Basil Lourié, and Alexey Ostrovsky. TSEC 16. Leiden: Brill, 2020.

———. "The First Two Discourses of the *Yačaxapatum* as a Single Discourse on the Most Holy Trinity." *HA* 132 (2018): 1–28.

———. "The Hellenizing School: Its Time, Place, and Scope of Activities Reconsidered." Pages 175–86 in *East of Byzantium: Syria and Armenia in the Formative Period*. Edited by Nina G. Garsoïan, Thomas F. Mathews, and Robert W. Thomson. Dumbarton Oaks Symposium 1980 (Washington, DC: Dumbarton Oaks, 1982)

———. "Mandakuni's 'Encyclical' on Fasting." Pages 185–95 in *Worship Traditions in Armenia and the Neighboring Christian East*. Edited by Roberta R. Ervine. AVANT 3. Crestwood: St. Vladimir's Seminary Press, 2006.

———. "Monastic Turmoil in Sixth-Century Jerusalem and the South Caucasus: The Letter of Patriarch John iv to Catholicos Abas of the Caucasian Albanians." *DOP* 74 (2020): 9–39.

———. "Rereading the Sixth-Century List of Jerusalem Monasteries by Anastas Vardapet." Pages 273–88 in *Sion, Mère des Églises. Mélanges liturgiques offerts au Père Charles Athanase Renoux*. Edited by Michael Daniel Findikyan, Daniel Galadza, and André Lossky. Semaines d'Études Liturgiques Saint-Serge, S1. Münster: Aschendorff Verlag, 2016.

Thomson, Robert W. "Armenia in the Fifth and Sixth Century." Pages 662–77 in *The Cambridge Ancient History, Volume XIV: Late Antiquity: Empire and Successors, AD 425–600*. Edited by Averil Cameron, Bryan Ward-Perkins, and Michael Whitby. Cambridge: Cambridge University Press, 2001.

———. *A Bibliography of Classical Armenian Literature to 1500*. Corpus Christianorum. Turnhout: Brepols, 1995.

———. "'Let Now the Astrologers Stand Up': The Armenian Christian Reaction to Astrology and Divination." *DOP* 46 (1992): 305–12. Repr. in his *Studies in Armenian Literature and Christianity*, XI. Aldershot, Hampshire (UK), and Brookfield, VT: Variorum, 1994.

———. *Saint Basil of Caesarea and Armenian Cosmology: A Study of the Armenian Version of Saint Basil's* Hexaemeron *and Its Influence on Medieval Armenian Views about the Cosmos*. CSCO 646, Subsidia 130. Leuven: Peeters, 2012.

———. "The Transformation of Athanasius in Armenian Theology." *Mus* 78 (1965): 47–69. Repr. in his *Studies in Armenian Literature and Christianity*, XIII. Aldershot, Hampshire (UK), and Brookfield, VT: Variorum, 1994.

Vaage, Leif F., and Vincent L. Wimbush, eds. *Asceticism and the New Testament*. New York: Routledge, 1999.

Vetter, Paul. "*Aristides-Citate in der armenischen Literatur*." *Tübinger Theologische Quartalschrift* 76 (1894): 529–39.

———. *Haykakan ašxatasirut'iwnk' hayagēt P. Fetteri* (sic) (*Armenian Studies by the Armenologist P. Vetter*). Translated by Yakobos Tashian. Azgayin Matenadaran 17. Vienna: Mxit'arean Tparan, 1895.

Vinel, Françoise. "La version arménienne des Homélies sur l'Écclesiaste de Grégoire de Nysse." *REArm* 21 (1988–1989): 127–43.

Vööbus, Arthur. *History of Asceticism in the Syrian Orient: A Contribution to the History of Culture in the Near East, I. The Origin of Asceticism: Early Monasticism in Persia,* CSCO 184, Subsidia 14; *II. Early Monasticism in Mesopotamia and Syria,* CSCO 197, Subsidia 17. Leuven: Secrétariat du CSCO, 1958.

———. *Studies in the History of the Gospel Text in Syriac.* CSCO 128, Subsidia 3. Leuven: Durbecq, 1951.

———. *Syriac and Arabic Documents Regarding Legislation Relative to Syrian Asceticism.* Papers of the Estonian Theological Society in Exile 11. Stockholm: PETSE, 1960.

Young, Robin Darling. "Syriac Christian Influence on Early Armenian Monasticism and the Evidence of the *Collected Homilies* Ascribed to Gregory the Illuminator." Paper presented at Syriac Symposium III: The Aramaic Heritage of Syria, The Summer Syriac Institute. University of Notre Dame, Notre Dame, IN, June 17–20, 1999.

———. "The Eucharist as Sacrifice According to Clement of Alexandria." Pages 63–91 in *Rediscovering the Eucharist: Ecumenical Considerations.* Edited by Roch A. Kereszty. New York: Paulist Press, 2003.

———. "*Xeniteia* According to Evagrius of Pontus." Pages 229–52 in *Ascetic Culture: Essays in Honor of Philip Rousseau.* Edited by Blake Leyerle and Robin Darling Young. Notre Dame, IN: University of Notre Dame Press, 2013.

Zekiyan, Boghos L. "Back to the Sources of Armenian Spirituality: Hachakhapatoum as a Doctrinal and Practical Vademecum for Introduction to Christian Life and Monastic Spirituality." Pages 139–53 in *In Search of a Precious Pearl. 5th Encounter of Monks from East and West (EMO V) at Dzaghgatzor Monastery (Valley of the Flowers) Armenia, Thursday, 31 May–Thursday, 7 June 2001.* Edited by Edward G. Farrugia. Rome: Pontificio Istituto Orientale; Riano: Cittadella Ecumenica Taddeide, 2005.

———. "Catechesi e inculturazione nel periodo formativo della Chiesa armena." *IJAIS* 12.1–2 (2014): 283–300 ("Christianity in Ancient Iran. Papers of the International Conference 'Ad ulteriores gentes:' The Christians in the East 1st to 7th century,' Rome, March 2009." Edited by Marco Bais et al.).

———. "La relation entre le sacrifice et la communion dans la théologie de Hovhan Mandakouni." Pages 81–93 in *The Eucharist in Theology and Philosophy. Issues of Doctrinal History in East and West from the Patristic Age to the Reformation.* Edited by István Perczel, Réka Forrai and György Geréby. Ancient and Medieval Philosophy, Series 1, 35. Leuven: Leuven University Press, 2005.

———. "Yovhan Mandakunii tesut'iunĕ Surb Hałordut'ean merjec'umi masin" ("La dottrina di Y. Mandakuni sulla Comunione frequente"). *Bazmavep* 132 (1974): 129–43.

PREFACE

My interest in studying this document was aroused by the fact that it is unique among the vast heritage of early Armenian literature and, in part, because of differing opinions on the beginning of coenobitic monasticism in Armenia. According to Professor Nina Garsoïan, there was no such development there before the turn of the seventh century. She not only ignores a substantial part of the documentary evidence and misconstrues some of the sources known to her, but also overlooks the larger factors contributing to the rise and spread of coenobitic monasticism in Armenia a century earlier: namely, the crosscurrents of monasticism that must have permeated Armenia prior to the Age of Justinian and for which there is documentary evidence. The *Discourses* presented here are but the last and textually the longest of that evidence from the fifth and sixth centuries, the rest of which I intend to publish in a forthcoming monograph, titled *A Documentary History of Early Armenian Monasticism.*

The *Discourses* abound in moral admonitions, supplemented with some generally outlined rules for ascetics; however, they are devoid of special rules that would be suggestive of differences in the way of life between one monastery and another, and thus provide no hint as to their exact provenance. Still, this is but a one-of-a-kind document in early Armenian literature, a witness to the monastic spread of the Church of the East.

The text of the *Discourses,* titled *Yačaxapatum čaŕk',* literally, *Oft-Repeated Discourses,* and traditionally transmitted in the name of St. Gregory the Illuminator, has consequently been accorded the first place in the first volume of a multi-volume series encompassing the writings of Armenian Church Fathers, the *Matenagirk' Hayoc'* (2003, dubbed *Armenian Classical Authors* by the series editors). *The Oft-Repeated Discourses* is neither the earliest nor the best representative document to introduce a magnificent and chronologically

xxvii

ordered series (to mark the 17th centenary of the Christianization of Armenia by St. Gregory, 301–2001) that may in time become known as *Patrologia armena*.

For the soul-satisfaction I have received in this labor of love, I want to thank several people. I begin with Professor Robin Darling Young for her continued interest in the *Discourses*, an interest sustained for decades. I was privileged to hear one of her perceptive presentations on the 23rd Discourse.* I want to thank her also for the suggestion to publish the monograph in the Fathers of the Church series. This could not have been accomplished without the kind consideration, guidance, and comments of Dr. Carole C. Burnett, editor of the series, to whom I am most grateful. I also want to thank my colleague, Professor Roberta R. Ervine, for her shared interest in the *Discourses* when the translation began at St. Nersess Armenian Seminary.

The monograph is dedicated to my daughter, Sonia Esther Terian Vo, for being the first reader of the translation and for her much-appreciated initial editing laced with valuable suggestions. I here take the opportunity to thank the Rev. Karl Wyneken for reading one of the early drafts of the manuscript and for identifying several biblical allusions I had missed.

This work would not have been completed were it not for the attentive administrators and librarians at the National Humanities Center in Research Triangle Park, NC, where I was privileged to spend the academic year 2018–19 as Robert F. and Margaret S. Goheen Fellow. I am deeply grateful to all.

Last but foremost, I must record my deepest thanks to my wife, Sara, also an academic, for being the person to whom I could turn with every turn of a page and without whom not a page could have been written (or translated).

Abraham Terian
Research Triangle Park
2019

---

* "Syriac Christian Influence on Early Armenian Monasticism and the Evidence of the *Collected Homilies* Ascribed to Gregory the Illuminator," read at "Syriac Symposium III: The Aramaic Heritage of Syria," The Summer Syriac Institute, University of Notre Dame, Notre Dame, IN, 17–20 June 1999.

INTRODUCTION

INTRODUCTION

The Armenian Church is heir to some of the richest and most ancient traditions of Early Christianity. In her treasure trove of spiritual writings is this collection of twenty-three ascetic discourses that abound in moral teachings with emphasis on the virtuous life. The discourses contain all the commonplaces of the early Church's moral teachings, including many of the Eastern Christian writers' favorite theological themes. No wonder the collection was traditionally attributed, along with other works, to St. Gregory the Illuminator, the Parthian-born evangelist of Armenia at the turn of the fourth century (d. 328), and in recent scholarship to St. Maštoc', the inventor of the Armenian alphabet and progenitor of the new literacy at the turn of the fifth century (d. 440).[1] That both

---

1. The last edition of the text, by Hakob K'ēoseian in the ongoing series Matenagirk' Hayoc', henceforth abbr. MH (Armenian Classical Authors), gen. ed. Zaven Yegavian, Armenian Library of the Calouste Gulbenkian Foundation (Antelias: Armenian Catholicosate of Cilicia, 2003–), 1:7–137, follows that of *Srboy Hōrn Meroy Grigori Lusaworč'i Yačaxapatum Čaṙk' ew Ałōt'k'* (*Oft-repeated Discourses and a Prayer of Our Holy Father Gregory the Illuminator*) (Venice: S. Łazar, 1954, a second printing of the 1838 edition). Of the other editions, the following is noteworthy for its early textual revisions: *Srboy Hōrn Meroy Eranelwoyn Grigori Lusaworč'i Yačaxapatum Čaṙk' Lusawork'* (*Oft-repeated [and] Enlightened Discourses of Our Blessed Father Gregory the Illuminator*), ed. Aršak Tēr Mik'elian (Vałaršapat / Ējmiacin: Mother See of Holy Ējmiacin, 1894); German trans. by Johann M. Schmid, *Reden und Lehren des hl. Gregorius des Erleuchters, Patriarch von Armenien* (Regensburg: Druck & Verlag von G. J. Manz, 1872), and by Eugene Sommer and Simon Weber, "Ausgewählte Reden aus dem *Hatschachapatum* vom hl. Mesrop," in *Ausgewählte Schriften der armenischen Kirchenväter*, ed. Simon Weber, 2 vols., Bibliothek der Kirchenväter, Series 1, 57–58 (Munich: Verlag Josef Kösel & Friedrich Pustet, 1927), 1:237–318 (incl. Disc. 1–2, 4–6, 14–15, numbered 1–7, with an introduction by Weber). Two translations in E. Arm. appeared in this century: one by Vazgēn Hambarjumian, *S. Grigor Lusaworič'. Yačaxapatum čaṙer* (Tehran: Arm. Prelacy, 2003), in which he combines readings from both the Ējmiacin 1894 ed. and the Venice 1954 ed.; and the other by Movsēs

3

of these attributions are unlikely for several reasons—regardless of the antiquity of content in inherited themes—will be shown in the ensuing discussion of authorship and date, where the anonymous discourses are relegated to the second half of the sixth century.

Although the document is replete with ascetic elements and the last discourse depicts an institutionalized form of monastic life, it will be somewhat inaccurate to think of the discourses as strictly ascetic. They are moral *paideia* to lead readers and hearers into a spiritual way of life, one that is disciplined by the Christian virtues and that finds its ultimate expression in asceticism. They are addressed to individuals as much as to segregated ascetic groups. In view, however, of their culmination with emphasis on monasticism and certain of its rules in Disc. 23, anticipated in the earlier discourses, there is reason to assume that they were intended for—though not necessarily limited to—novices who stood to be instructed spiritually by the monastic superior. The authoritative voice of the anonymous author is that of an abbot instructing those entrusted to his spiritual care and keeping. The document abounds with instruction about established ascetic or monastic practices such as love for the brothers, prayer, fasting, meditation for serenity of mind and body, the fight against the passions, and radical renunciation of the world. There is, however, no acknowledgment here of earlier, celebrated Fathers' sayings on various questions of the spiritual life. As a whole, the discourses provide a glimpse into the teaching of an anonymous Armenian abbot of the mid-sixth century. Of the commonly shared teaching in *ascetica*, the mystical influence of Evagrius Ponticus (d. 399) must be acknowledged, thus allowing a starting point of delineating tradition and theology in the document.

The handed-down rules are in accordance with the teaching of the Gospel. "It is always necessary to be instructed by the Gospel, which admonishes us with excellent mandates" (Disc. 2.143). The doctrinal and functional centrality of the Scriptures is emphasized

A. Načarian, *Yačaxapatum. S. Mesrop Maštoc'* (Aleppo: Tp. Arewelk', 2005), in which he poorly amplifies the Ējmiacin 1894 ed. An earlier, partial translation in E. Arm. covered Disc. 1–2, 16, and 19, with the concluding prayer attributed to the Illuminator, by Mesrop Aramian and Seta Stambōlc'ian, "S. Grigor Lusaworč'i «Yačax-apatumě»," *Ganjasar* 4 (1993): 134–64; it follows the Venice 1954 edition.

throughout the discourses, which are heavily punctuated with biblical quotations and laced with recurring biblical images and phraseology. These ubiquitous quotations, like the thematic commonplaces in the moral theology of the Fathers, have here acquired a degree of amplification to a point where most of them differ vastly from the biblical text. This may be the result of a long tradition of oral transmission of moral teachings derived from the Scriptures, the early councils, and the canonical letters of Nicene and post-Nicene Fathers—augmented by documentary sources mandating ascetic rules. The moral instruction of these admonitory discourses, based on vivid contrasts between virtue and vice, is aptly described as being "in accordance with God's righteous laws and the piety of the holy Fathers" (Disc. 5.47).[2] Still, by this time Christian communities and ascetics in particular had come a long way from earlier ethical concerns rooted in Judaism and Greco-Roman morality.[3] The continuity with the Decalogue's emphasis on love and the Greco-Roman ethical categories of virtue and vice notwithstanding, Christians were driven by the Johannine love-command and the Pauline Spirit-guided practice of virtuous living, ever maturing in the ethos of an in-group solidarity culminating in monasticism.

The rise of interest in classical philosophy, Greco-Roman morality, and late antique ethics is well attested in sixth-century Armenian translations from Greek—thanks to the mostly anonymous translators who persisted with their literary output through the eighth century. They are collectively referred to as "the Hellenizing School" for maintaining the Greek syntax of their sources, an

2. Paradoxically, the discourses do not name any of the Fathers and are devoid of sayings such as those attributed to the Desert Fathers; cf. Wilhelm Bousset, *Apophthegmata: Studien zur Geschichte des ältesten Mönchtums* (Tübingen: Mohr, 1923), giving the correspondence with texts in other languages, including Armenian and Syriac. For original sayings extant in the second part of *Vark' Haranc'*, the Armenian version of the *Apophthegmata Patrum* (*Vark' Srboc' Haranc'*, ed. Nersēs Sargisian, Matenagrut'iwn Naxneac', 2 vols. [Venice: S. Łazar, 1855]; E. Arm. trans. by Shahé Ananyan, Siranush Krikoryan, and Vagharshak T'angamyan [Ējmiacin: Mayr At'oṙ, 2016]), see Louis Leloir, ed., *Paterica armeniaca a P. P. Mechitaristis edita (1855) nunc latine reddita I*, CSCO 353, Subsidia 42 (Leuven: Secrétariat du CSCO, 1974).

3. On which see the various essays in *Early Christian Ethics in Interaction with Jewish and Greco-Roman Contexts*, ed. Jan Willem van Henten and Joseph Verheyden, Studies in Theology and Religion 17 (Leiden: Brill, 2013).

oddity in Armenian.[4] Except for echoes from the *Corpus Hermeticum*, the fragmentary translation of which belongs to the said period, the religious philosophy of the moral discourses here presented is not commensurate with these classical traditions known in Armenia at the time, and one must be warned against accentuation of classical elements here. The discourses, hereafter capitalized and italicized, and referred to in the plural, reflect the teaching of the New Testament on godly living or saintliness in the monastic milieu of their century. Nevertheless, their predominantly Armenian syntax often veers off to inversions more akin to Syriac literary tendencies than to Greek—notwithstanding the few striking similarities to the thought of Basil of Caesarea (d. 379) and some evidence of the author's dependence on the Armenian version of Basil's *Rules*, translated around the turn of the sixth century.[5] The implications of these and other observations for further questions on authorship and date are discussed below.

The Traditional Attributions

The primary source for the prevalent attribution of the *Discourses* to St. Gregory the Illuminator is the extant Armenian version of the *History of the Armenians* by a certain Agathangelos, whose account has become the received tradition about the Christianization of Armenia at the turn of the fourth century.[6] The *History* by the pseudonymous author, however, whose Greek name means "Messenger of Good News," exists in several other languages with differing versions,[7] certain of which derive from lost Armenian texts.

---

4. Abraham Terian, "The Hellenizing School: Its Time, Place, and Scope of Activities Reconsidered," in *East of Byzantium: Syria and Armenia in the Formative Period*, ed. Nina G. Garsoïan et al., Dumbarton Oaks Symposium 1980 (Washington, DC: Dumbarton Oaks, 1982), 175–86; Gohar Muradyan, *Grecisms in Ancient Armenian*, HUAS 13 (Leuven: Peeters, 2011). Valentina Calzolari, "Philosophical Literature in Ancient and Medieval Armenia," in *Armenian Philology in the Modern Era: From Manuscript to Digital Text*, ed. eadem (Leiden and Boston: Brill, 2014), 349–76.

5. Gabriella Uluhogian, *Basilio di Cesarea: Il libro delle domande (Le regole)*, CSCO 536–537, Scriptores Armeniaci 19–20 (Leuven: Peeters, 1993), t. 20, ix.

6. Robert W. Thomson, trans., *Agathangelos: History of the Armenians* (Albany, NY: State University of New York Press, 1976), Arm. text included; text also in MH 2:1302–1735.

7. Robert W. Thomson, trans., *The Lives of Saint Gregory. The Armenian, Greek,*

The extant Armenian version expands these earlier accounts into a grossly redacted account magnifying the achievement of the Saint while deleting the earlier, Syriac or Edessan contributions to Armenian Christianity. There is, nonetheless, sufficient reason to conclude that the extant Armenian version of the *History* by Agathangelos, as we have it, dates from the turn of the seventh century, the period that saw considerable architectural expansion in the former capital Vałaršapat (today's Ējmiacin) during the catholicosate of Komitas of Ałc'k' (in office 611/615–628).[8] Commensurate with this ecclesial development, the Agathangelian account aims at consolidating and expanding the seminal Gregorid traditions in Vałaršapat through legends and borrowed attributions claimed for St. Gregory.[9] This is also the period when the epithet "Illuminator" (*Lusaworič'*), derived from "illumination" as a synonym for "baptism" in the early Church, seems to have become popular when referring to the Saint.[10] One of the epithet's early uses is attested

Arabic, and Syriac Versions of the "History" Attributed to Agathangelos (Ann Arbor, MI: Caravan, 2010).

8. Ibid., 93–108; Abraham Terian, "A Compounded Interpolation in Koriwn's *Life of Maštoc'*," in *Mélanges Jean-Pierre Mahé,* ed. Aram Mardirossian, Agnès Ouzounian, and Constantin Zuckerman, Travaux et mémoires 18 (Paris: Centre d'Histoire et Civilisation de Byzance, 2014), 617–22.

9. The foundational myth of "the descent of the Only-begotten," to mark the cathedral establishment of Ējmiacin—purportedly anticipated through a vision by the Saint as narrated in the extant Armenian version (§§731–756; cf. *Vg* 77–82 and *Va* 54–62; Thomson, *Lives,* 337–52), seems to belong to an intermediate period—possibly to the second half of the fifth century, as Łazar P'arpec'i shows familiarity with it as well as with the *Teaching of Saint Gregory* inserted in the *History* of Agathangelos; Robert W. Thomson, trans., *The History of Łazar P'arpec'i,* Scholars Press Occasional Papers and Proceedings: Columbia University Program in Armenian Studies / S. D. Fesjian Academic Publications 4 (Atlanta: Scholars Press, 1991), 23, 255 (Arm. text in MH 2:2201–2376). Familiarity with the *Teaching* is palpable also in another fifth-century source, the *Biwzandaran Patmut'iwnk',* Arm. text in *P'awstosi Buzandac'woy Patmut'iwn Hayoc'* (Venice: S. Łazar, 1933; cf. MH 1:277–428), trans. Nina G. Garsoïan, *The Epic Histories Attributed to P'awstos Buzand (Buzandaran Patmut'iwnk'),* HATS 9 (Cambridge, MA: Harvard University Press, 1989), 26 and n. 108 (referring to 3.1; cf. MH 1:278). For yet another literary work claimed for the Illuminator, see below, n. 24.

10. Early Armenian sources speak of his "illuminating mission"; see Garsoïan, *Epic Histories,* 47 n. 222, 375–76 (referring to 3.2, 5; cf. MH 1:278, 281). For the use of the name *Lusaworič'* by subsequent authors, see the indices in MH 2:2522; 3:547. On the origin of the title, s.v. φώτισμα / φωτισμός in *PGL,* 1509–10.

in the *Seal of Faith* (*Knik' hawatoy*),[11] a doctrinal florilegium from the time of the said Komitas, where quite significantly, it is used in conjunction with an excerpt from the *Discourses* (Disc. 1–2), and that in the name of the Illuminator. This is also the earliest evidence for the use of the *Discourses*, thus establishing a *terminus ad quem* for dating our document—where the name of the Illuminator appears not only in the title of the work as a whole but hammered also into the title of every discourse as part of the transmission history of the text.

The ascription of the *Discourses* to the Illuminator belongs to the final redaction of the extant Armenian version of the Agathangelian *History*, where the continuator adds:

Then after such deeds [that is, adding to the Nicene Canons and evangelizing Armenia], with even more profound teaching blessed Gregory began to compose many discourses, difficult of language, profound parables, easy to listen to, many-faceted, composed by grace, composed from the matter and power of the prophetic writings, full of subtleties, and arranged and ordered in the truth of the evangelical faith. In these he set out many similes and examples from the transitory world, especially concerning the hope of the resurrection for the future life, that they might be intelligible and easily understood by the ignorant and those occupied with worldly affairs, in order to awaken and arouse and urge them on firmly to the promised good news.[12]

But this is one of several remarks on Maštoc', the founder of the Armenian alphabet at the turn of the fifth century, made in Koriwn's *Life of Maštoc'*, from where it was lifted with scores of other

---

11. Կնիք Հաւատոյ, ed. Karapet Tēr-Mkrtč'ian (Tēr-Mkertchian), (Ējmiacin: Mother See Press, 1914; repr. Antelias: The Armenian Catholicosate of Cilicia, 1998), 18 (MH 4:59).

12. *History*, §886 (trans. Thomson). «Ապա յետ այնպիսի գործոց դարձեալ առաւել բարձրագոյն վարդապետութեամբ սկսեալ երանելւոյն Գրիգորի ճառս յաճախագոյնս դժուարապատումս, առակս խորիմացս դիւրալուրս բազմադիմս շնորհագիրս, յարդարեալս ի զաւրութենէ և ի հլեթոյ զրոց մարգարէականաց, լի ամենայն ճաշակաւք կարգեալս և յաւրինեալս աւետարանական հաւատոցն ճշմարտութեամբ։ Յորս բազում նմանութիւնս և աւրինակս յանցաւորաց աստի, առաւել վասն յարութեանական յուսոյն առ ի Հանդերձեալսն յերիւրեալ, զի Հեշտընկալք և դիւրահասոյցք տխմարագունիցն և մարմնական իրաւք զբաղելոցն լինիցին, առ ի սթափիլ զլուարթացուցանէլ և Հաստահիմն առ խոստացեալ աւետիսն բաշալերել» (MH 2:1728 [127.6–7]).

remarks and appropriated for the Illuminator by the continuator of the pseudonymous Agathangelos.[13] Koriwn writes:

> Then, following this, the blessed Maštocʻ, given to his excellent and profound teaching, began to arrange and to compose discourses to be often repeated, easy to deliver, gracefully written, diverse, (culled) from the enlightenment and crux of the prophetic books, full of the whole fervor of the truth of the faith accordant with the Gospel. Into these he incorporated many analogies and examples from the transient things of the present, especially concerning the hope of resurrection for the things to come; that they might be intelligible and easily understood by the most ignorant and those occupied with carnal matters, in order to awaken and arouse and urge (them) on firmly to the promised good news.[14]

Primarily on the basis of the above-quoted passage from Koriwn, several scholars ascribe the *Discourses* either to Maštocʻ or to his circle of disciples, and some go on to consider the work the earliest example of Armenian moral philosophy.[15] What Koriwn seems to

13. Some fifty borrowings from Koriwn's *Life of Maštocʻ* are found in the Agathangelian *History* following the insertion of the *Teaching,* including several attributes of Maštocʻ claimed for the Illuminator (§§716–900); see Thomson, *Agathangelos: History,* lxxviii–lxxix, and notes, 482–503. For a list of the verbatim parallels, see idem, *Agathangelos: The Lives of Saint Gregory,* 526–27; and "Appendix III" in Abraham Terian, *The Life of Mashtotsʻ by His Disciple Koriwn: Translated from the Classical Armenian with Introduction and Commentary,* OECT (Oxford: Oxford University Press), forthcoming.

14. *Life,* 21.1–2 (MH 1:248–49) (20 [78.1–11] ed. Abełyan) (trans. mine). «Ապա յետ այնորիկ դարձեալ այնպիսի առաւել և բարձրագոյն վարդապետութեամբն սկսեալ երանելոյն Մաշտոցի ճառս յաճախագոյնս, դիւրապատումս, շնորհագիրս, բազմադիմիս ի լուսաւորութենէ և ի հինթոյ գրոց մարգարէականաց կարգել և յարինել, լի ամենայն ճաշակաւք աւետարանական հաւատոյն ճշմարտութեամբ։ Յորս բազում նմանութիւնս և աւրինակս ի յանցաւորացս աստի, առաւելագոյն վասն յարութեանական յուսոյն առ ի հանդերձեալսն, յերիւրեալ կազմեալ, զի հեշտընկալք և դիւրահասոյցք տխմարագունիցն և մարմնական իրաւք զբաղելոյն լինիցին, առ ի աթափել և զարթուցանել և հաստահիմն առ ի խոստացեալ աւետիսն քաջալերէլ»։

15. Paul Vetter, *Haykakan ašxatasirutʻiwnkʻ hayagēt P. Fetteri (sic) (Armenian Studies by the Armenologist P. Vetter),* trans. Yakobos Tashian, Azgayin Matenadaran 17 (Vienna: Mxitʻarean Tparan, 1895), 64–75, a pioneering work followed by several philologists, e.g., A(rmenuhi) N. Srapyan, "'Yačaxapatum' čaʻeri hełinaki harcʻē" ("The 'Yačaxapatum' Discourses' Authorship Question"), *Haykakan SSŘ Gitutʻyunneri Akademiayi Tełekagir: Hasarakakan Gitutʻyunner* 5 (1962): 25–38; Sen Arevshatyan, "Maštocʻ et les débuts de la patristique arménienne," in *From Byzantium to Iran:*

have had in mind, however, was most likely the *Teaching* (*Vardape-tutʻiwn*), a catechism that fits the laudatory description more than the *Discourses*, and which—like the latter—traditionally bears the name of St. Gregory, ever since its appropriation for the Saint by Agathangelos and incorporation into the text of the *History* (§§275–715).[16] Clearly, the *Discourses* do not fit the above description by Koriwn, for—unlike the *Teaching*, which they utilize—they are not "gracefully written."[17] Their compositional language, ridden with

---

Armenian Studies in Honour of Nina G. Garsoïan, ed. Jean-Pierre Mahé and Robert W. Thomson, Scholars Press Occasional Papers and Proceedings 8 / Columbia University Program in Armenian Studies–Suren D. Fesjian Academic Publications 5 (Atlanta: Scholars Press, 1997), 309–24; and Hračʻya Tamrazyan, "Stełcagorc anhati ew arvesti tesutʻyan xndirnerě Mesrop Maštocʻi 'Yačaxapatum čařerum'" ("Matters of Artistic Individuality and Art-Perception in the 'Yačaxapatum Discourses' of Mesrop Maštocʻ"), *BM* 19 (2012): 9–20, enumerating Vetter's arguments for the ascription to Maštocʻ. These porous arguments are systematically negated in the section on authorship and date. Thomson remarks: "It is likely that the homilies known as the *Yachakhapatum* and attributed to Gregory were in the mind of Koriwn (or the later redactor [*sc.* of Agathangelos, *Aa*])"; *Agathangelos*, 502, note to §866. Levon H. Ter-Petrosyan, *Daser Hay Eketecʻakan Matenagrutʻyunicʻ* (*E Dar*) (*Lessons from Armenian Ecclesiastical Bibliography [5th Century]*) (Sočʻi: Armenian Diocese of Nor Naxijewan and Russia, 1993), 22–23, 35–38, assumes their pre-Chalcedonian date.

16. First suggested by Barseł Sargisian, *Agatʻangełos ew iwr bazmadarean gałtnikʻn. Kʻnnadatutʻiwn* (*Agathangelos and His Enigmas of Many Centuries: A Critical Study*) (Venice: S. Łazar, 1890), 400–408. For an Eng. trans. of the catechism attributed to St. Gregory, see Robert W. Thomson, *The Teaching of St. Gregory*, rev. ed., AVANT 1 (New Rochelle, NY: St. Nersess Armenian Seminary, 2001); text in MH 2:1425–1646.

17. Arm. շնորհագիրս (*šnorhagirs*) in both authors; cf. the conflicting adjectives դիւրապատումս (*diwrapatums*, "easy to recount") in Koriwn and դժուարապատումս (*džuarapatums*, "difficult to recount") in Agathangelos. In his introduction to *The Teaching of St. Gregory* (56–57), Thomson mistranslates the above lines of Koriwn by taking the Agathangelian "difficult" for Koriwn's "easy" and expresses uncertainty about the written form of the composition referred to in the *Life;* yet Koriwn's wording suggests a written composition: the verbs *kargel ew yawrinel* are used by him both separately and in conjunction for that which is written down: 2.16; 8.4, 6; 29/28.1–2 (MH 1:231, 238, 256). Moreover, Thomson wrongly states that the earliest attestation for a verbatim quotation from the *Teaching* is from the beginning of the seventh century—referring to the above-mentioned florilegium titled *Seal of Faith* (ibid., 53–54). As we shall see, earlier dependence on the *Teaching* is evident in the *Discourses*, from which excerpts are likewise found in the *Seal of Faith*. Furthermore, Thomson's dating the *Teaching* "in its present form" to the latter part of the fifth century, thus calling into question

serious grammatical anomalies, is unlike that of known authors
from the fifth century, the immediate disciples of Maštocʻ, whose
writings mark the "Golden Age" of Armenian literature. Moreover,
they reveal a degree of coenobitic monasticism quite unlike the asceticism of Maštocʻ as described by Koriwn.[18] For this and other
reasons elaborated in the section on authorship and date, especially
the fact that the document utilizes translated sources dated to the
turn of the sixth century, we must pause before allowing its authorship to either Maštocʻ or his immediate disciples.

It is unnecessary here to go over the reasons for the rejection of
the traditional attribution of both the *Teaching* and the *Discourses* to
the Illuminator. Before dismissing the untenable ascription, however, there has to be some explanation for pairing the two documents in the first place. The linkage of these literarily dissimilar
works, composed more than a century apart, cannot be arbitrary;
obviously, they were considered as related works at some point in

---

its authorship by Maštocʻ, is rather ambivalent. To allow for the late fifth-century
Armenian authors' familiarity with the work, he is compelled to grant that "the
Teaching is a document that has undergone more than one stage of development"
(ibid., 52). Having earlier introduced the work's common themes and shared patristic tradition, Thomson turns his attention to the elusive yet early sources of
the work—all predating the 431 Council of Ephesus. He refers to verbatim parallels with an early and now lost Armenian text translated into Georgian: "On
the Faith," *De Fide,* attributed to Hippolytus (ibid., 51–52; citing the edition and
translation of the Georgian text by Gérard Garitte, "Le traité géorgien 'Sur la Foi'
attribué à Hippolyte," *Mus* 78 [1965]: 119–72). On questions about the identity of
Hippolytus, author of a catechism by way of questions and answers, a substantial
fragment of which, on the Holy Trinity, survives among the catena in the *Seal of
Faith* (7–15), see Léon-Marie Froidevaux, "Les Questions et Réponses sur la Sainte
Trinité attribuées à Hippolyte, évêque de Bostra," *RSR* 50 (1962): 32–73, who discerns a pre-Nicene core in this excerpt on the Trinity.

18. "And in keeping with the same spiritual practice, he would spend many
days in secluded places until notified by priests (*yericʻancʻ*) to come to help, by the
grace of Christ, in matters beneficial for the churches in those regions. And without further preoccupation, descending with his fellow workers to shoulder whatever happened to be the task, he would accomplish it through the strength given by
God. Through fluent speech [lit., 'with unshut mouth'] he would cause the overflowing and most abundant streams of his teaching to spread in the hearts of the
hearers." *Life* 23.9–10 (MH 1:250–51) (22 [82.9–15] ed. Abełyan) (trans. mine). The
passage suggests that the help given by Maštocʻ and his disciples was primarily in
teaching the laity (see also below, n. 75).

the course of their transmission. The *Teaching* and the *Discourses* seem to go hand in hand: the former, as catechism, is to prepare believers for baptism, and the latter, as moral exhortation, must have been thought of as essential to prepare the newly baptized to live virtuously, as expected of a Christian: to reinforce commitment and strengthen faith. To use biblical language, the former is like "milk" for infants, and the latter like "solid food" for the mature.[19] Perceived as such, the words of the anonymous author at the beginning of the seventh discourse are noteworthy: "When creatures grow from childhood into perfect adulthood and their wisdom increases with maturity, (then) they could hear satisfactorily the words of truth" (Disc. 7.1): that is, the truth as communicated through the *Discourses*. Equally noteworthy are the words near the end of the twenty-first discourse: "I speak wisdom to the mature" (Disc. 21.18).[20] The *Discourses* could thus have been considered a sequel to the *Teaching*. Their most obvious thematic connection is to be seen in their emphasis on the doctrine of the Trinity: whereas the *Teaching* concludes with emphasis that the Trinity is the most important doctrine (§§702–715), the *Discourses* begin with a treatise on the Trinity and abound with references to "the Most Holy Trinity."[21] The two works seem to have been deemed invariably related; and because the *Teaching* was already attributed to St. Gregory and had found its textual place in the *History* of Agathangelos (§§259–715), so too were the *Discourses* attributed to him. Or, as Arevshatyan thinks, just as several elements from Koriwn's *Life of Maštocʿ* were appropriated for St. Gregory by the continuator of the Agathangelian *History*, so were also these works of Maštocʿ.[22]

---

19. 1 Cor 3.2; Heb 5.12; cf. 1 Pt 2.2.

20. Drawing on 1 Cor 2.6.

21. The entire first discourse and the first paragraph of the second (1.1–2.6) are found as a single excerpt, evidently from an earlier recension of the *Yačaxapatum*, in *Knikʿ Hawatoy*, 18–22, where the text has been slightly refined; on this seventh-century compilation, see above, n. 11. Abraham Terian, "The First Two Discourses of the *Yačaxapatum* as a Single Discourse on the Most Holy Trinity," *HA* 132 (2018): 1–28. The appropriation of the Trinitarian theology of Gregory Nazianzen is obvious, throughout.

22. Arevshatyan, "Maštocʿ et les débuts de la patristique arménienne," 310. The attribution of the *Teaching* to either Maštocʿ or his circle of disciples is to be granted; not so with the *Discourses* on account of their later date, as we shall see.

The linking of the two works obscures the fact that the *Discourses* are basically a monastic text.[23] Also, its biblical quotations, even where they happen to overlap with those of the *Teaching*, are textually quite different and further removed from the extant Armenian Bible. Moreover, the compositional styles of the two works are very dissimilar, mitigating against the notion of common authorship. Whereas that of the *Teaching* is simple and in keeping with fifth-century works, that of the *Discourses* is complex and tediously garrulous.[24]

---

23. Boghos L. Zekiyan, "Back to the Sources of Armenian Spirituality: *Hachakhapatoum* as a Doctrinal and Practical Vademecum for Introduction to Christian Life and Monastic Spirituality," in *In Search of a Precious Pearl. 5th Encounter of Monks from East and West (EMO V) at Dzaghgatzor Monastery (Valley of the Flowers), Armenia, Thursday, 31 May–Thursday, 7 June 2001*, ed. Edward G. Farrugia (Rome: Pontificio Istituto Orientale; Riano: Cittadella Ecumenica Taddeide, 2005), 139–53; cf. idem, "Catechesi e inculturazione nel periodo formativo della Chiesa armena," *IJAIS* 12.1–2 (2014) ("Christianity in Ancient Iran. Papers of the International Conference '*Ad ulteriores gentes:* The Christians in the East 1st to 7th century,' Rome, March 2009," ed. Marco Bais et al.), 283–300.

24. A third work also wrongly attributed to the Illuminator is a brief, elenchic compilation called *Harc'umn ew patasxanik'* (*The Question[s] and Answers*), dealing with eschatological issues surrounding the Judgment. See N(ikołayos) Adontz, "Le Questionnaire de Saint Grégoire l'Illuminateur et ses rapports avec Eznik," *ROC* 25 [n.s. 5] (1925–1926): 309–57 (text = 312–22), who considers it one of the sources utilized by Eznik in the late 440s, in the latter's *Etc ałandoc'* (*Refutation of the Sects*); Levon Khach'ikyan, "Grigor Part'evin veragruac 'Harc'umě', orpes hay matenagrut'yan eraxayrik'" ("Le 'Questionnaire' attribué à Grégoire le Parthe, prémices de l'écriture arménienne"), *BM* 7 (1964): 301–30 (text = 315–28; cf. text in MH 1:147–53), attributes it to Maštoc'; reverting, however, to Adontz's position in "Otaralezu hay grakanut'iwně č'orrord darum" ("Foreign-language Armenian Literature in the Fourth Century"), *PBH* (1973): 3:27–51. For further emendations of the text, see Martiros Minassian, "Kanovn srboyn Grigori Part'ewi dardzeal harts'umn ew patasxanik' nora" ("Le 'Questionnaire' de Saint Grégoire l'Illuminateur"), *Bazmavep* 139 (1981): 57–72, who attributes it here, as elsewhere, to neither: "Grigor Part'ewi kam S. Maštoc'i veragruac 'Harc'umě' ew Eznik Kołbac'i" ("Le 'Questionnaire' attribué à Grégoire l'Illuminateur ou à Mesrop Machtotz n'est pas une source d'Eznik"), *HA* 85 (1971): 355–70, 463–82; 86 (1972): 73–94, 199–212, 347–54, 439–62; 87 (1973): 51–60. He sees it as an early canonical derivation from Eznik's *Refutation*, to the point of employing it to correct textual corruptions in the latter—following Galust Tēr-Mkrtč'ian's letter of 25 October 1911 to Nikoloaï Marr (cited, cols. 359–360). See, however, Michael E. Stone, "The Armenian Questions of St. Gregory: A Text Descended from *4 Ezra:* Edition of Recension I," *Mus* 131 (2018): 141–72, who rightly identifies three recensions (further articles by him to follow) and points to the apocalyptic book of *4 Ezra* (7:78–99) as their primary source.

Title, Headings, and Contents

The received title of the discourses is *Yačaxapatum Čaṙkʿ* (Յաճախապատում Ճառք), literally, "Oft-Repeated Discourses."[25] The adjectival compound *yačaxapatum* and the noun it qualifies bear close semblance to *čaṙs yačaxagoyns, diwrapatums* (ճառս յաճախագոյնս, դիւրապատումս / *"many discourses, easy to deliver"*) in Koriwn's description of the overall teaching of Maštocʿ, originally of oral derivation and subsequently committed to writing.[26] As noted, the whole designation was appropriated for St. Gregory the Illuminator by the continuator of the Agathangelian *History*, where it appears as *čaṙs yačaxagoyns, džuarapatums* (ճառս յաճախագոյնս, դժուարապատումս / *"many discourses, difficult to deliver"*). Paradoxically, the change from *diwrapatums* to *džuarapatums* alters the meaning from "delivered with ease" to "delivered with difficulty," and makes one ponder the possibility of a deliberate altering of the word by a learned scribe who, while endorsing the Agathangelian attribution of the *Discourses* to the Illuminator, seems to have sensed their many syntactical difficulties. Still, the word *yačaxapatum* remains a *hapax legomenon* (a word that occurs but once, and only with reference to the *Discourses*) in Armenian, and the possibility of its being a borrowed calque cannot be ruled out.

There is no reason to doubt the originality of the title given to the collection as a whole, even as one doubts the originality of most titles or headings of the discourses, with the name of the Illuminator appended to every heading. The title fittingly describes the overall character of the discourses with inherited themes and commonplace exhortations. The meaning of the adjectival compound *yačaxapatum* is sufficiently clear. The literal meaning is comparable

25. The title *Yačaxapatum* is at times rendered wrongly as *Stromata* or *Stromateis* ("Miscellanies" or "Patchwork"), following the Greek title Clement of Alexandria gave to the third work in his trilogy of works because it deals with a variety of subjects. It is interesting to note that the first edition of the *Discourses* has an expansive subtitle where the word *Yačaxapatum* is interpretatively rendered with a synonym, *Yognapatumkʿ*, meaning "much-repeated"; see below, n. 123.

26. See the preceding section on the traditional attributions and the references there. Koriwn's wording, as pointed out earlier (above, n. 17), suggests a written composition.

to Gk. *polylalētos* ("often said"). According to Malkhasian, who takes the word as a noun, it means "one who recounts [or] writes broadly and in detail, verbose";[27] but that would be equivalent to Gk. *polylalos*. He then cites as example the title *Yačaxapatum Čaṙk'* with its attribution to the Illuminator, without any further elaboration. The meaning he gives, while close, is misleading, for the term is used as an adjective alongside the noun *čaṙk'*, "discourses," "speeches," or "homilies." Following the literal meaning of the adjectival compound in conjunction with the noun it qualifies, the explicit meaning of *Yačaxapatum Čaṙk'* is "Oft-Repeated Discourses." However unique, the Armenian title is not altogether odd; it is a fitting designation for frequently delivered discourses of moral content. The repetitious use of comparable discourses in the early Church is well attested, especially in the epitomes and the less systematically organized variety of compilations that reached their high point in the Byzantine period. It was not uncommon to repeat moral discourses even when written by others.[28]

Contextually pertinent statements in several discourses lend themselves to the appropriateness of the title; for example, the concluding statement of Disc. 18: "Glorious are the teachers who take up this (exhortation) and teach the same" (§62). So too the concluding admonition of Disc. 5: "Now, be diligent in teaching this life-giving exhortation, to be heard regularly when rising up" (§120). And again, in the last discourse: "For this reason I often repeat (*yačaxagoyn asem*) the words of love, for this is good and acceptable to God, indeed his very command" (Disc. 23.117). Conversely, we read in Disc. 8: "Moreover, overseers should not hesitate to recount (*patmel*) the threats by the Lord God" (§83). Monastic over-

---

27. Step'an Malxasianc', *Hayerēn Bac'atrakan Baṙaran* (Arm. Explanatory Dictionary), 4 vols. (Erevan: Petakan Hratarakč'ut'iwn, 1944–1945), 3:385 («Ընդարձակ և մանրամասն պատմող՝ գրող, յաճախաբան»). He seems to follow somewhat the definition in *NBHL* 2:318.

28. The tradition of the necessity to repeat moral discourses is attested by Dio Chrysostom, *Oration* 17.1–11; cited by Abraham J. Malherbe, *Moral Exhortation: A Greco-Roman Sourcebook*, LEC 4 (Philadelphia: The Westminster Press, 1986), 154–57. For more on the transmission of moral traditions, see Wayne A. Meeks, *The Moral World of the First Christians*, LEC 6 (Philadelphia: The Westminster Press, 1986), 61–64.

seers or abbots had to exhort their followers, and some probably relied on such a sourcebook while others authored their own. Such teachers attracted those who were desirous for a Christ-like life, and taught not by word only but by their exemplary lives, which were deemed "perfect."

The titles of the discourses are long and not always descriptive of content; they seem to be secondary. While some titles or headings are rather inappropriate, others are altogether arbitrary. Disc. 2, on the Creator's beneficence and originally an integral part of Disc. 1, bears the title "On the Distinct Persons of the Holy Trinity," a title based on the opening paragraph of this severed discourse on the Trinity (according to the textual witness of *Knik' Hawatoy*).[29] Disc. 8, titled "Reproof of Heedless Living and (Admonition unto) Devotion to Virtue in General," is actually a diatribe against fornication. Disc. 11, the longest discourse, titled "On the Virtuous Life Crowned with Utmost Goodness by the Blessed One," is on the rewards of virtue, and deals with the benefits of faith, hope, and love (§§1–61); meekness (§§62–99); kindness, humility, and obedience (§§100–123); unity (§§124–131); compassion (§§132–139); thoughtfulness or discretion and the control of the senses (§§140–227), somewhat anticipating the diatribe against the wrongful use of the senses in Disc. 20.23–55, under the title "Guidance through Essential Counsel: Fundamentals of Knowledge and Understanding." Similarly, Disc. 12, irrespective of its lengthy title, "Teaching about the Provident Creator's Care, Condemnation of Disobedience and Defiance, and Guidance unto Morality—the Goodness of Morals," has virtually nothing about disobedience and/or rebelliousness; much of the discourse is about grieving over the dead, especially the unrepentant. So also Disc. 17; there is nothing there on discernment or discretion, irrespective of its title: "On Thoughtful Discretion (and the) Advantages of Readiness, with Honor for the Heedful and Punishment for the Heedless." In Disc. 21, titled "A Few Words on the Gift of Wisdom Bestowed by the Holy Spirit," the Spirit is not mentioned at all—in fact, not until the concluding line of Disc. 22, in the closing Trinitarian formula. Moreover, each title bears the name of St. Gregory as the author. These long titles,

29. See above, n. 21.

apart from the attribution, could be maintained in any translation of the text; however, revised and abridged titles could serve well for a table of contents or a synopsis.

In a medley of topics mostly related to the virtues and the virtuous life, it is interesting that after the initial discourse on the Trinity (Disc. 1–2) the author begins with the first of St. Paul's triad of virtues: faith, hope, and love, the so-called theological virtues (Disc. 3).[30] There is, however, some logical deficiency in the sequence of the discourses, even though four consecutive discourses deal with the virtuous life and its rewards (Disc. 10–13). Disc. 13 and 16, on memorial services and martyrs, are thematically related, yet separated by the thematically related Disc. 14–15, on human nature and the soul.

In the last discourse, titled "Counsel to Ascetics and General Directives That Promote Virtue," the word gnյgp (c'oyc'k', "directives" or, literally, "demonstrations") reminds one of the Syriac *Demonstrations* of Aphrahat (d. ca. 345), whose twenty-three "demonstrations" have some commonality with the *Yačaxapatum*, for example, Dem. 1: *On Faith;* Dem. 3: *On Fasting;* and elsewhere.[31] Indeed, Aphrahat's first ten "demonstrations" deal mostly with ascetic topics. Be that as it may, the division of the *Yačaxapatum* into twenty-three discourses is arbitrary, given the fact that the first two discourses constituted one discourse initially, and more than one major topic is squeezed under certain titles. The same pattern is discernible in the *Xrat Varuc'* (*Exhortation for Life*) homiliary, attributed by some to Catholicos Yovhan(nēs) Mandakuni (in office 478–490)[32] and by

30. 1 Cor 13.13; cf. Heb 11.

31. The extant Armenian version of the *Demonstrations*, wrongly attributed to Jacob of Nisibis, consists of nineteen homilies: *Srboy Hōrn meroy Yakobay Mcbnay Episkoposi Čaṙk': Sancti Patris Nostri Jacobi Episcopi Nisibeni Sermones*, ed. Niccolò M. Antonelli (Rome: Typiis Sacrae Congregationis de Propaganda Fide, 1756); see, however, Guy Lafontaine, ed. and trans., *La version arménienne des œuvres d'Aphraate le Syrien*, CSCO 382–383, 405–406, 423–424 (Leuven: Sécretariat du CSCO, 1977–1980), and Adam Lehto, trans., *The Demonstrations of Aphrahat, the Persian Sage*, GECS 27 (Piscataway, NJ: Gorgias Press, 2010). The comparison need not be pushed further, since the *Discourses* differ from the *Demonstrations* and *ascetica* in general that are addressed to novices in more or less dialogue form; e.g., Maximus the Confessor, *Liber asceticus* (PG 90:912–56; CCSG 40, ed. Van Deun).

32. First by Vardan Arewelc'i (d. 1271), followed by others in recent scholarship; see MH 1:1155–57, for a brief introduction and bibliography; cf. Levon B. Zekiyan,

others to Yovhan(nēs) Mayravanecʻi or Mayragomecʻi, the sacristan of the catholicosal cathedral at Dwin (d. ca. 640).[33] Even this work, the *Xrat Varucʻ* homiliary, seems to be a reduction from a much larger collection of homilies.[34]

Biblical Quotations, Allusions, and Echoes

The author's loose citations of Scripture make it difficult to draw lines of demarcation between exact quotations, paraphrases, allusions, and reminiscences or echoes of the biblical text. His biblical citations differ, even when the same passage is cited repeatedly, thus leaving no doubt that the citations are mostly by way of recall rather than strictly textual. By the same token, rampant amplification as part of the recall often blurs the distinction between exact quotations and amplifications. There are inconsistencies when the same passage is quoted again; for example, Mal 3.7, «Դարձարուք առ իս և ես դառնամ առ ձեզ», is quoted verbatim in Disc. 12.91. The same passage, however, is amplified as follows in Disc. 5.48: «Դարձարուք առ իս ի մեղաց և խոստովան լերուք և ապաշխարեցէք, և ես դառնամ առ ձեզ յողորմութիւն շնորհաւք ի բժշկել ի փրկել ի կեցուցանել». His loose citations, his cavalier way of handling the wording of his biblical quotations, raise the question of what constitutes a "citation," a much-discussed topic in recent study of ancient quotations. Such discursive manner in

---

"La relation entre le sacrifice et la communion dans la théologie de Hovhan Mandakouni," in *The Eucharist in Theology and Philosophy. Issues of Doctrinal History in East and West from the Patristic Age to the Reformation,* ed. István Perczel, Réka Forrai, and György Geréby, Ancient and Medieval Philosophy, Series 1, 35 (Leuven: Leuven University Press, 2005), 81–93. Cf. idem, "Yovhan Mandakunii tesutʻiunĕ Surb Hałordutʻean merjecʻumi masin" ("La dottrina di Y. Mandakuni sulla Comunione frequente"), *Bazmavep* 132 (1974): 129–43.

33. First by Stepʻanos Tarōnecʻi, also known as Asołik (d. ca. 1015), followed by few others in recent scholarship: see especially the study by Karapet Tēr-Mkrtčʻian and that by Nersēs Akinian and Petros Tēr-Połosian, cited in MH 1:1155–57; see also Abraham Terian, "Mandakuni's 'Encyclical' on Fasting," in *Worship Traditions in Armenia and the Neighboring Christian East,* ed. Roberta R. Ervine, AVANT 3 (Crestwood, NY: St. Vladimir's Seminary Press, 2006), 185–95.

34. Karapet Tēr-Mkrtčʻian, "Yovhan Mandakuni ew Yovhan Mayragomecʻi," *Šołakatʻ hayagitakan taregirkʻ (Šołakatʻ Armenological Annual)* (1913): 84–136.

which Scripture is quoted is common in Syriac, even in Syriac works translated from Greek—such as Basil's *Hexaemeron*.[35]

Two more examples of the rampant divergence from the biblical text will suffice. The Armenian text of Ps 119.113 (118.113 LXX and Arm.) reads: «Զանաւրէնս ատեցի, և զաւրէնս քո սիրեցի»; the author has «Զմեղս ատեցի և անարգեցի, և զաւրէնս քո սիրեցի» (Disc. 19.6; 20.30). The text of Ex 32.6 reads: «և նստաւ ժողովուրդն յուտել և յըմպել, և յարեան ի խաղալ»; the author has «(որովայնամուքն) որ նստան ուտել և ըմպել և յարեան ի խաղալ» (Disc. 19.41) and «(ժողովրդեանն) որ ուտելով և ըմպելով ի խաղս լիեալ» (Disc. 9.65).

Whether the author regularly quotes from memory or from a text at his disposal is hard to determine. The most that could be said, with a degree of reservation, is that he rarely seems to be quoting from a text at hand. Even so, this begs the question of identifying the underlying text(s) or *Vorlage(n): whether Greek, Syriac, or Armenian. Here, too, complexities abound, leading to despair of all efforts to distinguish between the versions, for the quotations—with rare exceptions—diverge from the wording of all three. In nearly a tenth of the quotations there is indication of some reliance on the Armenian Bible. One cannot help but observe with Vööbus that "The Armenian fathers often quote readings which occur only on grounds of Syriac text tradition,"[36] albeit rather lost tradition. Yet there can be no doubt that the author normally quoted loosely from memory, in keeping with the practices of writers in antiquity—just as scribes also tended to follow readings retained in their memory and not the wording of their exemplars.

There are but few cues or explicit formulae for the use of Scripture. Quotations are variously introduced. Only twice we encounter "It is written": in Disc. 2.6: "*'with a pure heart and a sincere faith,'* as written" (1 Tm 1.5); and in Disc. 20.30: "For it is written, saying: *'I hated and demeaned sin, but loved your Law'*" (Ps 119.113 [118.113 LXX]). Apart from instances where the biblical book or author is

35. Robert W. Thomson, ed., *The Syriac Version of the Hexaemeron by Basil of Caesarea*, CSCO 511, Scriptores Syri 223 (Leuven: Peeters, 1995).

36. Arthur Vööbus, *Studies in the History of the Gospel Text in Syriac*, CSCO 128, Subsidia 3 (Leuven: Durbecq, 1951), 150.

named, the usual introduction to a quotation is the conventional third-person-singular verb ասէ (*asē*), "it says," with "Scripture" as the presumed subject.[37] Paul is quoted some fifty times, though named but three times; his usual introduction is simply "the Apostle." Through it all, the author shows strong familiarity with the writings of Paul and much of the rest of Scripture. Only the major prophets are sometimes cited by name: Moses, Isaiah, Jeremiah, Ezekiel, and Daniel, so also David with his Psalms. His canon included The Wisdom of Solomon, from which he quotes three times, and certainly 1–2 Maccabees, judging from his repeated adulation of the Maccabean martyrs. Beyond the New Testament, with which he seems to have been very much at home, he shows some familiarity with the apocryphal Gospel of Nicodemus (Disc. 11.101).

The language of the author's presumed *Vorlage* must have been Armenian, even though the vast majority of the biblical quotations do not reflect his explicit use of the Armenian Bible. Three examples will help illustrate the former actuality. The citation of Prv 1.2 at Disc. 2.114 «ճանաչել զիմաստութիւն և զխրատ» (*"to know wisdom and discipline"*) is suggestive of the Armenian Bible, an early fifth-century translation that began with these words, according to Koriwn, *Life of Maštoc‘*, 8.7 (MH 1:238). No less suggestive is the citation of Ezek 18.2, «Հարք ագողի կերան, և որդւոց ատամունք առան» (*"The fathers ate sour grapes, and the children's teeth are set on edge"*), which reads as «Հարք ագողի կերան, և որդւոց ատամունք առին» at Disc. 8.76. So too is Eph 5.6, «վասն այսորիկ իսկ գայ բարկութիւն Աստուծոյ ի վերայ որդւոցն անհաւանութեան» (*"because of these things the wrath of God comes on the children of displeasure"*), which reads as «վասն այսորիկ [ասէ (says, viz. the Apostle)] գայ բարկութիւն Աստուծոյ ի վերայ որդւոցն անհաւանութեան» at Disc. 20.119. In each of these citations, the last word could not have been used apart from the Armenian Bible. Illustrative of the uncertain derivation of many more citations is Jer 48.10 (31.10 LXX) at Disc. 17.26: «Անիծեալ ամենայն որ գործէ զգործ Տեառն ծուլութեամբ» (*"Everyone who does the Lord's work idly is accursed"*). This differs somewhat from that of the Armenian Bible, which has «Անիծեալ լիցի որ գործէ զգործ Տեառն հեղգութեամբ» (*"Cursed*

---

37. Disc. 2.27, 151; 4.13, 62; 5.51, 121; 7.10, 11, 19; 8.55, 64; 10.7, 9, 119; 12.43; 13.38; 14.19; 16.30; 17.10, 21, 26, 40; 20.51, 159; 22.12; 23.38.

be the one who does the Lord's work carelessly"), better reflected in the Armenian version of Basil's *Rules,* «Անիծեալ ամենայն որ գործէ [var. գործեն] զգործ Տեառն հեղգութեամբ» (178), «Անիծեալ որ գործէ զգործ Տեառն հեղգութեամբ» (308), «Անիծեալ որ գործէ զգործ Տեառն յուլութեամբ [var. ծուլութեամբ, հեղգութեամբ]» (506), «Անիծեալ է որ գործէ զգործ Տեառն յուլութեամբ [var. հեղգութեամբ]» (515), and «Անիծեալ [var. + ամենայն] որ առնէ [var. գործէ] զգործ Տեառն [var. գործ զՏեառն] յուլութեամբ [var. հեղգութեամբ]» (551).[38]

The high frequency with which the author incorporates biblical citations into his composition is part of his aim to provide authoritative grounding for his counsel. Consequently, and quite frequently, his quotations are in clusters; for example, Disc. 2.19–23:

> For this reason, let us cease from vain and pointless criticism and let us follow the counsel of the Holy Scriptures, both Old and New. And let no one be left out of saying what is right: *"For in him we live and move and have our being"* (Acts 17.28). Listen to him and trust in him, the One who saved us from all dangers and who transfers us to the Kingdom of Heaven. He, who calls everyone unto obedience to the spiritual law, says in the Psalter: *"Come, my children, listen to me, and I will teach you the fear of the Lord"* (Ps 34.11 [33.12 LXX]). As the Lord says: *"He who keeps my commandments is the one who loves me; and he who loves me, my Father will love him, and we will come to him and make our home with him"* (Jn 14.21, 23). We have been honored with such ineffable love!

Most of the exhortations are based on catenae of scriptural quotations and allusions with little or no interpretation. "Earth" in Mt 5.5 is interpreted as "the Church" (10.34–35). A string of interpretations pertaining to Mt 16.18 is found in Disc. 17.27–28, with some indication of the author's ecclesiology:

> And the Lord said this to Peter in the Gospels: *"You are rock, and on this rock I will build my church";* that is, the faithful people of God. *"And the gates of hell shall not prevail against them";* (namely), the saints and the righteous by true

---

38. Hardly any of the scores of full biblical verses cited in both the Armenian version of Basil's *Rules* and the *Discourses* agree textually. Of the many citations see, e.g., those from Matthew's Gospel that are common to both documents (indexed here and in Uluhogian's edition of Arm. Basil's *Rules,* t. 20, 221–222): Mt 5.3, 6–7, 11–12, 14–16, 23–24, 29; 7.6; 10.26; 15.19; 18.10, 18; 22.37–40; 25.21, 30, 34–35, 40–42, 46.

faith,[39] those who were released from earth into heaven. *"And those you bind on earth"* are the unholy and the unjust and those who believe differently;[40] *"shall be bound in heaven,"* for the ominous punishments. The words spoken by the Lord to Peter are spoken to all holy overseers, those who really have the truth.

The "owner of a house" in the parabolic saying of Mt 13.52 is understood as the "church leader" (*arajnord*) in this discourse, which, closely anticipating the specifics of the role of the abbot in the final discourse, compels the author to warn his monastic community about the undesirable outsiders (Disc. 17.36–37):

He called the church leader "a house owner," one who has become a disciple of the true traditions. The "treasures" are the heart's wisdom, which holds positive knowledge of things "old and new," and graces those near and far with good thoughts, good deeds, and impeccable holiness. And the crop of evil deeds (is like) digging outside, where no remnants of good learning are left in the bad treasure, to sort the good from the bad.

Far more noteworthy is the author's systematic commentary on the "Beatitudes" (Mt 5.3–10) in Disc. 10.29–73.

Literary Style

The *Discourses* are not in the "high" literary style of Classical Armenian typical of fifth-century or "Golden Age" writings and translations employing the newly developed alphabet. As noted earlier, it is inconceivable that they are the "discourses" claimed for Maštoc' by Koriwn, whose laudation fits the *Teaching* more than the *Discourses*.[41] Yet, at different stages in the continuation of the *History* of Agathangelos, both the *Teaching* and the *Discourses* were claimed for the Illuminator, dissimilar as they are in both form and style of writing. Distinct from the earlier appropriation of the *Teaching*

39. Echoing Rom 3.28; Gal 2.16; 3.11, 24.

40. Or, "those of heterodox faith" (Arm. զայլահաւատս, *zaylahawats*), juxtaposed with "the faithful people of God" or "those who really have the truth."

41. Given the late sixth-century date of the *Discourses* and their grammatical shortcomings, distinctly different from the grammatically better structured works of the Golden Age (such as the *Teaching* and others from the idyllic period of early Armenian literature that saw the translation of the Bible), it seems unlikely that this work was in the mind of Koriwn. Moreover, the *Discourses* contain borrowings from the *Teaching*, as shown below.

for the Illuminator, the appropriation of the *Discourses* comes in the train of several attributes of Maštocʻ claimed for the Illuminator by the last redactor of the Armenian text of Agathangelos. The disconcerting style and grammatical shortcomings of the *Discourses* (as seen in the Venetian editions of 1838 and 1954) seem to have necessitated a slightly amplified redaction that was carried out partially (as seen in the Ējmiacin edition),[42] not unlike the earlier redaction observed in the opening discourse(s), adapted into a doctrinal statement on the Trinity (as seen in the *Knikʻ Hawatoy*, the *Seal of Faith*).

Even at first reading of the *Discourses* in the original language one could discern the notoriously pedantic style of Syriac prose. Following the Trinitarian formulae that characterize the first discourse(s), there comes a sudden departure from the lofty style with which the author begins.[43] There are grammatical errors of various sorts on every page that at times seem to call into question the Armenian authorship of the work. Were it not for the evidence for the author's use of the Armenian Bible, the *Teaching*, and the Armenian translation of Basil's *Rules* and that of the *Hermetica*, the grammati-

42. The Venetian Mekhitarists' editions are based on manuscript V1504, dated to 1673, the colophon of which states that it was copied from a manuscript written in uncials, *erkatʻagir*, dating from 929 and kept in Sis. The 1894 Ējmiacin edition, according to the introduction, is based on a manuscript dated to 1293 (old no. 1655, now M1479). Regardless of its comparatively early date, the latter manuscript is a witness to a slightly revised edition of the *Discourses*, indeed to an abortive attempt to render the whole in a more fluent style. The effort fizzles out after the first few discourses. An intermediate witness is a manuscript at St. James in Jerusalem, dated to 1215 (J94), the oldest of the known manuscripts of the *Discourses* (a detached half of M947), on which see N(orayr) Covakan (Połarian), "*Yačaxapatum* (1215): (Ĵeṛ. S.Y. Tʻ. 94)," *Sion* 35 (1961): 74–75, holding that it too follows the now lost manuscript of the year 929. There is a description with three photographs of a still older, lost manuscript provided by its last owner, Edward Aleanakʻian, "Hnagir 'Yačaxaptuam' (*sic*) mē" ("An Old-script *Yačaxapatum*"), in *Amēnun Tarecʻoycʻ, 21rd Tari (Almanack for All: 21st Year)*, ed. Tʻēodik (Tēodoros Lapʻčʻinčian) (Paris: Imprimerie Massis, 1927), 463–66. The manuscript is written in uncials, and the 23 headings are adorned in Kufic, the Arabic decorative script of the early Islamic period. None of these manuscripts is cited by Hakob Kʻeōsēian, the editor of the text in the MH edition, who follows the Venetian edition(s).

43. Disc. 1–2 constitutes the best example of a lofty style in the corpus; but even this seems to have been considered wanting by the radical redactor who drastically amplified the text, more so at the beginning (as witnessed in the manuscripts of the text comprising the 1894 edition).

cal complexity of his text—replete with non-scribal errors—would have suggested either (a) a work translated by an ill-prepared translator, or (b) an original work by a non-native speaker of the Armenian language. Clearly, the author's compositional skills do not measure up to those of fifth-century authors, collectively known as the Circle of Maštocʻ. Syriac influence could affect an Armenian writer at home in this Semitic language, and one could point to occasional instances of this in fifth-century writings of known Armenian authorship. The frequency of such instances in the *Discourses*, however, far exceeds that of the occasional, isolated irregularities in earlier writings.[44]

There is constant confusion between nouns and adjectives even when these are together, especially when these stand for abstract notions (ending with -թիւն, -թեան). Such grammatical inconsistency stems from the fact that Syriac is much more rigid than Armenian, compelling the borrower into adopting calques within the structure of sentences. And every so often, a construction started at the beginning of a sentence is not followed through, thus creating an anacoluthon. Given the verbosity of the author, or of the sources utilized by him, he seems to have had further difficulty: not foreseeing at the start the expression of additional thoughts, he obscures their connection to the structure with which he begins. The discourses are full of such anacoluthic instances, and it is this characteristic of the text that makes it difficult for a modern translator—especially for one unaware of the conflated syntactical dynamics of the two unrelated languages. Delineating the author's non-Armenian sources, however, remains a problem—more so,

44. Such as seen in the confused position of the adjective in relation to an expanded noun phrase, or the expansion of the adjective through a construct phrase, or the missed structural meaning of compound sentences. The grammatical and syntactical anomalies of the *Discourses* were observed by two distinguished philologists: Vardan Hacʻuni and Ełišē Durian, both of whom ruled out its authorship by either Maštocʻ or his immediate disciples, preferring to see it instead as the work of a second-generation disciple from the end of the fifth century; Hacʻuni, "Erb šaradruac en *Yačaxapatum Čaṙkʻ*" ("When were the *Yačaxapatum Discourses* Composed?"), *Bazmavep* 88 (1930): 401–6; Durian, *Patmutʻiwn Hay Matenagrutʻean* (*History of Armenian Literature*), Durian Matenadaran 2, Ambołǰ Erker Ełišē Patriarkʻ Duriani 1 (Jerusalem: St. James Press, 1933), 414–26. For more on these irregularities, see Appendix IV.

identifying them. This will be discussed below; but first more on the overriding style.

The author uses several different words for the dead or the departed: մեռեալք, ննջեցեալք, կատարեալք, վախճանեալք, հանգուցեալք, and at times հրաժարեալք, the word for penitents. In Disc. 12 զհրաժարեալսն (*zhražarealsn*, "the renouncers" or "the penitents") is used repeatedly (§§37, 38, 39, 58, 63, 64) in the sense of "the departed" or "those perfected" through death (զկատարեալսն, *zkatarealsn*, as in §15; cf. §89, եւ յայս աշխարհէս, *el yays ašxarhēs*, "[those] leaving this world"). The author seems to confuse such "departure" from the world with "withdrawal" from the world through "renunciation." The same confusion is seen in Disc. 13.66, 71, 72, where *zhražarealsn* is used instead of *katareloc'n*, as in §65. It seems to me that at times the author's inconsistencies result from misapprehension of borrowed passages.[45]

Consistency of style and thematic overlaps leave no doubt about a single authorship. The author was a master in the field of spiritual instruction, albeit redundant in the essentials of the faith and verbose in his hortatory admonitions. The discourses are marred by verbosity and repetitiveness, in part because of the author's drawing from a rich repertoire of mainstream Christian texts and traditions. Piling up divine titles and apposite attributes is a trait, resulting in a style that is often awkward and inelegant. More often than not, the awkwardness seems to be a result of heavy reliance on Syriac sources, seen in the rather clumsy construction of countless sentences. As noted, awkward phrases are found also in fifth-century Armenian writings, but not to the extent found in the *Discourses,* the result of Semitic constructs or Syriacism.[46] Coupled

45. A similar instance of an inconsistently translated source is found at Disc. 20.70. Satan's epithet "accuser" (բանսարկու, *bansarku*), which is the meaning of the Hebrew name, is used repeatedly (2.144; 5.34; 9.27, 32; 10.138; 11.59; 18.27; 21.19); but when the meaning of Satan's Hebrew name is given in Disc. 20.70 («Սատանայ... ըստ եբրայեցւոց բառից'ն հակառակ թարգմանի», *Satanay ... ēst ebrayec'woc' baŕic'n hakaŕak t'argmani*), the epithet "adverse" (հակառակ, *hakaŕak*) is used instead of "adversary" (հակառակորդ, *hakaŕakord*), a word used twice earlier with reference to Satan (Disc. 6.38; 10.68).

46. Some typical examples of intensification through emphatic repetition:– մեռանել զմեղացն մահ (*meŕanel zmeŕac'n mah*), Disc. 2.134–օրհնելով օրհնեցուք (*awrhnelov awrhnesc'uk'*), Disc. 3.23–զպէտս պիտոյից (*zpēts pitoyic'*), Disc. 4.27–

with ubiquitous grammatical errors, these point to an extraordinary reliance on Syriac sources—albeit poorly translated passages. There can be no question that the author was a passionate reader of Syriac and less so of Greek.[47]

From a literary perspective, the document leaves much to be desired. Its sparse use of imagery is limited to certain discourses only,[48] a far cry from the laudatory phrase in the above quotations from Koriwn (regarding Maštocʻ) and Agathangelos (regarding the Illuminator).[49] The document is replete with lists of virtues and vices, used paraenetically, as expected in an ancient document on moral instruction.[50] Commensurate with these, one finds ten mandates for the virtuous person (Disc. 18.29–39); ten mandates for the "virtuous ones who are witnesses for the Truth and living martyrs loved by the Lord" (Disc. 18.44–58); ten mandates that define repentance (Disc. 19.13–23); and others. There are twelve answers to question(s) on why the death of the righteous is honorable in the sight of God (Disc. 12.68–78). There is but little structure in the rest, where the author's irksome style dominates.

բարուցն բարութեանց (*barucʻn barutʻeancʻ*), Disc. 5.106–ազատութիւնն ազատ են (*azatutʻiwnkʻn azat en*), Disc. 7.32–խրատելով խրատէ (*xratelov xratē*), Disc. 7.63–կելով կեցցէ (*kelov kecʻcʻē*), Disc. 7.80 –նորոգեցին նորոգութեամբ (*norogescʻin norogutʻeamb*), Disc. 13.66–մեռանելով մեռանիցի (*meṙanelov meṙanicʻi*), Disc. 20.139–փառաւորութիւն փառաւոր է (*pʻaṙaworutʻiwn pʻaṙawor ē*), Disc. 20.163.

47. The use of sources alien in origin may be seen also in such instances as found in Disc. 11.41, among others. The glorification of the olive tree and the use of olive oil for anointing suggests a non-Armenian provenance. There is no mention in the *Discourses* of *miwṙon*, the consecrated fragrant oil derived from various plants and used as Holy Chrism in the Armenian Church. Nor should we ignore a shared Syriac religious culture in this period. See Ervand Tēr-Minasian, *Die Beziehungen der Armenischen Kirche zu den Syrischen bis zum ende des 6. Jahr-hunderts* (Leipzig: A. Pries, 1904); a revised version of this doctoral dissertation appeared in Armenian: *Hayocʻ Eketecʻu yaraberutʻiwnnerě Asorwocʻ eketecʻineri het* (Ējmiacin: Tparan Mayr Atʻoṙoy, 1908).

48. Disc. 6.1–3, 89–90; 10.30, 71–72, 97, 99 (proverbial), 110; 11.2, 80, 88, 129, 156, 159, 186, 193–194, 207–213; 14.35, 40; 15.32–33 (parabolic), 37; 19.48; 20.22, 97, 144.

49. Agathangelos uses the phrase «առակս խորհմացս» ("profound parables"). The word «առակս» is used but once in the *Discourses*, and that in the sense of "illustrations" to help comprehend the concept of a Triune God (Disc. 6.5).

50. See, e.g., Disc. 2.100; 11.145; 19.40; 20.20; 23.2, 14. On the prevalence of such lists in antiquity, see Malherbe, *Moral Exhortation*, 138–39.

For further stylistic and grammatical oddities, see the philological observations in Appendix IV.

Theological Ethics and Moral Philosophy

In the *Discourses* one finds nearly all the typical elements of moral exhortation of the early Church in late antiquity. Moreover, the recurring emphases on virtue and the virtues (Arm. *ar̄ak'inut'iwn[k']*) throughout the book, along with the imperative to pursue the virtuous life, cover all the meanings of the word *aretē* (from the cardinal virtues to the good and beautiful) in Greek moral philosophy—both intellectual and ethical, dating from Socrates and Plato.[51] The broad concepts associated with the term, both singular and plural, were endorsed and expanded upon not only by non-Christian moralists in the post-classical period but also by early Christian writers whose faith sought much of the same happy destiny, the highest good—the *summum bonum*—promised to all who espouse *aretē* or the *aretai*. In their religious use, wisdom, temperance, courage, and justice acquired broader meanings: ranging, respectively, from human prudence to divine or God-given wisdom, from sobriety to abstinence and renunciation of the world, and from fortitude to martyrdom. Justice (Gk. *dikaiosynē;* Arm. *ardarut'iwn*), being the same word as for "righteousness" or "uprightness," with legal meanings of "fairness" in both distributive justice and corrective (or retributive) justice, acquired many more meanings: from merited reward or punishment to vindication of right and annihilation of wrong. Christian moralists, as earlier in Hellenistic Judaism, could not have been indifferent to such Greek philosophical terms and concepts when presenting the moral excellence of their faith, the higher morality required in the struggle against vice (termed sin). While generally in agreement, there is a perceived inconsistency in the Christian sources between that which is a moral achievement and that which is a divine gift.[52]

---

51. The division of the virtues into intellectual and ethical or moral is Aristotelian (*Nicomachean Ethics* 1103a1–10).

52. The confusion goes back to pre-Christian times, to when *aretē* became a synonym of *dynamis* (excellence, power, efficacy) when speaking of the virtue of the gods and their powerful operation, their goodness and might. See Otto Bauernfeind, "*aretē*," in *Theological Dictionary of the New Testament* (*Theologisches Wörterbuch*

The author's theology derives from the Scriptures, with which he was very much at home, especially the Pauline corpus with its wealth of exhortation. His frequent, free, and paraphrastic citations are clear indicators of this. Biblical citations and allusions aside, echoes of biblical language are everywhere. He sums up his theology as "what we learned from the divines: the true traditions of the Holy Scriptures and the right fundamentals (of the faith)" (Disc. 20.125). The traditional theological categories of the Scriptures are recurring themes in the *Discourses:* the doctrine of God and the Trinity, the creation of the world, God's will for his creatures, the fall into sin, the necessity of Christ's incarnation for the redemption of humankind—with but one comment on his nature,[53] the necessity of repentance (with much repeated exhortation to repentance and contrition), and the Judgment. The author's sweep of salvation history in Disc. 2.120 sums it all up: "And thus we have been instructed: from opting for the Law to faith and light and love for justice, allegiance to the cumulative virtues and to the true Apostles and Prophets, to orthodox teachers and those who learned from them."

The emphasis on ethics, however, is paramount, as the discourses focus not on knowledge but on edification. They emphasize the renunciation of the world through self-denial, as a means of purifying the soul for union with God, and go on to address the rather mundane problems of ascetic and monastic life.

The moral teachings are a confused mixture of principles of right behavior in general, with supplementary instruction for monastic conduct in the later discourses. For our author, virtue is

---

zum Neuen Testament), ed. Gerhard Kittel, trans. Geoffrey W. Bromiley, 10 vols. (Grand Rapids, MI: Eerdmans, 1964–1976), 1:457–61. A substantial systematization emerges in the moral theology of the Cappadocian Fathers, in their soteriological expressions on the nature of God and the involvement of the will in human assimilation of or *approximation* to the *divine nature, in what is often termed as* "Semi-pelagianism."

53. Note the Miaphysite emphasis in Disc. 9.68. The statement in Disc. 2.4, «Մի է բնութիւն Աստուածութեանն» (*mi ē bnut'iwn Astuacut'eann,* "One is the nature of the Godhead"), is on the nature of God or of the Trinity in general, not a strictly Christological statement—much as it sounds similar to the Miaphysite dictum of Cyril of Alexandria, "One is the nature of the Incarnate Word," that had become the cornerstone of Armenian Christology since the Council of Ephesus.

continuance in a state of grace leading finally to a state of glory.[54] A somewhat systematic discussion of certain virtues is found in Disc. 11: meekness (§§62–99), kindness (§§100–125), unity of faith (§§126–131), and compassion (§§132–139); followed by warnings about passions and affections associated with the senses (§§140–227). These are but a distant echo of the moral exhortations of the Greco-Roman world, adopted by early Christian writers as of the second century, those who advocated a Christian life in terms of the Platonic cardinal virtues—albeit in their expanded and Christianized form.[55] In the discourses one does not find the philosophically reasoned moral theology of the post-apostolic period, such as that which is found in Clement of Alexandria's *Stromata*, or *Miscellanies*, for the ethical instruction and training of the Christian theologian. Of the more sophisticated questions, the author raises certain of the historic issues of theodicy; still, his brief responses fall short of the reasoned answers given in late antiquity.[56]

The author is a moral teacher whose aim is apparent in his exhortations. His repeated use of the hortatory "let us" is noteworthy; it is utilized to the end, with a penultimate emphasis on monasticism: "Let us fulfill sanctity with the fear of God.... And leaving worldly preoccupations, let us draw near to the angelic life without looking for earthly things" (Disc. 23.25, 120). He thus reiterates what he begins with: "Let us follow the counsel of the Holy Scriptures, both Old and New.... Let us flee from the filthy and abominable passions and the evils that threaten with painful consequences, and let us follow with clean lives the example of those above" (Disc. 2.19, 45). The Gospel must be expressed in a highly moral

54. For his canon(s) of virtue, see, e.g., Disc. 15.19; 23.2, 13.

55. On the Platonic tetrad of the cardinal virtues, based on Book IV of the *Republic* (419–445e), and its later versions, see Helen F. North, "Canons and Hierarchies of the Cardinal Virtues in Greek and Latin Literature," in *The Classical Tradition: Literary and Historical Studies in Honor of Harry Caplan*, ed. Luitpold Wallach (Ithaca: Cornell University Press, 1966), 165–83. The virtues in Christianity are not limited to St. Paul's triad of the so-called theological virtues: faith, hope, and love (1 Cor 13.13). Hellenistic philosophy—Middle Platonism in particular—helped shape the world-view in which the New Testament writers articulated the Christian faith and prepared the way for the synthesis of thought in Neo-Platonism, particularly in Plotinus and Pseudo-Dionysius.

56. See, e.g., Disc. 2.149–152; 4.95–97; 12.68–78; 18.12–13.

life. The biblical exhortations and those of the Church Fathers are very important to him, as he admonishes: "Let us not miss out on the gifts pledged in the Gospel.... Let us keep in mind, throughout our lives, the counsel of the saints" (Disc. 3.5, 8). "So, let us heed with the saints, in pure love, the One who calls. Let us seek, with fervent and ardent tears, that rest, through our labors here.[57] Let us quench the fire of the passions with the fire of the Holy Spirit.[58] '*Let us cleanse ourselves,*' even our senses and the invisible movements of the soul, '*from guilty conscience*'" (Heb 10.22; Disc. 16.21). "Let us lift up our minds daily to eternal blessings, decidedly away from vain opinions" (Disc. 20.125).

In his moral teachings the author seems to have been guided by Col 3.14: "And over all these virtues put on love, which binds them all together in perfect unity," but which he never quotes. He is fond of qualifying "love" with the adjective "holy" (Arm. *surb sēr*) to convey the true meaning of a foreign word for brotherly love, translating—so it seems—Syriac *hoba* or Greek *agapē* in his sources.

Given the author's repetitiousness and the overlapping themes throughout, I shall take but six of the *Yačaxapatum* discourses (nos. 3, 7, 11, 15, 19, 23) to illustrate the moral-philosophical content of the collection, touching also on the author's theology. In a medley of topics mostly related to the virtues and the virtuous life, it is interesting that after the initial discourse(s) on the Trinity the author begins with the first of St. Paul's triad of virtues: faith, hope, and love, the so-called theological virtues.[59] My choice to begin with the third discourse rests on this observation. As to the rest, I have taken every fourth discourse through the book. These should suffice to illustrate the author's moral philosophy against the background of the moral world of Greco-Roman times and that of the early Church in late antiquity.[60] I shall provide short synopses of

57. Tears continue the cleansing of the baptismal font (Disc. 9.29). On the varied implications of tears in religious context, see Gary L. Ebersole, "The Function of Ritual Weeping Revisited: Affective Expression and Moral Discourse," *HR* 39 (2000): 211–46.

58. As in the Byzantine monastic tradition, he uses the term "passion" (Arm. *c'ankut'iwn*) as the equivalent of vice.

59. 1 Cor 13.13; cf. Heb 11.

60. The primitive character of the initial discourses may be illustrated by the following quotation: "I always say [միշտ ասեմ]: 'Let us in all things be grateful

the six discourses and shall dwell on some essential points following each synopsis. As pointed out earlier, the discourse titles are not always indicative of content; more often than not, they are complex and appear to be of later derivation, and are at times misleading.

"Insights into Faith" (Disc. 3)

In this short discourse, *Mitk' Hawatoy,* literally, "The Mind of Faith," the author highlights the transcendence of God and his incomprehensibility even by heavenly beings. This transcendent God is nonetheless seen and apprehended by faith. Faith leads to the fullness of virtue that leads to God. His servants variously proclaim this God, "each according to one's grace" (§§1–12). To those who are enlightened about divine things and pursue virtue, the Lord himself becomes "the artisan of their art" (§§13–18). This God becomes comprehensible in so far as he allows himself to be seen: "For as the sunbeams extend and retract, so too (radiates) the truth of the Existent, the unchanging Essence, who is beyond the reach of the mind and its thoughts" (§§19–27). The One who is so boundless in the greatness of his glory and higher than all comprehensible and visible things, stoops down for his creatures, that he may become comprehensible and visible—to the extent that by faith we could comprehend and see him, or observe his providential care. Since angels, "who are sharper than the human mind," are unable to comprehend him even in part, how then could we, earthlings, be able to comprehend his glory? After all, he says: "No one knows the Father except the Son, and no one (knows) the Son and the Spirit except the Father" (Mt 11.27; §§28–30). God, however, created humans with free will, like angels, "so that by choosing the spiritual law they may attain change: from smallness to greatness, from dishonor to honor, from corruptibility to incorruptibility, from mortality to immortality, which is in Christ Jesus" (§§31–35).

---

for his benevolent care, and become confessors and profess the truth, and remain obedient to his ordinances, which pleases the Lord, abiding in love towards God in times of both trouble and calm. And let us not call creatures by the Creator's name, nor twist the truth into lies'" (2.15–16). The allusion to times of persecution and the denunciation of idolatry belong to a period of transition from paganism to Christianity, whereas the monastic issues raised in the last discourse certainly belong to a later time.

The point of the discourse is that we believe simply because we cannot comprehend, and we comprehend to the extent that we believe, and in so far as God reveals himself to us—who exercise our will to believe. Although the author presupposes a limit to reason and resorts to divine revelation to satisfy or to fulfill the measure of human comprehension and attainment of virtue, the role of reason is upheld, especially in the appeal to exercise one's free will to realize the desired transition to a virtuous existence. The end of virtue is God, or divine immortality in Christ. This last thought begins with the Platonic notion in the *Theaetetus,* that divine happiness is the pattern of human happiness, and that none could be happy who did not recognize the divine operation in the world.[61] Also, as in Stoic ethics (opposed to the Platonic doctrine of the cardinal virtues, which the Stoa believed to be attainable by very few), virtue is considered a gift from God.[62]

"On Mandates for Created Beings" (Disc. 7)

God has set this world as a school,[63] where created beings (specifically, maturing humans) learn about his providential care—especially as manifested in the process of creation, where they make progress in virtue, where they learn to distinguish between the beneficial and the harmful. Just as daylight enables people to work and night allows them to rest, so do opposites contribute to harmony. Fullness and deficiency equalize each other, but things go out of balance when either side tilts to the extreme. Building on this principle of complementary opposites, the author tries to surmount the hurdle of foolishness vis-à-vis wisdom: in earthly reality the former is at the service of the latter; however, on a higher plane, all are at the service of divine Wisdom. Even success and failure complement each other. Whether in gain or loss, the providential will must be acknowledged. The author then moves to the issue of life and death, and here, in the middle of the discourse, the constitution of created

61. *Theaetetus* 176a5–e4.

62. As epitomized by Hierocles (second century AD) and anthologized by Stobaeus (fifth century AD): *Ioannis Stobaei Anthologium,* ed. Curt Wachsmuth and Otto Hense, 5 vols. (Berlin: Weidmann, 1884–1912; repr., 1974), 1.3.53–54 (1.63,6–64,14, Wachsmuth).

63. A *topos* in ancient literature.

beings (specifically, humans, throughout) is consistently defined in dualistic terms (§§1–43). The focus is on how one can proceed unto eternal life. It has to do with the exercise of one's free will, the choice between good and evil: one leads to eternal life, and the other to eternal death (§44–49). The role of the senses in created beings is compared with certain elements in nature: heat and cold, occasional clouds, rain, hail, snow, and so forth. All these are good and beneficial, provided they do not go beyond a limit; so too with the senses (§§50–70). Transgressors, exercising their free will, could repent; but if they do not, they are self-condemned. God, however, always forgives those who truly repent (§§71–80). One has more power than one realizes, power to do either good or evil, and is judged accordingly. There is much to endure here: suffering and death for Christ's sake, even to the point of martyrdom, the honorable death.[64] Nonetheless, the ordinary death of those who are baptized and who have "put on Christ" (a Pauline phrase that became synonymous with chrismation, following baptism, which was viewed as death, burial, and resurrection with Christ)[65] is no less honorable than the death of martyrs (§§81–92). Finally, realizing one's weakness on earth and learning to rely on the power of Christ is a sure way of finding oneself in the realm of the blessed (§§93–99).

Throughout, the discourse manifests syncretistic thought typical of early Christianity: first, the Stoic doctrine of harmony through the equilibrium of opposites, then the Aristotelian mean, followed by the mandated choice between the two ways emphasized in Jewish dualism,[66] and finally God's longsuffering in forgiveness of the Christian penitent, the one who is considerate toward the suffering of others and is willing to suffer for Christ's sake, and who, through it all, is aware of his human condition—reminiscent of the Platonic knowing oneself.

---

64. On this common view, see Arthur J. Droge and James D. Tabor, *A Noble Death: Suicide and Martyrdom among Christians and Jews in Antiquity* (San Francisco: Harper, 1992).

65. Gal 3.26–27; Col 3.9–12; cf. Rom 6.3–4.

66. The image of a man at a crossroads, challenged to choose between a life of virtue and one of vice, is found in Prodictus's allegory of Heracles (Xenophon, *Memorabilia* 2.1.21–33) and appears repeatedly in the moral literature of late antiquity. A favorite *topos* in ancient Judaism, it is common in early Christianity (Mt 7.13–14; *Didache* 1–6; *Barnabas* 18–20). Cf. Disc. 4.73–78; 10.23–26.

"On the Virtuous Life Crowned with Utmost Goodness by the Blessed One" (Disc. 11)

This discourse, the longest in the collection, is the second of four consecutive discourses on the virtuous life and its rewards (Disc. 10–13), a dominant theme throughout the corpus. Collectively, the four discourses are structured, with overlaps, around a theological triad: God's will or the divine choice, God's love or the diffusion of the divine goodness, and divine justice and mercy in meting out rewards and punishments.

There are six expositions of unequal length in Disc. 11: the benefits of faith, hope, and love (§§1–61); the defining characteristics of meekness (§§62–99); those of kindness, humility, and obedience (§§100–123); unity in faith and accord in living a holy life (§§124–131); compassion (§§132–139); thoughtfulness or discretion and the control of the senses (§§140–227). The latter is comparable to the diatribe against the wrongful use of the senses in Disc. 20.23–55.

Following St. Paul's triad of virtues (faith, hope, and love), the author's amplification on love seems to provide the thematic connection between these expositions. He sees the Christian virtues—including the last of the four "cardinal virtues"—as quasi-faculties that enable a sanctified life, which in turn dictates the ethics of virtue. The importance accorded to sanctification shows that the author considers it essential for the rest. Given human limitations in the fallen state, he holds that more than human effort is needed for the otherwise attainable, almost natural virtues upheld for human rectitude and welfare, and that not without further reward: the supernatural state of eternal happiness. Like other Christian moralists, the author goes further than most moral philosophers in his understanding of virtue.

"Exposition on the Human Soul" (Disc. 15)

God, through his divine Providence, created angels and humans as rational beings. The former ones are ministering spirits attending to the redemption of the earthlings. As for human beings, they are providentially endowed to make the necessary progress in virtue, so as to attain to the higher calling (§§1–8). As Providence has it, some depart from this life in infancy, others in youth, others still as young adults, and others in old age. Those who depart in infancy or in youth are saved from the anguish of this world. Those left on earth need to pursue faith, love, and hope, so as to inherit eternal life. A paraphrase of the Matthean "Beatitudes" is given so as to underscore the blessedness of the souls of the righteous (§§9–22).[67] In contrast, the souls of the wicked will inherit all the dire opposites of this blessedness (§§23–29). The author then raises the question of whether bodiless souls could enjoy the heavenly bliss. His assuring answer is that that is what the saints in heaven are experiencing. The promises of God are for real (§§30–36). He then alludes to some people who teach that bodiless souls are like unborn children in the womb: that they are silent while alive, and have no sense perception, since they neither talk nor hear. Disagreeing, he goes on to talk about physical growth that follows birth, implying that departed souls go through a period of growth in comprehending divine things. They are neither silent nor devoid of sense perception, for they constantly praise God in heaven. Moreover, they will not always remain bodiless, as Ezekiel predicts—thanks to his vision of the valley strewn with dry bones that came together and were revived to the point of singing praises to God,[68] as shown also in the resurrection accounts in the Gospel (37–53). The soul remembers, recognizes, and—given its ties to the senses—also animates the body (§§54–58). The Lord has much in store for the believers (§§59–63).

The discourse is a concise exposition on the immortality of the soul. Although almost entirely Christian in its view of blissful heavenly existence, where the soul's progress continues, the pneumatology of the discourse carries reminiscences from classical and late antiquity, where the business of philosophy "is the soul."[69]

---

67. An exposition of the "Beatitudes" is found in Disc. 10.29–73.

68. Ezek 37.

69. Seneca, *Epistle* 75 (*On the Diseases of the Soul*). Cf. the Platonic notion in the *Philebus*, that the highest good is character development, the right cultivation of the soul, the well-being of life. "When a man's soul is in the state it ought to be in, then that man is happy"; Frederick C. Copleston, *A History of Philosophy, Vol. I: Greece and Rome* (Westminster, MD: Newman Press, 1962), 216.

"Admonition unto Repentance with Confession" (Disc. 19)

Beginning with Romans 8.30 ("Those whom he foreknew, he also called to the hope of eternal life, and justified and glorified them"),[70] the author applies the benefits of redemption to those who obey God and pursue the virtues. God does not ignore those who repent; rather, Christ himself visits them and restores them to doing good (§§1–9). The promise of Psalm 32.5 (31.5 LXX), "I said, 'I will recount my sins, and you will forgive all the guilt of my sins,'" is fulfilled for the one who abides by the following ten principles: (1) confesses his sins daily, with tears; (2) abhors sin and its associates; (3) loves the just and the virtuous and associates with them; (4) shuns the evildoer; (5) fears the Lord to the point of mortifying the passions; (6) looks for his personal salvation day and night; (7) does not forget the contrition of his soul; (8) having been healed, forgiven, and cleansed, listens to the inner man, mindful of the promises to those who truly repent; (9) observes all the spiritual commandments, heeds the Gospel, and eagerly anticipates the atonement through the Divine Liturgy, the *Patarag;* and (10) advances in every good deed, while contemplating the heavenly things (§§10–23). Repentance is for the soul what medicine is for the body. The healing effects of tears are discussed. Repentance is defined as turning from vice to virtue, with a list of contrasted transitions from one to the other (§§24–47). As a child cries for maternal attention, so should one cry for the attention of God, who is never slow to extend his love. After all, Christ came to summon sinners, not the righteous (§§48–56). David in the Old Testament and Peter in the New Testament are examples of those who repent with tears (§§57–61). A distinction is made between those who sin unwillingly and come to regret it and those who keep sinning willingly. More than remorse is needed on the part of the latter: they need to shed plenty of tears. The benefits of tears are compared to those of water in irrigating a parched land and in putting out fire. Another definition of repentance is "disapproval of oneself" and taking corrective action (§§62–76). A passionate appeal for repentance, upholding the heavenly promises, concludes the discourse (§§77–86).

In this good example of a discourse, there are several classical

---

70. Obviously an allusion, not a direct quotation of the Armenian Bible.

traditions, common to Hellenistic moralists: the mortification of the passions, the healing power of *metanoia*,[71] vice and virtue lists,[72] codes of ethics as paraenetic forms, and knowing oneself to the point of disapproval.

"Counsel to Ascetics and General Directives That Promote Virtue" (Disc. 23)

When read out of sequence, the last discourse seems to fall outside the author's system. It constitutes, however, the capstone of his hortatory endeavor in bolstering coenobitic monasticism; in effect, it constitutes his appeal. The discourse is packed with emphases on brotherly love, individual responsibility for others (drawing on the common metaphor of the one body with many members), the ethical conduct of the members, and that of the superior—called "spiritual father"—who ought to demonstrate more than parental care and concern for his spiritual children.

Addressed to novices, the discourse begins with a list of twenty-two vices and their exact opposites, the virtues embraced by all those engaged in spiritual warfare (§§1–4). The list is followed with another, of deadly sins and their opposites (§§5–14). After commending the ascetic life, touching on its main characteristics, the anonymous author goes on to promote communal or coenobitic monasticism and the necessity of obedience to the superior and loyalty to the brothers (§§15–18). He elaborates on these characteristics and repeats the call to obedience and loyalty (§§19–32). After stressing the qualifications of the superior and the necessity of obedience to him and loyalty to the brothers, he touches on the obligations of the latter to one another and to the monastic community as a whole (§§33–46). Further obligations include worship, adherence to the oath, and cooperation as members of one body (§§47–54). Turning to rules, he spells out conditions under which one may

71. Johannes Behm, "*metanoeō, metanoia*," in Kittel, *Theological Dictionary of the New Testament*, 4:975–80, 989–99, 1006–8.

72. The longest vice list, 147 characteristics of the lover of pleasure, is in Philo of Alexandria's (ca. 20 BC–ca. AD 50) *Sacrifices of Cain and Abel* 32. There are about fifty vice lists and thirty virtue lists in the orations of the Stoic orator Dio Chrysostom (ca. AD 40–115). On the use of such lists in the New Testament, see David E. Aune, *The New Testament in Its Literary Environment*, LEC 8 (Philadelphia: Westminster Press, 1987), 194–96.

be allowed to leave his monastery or, conversely, to seek further seclusion; and for all to carry out their assignments faithfully, under the supervision of superintendents (§§55–73). The latter have to be entrusted with the responsibilities given them; they are to be held accountable (§§74–87). The fatherly role of the superior is stressed, his care for his spiritual children, who are reminded of their filial and brotherly relations (§§88–95); so too his absolute authority, even to a point that "if anyone considers attaining virtue on his own, even if he were to achieve it to the uttermost, yet without the will of the superior and the brotherhood, it is unacceptable to God and is considered sinful" (§§96–121, esp. 115).

The virtues of the austere life and those of self-sufficiency, the disdain for all "externals," are well known in ancient philosophy, especially in what survives of Musonius's (c.30–c.100) dialogues and in the Cynic epistles.[73] The Therapeutae of Philo's *The Contemplative Life* and the Essenes of Qumran by the Dead Sea are noteworthy examples of pre-Christian monasticism.[74] Similar movements influenced early Christian asceticism in the East, including Armenia, by the end of the fourth century.[75] To these St. Basil of Caesarea

---

73. Cora E. Lutz, *Musonius Rufus: "The Roman Socrates,"* Yale Classical Studies 10 (New Haven: Yale University Press, 1947); Abraham J. Malherbe, ed., *The Cynic Epistles: A Study Edition,* SBL Sources for Biblical Study 12 (Missoula, MT: Scholars Press, 1977).

74. Philo calls the Therapeutae "philosophers"; see David Winston, trans., *Philo of Alexandria: The Contemplative Life, The Giants, and Selections,* CWS (New York: Paulist Press, 1981), 41 (§2). Josephus compares the Essenes with the Pythagoreans, as he also calls the various sects within Judaism "schools of philosophy"; see William Whiston, trans., *The Works of Josephus,* rev. ed. (Peabody, MA: Hendrickson Publishers, 1987), 422 (*Antiquities* 15.10.4).

75. Asceticism with Syrian characteristics, as described by Theodoret (see Richard M. Price, trans., *A History of the Monks of Syria by Theodoret of Cyrrhus,* CSS 88 [Kalamazoo: Cistercian Press, 1985]), was known in Armenia during this period, as attested repeatedly in Koriwn's *Life of Maštocʿ:* 4.1–7; 23/22.1–3, 9–10; cf. 13.4; 15/14.5, text in MH 1:229–57; cf. Manuk Abełyan, ed. and trans., *Varkʿ Maštocʿi* (Erevan: Haypethrat, 1941); Eng. trans., Bedros Norehad, *Koriwn: The Life of Mashtots* (New York: AGBU, 1965); both repr. with introduction by Krikor H. Maksoudian (Delmar, NY: Caravan Books, 1985). Cf. Edward G. Mathews, Jr., "Early Armenian and Syrian Contact: Reflections on Koriwn's *Life of Maštocʿ*," *SNTR* 7 (2002): 5–27; idem, "The Early Armenian Hermit: Further Reflections on the Syriac Sources," *SNTR* 10 (2005): 141–67. See also the brief eulogy on Gind of Tarōn in the *Buzandaran Patmutʿiwnkʿ* (6.16), trans. Garsoïan, *The Epic Histories,* 239.

(c.330–379) added his imprint of abbotship and learning, an asceticism that evolved into coenobitic or communal-type monasticism by the end of the fifth century—the type of monasticism reflected in the discourse written a century later.[76]

Contrary to the proverbial dictum since classical times, "virtue is its own reward," the *Discourses* promulgate reward-driven ethics, in keeping with traditional Judeo-Christian teaching, as summed up in a rhetorical pronouncement by Cyril of Jerusalem: "For when will an individual resolve to serve God, unless he believes that 'he is a giver of reward'? When will a young woman choose a virgin life, or a young man live soberly, if they do not believe that for chastity there is 'a crown that does not fade away'?"[77] Taken from the vocabulary of Greek moral philosophy, channeled through Hellenistic Judaism—where it acquired its religious meaning of "righteousness"—and baptized into the ethics of New Testament Christianity, the word "virtue" became synonymous with the applied faith of its adherents.[78] The Christianized meanings of "virtue," numerous as they are, hinge around the predominant meaning of "excellence" in the Christian way of life and all that it encompasses, both physical and spiritual—with a heavenly orientation. It thus became the means to attain the *telos*, the promised better life with Christ in heaven, its destination or goal. When applied to monastic life, "vir-

---

76. On the author's familiarity with the Armenian version of Basil's *Rules*, see below, on authorship and date.

77. *Catechetical Lectures* 5.4, quoting 1 Pt 2.4 (trans. Gifford, *NPNF*[2] 7:29–30). Not so with Chrysostom: "Wherefore, I exhort you also who are uninitiated, be sober. Let no man follow after virtue as a hireling, no man as a senseless person, no man as after a heavy and burdensome thing. Let us pursue it then with a ready mind, and with joy. For if there were no reward laid up, ought we not to be good? But however, at least with a reward, let us become good. And how is this anything else than a disgrace and a very great condemnation? Unless thou givest me a reward (says one), I do not become self-controlled. Then am I bold to say something: thou wilt never be self-controlled, no not even when thou livest with self-control, if thou dost it for a reward. Thou esteemest not virtue at all, if thou dost not love it. But on account of our great weakness, God was willing that for a time it should be practiced even for reward, yet not even so do we pursue it" (*Homilies on Hebrews* 13.9, commenting on Heb 7.28; trans. Gardiner, *NPNF*[1] 14:622).

78. See, e.g., the citation of the four cardinal virtues in Wis 8.7; the amplified valor—with reliance on God—in the Books of the Maccabees; and Philo's treatise *On the Virtues.*

tue," embodied in the abbot (Disc. 23), governed all the rules, all moral sensibilities within the community.

Thus, when viewed in the tradition of the moral exhortations of the Greco-Roman world in late antiquity, a tradition passed on through the moral theology of the Cappadocian Fathers, the *Discourses* could be considered the earliest development of Armenian moral philosophy. Yet, like many anonymous Fathers of the Church, the author was more anxious for the purity of faith and the moral development of believers than for the production of literary or philosophical treatises. More specifically, his work is to be viewed as an abbot's *enchiridion* for the repeated instruction of novices; hence the acquired title.

The unattractive and often inconsistent manner of expression tends to distract from the beauty of the text's theological content. Beginning with the all-important subject of the Holy Trinity, there is a degree of progression in the author's imparting of knowledge, in his burden to give moral / ethical counsel. There is, to be sure, a logical weakness in the linkage of the discourses, which to a certain degree is compensated for through repetitious themes with little and at times no connection to the titles given to the respective discourses. Of these themes, virtue and vice with their constituent parts are tailored for practical, moral life in Christ.

Church leaders (*aṙajnordkʻ*), described as "high-ranking" officials and identified with "the house owner" of Mt 13.52 (Disc. 17.32, 36), are preachers and teachers whose role on earth corresponds to that of archangels in heaven, but who stand to fall like Satan (Disc. 20.86, 91, 93, 95; cf. 10.138). In Disc. 23, however, the term *aṙajnord* is used synonymously with *verakacʻu* for the monastic superior or abbot in charge of the brotherhood.[79] His role is distinguishable from that of the *tesučʻ(kʻ)*, the superintendent(s) responsible for various duties related to the life of the monks, including the care of guests, animals, and farming implements.[80]

The author gives counsel to superiors or abbots as well (Disc. 10.124–142; 23 *passim*). The moral qualifications expected of them hardly differ from those of a bishop, as spelled out in 1 Tm 3.1–7,

---

79. *Aṙajnord*, §§19, 20, 27, 35–37, 46, 51, 56, 57, 61, 115; *verakacʻu*, §§28, 33, 44, 47, 50, 52, 55, 58, 64, 68, 76, 88, 91; cf. Gk. *hegumenos;* Syr. *rysh dyr'*.
80. *Tesučʻ*, 74, 78; cf. Syr. *sʻwr'*.

a passage applied to the worthiness of heads of monastic communities (implied but not quoted in the *Discourses*). His counsel is reminiscent of one of Basil's *Ascetical Discourses* emphasizing "that the one chosen as guide in this state of life [that is, the monastic community] be such that his life may serve as a model of every virtue to those who look to him, and, as the Apostle says, that he be 'sober, prudent, of good character, a teacher' (vs. 2)." Basil adds that a potential future abbot should be examined with regard to his moral and spiritual maturity to make sure that "everything said and done by him may represent a law and a standard for the community."[81] So also our author urges all in the community to follow the example of the superior in dedication to God (Disc. 23.51).

Although addressed to ascetic communities or monastic brotherhoods, the moral precepts of these discourses are applicable to all Christians. Both the appeal to moral action and the call to renounce the world are mandates of Scripture. Concern for the poor, drawn as a lesson from the theology of the Eucharist[82] as expression of God's utmost love for humankind (Gk. *philanthrōpia*), is one such profound, repeated teaching that finds its most immediate application within the community of the equally poor.

Authorship and Date

Having rejected the attribution of the *Discourses* to Gregory the Illuminator, a tradition engraved in the textual transmission, I now turn my attention to the question of authorship and date of composition. The anonymous author's use of identifiable sources is central to establishing the latter. As these are pointed out, the

---

81. Basil, "An Ascetical Discourse" (PG 35:876B–C; trans. Wagner, *Ascetical Works*, FC 9:210–11); cf. *LR* 43. Claudia Rapp, *Holy Bishops in Late Antiquity: The Nature of Christian Leadership in an Age of Transition*, TCH 37 (Berkeley: University of California Press, 2005), 17–22, 32–37.

82. In addition to dispersed euchological words in references to Christ's atoning sacrifice, various terms are used when referring to the Eucharist—especially as պատարագ (*patarag* / "sacrifice"), խորհուրդ (*xorhurd* / "mystery"), and յիշատակ (*yišatak* / "anamnesis"). The latter term occurs with varying modifiers of Christ's "remembrance"; e.g., յիշատակ անճառիցն (*yišatak ančaric'n;* "remembrance of the ineffable"), Disc. 6.88; յիշատակ սիրոյն (*yišatak siroyn;* "the remembrance of [Christ's] love"), Disc. 11.6; յիշատակ սրբութեանն (*yišatak srbut'eann;* "the remembrance sacrament"), Disc. 11.20. For more, see the introductory note to Disc. 13.

attribution to Maštocʻ will again be rejected for two reasons: the author of the *Discourses* makes use of the *Teaching*, a fifth-century work attributable to Maštocʻ, as already discussed, and draws upon two translations into Armenian that did not exist before the turn of the sixth century.

Except for biblical authors and their writings, the author never mentions any of his sources. He alludes, however, to the tradition of the "holy fathers" (Disc. 5.47; 9.34; 23.1, 51, 58), and is certainly aware of prior moral teachings in the early Church. He seems to draw on a wide range of Greek and Syriac Fathers, albeit their commonplaces, which makes the identification of his patristic sources rather difficult—and so too the dating of the work. The task would have been much more difficult were it not for the rare instances where his sources are identifiable.

Of the immediate sources in the native tradition, the *Teaching* was paramount. Thus the dependence on it is not surprising, as this is demonstrable in at least three instances:[83]

Teaching §668

Ընդ պապտումք պատուհասիւք անկեալ յարդարութեան դապասապանին, գրաւեաւ ի ներքոյ մահու:

Disc. 5.32–33

Զնոյն պապիդս տայցեն յալիտենից տանջանացն: Որք աստէն են գրաւեալք ի ներքոյ աճաւոր սպառնալեաց արդար դապասապանին:

Teaching §522

Արդ՝ պարտ է ձեզ կակրել վանդս մրայ ձերոց, և խլել զմեղսն գայթակղեցուցիչս յանձանց ձերոց, որ խափան առնեն արդարութեանցն ի ձեզ բուսոյն:

Disc. 8.46

Եւ յորժամ Փրկիչն զառաքեալսն յաշխարհ առաքէր սերմանել զբանն ճշմարտութեան յանդս մրայ հաւատացելոց, և նովաւ աճել ի կարգ ուղղութեան, նախ զխիւսն խլել զգանկութիւն բուսոյն հրամայէ, զկամս մարմնոյ և զմտաց:

---

83. These were first observed by Albert V. Mušełyan, "Koriwn tʻe Agatʻangełos: Bnagreri kʻnnutʻyun nor tesankyunicʻ" ("Koriwn or Agathangelos? Textual Analysis from a New Perspective"), *Lraber* (1996/2): 51, albeit in an entirely different context, arguing for Koriwn's dependence on Agathangelos (a debunked view).

Teaching §678

Երկու ինչ իրք պաշտեցաւ. մին կենաց աւետիք, և միւս արհաւիրք
սպառնալեաց պատուհասից:

Disc. 8.97

Իրաւանցն արդարութեան երկու բարբառք են, որ յարգեն և պատուեն
զիրաւախորհան աւետեաւք պարգևացն, և սպառնալեաւք և պէսպէս
նեղութեամբք պատժեն զապախտաւորսն և զանիրաւսն:

The Basilian influence is transparent. Thanks to Gabriella
Uluhogian's meritorious work on the Armenian version of Basil's
Rules, direct dependence on the Armenian text could be pointed
out, in at least one instance—even though Uluhogian draws attention to two others. Still, this was sufficient for her to observe and to
conclude rather correctly:

> The last sermon of the collection [Disc. 23], addressed to those who want
> to practice the ascetic life, not only takes up a few concepts, almost liter-
> ally, the DOM 33 [= *LR* 37], 34 [= *LR* 38–42] and 125 [= *SR* 144], but in
> general has an extraordinary affinity of thought and terminology with
> the Armenian translation of the Basilian work, much that cannot be put
> beyond doubt that the unknown author of the *Yačaxapatum* knew well the
> *Book of Questions*. We could even consider his familiarity with the concepts
> and the language expressed there as derived from an in-depth knowledge
> of the latter, which allows him to personally elaborate on already assimi-
> lated subject matter.[84]

I agree with Uluhogian's assessment of the anonymous author's
familiarity with and extensive utilization of the Basilian work, to
the extent that he was so imbued with the text that he could "elaborate on already assimilated subject-matter." Only one, however,
of the three Basilian passages to which she refers (Q125 = *SR* 144)

---

84. "L'ultima omelia della raccolta, indirizzata a chi vuol praticare la vita ascetica, non solo riprende alcuni concetti, quasi alla lettera, delle DOM 33, 34 e
125, ma in generale presenta una straordinaria affinità di pensiero e di terminolo-
gia con la traduzione armena dell'opera basiliana, tanto che non può essere mes-
so indubbio che l'ignoto autore del Yacaxapatum conoscesse bene il Libro delle
Domande. Anzi vien fatto di pensare che la sua dimestichezza con i concetti e
il linguaggio ivi espressi derivi da una conoscenza approfondita che permette la
rielaborazione personale di materiale già assimilato" (tomus 20, viii–ix); following
Kiwregh K'iparian, "'*Yačaxapatum*' čařeru hełinaki harc'ě" ("The '*Yačaxapatum*'
Discourses' Authorship Question"), *Bazmavep* 120 (1962): 237–42.

shows textual affinity with the *Discourses* (Disc. 23.67), and this has to be exhibited in parallel lines, beginning with the Greek text in the foreground:

SR 144

ΕΡΩΤΗΣΙΣ ΡΜΔ΄. Ἐὰν δέ τις ἐζ ἀμελείας ἀπολέσῃ τι, ἢ ἐκ καταφρονήσεως καραχρήσεται. ΑΠΟΚΡΙΣΙΣ. Ὁ μὲν παραχρησάμενος ὡς ἱερόσυλος, ὁ δὲ ἀπολέσας ὡς αἴτιος ἱεροσυλίας κρινέσθω, πάντων τῷ Κυρίῳ ἐπονομασθέντων, καὶ τῷ Θεῷ ἀνακειμένων. (PG 31:1177C)

Arm. Q125

ՀԱՐՑ. ՃԺԵ. Եթէ ի ծուլութեանէ կորուսցէ և կամ յարհամարհանաց արդիազս վարեսցէ․ ԱՍՈՂ. Որ արտաքս վարեաց, որպէս սեղանակապուտ,[85] իսկ որ կորուսն, որպէս պատճառք կողոպտողի դատիցի․ զի ամենայն որ Մեսանն անուանեալ է, Աստուծոյ անիրեալ է (vol. 19, 177).

Disc. 23.67

Այլ որ տունտենն է՝ հաւաներցի զինքն Աստուծոյ մատակարար. աշիւ և երկիւղիւ տունտենեսցէ զզաւատացեալըն յԱստուծոյ աւանդն, և զգուշացի աներթգն. մի՛ ի ծուլութեանէ կորուսցէ և կամ յարհամարհանաց արդիազս զնկեսցէ. և անփութ արարեալ աւանդիցն յաձախի ի ծախս արից ոչ ի հաճոյս Աստուծոյ, և կրեսցէ դատապարտաւ ի Մեսանն՝ որ ի մին առաւել զամենայն զխորհուրդս և զգործս. զի ամենայն ինչ յԱստուծոյ է անիրեալ յաղագս պիտոյից եղբայրութեանն:

The evidence here for textual dependency, however scant, is fairly adequate. As for the other two instances to which Uluhogian draws attention, their evidence for any direct textual dependency is nil;[86] like a score of other passages, they suggest close familiarity with the Basilian work. Nevertheless, the Armenian translation of Basil's rules, dated by Uluhogian to the turn of the sixth century,[87] provides the *terminus post quem* for the composition of the *Discourses*.

85. Variant: սեղանակողոպուտ; a further corruption of the word մեղեանակապուտ, as in Acts 19.37 (pl. acc. մեղեանակապուտու; Gk. ἱεροσύλους).

86. Arm. Q33 [= *LR* 37] and Q34 [= *LR* 38–42] have non-verbatim equivalence in Disc. 23.48.

87. In her second volume, Uluhogian concludes: "The convergence of all the data obtained from the work, both internal and external, seems to narrow down its translation into Armenian most probably to between the end of the fifth century and the beginning of the sixth century." ("La convergenza di tutti questi dati, esterni ed interni all'opera, sembra circoscrivere tra la fine del V sec. e l'inizio del VI l'epoca più probabile della sua traduzione in armeno") (vol. 537, ix).

This, in turn, agrees with (1) their late attribution to the Illuminator by the last redactor of the Armenian Agathangelos; and (2) the earliest attestation to their having been excerpted in the *Seal of Faith* (*Gnikʻ hawatoy*) florilegium early in the seventh century, the *terminus ante quem*.[88] Two other identifiable sources used by the author corroborate this conclusion: (1) the document known as "The Descent of Christ into Hell," some elements of which are found in Disc. 11.101;[89] and (2) reverberations of Pseudo-Dionysius the Areopagite in Disc. 10.125; 20.85–86, 91–93, 96, 154; 23.100.[90]

The anonymous author's familiarity with Basil's *Rules* is a given. His dependence on its Armenian translation could be seen also in his interchangeable use of the terms *verakacʻu* and *aṙaǰnord* when referring to the superior or abbot, similar to their interchangeableness in the translation. Fedwick observes,

Direct borrowings from the *Asc. 2h* are found in the homily called *Yačax-apatum 23*, attributed by some to Gregory the Illuminator, by others to Mashtots, but which in reality seems to be from 630. Here are its main ideas for which it is not difficult to find parallels in the work of Basil: the ascetic community as the body of Christ; necessity to obey the leader and the community; practice of prayer as memory of God, etc.[91]

---

88. See the above discussion on the rejected attributions.

89. An Armenian version of which must have been known in the fifth century. For more, see note to Disc. 11.101.

90. The author's familiarity with the Areopagetic tradition, not known prior to the sixth century, could not have been dependent on an Armenian translation of the Ps.-Dionysian corpus. The extant Armenian translation was done by Stepʻanos of Siwnikʻ (d. 735); see Robert W. Thomson, ed. and trans., *The Armenian Version of the Works Attributed to Dionysius the Areopagite,* CSCO 488–489, Scriptores Armeniaci 17–18 (Leuven: Peeters, 1987).

91. "The Translations of the Works of Basil before 1400," in *Basil of Caesarea: Christian, Humanist, Ascetic. A Sixteen-hundredth Anniversary Symposium,* Part One: *Vita, Opera, Doctrina;* Part Two: *The Tradition,* ed. Paul J. Fedwick, 2 vols. (Toronto: Pontifical Institute of Medieval Studies, 1981), 2:475. The date given by Fedwick is considerably late, since the use of the *Discourses* is attested in the *Seal of Faith* florilegium from the turn of the seventh century. Fedwick goes on to invite attention to the founding of the monastery at Sevan in accordance with Basil's *Rules,* by the future Catholicos Maštocʻ (in office for only a year, 897/8; better known for his edition of the *Euchologion* still in use and which bears his name for its title), as recorded by the historian Stepʻanos Tarōnecʻi Asołik (d. ca. 1015). On the last thought in this quotation, the recurring Eucharistic *anamnesis* in the *Discourses,* see the "Subject Index." For Basil's works in Armenian, see also Petros Tēr Pōłosean,

While the discourses show close familiarity with the Basilian *Rules* and reiterate certain of the admonitions, they do not follow most of its precepts. A good example is the superior's limited authority in the *Rules:* he stands to be admonished by "aged and wise" monks (*LR* 27, 48); whereas in the discourses the superior wields absolute authority and stands to be challenged by none (Disc. 23.33–36).

Another identifiable source is the fragmentary Hermetic text of the *Definitions* (especially *DH* frag. VI.2–3; VII.3),[92] echoed in four discourses: 2.40; 12.9, 44–46; 15.37–56; and 20.22.[93] The pertinent fragments, possibly in Armenian translation from the middle of the sixth century, with the relevant passages from these discourses, are consigned to the end of this book (Appendix III).[94]

There can be no question about the author's use of other, hitherto unidentified Greek sources.[95] As for his use of unidentifiable Syr-

---

"S. Parseł Kesaracʻi ew ir grutʻiwnnerĕ hayerēn tʻargmanutʻeamb" ("S. Basil of Caesarea and His Works in Armenian Translation"), *HA* 82 (1968): 385–418; 83 (1969): 129–58, 257–92, 385–98.

92. Jean-Pierre Mahé, *Hermès en Haute-Égypte*, 2 vols. (Quebec: Presses de l'Université Laval, 1978–1982), especially 2:327–28.

93. The last of these (Disc. 20.22) was first noticed by Joseph Paramelle and Jean-Pierre Mahé, "Nouveaux parallèles grecs aux *Définitions* hermétiques arméniennes," *REArm* 22 (1990–91): 115–34, especially 117 n. 7a, 120–23; cf. Mahé, *Hermès en Haute-Égypte*, 2:376–80. Also by the same authors: "Extraits hermétiques inédits dans un manuscrit d'Oxford," *REG* 104 (1991): 109–39; and by Hacʻuni, "Erb šaradruac en *Yačaxapatum Čaṙkʻ*," 403.

94. Aware of the observations made by Uluhogian and Mahé with Paramelle, Bernard Outtier observes correctly, with reference to the *Yačaxapatum,* that "there are implicit quotations of texts that were not translated into Armenian before the sixth century (Basil, *Books of Questions;* Hermes Trismegistus)," "The Church Fathers in Armenia and the Armenian Fathers," in *Armenian Philology in the Modern Era: From Manuscript to Digital Text,* ed. Valentina Calzolari with the collaboration of Michael E. Stone, *Handbook of Oriental Studies,* Section 8, Uralic & Central Asian Studies 23/1 = History of Armenian Studies 1 (Leiden and Boston: Brill, 2014), 299.

95. For a remote possibility of some reliance on Aelius Aristides (AD 117–181), see Disc. 4.1–11 and note. For an instance of the author's use of a Greek source with a likely corruption of the word μέρη to χρή, see Disc. 7.39 and note. Further source-criticism of the *Yačaxapatum* remains to be done, with special attention to the works of the Cappadocian Fathers—the homilies of Gregory of Nyssa in particular, especially those on the Beatitudes and Ecclesiastes, and his ascetical theology in general. See Françoise Vinel, "La version arménienne des Homélies

iac sources, this is assumed from his pleonastic style, as discussed above.[96] Given his unmistakable familiarity with Basil's works and the absence of evidence for direct reliance on Basil's Greek text—and the little evidence for direct reliance on the Armenian translation—it is reasonable to surmise reliance on the incredibly loose Syriac translation of Basil's "rules" or of works dependent on them.[97]

The late sixth-century date of the *Discourses* nullifies its attribution to Maštoc' in more recent scholarship that simply reiterates the dismissible arguments set forth by Paul Vetter near the end of the nineteenth century.[98] Vetter's old arguments, which can no longer be maintained, are summed up by Tamrazyan[99] as follows (in *italics*):

---

sur l'Ecclésiaste de Grégoire de Nysse," *REArm* 21 (1988–1989): 127–43; also Hubertus R. Drobner and Albert Vicciano, eds., *Gregory of Nyssa, Homilies on the Beatitudes: An English Version with Commentary and Supporting Studies: Proceedings of the Eighth International Colloquium on Gregory of Nyssa, Paderborn, 14–18 September 1998*, Supplements to Vigiliae Christianae 52 (Leiden: Brill, 2000); and Raphael A. Cadenhead, *The Body and Desire: Gregory of Nyssa's Ascetical Theology*, Christianity in Late Antiquity 4 (Oakland, CA: University of California Press, 2018). The author's Trinitarian theology is mostly that of Gregory Nazianzen.

96. See also Appendix IV for syntactical oddities in possibly translated borrowings.

97. On the Syriac recension, see Jean Gribomont, *Histoire du texte des Ascétiques de S. Basile*, Bibliothèque du Muséon 32 (Leuven: Publications universitaires, 1953); see also the bibliography in Philip Rousseau, *Basil of Caesarea*, TCH 20 (Berkeley: University of California Press, 1994), esp. 378. For a more recent assessment of the Syriac reception of the "rules," see Anna M. Silvas, *Basil of Caesarea. Questions of the Brothers: Syriac Text and English Translation*, TSEC 3 (Leiden: Brill, 2014): 1–45, 22–31 in particular, on the translator's style and own contribution to the text; cf. eadem, "The Syriac Translator of Basil's *Small Asketikon*: Translation Techniques and Personal Identity," *ParOr* 40 (2015): 404–15.

98. See above, n. 15. Vetter's arguments were in part—yet fairly—negated by Durian, *Patmut'iwn Hay Matenagrut'ean*, 420–22.

99. Tamrazyan, *"Stełcagorc anhati ew arvesti tesut'yan xndirnerě,"* 19.

1. *Koriwn's testimony, that Maštoc' composed "many discourses, easy to deliver, gracefully written, etc."*

As I have indicated earlier, in the section on attributions, Koriwn's testimony seems more fitting when applied to the *Teaching* and not to the *Discourses;* more so since the latter lacks the finesse Koriwn speaks of, and makes use of the *Teaching* along with translated sources not known prior to the turn of the sixth century.

2. *Correlation between the document's biblical citations and the newly translated Armenian Bible*

Similarly, as I have shown at the beginning of the discussion on sources, the vast majority of the biblical citations do not agree with the text of the Armenian Bible. Only rarely one finds a token of such correlation. The evidence indicates nothing more than the existence of the Armenian Bible and the later Armenian authorship of the *Discourses;* a *terminus post quem.*

3. *The anti-Zoroastrian sentiment in the document*

No such sentiment is expressed in the *Discourses,* where there is no mention of any pagan religion other than a passing reference to the Persians as a people without law, like Barbarians, who nonetheless know about rewards and punishments, as do the Greeks and other nations privileged with legislation (Disc. 8.91, 95–96).[100] The thought is taken—albeit with a twist—from Book V of Aristotle's *Nicomachean Ethics,* where Aristotle goes on to comment on the relationship of natural justice or law and positive justice or legislation, where Persia is cited as an example of places where natural law is as much at work as with or without legislation (that is, without law, a meaning taken by our author—or his source—with a twist, as lawlessness). Moreover, all five references to *het'anos(k')*, "pagans," are generic: Disc. 2.93, mentioned with demons and the wicked; Disc. 2.132, mentioned with Jews vis-à-vis "Gentiles"; Disc. 8.48,

---

100. The context deals with the Aristotelian dual application of justice: distributive or constitutional (honoring citizens' merits by the *polis*) and corrective or judicial (rectifying injustices through liability), elaborated in Book V of the *Nicomachean Ethics* (1130b30–1133b28). Aristotle continues: "Some people think that all rules of justice are merely conventional, because whereas a law of nature is immutable and has the same validity everywhere, as fire burns both here and in Persia, rules of justice are seen to vary" (1134b25–27, trans. Rackham; see Bibliography).

mentioned with Jews vis-à-vis "Gentiles" in a biblical citation; Disc.
12.64, mentioned in a biblical citation; Disc. 22.14, as an adjective
(*het'anosakan*) to describe astral superstitions regarding chance.[101]

4. *The Trinitarian theology of the document reflects the conciliar pronounce-
ments of Nicaea and Constantinople, just as the absence of Christological
polemics suggests a pre-Chalcedonian period.*

The first part of the statement is true to the orthodox trajecto-
ry of the Christian faith. Moreover, after the first discourse(s) the
Trinitarian statements are formulary, marking the beginning and
the end of every discourse. The second part of the statement is in-
correct, for the author reveals his Miaphysite leaning in Disc. 9.68:
«Աստուածախառն մարմնովն» ("with his body, commingled with
divinity").

5. *The commendation in Disc. 20 of the Arsacid Dynasty of Armenia, which
ended with the dethronement of Artashēs or Artashir III in AD 428*

Disc. 20.163–164 reads: "This is clear: with God there is no exalting of dynastic prestige except for the good dynasty of virtue—
even though in Armenia and Persia none (was) greater than the
Arsacid Dynasty that had descended here, from Abraham, as also
the kings of all nations on earth."[102] The context implies that the
downfall of the dynasty was a divine retribution. The passage goes

---

101. Astral superstitions, well known in the ancient world, are discussed at
length in Philo's *On Providence* (1.77–88), a work extant only in a sixth-century
Armenian translation; see *Philon d'Alexandrie: De Providentia,* trans. Mireille
Hadas-Lebel, Les œuvres de Philon d'Alexandrie 35 (Paris: Éditions du Cerf,
1973), 190–201. Yet neither Philo nor our author makes any reference to Zoroas-
trianism, the old religion of the Armenians (see James R. Russell, *Zoroastrianism in
Armenia,* Harvard Iranian Series 5 [Cambridge, MA: Harvard University Press,
1987]). For a fifth-century Armenian denunciation of the latter, see Eznik of Kołb,
A Treatise on God Written in Armenian by Eznik of Kołb, trans. Monica J. Blanchard and
Robin Darling Young, ECTT 2 (Leuven: Peeters, 1998), 101–24; also Robert W.
Thomson, "'Let Now the Astrologers Stand Up': The Armenian Christian Re-
action to Astrology and Divination," *DOP* 46 (1992): 305–12; repr. in his *Studies in
Armenian Literature and Christianity* (Aldershot, Hampshire, and Brookfield, VT: Var-
iorum, 1994), XI. For more on the *topos* in the author's milieu, see David Pingree,
"Classical and Byzantine Astrology in Sasanian Persia," *DOP* 43 (1989): 227–39.

102. "... *Zi i Hays oč' inč' mecagoyn ew i Pars k'an zAršakuneac' tohm*" («... Զի ի Հայս
ոչ ինչ մեծագոյն և ի Պարս՝ քան զԱրշակունեաց տոհմ»). Except for the proper
names here, all proper names in the *Discourses* are linked with biblical association.

on to draw a moral lesson for rulers in general, that a greater punishment than this awaits them should they not exercise good, moral
judgment. The illustrative commendation of the Arsacid Dynasty
is tempered with preference for the "dynasty of virtue" on the one
hand and with the warning that follows. The statement reveals a
nostalgic expression by an Armenian author, writing in Armenian
territory and lamenting a bygone era.[103] Moreover, early Armenian
authors are not as enthusiastic about the Arsacids because of their
pro-Arian policies. In P'awstos (iv. 15), Nersēs the Great predicts
the downfall of the dynasty, never to rise again. There is no con-
temporaneity here; and as for dating, nothing more than another
post quem reference, superseded by yet other *post quem* indicators: the
author's utilization of the Armenian translation of Basil's *Rules* as
well as that of the Hermetic writings among others.[104]

As noted above, the anonymous author is a moral teacher in
the mainstream of ascetic tradition, a traditionalist who is equally
conversant with Greek and Syriac monastic texts. As Thomson observes, "Extensive knowledge of Greek and Syriac literature in an
early Armenian author is neither surprising nor unusual."[105] While
the author's familiarity with the Basilian *Rules* in Armenian translation is demonstrable, it is safe to assume on syntactic and stylistic
grounds his greater dependence on and utilization of Syriac sources
for the most part. The *Discourses* depict an asceticism clearly rooted in early Syrian tradition, except that they do not reflect its one
important trait of active involvement in the affairs of the community,[106] a trait that clearly predates the composition of the *Discourses*.

The author uses the first-person-singular thirteen times,[107] but
always rhetorically, without indicating anything specific about

103. The Arsacid Dynasty's rule in Armenia ended in 428, with the Sasanian
recall of the last Arsacid king, Artashēs or Artashir III (422–428), upon the request
of the Armenian tribal lords known as *nakharars*. This also led to the deposition
of St. Sahak from the patriarchal office in that year (d. 439). As for the Persian
branch of this Parthian dynasty, it was overthrown by the Sasanians in AD 224.

104. The allusion to the invention of letters in one of the discourses (7.9) does
not necessarily imply the invention of the Armenian alphabet (as some presume).

105. Thomson, *Teaching*, p. 50. See also Edward G. Mathews, Jr., "Syriac into
Armenian: The Translations and Their Translators," *JCSSS* 10 (2010): 20–44.

106. A trait discernible in earlier Armenian sources; see above, nn. 18 and 75.

107. Disc. 2.15; 8.30; 9.36, 107; 10.1; 11.62, 132; 12.4; 17.1; 19.61; 20.55; 23.72, 117.

himself. Two of his discourses begin in a somewhat charismatic way: Disc. 10.1: "I have received grace from the benevolence of the Holy Trinity's eternal Lordship ..."; and Disc. 17.1: "I write endeavoring to teach you, my brothers and children whom '*I begot in Christ, through the Gospel,*'" appropriating to himself Paul's words in 1 Cor 4.15. Similarly, his use of the first-person-plural shows nothing more than a hortatory spirit, exhorting others in an institutionalized form of ascetic life. That he speaks authoritatively is clear, and that from a position of a monastic abbot. Near the end of the last discourse, he declares: "For this reason I often repeat the words of love, for this is good and acceptable to God, indeed his very command" (Disc. 23.117).[108]

The Historical Context: An Overview

Unfortunately, there is no comprehensive history of early Armenian monasticism for a historical context wherein to place this collection of ascetic discourses.[109] I will have the deficiency filled

108. Cf. Jn 13.35; 14.23–24 (quoted earlier in the discourse, §§23, 90, 114). There is reason to believe that the statement is invariably related to the title given to this collection of discourses. See also Disc. 20.31, a likely reflection on the author, his self-perceived role as a counselor in the tradition of biblical authors.

109. For a brief survey, see Garabed Amadouni, "Le rôle historique des hiéromoins arméniens," in *Il monachesimo orientale: Atti del Convegno di studi orientale che sull predetto tema si tenne a Roma: sotto la direzione del Pontificio Istituto orientale, nei giorni 9, 10, 11 e 12 aprile 1958 allocuzione di S.S. Pio XII*, ed. Irénée Hausherr et al., OCA 153 (Rome: Pontificium Institutum Orientalium Studiorum, 1958), 279–305; cf. idem, "Armeno (monachesimo)," in *Dizionario degli Istituti di perfezione*, ed. Giancarlo Rocca and Guerrino Pelliccia, 10 vols. (Rome: Edizioni Paoline, 1974–2003), 1:879–99. For an equally brief survey of the history of Armenia in this period, see Robert W. Thomson, "Armenia in the Fifth and Sixth Century," in *The Cambridge Ancient History, Volume XIV: Late Antiquity: Empire and Successors, AD 425–600*, ed. Averil Cameron, Bryan Ward-Perkins, and Michael Whitby (Cambridge: Cambridge University Press, 2001), 662–77; Anne E. Redgate, *The Armenians*, The Peoples of Europe (Oxford: Blackwell, 1998), 140–65. For unacceptable arguments placing the introduction of coenobitic monasticism in Armenia in the beginning of the seventh century, see Nina G. Garsoïan, *L'Église arménienne et le grand schisme d'Orient*, CSCO 574, Subsidia 100 (Leuven: Peeters, 1999), 87 n. 156; see also 439–40 n. 11; cf. eadem, *The Epic Histories*, 566–67 (cf. 47 n. 221, 272 n. 19). She holds a somewhat modified view in eadem, "Le témoignage d'Anastas *Vardapet* sur les monastères arméniens de Jérusalem à la fin du VIe siècle," in *Mélanges Gilbert Dagron*, ed. Vincent Déroche et al., Travaux et mémoires 14 (Paris: Association des amis du

with a forthcoming monograph, titled *A Documentary History of Early Armenian Monasticism.* Already I have translated the pertinent documents from the fifth and sixth centuries, nearly all predating the *Discourses* dated to the second half of the sixth century. While this is not the place to review each of the documents to appear in the forthcoming monograph, I would like to draw attention to two letters in particular, but not before surveying briefly three significant movements in the spread of coenobitic monasticism that must have reached the southern Caucasus, distinct from—yet owing to—the earlier Pachomian-Basilian influences.

First, there was the development in the Holy Land, beginning with the Euthymian establishment of monasticism in the Judean desert in the fifth century[110] and culminating in vast clusters of crowded monasteries—especially in Jerusalem—where compatriots from the southern Caucasus lived together with Greek and Arab monks without losing touch with their respective homelands.[111] Second, there was the development in northern Syria and Mesopotamia, and farther east, in the Persian Empire,[112] thanks to

---

Centre d'histoire et civilisation de Byzance, 2002), 257–67, that coenobitic monasticism entered Armenia at the turn of the seventh century, and that from Palestine and not Cappadocia. See also her further modifications in "Introduction to the Problem of Early Armenian Monasticism," *REArm* 30 (2005–2007): 177–236; both articles repr. in eadem, *Studies on the Formation of Christian Armenia,* Variorum Collected Studies Series CS959 (Farnham: Ashgate / Variorum, 2010), chs. VIII, IX.

110. On Euthymius, an Armenian from Melitene / Malatia, see *Kyrillos von Skythopolis, Leben des Euthymius,* ed. Eduard Schwartz, TU 49.2 (Leipzig: Hinrichs, 1939); Eng. trans. by Richard M. Price, *Cyril of Scythopolis: Lives of the Monks of Palestine,* CSS 114 (Kalamazoo, MI: Cistercian Publications, 1991). On the archaeological remains, see Yizhar Hirschfeld, "Euthymius and His Monastery in the Judean Desert," *LASBF* 43 (1993): 339–71, Plates 19–24; idem, "Spirituality in the Desert: Judean Wilderness Monasteries," *BAR* 21.5 (1995): 28–37, 70.

111. John Binns, *Ascetics and Ambassadors of Christ: The Monasteries of Palestine, 314–631,* OECS (Oxford: Clarendon Press; New York: Oxford University Press, 1994); on the widespread monasticism in Jerusalem with significant Armenian presence, see Abraham Terian, "Rereading the Sixth-Century List of Jerusalem Monasteries by Anastas Vardapet," in *Sion, Mère des Églises. Mélanges liturgiques offerts au Père Charles Athanase Renoux,* ed. Michael Daniel Findikyan, Daniel Galadza, and André Lossky, Semaines d'Études Liturgiques Saint-Serge, S1 (Münster: Aschendorff Verlag, 2016), 273–88.

112. Arthur Vööbus, *History of Asceticism in the Syrian Orient: A Contribution to the History of Culture in the Near East, I. The Origin of Asceticism: Early Monasticism in Persia,*

the extensive spread of East Syrian monasticism, which must have left its imprint on Armenian monasticism in these regions where the Armenian Church was in competition with the Nestorians. It should be pointed out that since 428 most of Armenia was under Sasanian rule while the lesser, western part was annexed by Byzantium—until the situation was reversed in 591, with the Sasanians ceding Armenia to Byzantium.[113] Third, there was the development in Asia Minor led by John of Ephesus, the non-Chalcedonian trustee of Justinian I (reigned 527–565), who zealously and with imperial backing championed the spread of monasticism since 540/42, beginning with the monastic establishment at Tralles and throughout the southwestern part of the land. Bent on eradicating paganism on the one hand and spreading monasticism on the other, John carried his dual mission through much of the rest of the land.[114] As a historian of the saints, John had been to Palestine in 534 and was well acquainted with its monasticism and the troubles there over Chalcedon, culminating with the expulsion of the non-Chalcedonian monks, who then congregated around ascetic communities in Gaza and the Negev. Expulsions were not limited to the Holy Land; they were carried out in various parts of the Empire and helped add to the monastic institutions in the southern Caucasus. John speaks of a certain Thomas, an Armenian and son of a satrap, who founded a non-Chalcedonian monastery in Arme-

CSCO 184, Subsidia 14; *II. Early Monasticism in Mesopotamia and Syria*, CSCO 197, Subsidia 17 (Leuven: Secrétariat du CSCO, 1958).

113. Nikoghayos Adontz, *Armenia in the Period of Justinian*, ed. and trans. Nina G. Garsoïan (Lisbon: Calouste Gulbenkian Foundation, 1970), 7–24, on the history of the partition and its later adjustments.

114. In his introduction to John of Ephesus's *Lives of the Eastern Saints,* E[rnest] W. Brooks observes: "In 542 John (born about 507 in the territory of Ingila in the territory afterwards known as Armenia IV) was selected by the emperor for the task of converting the pagans in Asia on condition that he should convert them to the Chalcedonian faith. Probably, however, he did not wholly neglect the opportunity for propagating Monophysitism" (PO 17 [1–307], 18 [513–698], 19 [151–285] [Paris: Firmin-Didot, 1923–1926]), here 17: iv–v. On the zealous acts of John of Ephesus, see Susan Ashbrook Harvey, *Asceticism and Society in Crisis: John of Ephesus and The Lives of the Eastern Saints,* TCH 18 (Berkeley: University of California Press, 1990), *passim,* esp. 13–21, 43–56, 94–107. For more, see Jan J. van Ginkel, *John of Ephesus. A Monophysite Historian in Sixth-century Byzantium* (Groningen: Rijksuniversiteit Groningen, 1995).

nia around 514, with some eight hundred followers from among the locals, including priests and a chorepiscopus.[115] But this was not a lasting settlement, for John goes on to tell about Chalcedonian resistance instigated by the Orthodox Patriarch of Antioch, Ephrem of Amida (in office 526–546), following the Synod of Constantinople in 537, which compelled the satrap to ask Thomas to leave the district lest there be bloodshed.[116]

The Armenian documentary evidence is commensurate with the established historicity of these movements. Here I should first mention the letter of Patriarch John IV of Jerusalem (in office 575–594) addressed to Catholicos Abas of the Caucasian Albanians (in office 552–596).[117] This rare document alludes to earlier contacts

115. On Thomas and his education, see John of Ephesus, *Lives of the Eastern Saints*, §21, ed. and trans. Brooks, PO 17:283–98, esp. 284: "(His father) bestowed great care upon him that he might receive the best possible education in the wisdom of the Greeks, placing him at Berytus and at Antioch and at other places." In all probability, the monastery founded by Thomas was in Byzantine Armenia. Cf. Bernard Flussin, "Palestinian Hagiography and the Reception of the Council of Chalcedon," in *Languages and Cultures of Eastern Christianity: Greek*, trans. Emily Corran, ed. Scott Fitzgerald Johnson, *The Worlds of Eastern Christianity, 300–1500* 6 (Farnham, UK: Ashgate Variorum, 2015; New York: Routledge, 2016), 261–80; trans. of "L'hagiographie palestinienne et la réception du concile de Chalcédoine," in *Leimôn: Studies Presented to Lennart Rydén on His Sixty-Fifth Birthday*, ed. Jan Olof Rosenqvist, Studia Byzantina Upsaliensia (Uppsala: University of Uppsala, 1996), 25–47. See also Volker L. Menze, *Justinian and the Making of the Syrian Orthodox Church*, OECS (Oxford and New York: Oxford University Press, 2008), 130–31.

116. In his review of Michael Tarchnišvili and Julius Assfalg's *Geschichte der kirchlichen georgischen Literatur, auf Grund des ersten Bandes der georgischen Literaturgeschichte von K. Kekelidze*, ST 185 (Vatican: Biblioteca Apostolica Vaticana, 1955), David M. Lang remarks: "Father Tarchnišvili thinks (pp. 61, 107–9, 412) that the Syrian Fathers, who are supposed to have brought monastic institutions to Georgia in the sixth century, were orthodox Chalcedonians; the reviewer is inclined to think of them as Monophysite refugees from Byzantine persecution, however unpalatable this view may be to the staunch protagonists of Georgian Orthodoxy and doctrinal purity"; *BSOAS* 19.1 (1957): 179–81, here 181.

117. The Armenian text extant in a single manuscript, a miscellany at the Matenadaran in Erevan (M500, fol. 428r–35v), copied in 1305 for the pro-Chalcedonian Catholicos Grigor VII Anawarzec'i (in office 1293–1307), was published by Karapet Tēr-Mkrtč'ian, "Erusałēmi Yovhannēs episkoposi t'ułt'ē," *Ararat* 29 (1896): 252–56, intro. 214–15 (has the old Ējmiacin number of the ms., 517); described in *Mayr c'uc'ak hayerēn jeṙagrac' Maštoc'i anvan matenadarani* (*General Catalogue of Armenian Manuscripts of the Maštoc' Matenadaran*), ed. Ō(nnik) Eganyan et al., ongoing series (Erevan: "Nairi"

between the two hierarchies and the conveyance of liturgical and canonical texts from Jerusalem. It also presents a vivid picture of the post-Chalcedonian turmoil in sixth-century Jerusalem and the seeding of antagonism among the churches of the southern Caucasus. Employing the historical influence of the Patriarchal See of Jerusalem, John attempts to draw Abas into the Chalcedonian camp by urging him to sever all ties with the neighboring Armenian Church and to expel Armenian monks from monasteries under his jurisdiction—just as he himself had succeeded in purging the monasteries under his jurisdiction of their heretical, Miaphysite Armenians. Contemporaneous documents bear witness not only to Chalcedonian persecutions in Palestine and elsewhere in the Empire but also to the resultant growth of Miaphysite monasticism from southern Palestine to the southern Caucasus.

The other letter to which I wish to draw attention is that of the historian Łazar P'arpec'i (thrived ca. 500) addressed to his patron, the Marzpan Vahan Mamikonean, who had appointed him head of the monastery at Vałaršapat (Ējmiacin). In this "Letter" appended to Łazar's *History*,[118] he describes in substantial detail the monastic community with which he was at odds because of "slanderous monks." He refers several times to the monastery, adjacent to the cathedral church, and to its residents in subgroups and collectively. His "Letter" emerges as the last piece of evidence in the development of coenobitic monasticism in Armenia by the end of the fifth century, when viewed alongside the earlier documents, beginning with Koriwn's passages on the ascetic life of Maštoc' and the groups organized by him at the turn of the fifth century,[119] the ca-

---

Hratarakč'ut'iwn, 1984–), 2:1009–18. Latin trans. by Aristaces Vardanian, "Des Johannes von Jerusalem Brief an den albanischen Katholikos Abas," *OC* n.s. 2 (1912): 64–77. Eng. trans. by Abraham Terian, "Monastic Turmoil in Sixth-Century Jerusalem and the South Caucasus: The Letter of Patriarch John IV to Catholicos Abas of the Caucasian Albanians," *DOP* 74 (2020): 9–39.

118. Thomson, *The History of Łazar P'arpec'i*, 247–66 (Arm. text in MH 2:2377–94). See especially Thomson's accurate assessment of the evidence for monasticism in the "Letter," 269–71.

119. *The Life of Maštoc'*, 4.1–7; 23/22.1–3, 9–10; cf. 13.4; 15/14.5 (MH 1:229–57), trans. Terian, *The Life of Mashtots' by His Disciple Koriwn* (forthcoming). Cf. the contemporaneous description of the fourth- and fifth-century ascetics in northwest Syria by Theodoret of Cyrrhus (see above, n. 75).

nonical injunctions directed at ascetics and monks since the middle of the fifth century, and the colophonic and hagiographic evidence contemporaneous with Łazar.[120] His "Letter" also shows that earlier forms of asceticism and coenobitic monasticism coexisted in Armenia at that time,[121] whereas the *Discourses* show a growing intolerance with the earlier forms; they were opposed and coenobitic monasticism was encouraged.[122] "For on your own you cannot perceive the greatness of divine glory" had become a dictum (Disc. 3.9), anticipating the repeated appeals made in the last discourse.

Text and Translation

I have discussed the characteristics of the Armenian text, above, under the rubric of "Literary Style," where I have underscored its complexity, with added examples and philological observations provided in Appendix IV. The difficulties of the text are further reflected through the not infrequent errors of punctuation in the printed editions,[123] and more so by the frequently wrong and some-

120. Documents in my forthcoming monograph: *A Documentary History of Early Armenian Monasticism.*

121. Garsoïan fails to see the overlap of ascetic and early monastic institutions, and the fact that the latter did not altogether supplant the earlier features of Armenian asceticism. Our sources show that the situation in Armenia was no different from that in the Syrian Orient from the fourth through the sixth centuries (cf. Ashbrook Harvey, *Asceticism and Society in Crisis*, 8–21).

122. Beginning with Canons XV and XVI of the Armenian Church Council of Shahapivan (AD 444), similar to Canon IV of the Council of Chalcedon (AD 451). For a history, see Garabed Amadouni, ed., *Disciplina Armena: Testi vari di diritto canonico secolo IV–XVII,* Codificazione canonica orientale, fonti; ser. 1, fasc. 7 (Vatican: Tipografia poliglotta vaticana, 1932).

123. The first edition, replete with abbreviations, has a lengthy subtitle, as follows: *Girk' or koč'i Yačaxapatum, Asac['ea]l S[urb] hōrn meroy eranelwoyn Grigori Lusaworč'in: Yorum parunakin čaŕk' yognapatumk' k'sanerek': V[a]s[n] anhas ēu[t']e[an]n a[stuco]y ew xnamoc'n ew siṙoyn or aṙ stetcuacs: Ew varuc' uṫuṫ'ean ew hatuc'man gorcoc'* (*Book Which Is Called Yačaxapatum, Spoken by our Father the Blessed St. Gregory the Illuminator, which Contains Much-Repeated Twenty-three Discourses, about God's Unreachable Essence and Care and Love for Creatures, and Just Lives and Reward for Deeds*) (Constantinople: Tparan Astuacatur Kostandnupolsec'u, 1737; repr. Calcutta: Tparan Awet Jĕnt'lumeani, 1813; Constantinople: Gorcaran Abraham Amirayi, 1824).

times illogical division of the text into sections by its latest editor.[124] Nonetheless, I have retained the numbers assigned to the section divisions in order to facilitate correlation with the text. I have not corrected the erroneous biblical references found in the various editions; these are insignificant in view of the scores of biblical references and allusions editors have failed to recognize.

I have made every effort to provide a highly readable translation without sacrificing the literal meaning of the text, while trying to be faithful to the words, style, and tone of the original. Where I have added pivotal words or phrases for sentence clarity in translation, these I have enclosed in parentheses: ( ). The text is rarely in doubt; however, where words are used sparingly, the completions of thoughts are also enclosed in parentheses. Except in biblical quotations, I have not placed parentheses around conjunctions and prepositions, nor around pronouns and auxiliary verbs added for fluency. On the whole, I have followed the standard maintained by translators of sacred texts, providing "as literal as possible" and only "as free as necessary" translation.

Regarding words with broad Greek meanings, such as terms associated with the virtues, I have tried to translate them with consistency. For example, the fourth cardinal virtue of self-control or temperance (Gk. *sōphrosynē*; Arm. *zgastutʻiwn*) could also mean alertness, cautiousness, circumspection, being on guard, watchfulness, discretion, discernment, sobriety, and so forth. While all these meanings are encompassed in the Armenian word, I have often rendered it as "discretion" and occasionally as "circumspection" or "thoughtfulness"—where these terms make better sense in context. Such consistency in translation is demanded also by the dictates of indexing, especially when preparing a topical index.

As much as possible, I have avoided textual comments in the notes for the simple reasons that these would have added considerably to the paratext and annoyed readers not interested in philological minutiae. More than a dissertation could be written on philological matters encountered in the text, especially its grammatical discrepancies. Because our author is a highly repetitive writer, I

---

124. See above, n. 1. Except for the editor's section divisions, the text is that of the 1954 Venice edition.

have kept cross-references to a minimum, assuming that the "Subject Index" will compensate for this measure.

Since all manuscripts and published editions include the prayer attributed to St. Gregory the Illuminator at the end of the *Discourses,* I have provided a translation (Appendix I). As with the general attribution, there is good reason to suspect the authorial authenticity of the prayer.

MORALIA ET ASCETICA ARMENIACA: THE OFT-REPEATED DISCOURSES

DISCOURSE 1

ON THE MOST HOLY TRINITY

THE NATURE and being of the Most Holy Trinity are one, and of the selfsame essence—not from another being. ₂The Father, who is without beginning, possesses the causation of the Son and the Spirit. ₃He is unbegotten entity and existence without beginning, boundless eternity and immutable truth, the life and sustainer of all living beings. ₄He is the Father of the Son and the Source of the Spirit.[1] He is God and Creator of creatures, seen and unseen. ₅He is said to be the Cause of the Son through birth and the Source of the Holy Spirit. ₆He himself is the unbegotten Existent, begetting the One who is without beginning; begetting the immutable Truth of the boundlessly eternal; begetting the Giver of life, the Life that bestows life; begetting the living Light, the Light of living beings; begetting the Benefactor of goodness; the Creator begetting the Creator of all creatures, seen and unseen,[2] ₇the Founder of heaven and of the heavenly powers, of earth and the creatures therein. ₈He is replete (with everything) and perfect, and *"accomplishes all in all"* (Eph 1.23). He is not wanting; who is neither renewed nor aging; who is neither replenished nor consumed; who is always the same in his fullness and unboundedness. ₉And into his unlimited and unattainable and boundless and most perfect nature there is neither infiltration nor addition. ₁₀The mind cannot attain him, nor could angels comprehend him, even though they are of the same hue as the human mind. Rather, the heavenly and earthly beings assume their service wherever the Creator's will assigns them. ₁₁Just as heaven and all its adorn-

---

1. Cf. §§5, 23; Disc. 5.3; 6.1, 23.
2. The Son's traditional epithets and role in creation are stated in mostly Johannine terms in this section; cf. Disc. 3.4, with reference to the Trinity.

ments are established by God's Word and Spirit,[3] so is earth, with its mountains and plains, seas and rivers, and dense forests.

₁₂And there is no other Creator but the Holy Trinity, the almighty Lordship, the clear, plain, and all-capable Power, *"who spoke and they came to be; commanded and they stood firm"* (Ps 33.9 [32.9 LXX]); ₁₃who sits in the heaven of heavens and cares for all creatures; who in his foreknowledge and infinite wisdom manages all the heavenly and earthly beings. And he is the life and sustainer of all; unlimited, unreachable, and unfathomable in all things. ₁₄He is love,[4] full of vital blessings; unapproachable light,[5] awe-inspiring and wonderful. ₁₅Knowledge and wisdom are ascertained through him; he lives and is life-giving, merciful and benevolent in grace, longsuffering and sustainer. ₁₆He is the Most Holy to those who approach him in holiness and righteousness, constant Enlightener of those rational by nature. And he is the Truth in all things: in rebuking and exhorting sinners that they may survive the wrath that will befall the wicked. ₁₇Moreover, he exhorts with promises of good things, that we may become worthy of gaining the eternal crowns of glory. ₁₈For he is a comforting harbor to those who persevere patiently under the care of his sacred love; he graces with ineffable blessings those who are virtuous in spirit. ₁₉His greatness is inscrutable; the Existent without beginning is beyond comprehension, being unlimited and unbounded. Through his overseeing care he satisfies all creatures. ₂₀He knows the thoughts of the heart and searches the innermost parts,[6] and leads through the law of the life-giving and immortal Spirit to the remarkable joy, the endless rejoicing, the ineffable and untold goodness (that comes) by inheriting the Kingdom of God.

₂₁Now, all these self-generating acts of the unboundedly eternal One, done by virtue of his benevolence, are for the well-being of his creatures; for he, the infinite and inscrutable One, is their sustainer through his care. ₂₂Those incapable of comprehending the Father, the Son, and the Holy Spirit because of their own lack of spiritual wisdom, should know and recognize the almighty Lordship of

---

3. Allusion to Ps 33.6 (32.6 LXX).
4. Allusion to 1 Jn 4.8, 16.
5. Allusion to 1 Tm 6.16; cf. Ps 104.2 (103.2 LXX).
6. Allusion to Ps 139.23 (138.23 LXX).

the One Godhead through his works and beneficence.[7] 23For as
sunshine and light and warmth are attributable to one sun and no
other, and as fountain and water and river are said to be of one nature, as also mind, reason, and spirit[8] are understood in man, so
(one may) also understand here the one nature and Godhead of the
Father, Son, and Holy Spirit.[9] 24For the sun is not without light
and warmth, and a fountain is not without water and source, and
the mind is not without reason and spirit. 25Likewise, the Father is
neither without the Son nor without the Holy Spirit.[10]

7. A rudimentary form of mystical understanding of God, who remains inscrutable; cf. §§10, 19. An echo of Rom 1.18–19 is discernible here.

8. The latter triad draws on the synonymity of these terms, a *topos* in classical
philosophy and the anthropological theology of the Fathers.

9. The same analogy is found in Disc. 6.3. For such metaphorical images in
describing the relationship of the three persons of the Trinity, especially in the
Orations of Gregory of Nazianzus, see Rosemary R. Ruether, *Gregory of Nazianzus:
Rhetor and Philosopher* (Oxford: Clarendon Press, 1969), 86–105; Manfred Kertsch,
*Bildersprache bei Gregor von Nazianz: Ein Beitrag zur spätantiken Rhetorik und Popularphil-
osophie*, Grazer Theologische Studien 2 (Graz: Eigenverl. des Inst. f. Ökumenische
Theologie u. Patrologie an d. Univ. Graz, 1978), *passim*.

10. Disc. 2 constitutes the continuation of Disc. 1, disrupted in the course of
the textual transmission of the document. This observation is based on two facts.
First, the opening paragraph of Disc. 2 (§§1–6) appears as an integral part of
Disc. 1 in the earliest florilegium of credal extracts known as *Knikʻ Hawatoy* (Կնիք
Հաւատոյ, *Seal of Faith*), compiled belatedly in response to Chalcedon (451) prob-
ably by Yovhan(nēs) Mayravanecʻi or Mayragomecʻi "in the days of Catholicos
Komitas" (in office 611/15–628); ed. Karapet Tēr-Mkertčʻian (Ējmiacin: Mother
See Press, 1914; repr. Antelias: The Armenian Catholicosate of Cilicia, 1998; repr.
under the title *Le Sceau de la Foi* and attributed to Catholicos Komitas, Bibliothèque
Arménienne de la Fondation Calouste Gulbenkian, Leuven: Peeters, 1974), 18–22;
cf. MH 4:59–62. Second, Disc. 2, like all the rest of the discourses, ends with a
formulaic Trinitarian invocation followed with the concluding "Amen," a feature
not found at this juncture. Obviously, the Trinitarian statement here was mistaken
for such a conclusion by an early scribe, whose manuscript became the archetype
of subsequent copies of the document.

DISCOURSE 2

ON THE DISTINCT PERSONS OF
THE HOLY TRINITY[1]

HE FATHER is perfect in personhood and power, knowledge and wisdom, creation and benevolence, and possesses within himself the unbegotten entity. ₂The Son is perfect in personhood and power, knowledge and wisdom, creation and benevolence, who also possesses within himself the existence without beginning. ₃The Holy Spirit is perfect in personhood and power, knowledge and wisdom, creation and benevolence, and possesses within himself the utmost existence without beginning. ₄One is the nature of the Godhead and of the immutable Entity. One creation and one benevolence, one Lordship and one Power; and there is neither shortage nor excess of glory in the Trinity without beginning. ₅For he is the fountain of every goodness, and by him all the gifts of creation are distributed among all creatures. ₆He makes, sustains, and nurtures by his benevolence those seen and unseen; and those who believe in him and continue in holiness, in the fear of God and *"with a pure heart and a sincere faith,"* as written (1 Tm 1.5), he leads by the Spirit and right doctrine towards his Kingdom and glory.[2]

1. On §§1–6 and the rest of the discourse, once the continuation of Disc. 1, see the last note there (n. 10). In the manuscripts as well as in the published editions, the inappropriate, secondary title given to this part of the discourse is based on the Trinitarian reaffirmation in §§1–6. This part of the discourse, however, is mostly on the Creator's beneficence (cf. the title of Disc. 10).

2. Although the appropriation of the Trinitarian theology of the Cappadocian Fathers is obvious throughout, a substantial Armenian fragment with a pre-Nicene core on the Holy Trinity survives among the catena in the *Seal of Faith* (7–15), attributed to Hippolytus of Bostra, author of a catechism by way of questions and answers; see Léon-Marie Froidevaux, "Les Questions et Réponses sur la Sainte

7Thus we have received the word of faith, and thus you believed[3] in the Most Holy Trinity: in God who creates, in the Lord who establishes, and in the Grace that gives life;[4] 8who by his life-giving light and sacred love prepares heirs of his ineffable Kingdom, and prompts recollection of the promised, ineffable gifts that are kept in store for those who trust in him in faith and love. 9For the love of creation compelled the Creator to make all creatures, seen and unseen. He did not make them for the needs of the Deity but *"for his glory to be revealed, to be understood through the things that are made visible"* (Rom 1.20) to incorporeal and corporeal beings.[5] 10Not as if receiving anything from living beings but rather giving them life; not (just) the light for the eyes but that they be enlightened by his light in order to behold him. Thus the Lord gives life to his creatures, and enlightens them, those intelligent and rational beings, and distributes spiritual gifts to them as he wills. 11*"Though there are categories*

Trinité attribuées à Hippolyte, évêque de Bostra," *RSR* 50 (1962): 32–73. The now lost Armenian text was translated into Georgian under the title "On the Faith," *De Fide* (Gérard Garitte, "Le traité géorgien 'Sur la Foi' attribué à Hippolyte," *Mus* 78 [1965]: 119–72; cf. idem, "Une nouvelle source du 'De fide' géorgien attribué à Hippolyte," *RHE* 43 [1968]: 835–43), and was a source utilized in the *Teaching* once attributed to St. Gregory the Illuminator (Thomson, *Teaching*, 51–52). Still, the figure of Gregory of Nazianzus (329–390), "the Theologian," looms large as the foremost teacher on the Holy Trinity in Eastern Christian tradition. For his profound theology on the subject, see Christopher A. Beeley, *Gregory of Nazianzus on the Trinity and the Knowledge of God: In Your Light We Shall See Light,* Oxford Studies in Historical Theology (Oxford: Oxford University Press, 2008). On his influence on the Armenian Church, see Kim Muradyan, *Grigor Nazianzac'in hay matenagrut'yan méj* (*Gregory of Nazianzus in Armenian Writings*) (Erevan: Haykakan SSH GA Hratarakč'ut'yun, 1983). Cf. the dialogues *On the Holy Trinity* by Theodoret of Cyrrhus (wrongly ascribed to Cyril of Alexandria, PG 75:1147–1189) and those by pseudo-Athanasius (PG 28:1115–1286), contemporaries of "the Theologian." On the Armenian version of the latter's "Fourth Dialogue" see Alessandro Capone, ed. and trans., *Pseudo-Atanasio: Dialoghi IV e V sulla santa Trinità: Testo greco con traduzione italiana, versione latina e armena,* CSCO 634, Subsidia 125 (Leuven: Peeters, 2011), 49–61; cf. Robert W. Thomson, "The Transformation of Athanasius in Armenian Theology," *Mus* 78 (1965): 47–69; repr. in his *Studies in Armenian Literature and Christianity* (Aldershot, Hampshire, and Brookfield, VT: Variorum, 1994), XIII.

3. Echoing 1 Cor 15.11.

4. Grace as metonym for the Spirit is a *hapax* in these discourses. The form is reminiscent of later formulae, e.g., "The Father is the Creator; the Son, the Redeemer; the Holy Spirit, the Sanctifier"; cf. Disc. 6.7; 12.37.

5. Cf. Disc. 11.14.

of gifts ... but the same God who facilitates them all in everyone" (1 Cor 12.4–6). ₁₂And he bestowed honor upon angels and humans, the princely will, so that they may glorify God who is benevolent, who brought about existence out of no existence and through the Holy Scriptures taught the principles of piety so that they may flee from evil and embrace the good, and to be renewed from glory to glory.

₁₃God's love is revealed to us in this: it was for our sake that he made the heavens and the earth and the created things therein, and through such care he continues to reveal his benevolent love. ₁₄For this reason, created beings should draw near to God with true love, with faith and hope,[6] and with obedience to his commandments; and he will reward them. ₁₅I always say: In all things let us be grateful for his benevolent care, and become confessors, professing the truth, and remain obedient to his ordinances, which pleases the Lord—(our) abiding in love towards God in times of both trouble and calm. ₁₆And let us not call created things by the Creator's name,[7] nor twist the truth into lies. ₁₇Rather, let us be receptive to the beneficence of his spotless, immaculately pure love. ₁₈The Creator has set all these just and righteous rules perpetually for his creatures.

₁₉For this reason, let us cease from vain and pointless criticism and let us follow the counsel of the Holy Scriptures, both Old and New. ₂₀And let no one be left out of saying what is right: *"For in him we live and move and have our being"* (Acts 17.28). ₂₁Listen to him and trust in him, the One who saved us from all dangers and who transfers us to the Kingdom of Heaven. ₂₂He, who calls everyone unto obedience to the spiritual law, says in the Psalter: *"Come, my children, listen to me, and I will teach you the fear of the Lord"* (Ps 34.11 [33.12 LXX]). ₂₃As the Lord says: *"He who keeps my commandments is the one who loves me; and he who loves me, my Father will love him, and we will come to him and make our home with him"* (Jn 14.21, 23).[8] ₂₄We have been honored with such ineffable love!

---

6. Echoing 1 Cor 13.13, quoted in §48.

7. Pointing to the veneration of idols and/or animals, as in ancient Egypt; cf. Rom 1.25. Note the use of the word *ararack'* in several senses: from created things or beings to creatures in general and humans in particular.

8. The Johannine passage quoted here and elsewhere (Disc. 11.21; 23.23 and 116) is foundational in the formation of the Evagrian / Macarian mystical

25Now, let no one be found *"hostile to God"* (Rom 8.7), lest we forfeit the blessed life that he promised to the saints. 26For the righteous shall inherit the good things, and sinners shall bear punishment. 27*"Those who live in accordance with the Spirit of God,"* (Scripture) says, *"they are the children of God; and those who persist in the flesh, cannot please God"* (Rom 8.13–14, 8). 28For by living such a spiritual life we shall enjoy the whole goodness of heaven. 29The breadth and span of that eternal life is beyond measure, unlike (anything). That which the Creator has prepared because of his love, through the Holy Spirit, is beyond description. That which God shall give to those who love him is beyond what could be heard or understood. Because of his life-giving love, they shall enjoy these good things that are over and above any thought or understanding, even past the heavenly hosts. He shall make them rest among the ranks of the immortal. 30There, the elect will be in mansions,[9] in unfathomable joy, as they are worthy.

31As rational souls, they are living and immortal, and have no limit to the extent or distance of their mobility—whether they ascend above heaven or descend into the sea—by virtue of their remarkable wisdom and knowledge that comes first from the Holy Scriptures. In the twinkling of an eye they are gathered into the state of a living body.[10] Likewise our bodies will be transformed into that unfathomable and ineffable life, into radiant beams and living light and unto glory at the resurrection time; they will be absorbed by the Spirit's fire into that light which does not go out.[11] 32Our physical sight is so dim and pathetic when compared to that of the immortal souls. Every bit of light or even the brightest beam will vanish for us creatures;[12] it cannot be compared, it passes away. Whereas the living beams of the glory of the Sun of Righteous-

---

tradition in ascetic circles. See Leif F. Vaage and Vincent L. Wimbush, eds., *Asceticism and the New Testament* (New York: Routledge, 1999); Samuel Rubenson, "Asceticism: Christian Perspectives," in *EncMon*, 92–94; and Alexander Golitzin, *Mystagogy: A Monastic Reading of Dionysius Areopagita: 1 Cor 3:16, John 14:21–23*, with the collaboration of Bogdan G. Bucur, ed. Bogdan G. Bucur, CSS 250 (Collegeville, MN: Cistercian Publications, 2013); see also note at Disc. 5.26, on 1 Cor 3.16.

9. Allusion to Jn 14.2.
10. Echoing 1 Cor 15.52.
11. Referring to the primordial light of Gn 1.3.
12. Allusion to Mt 24.29 (cf. Mk 13.24).

ness,[13] with which the saints will be clothed in eternal life,[14] do not pass away. The sun's light, with which we—of ordinary soul and body—clothe ourselves and are satisfied, seeing it from east to west, is a vanishing light according to the word of the Lord: *"The sun and the moon will be darkened … and the stars will be covered,"* he says, *"and the righteous will shine like the sun in the Kingdom of God"* (Mt 24.29; 13.43). ₃₃*"For when Christ, your life, appears,"* says the Apostle, *"then you also will appear with him in glory"* (Col 3.4). We will be absorbed by the divine fire into that light which does not go out and which is holy. ₃₄And when he clothes us with his inextinguishable light, the light of the Sun of Righteousness, which befits the happy countenance of the saints, it will quicken and illumine us continuously. ₃₅Of those blessed with the good news of his sacred love, who are altogether glorified with the fullness of Christ and more,[15] none could restrain oneself from saying: *"God will be all in all"* (1 Cor 15.28). ₃₆Such a one is filled with the eternal good, according to the word of the Lord, as he asked of the Father: *"As you and I are one, may the believers and the saints also be in us"* (Jn 17.21). ₃₇For God so loved humanity that he bestowed upon us the honor and glory of the Divinity.[16] ₃₈God made this world for humans: to beget, to be sustained, and to live justly, righteously, and virtuously. He bestowed upon it his delightful and divine grace, like a decree, ever-renewing its eternal blessings and endless joys.

₃₉This, which we have discussed, is only a fraction of the plenitude of goodness. ₄₀Just as infants in their mothers' wombs do not know how they are about to grow and see and enjoy God's creation, so we are unable to comprehend. ₄₁This is in keeping with the word of the Apostle, which says: *"For we know in part and we prophesy in part, but when perfection comes, the imperfect disappears"* (1 Cor 13.9–10). ₄₂This (goodness) is more than the plenitude of things and is ineffable, incomprehensible even to incorporeal beings—certainly inexpressible for the grasp of the mind of corporeal beings. ₄₃For just as darkness flees away from light, earthlings (shy away) from heavenly and immortal beings. ₄₄To attain this goodness every positive

---

13. A recurring messianic title derived from Mal 4.2.

14. Cf. Disc. 12.41.

15. Allusion to Eph 4.13.

16. Echoing Ps 8.5 (8.6 LXX); cf. 82.6 (81.6 LXX). See §140 and note.

effort should be made on our part, to continue in the husbandry that pleases God, that culminates in (receiving) the promised good things.[17] ₄₅Let us flee from the filthy and abominable passions[18] and the evils that threaten with painful consequences, and let us follow with clean lives the example of those above. ₄₆To be beneficent, with love towards brothers, for their necessities of life;[19] to cultivate the good traditions for the redemption of our souls and bodies, for we have been invited and called unto the grace of adoption.[20] ₄₇For goodness has been planted in us by God, even the sovereign will, so that we may always do willingly what is good. ₄₈For the spiritual law has been established in our hearts: *"hope, love, and faith"* (1 Cor 13.13), along with that sovereign angelic and human will, ₄₉so that we may become heirs of the glorious life and be honored by the Creator with the inexpressible blessings.[21]

₅₀And to creatures with sovereign mind he appointed two tutors, as for one's child: threats and promises of good things;[22] to fear the threats and run away from harms, and to desire the promised good things and follow righteousness; ₅₁to obey—following the right counsel of the Holy Scriptures—the authorities that administer justice for the sake of moral behavior.[23] ₅₂For this reason he gave us the Prophets and the Apostles, (also) patriarchs, *vardapets*,[24] and teachers, to make us aware of and knowledgeable and well-informed about God's good will, so that whoever chooses may come to the knowledge of truth and live,[25] and through their righteous deeds

17. Remotely alluding to Mt 25.21 ("Well done ..."), an often quoted verse (see Disc. 4.78; 5.122; 6.83; 11.95; 18.59; 23.79).

18. The term "passion" (Arm. ցանկութիւն [*c'ankut'iwn*]) throughout, as in the Byzantine monastic tradition, is used as the equivalent of vice.

19. Fraternal love and care, including correction, is a traditional monastic requirement for the good of others; see Disc. 5.106, 6.72, 96; 11.33; 23.32, 44, 57, 71, 86.

20. Allusion to Eph 1.5–6; cf. Rom 8.14–17, 23; Gal 4.1–7. In §§129 and 133, as elsewhere, adoption is linked to baptism (Disc. 3.17; 9.29–30; to baptism and the Eucharist in 5.45; 9.23; 13.31–35; 14.17). See also Disc. 3.16; 6.17; 9.30; 10.48, 88 (on adoption as grace); for more, see the Subject Index.

21. Allusion to the "Beatitudes" in Mt 5.1–16.

22. Cf. Disc. 18.3.

23. Allusion to Rom 13.1–5; cf. Ti 3.1; 1 Pt 2.13–14.

24. Arm. word for ecclesiastical teacher; later, doctor of divinity; here used redundantly with the synonymous word *usuc'ič's* ("teachers").

25. Allusion to 1 Tm 2.4.

show gratitude to the heavenly Father and to the only-begotten Son
and to the Holy Spirit, who grants life to his creatures to collaborate with God's good will. ₅₃He shall bring those who truly and
righteously abide by these (mandates) into his divine inheritance, as
the Apostle says: *"Heirs of God and co-heirs with Christ;* ₅₄*(if) we become
like Christ (we may) also share in his glory"* (Rom 8.17). ₅₅Therefore, let us
not be sluggish in our lives, but let us give heed to our calling, with
an earnest haste to learn and do his will, *"so that one may be called
great in the Kingdom of God"* (Mt 5.19).

₅₆We, whom he created and instructed, the elect of his Lordship,
were taught that by observing the ways of our Savior we may become like him.[26] ₅₇Thus, through the prophetic word, the apostolic
preaching, and the patriarchates,[27] we have come to recognize the
Father almighty, the Son equal in power, and the Holy Spirit their
co-worker. ₅₈And by the right faith[28] we have come to recognize
and to know the Creator and to abide by what pleases him; to remain inseparably bound to his love in both dire and tranquil times;
and (in doing so) we shall be justified according to the Benefactor's will. ₅₉To bear unfailing witness to God, to bless cordially the
Lord, the Giver of all good things, and to praise him with thanksgiving. ₆₀And the Lord himself holds his beneficence as proof of
his love and benevolence towards his chosen and perfect ones, in
whom God's grace overflows. ₆₁He mercifully pardons, cares for,
and heals those who repent and with confession turn to his beneficence; and he forgives their sins according to his immense compassion. ₆₂He is longsuffering towards the wicked and the unjust, the
arrogant exceeding in vice, whose minds are in darkness and who
are estranged from holy and righteous living, that they may have

---

26. Possible allusion to Eph 5.1, quoted below, §127; cf. 1 Jn 3.2.

27. The pl. *hayrapetut'eambk'n* most likely refers to the four ancient patriarchates
of Orthodoxy: Constantinople, Alexandria, Antioch, and Jerusalem.

28. Arm. ուղղափառ հաւատոյ (*uttap'ař hawatoy*), suggestive of orthodoxy, is
used four times (§§58, 143, and Disc. 5.26; 23.58; cf. ուղղափառութիւն [*utta-
hawatut'iwn*], Disc. 5.97). The simpler form, ուղիղ հաւատով (*utit hawatov*), with
the same meaning of "right faith," is used seven times (Disc. 3.4; 5.34; 6.98; 13.31;
15.62; 18.58; and 20.156). The adj. *uttap'ař* is used likewise, in the sense of "orthodox," with reference to teachers (§120; cf. *utit* in Disc. 12.6), confession of faith
(§138; cf. ուղիղ հանգամանաց [*utit hangamanac'*], with reference to its fundamentals, in Disc. 20.125), and episcopal synods or councils (Disc. 23.58).

remorse. ₆₃Otherwise, *"the Creator's wrath and fury will remain upon them all,"* according to the saying of the Apostle (Rom 1.18).

₆₄Such are the issues of life for the Giver of Life and for the recipient; he cares for his visible and invisible creatures daily through his sustaining love. ₆₅And he directs his benevolence to nurture and sustain—through the diverse gifts of his knowledge and wisdom, which compel the attentive and diligent to guard his commandments. ₆₆And by his power he enables them and keeps them steadfast; for, being strengthened, they withstand the machinations of Satan; and they remain unmoved and steadfast in their love for the truth. They are stimulated in the excellent virtues and essential works that crown with glory. ₆₇Such are those who revel in good things. ₆₈For they pursue their convictions with true faith and hope, for the sake of the blessings of the life-giving good news, lovingly cherishing the life to come, which is beyond measure and scrutiny. For they shall enjoy his blessings with him, and shall dwell with him in his ineffable joy. ₆₉For in his great mercy he compassionately cares for their spiritual and physical needs. ₇₀Being strengthened in grace and with God-given gifts, they revel in good health and peace.

₇₁And because of the renewal by the longsuffering goodness of God, one is able to confront the visible and invisible (evils); and being cleansed from filth by a holy God, the person is freed and enlightened about the glory of the redeeming Lordship and remains untouched by the enemy. And he stays pure and impeccable, immune from deadly sins, being enlightened about the hope of the resurrection. ₇₂And he is uplifted by the glory of humility, by which arrogance is vanquished, by honoring the Lord. ₇₃For the humble, the obedient, and the meek shall be uplifted, but the arrogant, the oppressive, and the faithless shall be vanquished before the fear of the Lord. ₇₄And the just shall be crowned and glorified in every way by the Creator in the Kingdom of the righteous. ₇₅For every utterance of the good news is an invitation to believers, those who are good and virtuous, to (enter) the gates of righteousness, to enjoy the honors and crowns of glory from him. ₇₆For because of his mercy, compassion, and caring, those who truly repent shall receive forgiveness from his almighty Lordship.

₇₇But terrifying words of chastisement summon the wicked—the prodigals, those who love the passions, the disobedient, and those who persist in sin—to eternal torments and perpetual death and hell. 78For they disdained the Creator's compassion and care and strayed far from true repentance, which would have cleansed, justified, and drawn them closer to eternal life. 79They will therefore receive shame and *"the unquenchable fire which is prepared for Satan and his demons"* (Mt 25.41).

80All these are ordained for our needs and concerns by the benevolent will of God. 81To those on the sanctified and good side, the promised good things from the Lord; 82but to those on the evil and disobedient side, the chastisement with wrath and fury that they will receive, the vengeance at the hand of the angel of evil.[29] 83For had they been willing, they could have avoided the tangible wrath and had it removed through genuine repentance, according to the great mercy of the Creator. 84And he deals with such promises of blessings and chastisement in order to correct, so that all would be willing, that they might have life and reach the Kingdom; 85also to reveal those who are the elect among us, who conduct their lives by his righteous laws. 86For the one who is good by nature, and truly so, will remain always good, lacking nothing in absolute goodness.

87These things that are called God's fury, wrath, or (chastening) threats, are said to be the justice of his law, since the unjust and the senseless are corrected with (such) threats bursting with wrath. 88Surely, there is no blemish or stain in the One who is perfect in benevolence and kindness. Neither does evil emanate from him, nor is there any tinge of it in him; he is in essence good, and not a trace of vice is to be found in him. 89For it is our sins that annoy God, and he admonishes us with punishments, though mindful of mercy in his wrath. For those who are admonished are being visited by the Creator. 90For it behooves us to abhor sin and to love justice, holiness, and truth, which make the Creator happy along with his hosts.

91These are demonstrations of his love, for he rejoices over the conduct and morals of men who repent of their evil lives. 92For he is life and sustainer of life, and love brimming with gifts. No one

---

29. Here and in the next paragraph, as in Disc. 17.32, the author endeavors to absolve God from any evil, even inflicting punishment: an argument of theodicy. Cf. Basil's *Quod Deus non est auctor malorum* (*Hom.* 9).

could accurately describe his all-powerful greatness: none of the countless powerful heavenly hosts or anyone from among humans, from whom he is pleased to receive blessing and worship with prostration. ₉₃All the blasphemy by demons, the heathen, the wicked, and sinners does not have the slightest effect on the untouchable light of the Godhead. ₉₄All the armies of myriads of angels, who persist in ceaseless praise, and those chosen by the Lord from among humans, are incapable of blessing God worthily. ₉₅For the Godhead is neither honored nor dishonored by anyone; nothing of his glory is changed by that, for he is Life and immutable Light that does not pass away.

₉₆What is amazing is that he who is Nameless has acquired a name because of his utmost love; for there was nobody with the One without beginning to call him by name.[30] Yet his creatures call him Creator because of his benevolence and benevolent will. ₉₇It is because of his care for creatures that he is called Creator and Benefactor and Light and Life. As to his name, he alone knows it. ₉₈For he is the inextinguishable Light of Light, Life of the Living, Immaterial Fire, and Creator of the material fire.[31] ₉₉For as he was, he is, and remains so forever. He alone is omniscient. He revealed himself to his creatures because of his love, and made himself known through his care.

₁₀₀And he called his creatures, all sorts of people, to the discipleship of his benevolence: *"First apostles,"* as Paul says, *"then prophets, then teachers,"* and others that follow (1 Cor 12.28), ₁₀₁those to whom the Holy Spirit distributes gifts according to their calling—those whom he has invited to his Kingdom. ₁₀₂He revealed the watchfulness of his love so that we may be justified in believing it, whereby we shall enter into Christ our God's glorious inheritance. ₁₀₃For he has called those who believe, his "vineyard"; and the heavenly Father, the "Gardener,"[32] by whom the disciples—the "gar-

30. An indicator of *apophatic* theology, which is slow to identify God with any human concept capable of defining him.

31. The first of these epithets recalls one in the Nicene Creed; others echo biblical ascriptions to God as "consuming fire" (e.g., Ex 24.17; Dt 4.24; Heb 12.29; cf. Ex 3.1–6, on Moses and "the burning bush") more than echoing Greek mythology surrounding the fire-god Hephaistos and/or Prometheus.

32. Reference to Jn 15.1.

deners"—are sanctified and gathered into the eternal storerooms: 104those who labored from the first hour to the last, those willing (late-comers) who were rewarded by the (All)-knowing as much as those who were (hired) first.[33] 105But those who alienated themselves from the love of God, *"who makes the sun shine upon the wicked and the good"* (Mt 5.45), and estranged themselves, cannot be rewarded like the children of God—106all those saints who pursued righteousness and spiritual husbandry, who through preaching the truth attained the promised good things that are in Christ Jesus, to the glory of the Most Holy Trinity, 107and who filled the universe with the Word of Life[34] and renewed believers with water and Spirit.[35] 108Moreover, they preached salvation by the grace of the Son of God, through confession and repentance.

109For by nature he is the Father of his only-begotten Son, and Life of Life, Light of Light, and the Good of Goodness. 110And by grace he is called our Father also; and Light, who enlightens us through the faith; and Life, who works life in us. 111He reveals himself to people through true manifestations: to some through nature[36] and to others through providential care, (like) a father to orphans.[37] 112He thus draws us near, moreover, to imitate his creative, providential care; to turn the misguided to the knowledge of God, by the grace of the benevolent Father; 113more so, regarding benevolence, to become like him in compassionate love.[38] 114He teaches sinners so that they may not be lost eternally; rather, to proceed thoughtfully in the right path, (guided) by divine laws; to study, to learn, *"to know wisdom and discipline"* (Prv 1.1),[39] and to guide the lost

33. Reference to "The Parable of the Workers in the Vineyard," Mt 20.1–16; cf. Disc. 11.118.

34. Echoing 1 Jn 1.1.

35. Echoing Jn 1.33; 3.5. Describing Christian baptism as rebirth through "living water" and "spiritual fire" is common in patristic writings; e.g., Basil, *De Spiritu Sancto* 15, 35–36 (PG 32:128C–133A); Didymus the Blind, *De Trinitate* 2, 12 (PG 39:667–674).

36. Echoing Rom 1.20.

37. Echoing Jn 14.18; Jas 1.27.

38. Echoing Lk 6.36.

39. The words here are identical to those of the Arm. Bible, an early fifth-century translation that began with these words according to Koriwn, *Life of Maštocʿ*, 8.7 (MH 1.238).

with signs and wonders; 115to establish the disciples in the faith; to remain unmoved in the truth; to be very patient through all tribulations. 116Moreover, following the example of the Lord's love, to urge (others) to respond to his love, to care for and sustain (others) with compassion, to lift the burdens and aches of many, and to summon them to grace through repentance and the (baptismal) font. 117Also to fish tirelessly and skillfully, with the spiritual net, (to draw) many to piety;[40] 118to enlighten those in the darkness of sin and injustice; to cleanse, sanctify, and free (people) from servitude to Satan; to renew them in the renewal according to God: enlightenment, justice, and truth; and to (help them) take off the old self with its evil works,[41] so that they may be worthy of crowns and glory.

119We have learned this line of work from the Father and from the Son and from the Holy Spirit, who always takes us as collaborators with his benevolent will, in accordance with the true traditions that keep the faithful people inerrant and close to the saints' resting places.[42] 120And thus we have been instructed: from opting for the Law to faith and light and love for justice, allegiance to the cumulative virtues and to the true Apostles and Prophets, to orthodox teachers and those who learned from them: witnesses (taught) patient endurance of torture; confessors, self-restraint; ascetic virgins, sanctity and virtue; penitents, forgiveness. 121For these reasons, God chose his people from humankind so that they may be zealous in good works and obtain from his benevolence the imperishable crowns;[43] 122since they love the Creator and are loved by him, who by his grace did wondrous and remarkable things on earth and in heaven, and who abides forever.

123For had there been no election by the Lord, in keeping with his righteous laws, the desirability and preciousness of the virtues would not have been (so) prominent. Moreover, the martyrs' example of the way to the blessed life, that of the saints whose lives

---

40. Echoing Mt 4.19.

41. Allusion to Col 3.9; Eph 4.22.

42. Generally, Arm. աղլնանս սրբոց (*awt'evans srboc'*) points to heavenly places, not to *martyria* (Arm. վկայարան, վկայանոց [*vkayaran, vkayanoc'*]). On the terminology for the latter, see Garsoïan, *Epic Histories*, 543.

43. Echoing 1 Pt 5.4.

were cut short (in their endeavor) to inherit the blessings, and that of the spiritual hosts who stayed in God's love[44] would have been for naught. 124Those who strayed from the Creator's care shall be punished by the fearsome Judge, who shall recompense as deserved, for *"the righteous shall go to eternal life, and the wicked to eternal punishment"* (Mt 25.46). 125The divine Word identifies both groups: *"Come,"* he says, *"you who are blessed by my Father; inherit the Kingdom of God"* (Mt 25.34), and *"Depart from me, you who are cursed, into the eternal fire prepared for Satan and his angels"* (Mt 25.41). 126He first admonishes and calls unto good works. *"Come,"* he says, *"to me, all you who are weary and burdened, and I will give you rest. Take my yoke upon you and learn meekness and humility from me, and you will find rest for your souls"* (Mt 11.28–29). 127And the Apostle says: *"Be like God, as dearly loved children, and persist in love, just as Christ loved us and gave himself up for us[45] as a sacrifice to God"* (Eph 5.1–2).

128For the Son of God made humans his heirs, and lavishly bestowed upon us the grace of the Holy Spirit. 129For with kind entreaties he called sinners to repent through confession and to obey the Gospel of Life,[46] in order to renew the believers through the luminous font for adoption by his Father.[47] 130He, who by nature is Son, has received us as his brothers by grace.[48] 131He removes sin's countless stains from those who are reborn in the (holy) font by the Spirit and frees them from servitude to the evil one. 132*"For those who were baptized into Christ were clothed with Christ, whether male or female, whether Jew or Gentile, whether slave or free; for, by the same grace, they are children of God and co-heirs with Christ"* (Gal 3.27–28). 133Those who descended into the womb of the spiritual font as a gift from the Most Holy Trinity, with priestly blessing and consent, were enlightened in Christ by the anointing and the Spirit,[49] according to the Word of

44. Allusion to the loyal angels of Rv 12.7–9. In verses 10–12, the revisited defeat and casting down of Satan (cf. Is 14.12–15 on the king of Babylon; Ezek 28.1–19 on the king of Tyre; Lk 10.18 on Satan), as a result of Christ's triumphant death on the cross, are reaffirmed through the martyrs' testimony to the blood of the Lamb. See also §§148–152, where the subject is somewhat amplified.

45. Text has ձեր (*jer*, "your" pl.) instead of մեր (*mer*, "our"), a common scribal error.

46. Cf. Disc. 19.79.

47. On the linkage of divine adoption with baptism, see note to §46.

48. Allusion to Mt 12.49.

49. Distinct from post-baptismal Chrismation, associated with the bestowal of

the Lord: *"Receive the Holy Spirit"* (Jn 20.22) unto adoption by the Father of Christ. ₁₃₄For from him the priests received authority to bind and release (from sin);⁵⁰ for they make those who are being baptized renounce Satan and die the death unto sin, so that they no longer live in sin on earth.⁵¹ ₁₃₅Just as the dead cease from all works, the one who is baptized becomes dead to sin and alive unto righteousness, for he receives the image of Christ by the grace of the Holy Trinity.⁵² Thereafter, *"setting your minds on things above"* (Col 3.2), in accordance with the truth of the proclaimed Gospel and with what is pleasing to the immortal King, and with just and true and holy lives, you may reach the mansions of eternal life, which is in Christ Jesus. ₁₃₆For such is the rebirth from the spiritual font, whereby those born into filth may obtain what is free from filth by the grace and loving kindness of the Most Holy Trinity: ₁₃₇*"Those who are born neither of blood nor of human will, but of God"* (Jn 1.13) for the promised inheritance of Christ. ₁₃₈For thus are born the children of God, in the image of the Son of God. And they testify to the truth in times of trouble and peace, and they remain steadfast in the love of God, with right hearts and right confession. And the children of the life-giving Father become recipients of the ineffable heavenly gifts. ₁₃₉Thereafter they do God's work and fulfill his will, in accordance with the Benefactor's beneficence. And they become partners with the heavenly hosts in the service of humankind, by the grace of the Creator, to those who would inherit eternal salvation, which is in Christ.⁵³

---

the Spirit, the baptismal rite in the early Armenian Church included pre-baptismal anointing, following the East Syrian practice; see *Macarius of Jerusalem: Letter to the Armenians, AD 335*, trans. Abraham Terian, AVANT 4 (Crestwood, NY: St. Vladimir's Seminary Press, 2008), 104–5. A likely allusion to this practice, apparently maintaining the distinction between pre- and post-baptismal anointing, may be discerned here; cf. Disc. 5.26; 11.41, both with likely allusion to the pre-baptismal part of the rite.

50. Allusion to Mt 16.19; 18.18. The author here makes a leap from baptismal anointing to priestly anointing or consecration and the assumed authority it bestows; cf. Disc. 5.45, in context.

51. Echoing Rom 6.1–14.

52. Note the twin images of baptism as birth and death, owing to Jn 3.3–8 and Rom 6.1–7 respectively. While the former was stressed in the East and the latter in the West, the two images are often found side by side in early Christian writings (the distinction in the East-West use of these images is overdrawn in liturgiology). Elsewhere, see Disc. 7.89; 13.31 (death); 6.36; 23.91 (birth).

53. Allusion to Heb 1.14.

₁₄₀Just as the Son of God became Son of Man and took our nature and pursued righteousness with all his soul and body,[54] so ought we to put on what is right and pursue all righteousness in Christ, so that through love we may become children of God and gods.[55] ₁₄₁For (as) the Son of God willingly took body and appropriated every aspect of our human nature except sin, ₁₄₂so too should we be able, by the power of God, to pass through everything without sinning, so that we may be able to reach the measure of Christ's perfection and, being truly in the image of God, inherit the Kingdom of Christ. ₁₄₃And it is always necessary to be instructed by the Gospel, which admonishes us with excellent mandates. So that being individually endowed by the grace of the Holy Spirit, we may truly multiply the endowment of truth with a pure heart and right faith in God. ₁₄₄And under the supervision of God's providential love let us always be alert and watchful against the fallacies of the accuser,[56] so that with steadfast hope and virtue, with holy life and pure spirit and body, we may reach the harbor of peace, the eternal life, the unbounded place prepared for the saints by God's ineffable love. ₁₄₅And just as this sun gives light to the world and to the creatures therein, those seen in the sea and on land, so may the word and the sanctity of the true faith also illumine the minds of those who long for God. ₁₄₆And may the heavenly and earthly beings of sovereign will, both humans and angels, continue to be teachers of the truth by the grace of the Holy Spirit, with sure knowledge and unerring wisdom, abiding by the righteous laws. ₁₄₇And thus being led by the Trinity's light, the sure account of that creative essence, may heaven and earth be filled with rays like those of the sun's light, for the life and glory of heavenly and earthly beings. ₁₄₈As for Satan, who wanted to become god, he erred in thought in his glory;

54. Echoing Phil 2.7.

55. For an equally pointed notion of deification (*theōsis*), see Disc. 10.48. The scriptural basis of the doctrine is in Ps 82.6 (81.6 LXX), quoted in Jn 10.34; cf. 2 Pt 1.4. See also Rom 8.14–17, 29; 1 Cor 15.28; 2 Cor 3.18; Eph 4.24; Phil 3.21; 1 Jn 3.2. On the emergence of the doctrine in the early Church, see the various articles in *Theōsis: Deification in Christian Theology*, ed. Stephen Finlan and Vladimir Kharlamov, Princeton Theological Monograph Series (Eugene, OR: Pickwick Publications, 2006).

56. A recurring epithet for Satan (name in Hebrew means "accuser"); see Jb 1.9–11; Zec 3.1; 1 Pt 5.8; Rv 12.10.

seeing his brightness, he became proud and fell from his honor.[57] He began hunting down humans for perdition, enslaving them by vain hopes, by the misleading spirit of alienation—drawing them away from the love of God into diverse passions for wickedness.

149Should someone ask, "Why did God allow Satan to spread so much misleading lawlessness?" Listen. It is up to the sovereign will of angels and humans, granted by God. It is their prerogative to do what seems best to them; and accordingly, they shall receive their recompense from the Creator of all creatures, as time will tell, either for glory or for torture. 150Just as death came to reign because of Adam's transgression,[58] so Satan lords it over sinners. 151*"For men preferred delusion,"* (Scripture) says, *"for this reason God sends them the effects of delusion ... so that they will be condemned ... for they delighted in wickedness"* (2 Thes 2.11–12). 152Because of his providential love, however, he did not leave his creatures to perish: by the coming of his Son, who came into the world to save sinners from servitude to Satan, through faith in the redemption by the glorious Son of God. The tyranny of sin's reign over humans ended with the appearance of the Savior. 153And by grace, by faith in the Holy Trinity, they shall reign, those who have found forgiveness through the (baptismal) font and through the body and blood of Christ, having received the Holy Spirit, who spreads gifts in streams to his creatures. 154Thereafter, those justified by faith shall stand in peace before God,[59] those who believed in the inheritance attained through Jesus Christ, whose immutable glory is reaffirmed by his willing crucifixion. Through death he abolished death,[60] and through his resurrection he raised us from death because of sin, so that we may stand in the newness of life and abide in the hope of the resurrection;[61] to the glory of the Most Holy Trinity, now and always and to the ages of ages. Amen.

---

57. Allusion to Is 14.12–15; Ezek 28.1–19. Cf. Disc. 6.25–41 and 20.70–84, on Satan's fall as a result of free-will choice.

58. Allusion to Gn 3.17–19; cf. Rom 5.12–21; 1 Cor 15.21–22.

59. Echoing Rom 3.28; Gal 2.16; 3.11, 24 (cf. Disc. 15.62 and 18.43, where *tsmartealk'* is used instead of *ardarac'ealk'* as here and in Disc. 23.108; and Disc. 17.27, where the equally specific *ardars hawatov* is used).

60. Allusion to Heb 2.14.

61. See Rom 6.3–5; Phil 3.10–11; cf. 2 Tm 1.10.

DISCOURSE 3

INSIGHTS INTO FAITH[1]

RUE FAITH is light to the eyes of the mind, for the process of thoughtful reflection; it is the perceptible light of
knowledge and wisdom, gifts of the Holy Spirit. ₂It enlightens the ruling part of the mind and poises it to assess abstract
notions, in keeping with the Holy Scriptures. In the manner that
the eyes perceive sunlight and other luminaries, likewise the inscrutable mighty acts of the Lord God are revealed. ₃For he is unique
and beyond comparison, boundary, or definition; unreachable and
immeasurable. By faith, by unwavering faith, he is seen, comprehended, and praised by creatures in distress and in tranquility. The
one with strong faith in the Holy Trinity abides immovable against
the antagonists of faith. ₄For being enlightened in the right faith in
the Existence without beginning, the eternal Light, the life-giving
Life, and the Truth that does not change, we shall no longer be led
astray by vain talk, which is blasphemy against the Father, the Son,
and the Holy Spirit.

₅Let us not miss out on the gifts pledged in the Gospel,[2] but receive the promised blessings—immortality and incorruption, ₆so
that we may always experience the salutary love of the Lord's benevolence. Let us cherish hope for the Kingdom daily in our hearts,
and let us not forget the Lord's life-giving gifts. And let us cherish
his affectionate care in aiding our weakness and ignorance of the

1. The Arm. title, «Միտք Հաւատոյ» ("Mitkʻ Hawatoy"; lit., "The Mind of
Faith") could equally mean an intellect-deepened faith, a faith disciplined by the
intellect, or the ability to reason and believe. Contextually, however, the discourse
is on the perception of faith, its capacity and attributes. Like Basil's *De fide* (Hom.
3), the discourse does not deal with any dogmatic formula but with the believer's
frame of mind. Cf. Aphrahat's building of faith, wherein Christ dwells, *Dem.* 1.

2. Lit., "the good news."

plots of Satan, who is a constant enemy. ₇And being strengthened by the counsel of the Prince of life,³ let us strive to grow in faith, toward the fullness of virtue. ₈Let us keep in mind, throughout our lives, the counsel of the saints regarding the visible and invisible things, that we may thus know the Truth. ₉For on your own you cannot perceive the greatness of divine glory; nor could the spiritual beings, the armies of angels, Seraphim, and Cherubim. None of the heavenly wakeful beings could perceive the divine glory.

₁₀Moses, the faithful servant of God, proclaimed the Existent to us; (this was done) not by him but rather by God himself, ₁₁who says: *"I am God, the Existent"* (Ex 3.14). ₁₂Thus the light of divine existence was spread to creatures, that they may confess, with unwavering knowledge, the immeasurable greatness of his glory, the uncreated Essence, and the truth about the Existent who is without beginning, the eternal One who does not change, the unattainable and unerring Wisdom, whom lawgivers and law-abiding folk proclaimed, each according to one's grace. ₁₃That one may root out the adverse, appalling, and detrimental ingratitude and promote the luminous, beneficial, and helpful (acts of) beneficence till the end of time. ₁₄For this reason the Benefactor's helpers were glorified and honored. ₁₅For when God sent Moses to the ungrateful people, he showed the tenderness of his loving care; for he says, *"I am compassionate and merciful, longsuffering and abundant in mercy, and have pity upon creatures"* (Ex 34.6). ₁₆He thus leads those who err from grace, those who were (once) called to the grace of adoption,⁴ and restores them again by his almighty power and most generous, rewarding love. ₁₇And with such longings for impeccable sanctity through unhampered virtue, the Most Holy Trinity unites the enlightened ones⁵ in the world, and with unchanging truth appoints them for adoption. ₁₈For the Lord himself is the Artisan of their art, the One who welcomes disciples, virtuous martyrs, his co-workers for truth from among his creatures. And through God's love they become superintendents⁶ of souls and bodies, both far and near.

3. Title of Christ in Acts 3.15 (Arm. Առաջնորդ Կենաց, *Aṙajnord Kenac*ʻ).

4. Cf. §17. Allusion to Eph 1.5–6; cf. Rom 8.14–17, 23; Gal 4.1–7. See also Disc. 2.46; 6.17; 9.30; 10.48, 88 (on adoption as grace); for more, see the Subject Index.

5. A metonym for the baptized; cf. Disc. 2.129, 133; 5.45; 9.23, 29–30; 14.17.

6. Arm. տեսուչ (*tesuč*ʻ), a term used in Disc. 23.74 and 78 for someone responsible for some practical aspect of monastic life (cf. Gk. *epitērētēs;* Syr. *rabbaitā*).

19Now by faith, in all truth and virtue, in righteousness and sanctity, let us be firmly established in the invisible Greatness, in the Glory that is inscrutable and unbounded, commensurate with the announced good things—endless and ineffably glorious. 20And with our whole heart and true confession (let us) praise the inscrutable Creator, and (let us) abide unshaken in the living hope[7] and that delightful rest, as having seen that which *"the eye has not seen, nor has the ear heard, nor has it occurred in the human heart, what God has prepared for those who love him"* (1 Cor 2.9).[8] 21For the good things that the saints enjoy, by virtue of the overabundant care and life-giving love of God, are ineffable.

22We ought to thank (God) always for all these things: for his creative care, for allowing so many good things, both by visible and invisible means. 23And let us always bless the immortal Lordship: day and night, with pure love, genial willingness, and impeccable sanctity—bearing in mind the sacred canon of the unforgettable remembrance, with praise to God's glory and the confession (of faith) that pleases him.[9] 24For as the sunbeams extend and retract, so too (radiates) the truth of the Existent: the unchanging Essence, who is beyond the reach of the mind and its thoughts, whose account is from before there were creatures and past the eternal ages, who is higher than heaven, who is from earth and deeper than the depth of the sea, who is and remains boundless. 25Yet creatures are visited by the good will of the Creator, the One without beginning, the Existent. For he is unlimited, immeasurable, and boundless; an unclouded Source, Omnipotent and Almighty. 26He is Life and Sustainer of life, eternal Light, awe-inspiring, mighty, all-wise, and foreknowing, Benefactor bestowing good things, compassionate and merciful, forgiving and longsuffering, Most Holy—sanctity

7. Echoing 1 Pt 1.3.

8. Cf. Is 64.4; 65.17.

9. The liturgical language is unmistakable here. "The sacred canon of the unforgettable 'remembrance' (*yišatak*)," as in Disc. 11.6, 20, 76, 127, and elsewhere (see "Eucharist" in the Subject Index), refers to the *Anamnesis*, the recalling of Christ's atoning sacrifice through the Liturgy of the Eucharist (based on his words at the Last Supper, Lk 22.19; cf. 1 Cor 11.24–25). "The praise to God's glory" (*govest p'aṙac'n Astucoy*) is the psalmodic vigil followed by the cathedral service of praise. The "confession" (*vkayut'iwn*, elsewhere *xostovanut'iwn;* see term in the Subject Index) is the credal Confession of Faith in the Liturgy of the Word.

to all creatures. ₂₇For even if the countless armies of incorporeal beings, the luminaries in heaven—those visible and invisible—humans and others on earth, the innumerable creatures of the sea and the non-breathing creatures therein were to be able to speak, they could not offer sufficient praise befitting the greatness of his glory.

₂₈Now, the One who is so boundless in the greatness of his glory and higher than all comprehensible and visible things, stoops down for his creatures, so that he may become comprehensible and visible, to the extent that we are able to receive his loving care. ₂₉(Since) angels, who are sharper than the human mind, are unable to comprehend (even) in part, how could we earthlings be able to comprehend his glory? ₃₀For he says: *"No one knows the Father except the Son, and no one (knows) the Son and the Spirit except the Father"* (Mt 11.27).

₃₁As for the care (shown) by God's benevolent love, laden with manifold cures, it derives from the Existent who is without beginning and immutable from eternity. The Most Holy Trinity, who abounds in every goodness, rules over the creatures, overseeing and caring. ₃₂For by his bountiful grace and life-giving and overwhelming virtue, he gathers the virtuous elect into his blessed rest and crowns them with glory, with eternal and unfading gifts. ₃₃It was for this reason that the Creator made the armies of angels and human beings with free will, so that by choosing the spiritual law they may attain change: from smallness to greatness, from dishonor to honor, from corruptibility to incorruptibility, from mortality to divine immortality, which is in Christ Jesus. ₃₄In the Kingdom of God there will be neither change because of time nor withdrawal of the good things to be given. ₃₅The endless blessings will be enjoyed there to the glory of the Most Holy Trinity: Father, Son, and Holy Spirit, forever and ever. Amen.

DISCOURSE 4

HE MOST HOLY Trinity is incomparably almighty. By the Existent without beginning were all creatures established, both visible and invisible. ₂Heaven and earth and everything in them were created by the only Creator, the almighty Power, the most luminous Light and life-giving Lordship; all creatures are full of his glory: ₃of him who cares for his creatures through his all-wise, all-knowing, and all-seeing benevolent will, who from nothing and non-existence brought into being the spiritual and corporeal beings, breathing and non-breathing. ₄And all the elements were ordered into four categories, in height and depth, breadth and length. ₅ He also brought forth the living, immortal, intelligent, and rational beings, who are the angelic armies, the heavenly hosts, ranked in honor, in duty, and in their ceaseless glorification of his almighty Lordship. ₆He also placed the luminaries in heaven for guidance and the succession of days and seasons, and for the nourishment of people and all animals, plants and (all) flora. ₇Likewise he established fire and water, clouds and winds, as necessary for plants and (all) flora after their kind, all of which were created for human needs. ₈The water creatures, shellfish and fish, and the various beasts of diverse natures and appearances in the sea and on the land: large and small, wild and domestic, beneficial and unbeneficial. ₉It is the same with plants and (all) flora, which were created for human needs and not for (the sake of) the Creator. ₁₀He made gold and silver, copper and iron, precious and common stones for the needs of humans. These were made as a testimonial for the great God. ₁₁And out of the four elements he brought forth

84

the visible things. The moist and dry things, the cold and the hot, were made by God.[1]

₁₂And out of the same substance he made man and breathed into him the breath of life: immortal, intelligent, and rational. ₁₃And he mixed the spiritual with the physical in order to indicate the outcome's close affinity to the Creator: to observe his commandments with self-restraint, spiritual love, and fear, so that by pleasing God one may become an heir to the everlasting blessedness. For (Scripture) says: *"He created man in his own image and appointed him lord over everything, for he had created him in his own image"* (Gn 1.27), which is to be understood as the Incarnation of Christ.[2] ₁₄And he privileged humans with a sovereign will, just like the angels, and filled them with wisdom and knowledge and familiarity with every condition and spiritual counsel, as it pleased his Lordship; so that they may follow the Creator's command to become stewards of his creation.[3] ₁₅And that through their ingenious artistry people may utilize all the elements for the development of the world, its provinces and cities; ₁₆and to make through their creative ability furniture, structures, and vessels that are necessary for life in the world, for essential needs.

₁₇And he gave breathing creatures, beasts and birds, certain blessings and attention to their needs. ₁₈These blessings activate, through inner working, their attentiveness. And he (set) the human intellect (as) an instructor, both for their well-being and for our servitude. ₁₉Among them are found the small and the large, the ignoble and the beneficial, the useful and the useless, the ugly and the pretty, so that the good may be differentiated from the bad, and

---

1. Paul Vetter sees in this paragraph some amplification of a fragment of Aelius Aristides's *Ex Apologia ad Adrianum Imperatorem* preserved in Armenian; "Aristides-Citate in der armenischen Literatur," *Tübinger Theologische Quartalschrift* 76 (1894): 529–39. For the assumed source, see Félix A. P. Dupanloup, ed. and trans., *Xōskʻ srboyn Aristideay Imastasiri Atʻenacʻwoy / Sancti Aristides Philosophi Athieniensis sermones duo* (Venice: Patres Mechitaristae, 1878). Reprinted in Joannes Baptista Pitra, ed. and trans., *Analecta Sacra, Tom. IV: Patres Antenicaeni* (Paris: Ex Publico Galliarum Typographeo, 1883), 6–8 (for frag. I, *Apologia*, trans. 282–84), 9–10 (for frag. II, *Homiliae in Sanctum Latronem Fragmentum*, on Lk 23.42–43, trans. 284–86), 11 (for frags. III–IV, consisting of two lines each, on the Incarnation, trans. 287).

2. A likely gloss.

3. See Gn 1.26. Arm. սեպունչը (*tesučʻkʻ*); elsewhere, a monastic term (Disc. 23.74 and 78) for "superintendents" assisting the superior.

the dishonorable from the honorable. ₂₀Just as light appears in the midst of darkness, so too the domesticated[4] among the beastly, the harmless among the venomous, and the beneficial among the detrimental. It is the same with plants and vegetation, with varying aroma and taste: sweet and bitter, delicious and tasteless, so that the bad may be discernible from the good, those that are set apart for healing and sustenance by the inner working of God. ₂₁And there are those that are unknown and those that are known in particular regions. ₂₂There also are the reptiles—some of which are useful, as snakes are said to provide medicines.

₂₃The Creator has thus created his creatures providentially, those visible and those invisible. And he placed man with his noticeably creative mind (as) lord and ruler over them and heir to all.[5] ₂₄He created all things out of nothing, and he placed man over them, honoring him as king, so that through him the Creator would be made known and always glorified, and that man himself would acknowledge the honor bestowed upon him while in a dishonorable state, from among all creatures. ₂₅Through his creative genius, which is from the Creator, he was enabled to utilize the breathing and the non-breathing so that the wise works (of God) should become fully manifest, as to how they all are compliantly laid down by the Lord for their necessary function: be it for construction, adornment, or certain enrichment. ₂₆The Benefactor will always be glorified by those richly privileged with a sovereign (mind). ₂₇He bestowed as much honor upon those corporeal beings as upon the incorporeal and immortal spirits. He made those privileged (beings) who would praise him for his creation,[6] who would always bless him across their appointed ranks,[7] those who by their own free will have been established in the true faith, who can differentiate between the Creator and the creatures, the Sustainer and those sustained by the Giver of Life to all beings—who fulfills the needs of all creatures.

---

4. The word *gaw* is a rare loan word from Persian *gāv* (lit., "cow").

5. Allusion to Gn 1.26, 28.

6. The original text probably had աղարիչն (*ararič'n*, "the Creator") instead of աղարչութեանն (*ararč'ut'eann*, "for the creation," with the last syllable abbreviated).

7. Lit., "through the set rules (or, law)."

₂₈It is proper to pray to him at all times and to ask for one's spiritual and physical (needs), and to collaborate with his benevolent will, becoming attentive to the beneficent God. ₂₉And to be transformed,[8] by (following) this mandate, from bad to good, from the ignominious to the honorable, from slavery to freedom in the Son of God, being familiar with the true faith in the Father, the Son, and the Holy Spirit; to become an heir to the Kingdom of Heaven and the everlasting blessedness. ₃₀For he is the Creator of all, *"who makes his servants spirits and his armies on high flames of fire"* (Heb 1.7). ₃₁And earthborn people, though inferior, exist through sustenance; ₃₂for they shall be instructed in the spiritual life by angels, by the providence of God who gave as an aid *"the law proclaimed by angels"* (Acts 7.53).

₃₃For it pleased God to be proclaimed by people (abiding) in the true traditions, by those who were found faithful to his commandments and became pleasing to God. They turned many to the knowledge of God, to the right way, according to the will of the Creator of life. ₃₄But those who were found to be abhorring God and misguided in their thoughts *"and their hearts darkened in their misunderstanding"*—as the Apostle has said (Eph 4.18)—deprived themselves of the most bounteous benevolence. ₃₅They not only deprived themselves of the Creator's care through their disobedient conduct and backwardness but also provoked God's wrath toward them, from the righteous Judge who loves humankind. ₃₆They are the ones who fell from glory and honor, from the providential care of his benevolent will, and from being instructed by angels who were their helpers.

₃₇But those who abide considerately, patiently enduring all troubles, shall enjoy his attentive care both here and in the world to come. ₃₈And those who stray from the truth shall have God's wrath constantly upon them. ₃₉For they made gods out of the elements, out of the breathing and the non-breathing, out of water and fire. ₄₀Yet God made water for the needs of living beings, to water the earth; and they suffer by its excess and shortage. ₄₁And he made fire for our needs, to be kindled for our sustenance and use, and unless it is fueled, it dwindles and goes out. ₄₂The same is with the

8. Echoing Rom 12.2; 2 Cor 2.13.

winds and the clouds. These too were made for the needs of creatures; they did not come into existence by themselves. And they die out. They help and they harm by their increase and decrease, showing weakness. ₄₃Nor have heaven and earth come into existence on their own, nor the vibrant and breathless things in them; they were made by God and are perishable. ₄₄The luminaries in heaven, the creatures, plants and vegetation on earth, and all hand-crafted gods in the image of creatures made by the God of gods are false and perishable, as philosophers have clearly demonstrated. ₄₅So are silver and gold and the precious gems, copper, and iron. They were made to be crafted by people for their various needs, or for adornment. Whatever the substance, it was made by the Creator, by the providential wisdom of God. ₄₆For heaven and earth and all their adornments were made by God out of nothing. The elements, one and all, are not gods; they were created by the Creator of everything.

₄₇The luminaries: the sun, the moon, and all the stars are created beings, which through their changes indicate their defined servitude to other creatures as well. ₄₈They show us that they are created beings, whether through their helpfulness or through their unhelpfulness by reason of the scorching heat in summer and coldness in winter. Their advantages and disadvantages are numerous, as is well known. ₄₉As when people do not observe God's commandments or (follow) the healer's orders to enjoy their benefits—but become weary of these remedies for creatures—their benefits turn to harms. ₅₀As surely as winter cools, it also kills; and summer not only warms but also scorches. And fire not only heats and helps but also burns and destroys. And water not only wets the earth but also inundates and damages. ₅₁Such also are all the remedies, such as oil and honey, and wine and all the rest of this sort of things. ₅₂Remedies help when taken in their proper amount, but in excess cause misery and death. The insolent and audacious will, the inclination to greediness, the course of the unrestrained will, and the spread of lawlessness and outright vice have to be controlled, this *"broad way that leads to destruction"* (Mt 7.13). ₅₃But narrow and straight is the way of love and righteous laws that leads to life, for sanctity and righteousness bring the sojourner[9] to the gate of life and salvation.

---

9. Arm. Ճամբորդ (*čambord*, a *hapax* in singular here, with another *hapax* in plu-

₅₄Thus, in things seen and unseen, in the fear of the Lord, one has to restrain oneself through discernment; to rid one's sovereign will from the evil of disagreeableness and immodesty and to direct it unto goodness, to have it admonished in accordance with his laws; ₅₅to be considerate and thoughtful, to say and do what is pleasing to God, accomplished by the true testimony of the Holy Scriptures; ₅₆not to be embroiled in controversial issues that lead astray from sure doctrine, ₅₇so that one may always be filled with true knowledge, wisdom, life-improving rewards; and to remain steadfast in the spiritual doctrine, strengthened by the safeguarding commandments ₅₈*"that demolish every stronghold of pride ... which sets itself up against the knowledge of God"* (2 Cor 10.4–5), and bring about an affirmation of the faith.

₅₉(There was a time) when man was obedient to God's laws and venomous beasts were obedient to man as their lord and king, ₆₀as when Daniel remained steadfast in (keeping) the commandments and the three young men were in the fiery furnace,[10] as when the sea (obeyed) Peter[11] and all saintly beings obeyed God's will.[12] ₆₁But with the rebellion against the commandments of God, all creatures—breathing and non-breathing—experienced the opposite: the whole earth with all its plants and vegetation slipped into corruption. ₆₂(Scripture) says: *"Fruitful land turned into a salt waste because of the wickedness of its inhabitants"* (Ps 107.34 [106.34 LXX]). ₆₃And how much effort was made by the saints to direct men in the path of the Law and the Gospel of Christ! Similarly, men, by the grace of God, contrived ways to bring beasts and (other) animals and birds into obedience, to serve as needed, to work the land as necessary; ₆₄even to utilize fire, water, and wind through contrivances for our service. They were guided by the wisdom of God. ₆₅The Creator's providence works invisibly on beasts and (other)

---

ral at Disc. 23.70) is also the homeless or the exiled from home. For its spiritual sense, see Robin Darling Young, *"Xeniteia* According to Evagrius of Pontus," in *Ascetic Culture: Essays in Honor of Philip Rousseau,* ed. Blake Leyerle and Robin Darling Young (Notre Dame, IN: University of Notre Dame Press, 2013), 229–52.

10. Allusion to Dn 6 (esp. vs. 27) and 3 (esp. vs. 27). The same connection with the time before Adam's transgression, when animals did not harm humans (Gn 2.19–20), is made also by Eznik, *Refutation* 113 (22.16; MH 1:455–456).

11. Allusion to Mt 17.24–27.

12. Allusion to the harrowing of hell (1 Pt 3.19–20; 4.6).

animals, birds and reptiles and (other) creeping creatures, whether in the sea or on land, to obey us. 66If it were not for the fear of the Lord (hovering) over them all, they would kill us. 67And whenever they hurt us, they are moved by the fear of God, so that we may always hasten to change from viciousness to a life of virtue. 68For beasts are not made evil by nature, as trainers demonstrate by domesticating them. Lions, leopards, and bears obey man, like bulls and dogs and others under yoke or coaxing. Whereas those that are not tamed, they become wild and cause death and wounds to strangers.

69Similarly, for some reason, delirium strikes the mind to a point beyond remedy, as when among the well-behaved[13] some become wild to their own detriment or that of others. Erroneous learning, just like delirium, affects the mind and causes bewilderment; it estranges from the truth, giving way to wicked and licentious living that goes beyond the bounds of nature. This, nonetheless, is curable—like delirium. 70For this reason great caution is necessary to safeguard the hearing and the mind from harmful effects, "to meditate day and night on the law of the Lord" (Ps 1.2), which is replete with salvation and life. 71Yet man is a rational and articulate being by the grace of God and capable of staying resolute, intimate in the goodness of the faith and in pursuit of a pure life; 72of being rehabilitated from what is harmful to what is best; of being worthy of spiritual wellness by the beneficence of God's true love, impeccably pure; of receiving the gifts of apostleship, prophecy, teaching, and priesthood;[14] of accepting this grace willingly, worthily, illuminating the thoughts of his mind with the light of knowledge and wisdom; of reaching the haven of life worthily and gratefully.

73The will to control oneself has the power either to abide intimately in God's sacred love or—due to disobeying the spiritual law and its advantages—to plunge into the depths of wickedness, to inherit the notorious dishonor of the lawless, wicked, and filthy. 74The incorporeal beings likewise exercise their will either to remain within (the realm) of God's command or to rebel against the Lord. 75As it is understood, the spiritual beings abide in God's love

13. Or, "domesticated."
14. Alluding to the spiritual gifts, the *charismata* of 1 Cor 12.28; Eph 4.11; cf. Disc. 5.15; 20.154.

eternally, praising their Creator endlessly. ₇₆Yet Satan made some of them revolt,[15] and those who joined his army are called filthy and lovers of wickedness. ₇₇They thus possess from the beginning[16] the qualities of both natures: of good and evil, showing us both the good and the bad. ₇₈Each of us is acquainted with the honorable and the dishonorable. Let us follow what is good and hate what is evil, so that we may hear the blessed saying: *"Kind, good, and faithful servant; because you have been faithful over a little, I will set you over much; enter into the joy of your master"* (Mt 25.21).

₇₉And those who are sick, if they truly repent, they will attain the salvation that is in Christ Jesus. ₈₀The (unrepentant) sick should not enjoy the remedies for the righteous; nor should the bad and the good, the sinners and the sinless, the unholy and the holy be treated equally. ₈₁Each should have one's place in learning: some to learn and others to teach. ₈₂For in this manner all are invited into his Kingdom. Early on, he knowingly chose the Apostles for the ministry of worshiping the Creator by preaching the truth to all people. ₈₃Through them he prepared many to inherit the knowledge of God. ₈₄For this reason he is called Benefactor, King of Kings, and Lord of Lords, who alone possesses foreknowledge. To those who trust in him, to his faithful and virtuous servants, he manifests help during trouble and during peace. ₈₅For he is a righteous Judge, above the law; Healer of the sick, those inflicted by diverse illnesses and afflictions, when they turn in repentance, with confession. ₈₆For those who are willing, there are various spiritual remedies in the Holy Scriptures: counsels for well-being, good news of forgiveness and blessedness to come. ₈₇Just as clouds carry hail and lightning[17] and sometimes gentle rain, the Lord's command carries wrath upon the unworthy and kindness upon the worthy, according to his just judgment.

₈₈God, the Creator and the Lord who establishes, is to be praised with accolades for his works and his sustaining beneficence: Benefactor, Merciful, Compassionate, the Holy One, Longsuffering, the Constant, the True, the Invisible Power who stands to counsel

---

15. Allusion to Rv 12.7–9; cf. Is 14.12–15 and Ezek 28.11–19 and their interpretation in Jewish apocalypticism, e.g., 2 (Slavonic) Enoch 29.4–6; 31.3–6.

16. Lit., "from the naming."

17. Lit., "fire."

and to guide through discernible things both the invisible spiritual beings and the visible human beings—through election, goodness, virtue, and sacred deeds. 89Also the Creator's life-giving means, which work together with his grace, are to be praised. 90And (how could) the created receive the same accolades as its Creator? The one who extols (the Creator) shall enter into the inheritance of the Son of God, the lover of humankind, and shall enjoy his goodness, the eternal and unending blessings, with the immortal King, forever, always.

91A few words of exhortation are sufficient to guide the gracious, thoughtful ones who believe; but to unbelievers, those who are devoid of grace and erratic, those whose minds are in darkness and alienated from grace, words of exhortation are useless. 92Now, let none forget this divine exhortation by which we are enlightened, the intelligible light that casts no shadow—devoid of any hue of darkness. 93He made us rational and thoughtful so that we may recognize the Creator and do what pleases him, the One who drew (everything) out of nothing and from nonexistence into existence. 94And having nurtured those who abide within his commandments, he shall change them physically, to be sheltered in the divine glory of Christ. 95Those who say, "Why then did he make us corruptible and not incorruptible?" (ought to remember): *"Shall what is formed say to him who formed it, 'Why did you make me like this?'"* (Rom 9.20). 96For we shall learn on our own, by virtue of our sovereign will, that we are sinners and corruptible, as well as sinless and incorruptible. 97For to each is prepared (as deserved): death to sinners and life to the sinless, to be rewarded in the hereafter, where life and death are irrevocable. 98The state of blessed existence wrought by the love of God is unchanging. *"No eye has seen, no ear has heard ... what God has prepared for those who love him"* (1 Cor 2.9), says the divine Apostle.

99At that end-time (everything) will be revealed, on the day of revelation and resurrection, when the frightening tribunal of the Son of God will be seen in glory; *"for heaven and earth shall pass away"* (Mt 5.17), but he remains immortal, eternal, and unconsumed, forever and ever. 100Eternal torments await the disobedient and unbelieving ones, the wicked and sinners, like those for Satan and his demons; 101since on earth they swarmed and fanned out in sin, as if on the sea. ₁₀₂But the faithful, those enlightened by grace, remained steadfast in the commandments of the Creator. For their lives shone; and *"those who saw their good works glorified the Father who is in heaven"* (Mt 5.16), according to the words of the Gospel. ₁₀₃No one can comprehend the Creator, the Lord of all and of everything; nor could enough be said about the greatness of his all-creative power and wisdom. ₁₀₄Through his benevolence he opened the gate of life for his faithful creatures, through Jesus Christ and his saints. ₁₀₅By becoming their disciples, we shall keep on to the same (destiny), in faith, love, and hope.[18] With them, we shall inherit the eternally good things in Christ Jesus our Lord, to whom be glory forever and ever. Amen.

18. Echoing 1 Cor 13.13.

DISCOURSE 5

AFFIRMATION OF TRUTH AND GUIDANCE
THROUGH LIFE-GIVING COUNSEL

T IS CLEAR to the holy sages who are knowledgeable in the books of the Prophets, the Apostles, and the teachers (of the Church)[1] that the Most Holy Trinity is one in nature, power, glory, and eternity; 2infinite being, essence without beginning, immutable Truth, Life and Life-giver to living beings. 3He is Father, the Father of the only-begotten Son and the Source of the Holy Spirit;[2] the Cause of their essence, of the same nature. 4The Trinity is perfect and One in Divinity, always glorified by the heavenly hosts and humans for being God and Creator. 5For he made them out of nothing, as with everything visible and invisible in heaven and on earth. 6To spiritual and rational beings was given the sovereign will, with which they are privileged, and (thus) they exhibit the excellence of intimacy with the Father, glorifying the Lord of Glory[3] and doing what pleases him: being familiar with and studying his handiwork in purity and holiness; 7being beneficent, for the sustenance of fellow humans, shepherding and healing and guiding them in both visible and invisible necessities, with the help of the Holy Spirit in every (act of) benevolence and according to the (spiritual) law. 8Through good will and good thoughts and good works, let us exhibit this essential work. 9Being made and established in his goodness, let us abide in the same. 10For he is the Fountain of every good thing and Giver of salutary and holy admonitions that enlighten the minds of all who collaborate thoughtfully

---

1. Arm. վարդապետաց (*vardapetac‘*) also refers to the doctors or theologians of the Church; here, the received patristic tradition.

2. Cf. Disc. 1.4–5, 23; 6.1, 23.

3. Echoing 1 Cor 2.8.

with his benevolent will through holy works, in order to inherit the Kingdom that extends through eternal life. ₁₁This is a synopsis of his benevolence. He is affable and generous toward his creatures; for he invites everyone to his glory and blessedness through their compliance with his benevolent will.

₁₂And his good will has been communicated through the established Law: his will for his creatures, so that they will become disciples of the Word of Life.[4] ₁₃The unique acts of his almighty power, benevolent will, and omnipresent love were made manifest, in the first place, when from nothing he made heaven and earth and the creatures there—both seen and unseen; ₁₄and again through the excellence of those endowed with intellect and reason, who consequently exhibit considerate deeds out of obedience, intimacy, and love, for they will be elevated to the honor reserved for angels, archangels, the Seraphim, the Cherubim, the wakeful ones, the entire host of heaven who glorify him.[5] ₁₅We earthlings were given the gifts of apostleship, prophesying, priesthood, evangelism, orthodox teaching, martyrdom, virginity, sanctity, and complete renunciation;[6] ₁₆since both camps, the hosts above and we humans, are stewards and disciples of the one benevolent will. ₁₇For God the Father is one, from whom is everything; and one Lord Jesus Christ, by whom are all things; and one Holy Spirit, who restores—Holy Trinity. ₁₈As the Prophet has said: *"For by the word of the Lord were the heavens and earth established, and by the breath[7] of his mouth all the hosts in them"* (Ps 33.6 [32.6 LXX]), so that he may be praised by his creatures.

₁₉There are distinct ranks and honors from God for angels and humans, in accordance with their devotion and love for God. ₂₀Those heavenly and earthly ones of great renown teach us to be deeply concerned and solicitous about good deeds; to admonish others in what is good and pleasing to his almighty Lordship and have them eradicate their filthy habits; ₂₁to think of the angels

---

4. Echoing the theology of Rom 10.4, with Christ as the *telos* of the Law.

5. For more on the elevation of humans to the ranks of angels, see below, §21; Disc. 16.13 and note; 20.152; 23.102.

6. Lit., "repentance." While the earlier gifts are a reminder of the *charismata* of 1 Cor 12.28, the later gifts are those associated with asceticism.

7. Or, "spirit."

above, so that we may attain the same glory and honor and become stewards of the Word of Life,[8] truly proclaiming the Creator's will; to spread inerrant knowledge in the hearing of men; to wake them up for good deeds; and to use as restraint our sovereign will to keep the commandments and statutes of the Lord. [22]Whoever does these things resembles a Cherub and receives the same honor from the Creator. [23]And whoever counters the adversarial life by pursuing obedience, humility, and impeccable purity, rooting out of one's mind and body the weeds of vice,[9] iniquity, cunning, deceit, and every harm, and longs for the righteous and divine laws, has the rank and honor of a Seraph.[10]

[24]The one who remains vigilant in virtue, holy and impeccable, and does not forfeit his spiritual and physical advantages, has the rank, glory, and blessedness of an angel.

[25]The one who finds the lost and keeps the one found, and reduces the wrath and the rancor[11] of a mob to peace, humility, and reconciliation, will be likened to the Son of God and will be his co-heir, according to his word: *"Blessed are the peacemakers, for they will be called sons of God"* (Mt 5.9).

[26]As for those who welcome the estranged ones and restore those fallen in sin, and heal with right faith and good deeds those in sickness of unbelief and doubt, and anoint with exact confession—in accordance with that of the baptismal font—those mired with spiritual and physical filth, and lead them to repentance, they are co-workers with the Holy Spirit and are his habitat, according to the saying: *"You are the temple of God, built in truth and sanctity,"* adding, *"and the Spirit of God dwells in you"* (1 Cor 3.16), (as it does) in those sanctified by his divine glory.[12]

[27]As for the one who restores the hopeless ones in the hope of eternal life, and calms down the alienated ones and the apostates

8. A designation for Christ in 1 Jn 1.1.

9. Interpretively, vices are the weeds sown by Satan, the "enemy" in "The Parable of the Weeds" (Mt 13.24–30); see below, §§95, 101; cf. Disc. 11.145; 18.27–28; 20.19, 69.

10. Cf. Disc. 20.154.

11. Lit., "arrogance."

12. The 1 Corinthians passage quoted here and elsewhere (Disc. 8.56; cf. 17.41) is foundational in the formation of the mystical tradition in ascetic circles. See note at Disc. 2.23.

and brings them to longsuffering in patience, and cares for them with compassionate caring, and directs them with the grace of mercy to the best of things, to enlightenment in divine knowledge and to pure life, he will be an heir of Christ's heavenly Kingdom. ₂₈The one who models him in love for humankind, in every way, will enjoy the blessed life by the grace of the Holy Trinity. ₂₉For he was faithful in little things entrusted by God, for both spiritual and physical sustenance; as he says: *"I was hungry, and you gave me to eat; I was thirsty, and you gave me to drink"* (Mt 25.35), and the like. ₃₀He adds: *"Since you did it for one of the little ones, you did it for me"* (Mt 25.40). ₃₁Such is his caring love for us.

₃₂But as for those who are sluggish in good works and really abhor[13] the Lawgiver, distancing themselves from the Lord through pride and unfaithfulness, rebelling against the Word of Life, sinning arrogantly against the forgiving Lordship of the almighty Power, being the cause of perdition for many, erring from the eternally good things and the blessed hope,[14] resembling Satan, they will receive the same punishment, being handed over for eternal torments. ₃₃These are the ones who have surrendered themselves to the frightful perils of that just judgment because of their reckless and dissolutely evil works.

₃₄As for those who are defiant and stray into wickedness and by treachery become (agents of the) accuser,[15] misleading (others) from the right faith and saintly life, becoming envious of the doers of good, becoming controversial and angry and agitators of the simple-minded, they possess the will of demons and will become their heirs in eternal torments, whether in the realm of incorporeal beings or that of corporeal earthlings.

₃₅As for the one who is indecently into filthiness, indiscreetly into recklessness, and given to diverse passions because of delusion, multiplying his lawlessness with theft, lying, swearing, and becoming through many pernicious ways the cause of perdition for many, such a person will inherit the name of the filthy and the impure. Having rejected the living Light and glorious sanctity, he will be cast out into the outer darkness mixed with fire, *"where their worms*

13. Lit., "abhor with abhorrence"; an indicator of Semitism.
14. Allusion to Ti 2.13.
15. A recurring epithet for Satan; see Jb 1.9–11; Zec 3.1; 1 Pt 5.8; Rv 12.10.

do not die and the fire is not quenched; and they will be a spectacle to all humankind" (Is 66.24).[16]

₃₆As for those who engage in outright vice and are full of injustice, in things seen and unseen, who are lawless and senseless, afflicting and depriving, torturing, abducting, and killing, such ones will receive the punishment (reserved) for the mercilessly wicked, for the wicked shall perish in wickedness.[17]

₃₇Have you heard of the recompense according to God's scales of justice for every thought and deed? ₃₈For he commanded man to remain unmoved in utter purity and to do what is worthwhile and just, and *"to hold tightly to the best of things,"* as has been said (Rom 12.9). ₃₉This way they will be able to receive the gift of prophecy and become intimate with the Lord's benevolent will: to preach the truth and to awaken every mind from slumber for anticipation of the hope, to await the promised, real things of the good news, and to become heirs of the inscrutable glory that is for the righteous ones.

₄₀Those who renounce the deluding deceit of life lived for the flesh, cleansing their minds from guilty conscience[18] by the grace of true remorse and repentance with tears,[19] hating evil and loving the good, thwarting the treachery of deceit and dedicating themselves in true faith to the Most Holy Trinity, they will be deemed worthy to be called apostles of the good news of the New Testament.[20] ₄₁Those who early on dedicated themselves to the true proclamation, whose works attest to the proclamation and are pleasing to their listeners, who have dispelled from their minds the fallacious and deluding deceit, they will become heirs of the Kingdom of Heaven. ₄₂For the Apostle says: *"Those who are Christians have crucified their bodies with the desires and the passions"* (Gal 5.24). ₄₃Such are the abodes of the Divinity and the witnesses of the Truth for all believers.

₄₄As for those who choose to cleanse through single-mindedness

16. Cf. Mk 9.48.

17. Cf. Eccl 8.8; Jer 2.19; Ezek 18.20.

18. Allusion to Heb 10.22; cf. §44.

19. Here the author introduces the concept of *penthos:* the mourning with tears that accompany repentance, conversion, and inward renewal (cf. §52). For more, see note to Disc. 10.48.

20. Paralleling "the gift of prophecy" (§39). Note the direct reference to the *kerygma* in what follows.

and purity their minds and bodies from all guilty conscience,[21] from things seen and unseen, they will be worthy of the calling of the Holy Spirit. They will be beatified like the brave martyrs, for always being in control of bodily movements in pure sanctity, tearing down the bodily obsessions and developing the spiritual: chastity and every coveted and absolute righteousness for the meritorious finding and salvation of those near and far. 45For those who live in this way are worthy of the Holy Spirit's unction, to become priests of God and to present the Lord with a people zealous for good works,[22] attendants of the Holy Trinity by the grace of the holy font and the body and blood of Christ, to whom they are related through adoption.[23] For they have taken off the old man and have put on the new,[24] who is after the likeness of God: just and holy, removed from evil. 46As for those who intend to relinquish the transient things and cherish the eternal as inheritance, they abhor the bodily life and love the spiritual life; (even) martyrdom with its many virtues, for they will receive the appellation of confessors and witnesses, of holy martyrs, those crowned with blessedness.

47As for those who have clothed themselves with the immaculate sanctity of virginity and the single-mindedness of pleasing his benevolent will, in accordance with his righteous laws and the piety of the holy Fathers, they are the ones who enter the nuptial chamber of light and enjoy the glory of the immortal King.[25] 48As for those who have fallen into temptation, the filth of sin, and the perils caused by Satan's deceptions, they will remember the living word that says: *"Return to me from sin and confess and repent, and I will return to you with mercy (and) grace to heal, to save, and to bestow life"* (Mal 3.7).[26] For the one strengthened by the Lord shall overcome the common passions and the deceptions of the evil one, who wages war against

---

21. Allusion to Heb 10.22; cf. §40.

22. Echoing Ti 2.14.

23. Allusion to Rom 8.14–17, 23; Gal 4.1–7; Eph 1.5–6. Adoption is likewise linked to the twin Sacraments, of baptism and the Eucharist, in Disc. 9.23; 13.31–35; and 14.17; elsewhere, to baptism only: Disc. 2.129, 133; 3.17; 9.29–30.

24. Allusion to Eph 4.22–24; Col 3.9–10; cf. Rom 13.14; Gal 3.27.

25. For more on this subject, see Susanna Elm, *"Virgins of God": The Making of Asceticism in Late Antiquity,* Oxford Classical Monographs (Oxford and New York: Oxford University Press, 1994).

26. Mostly amplified.

both soul and body.[27] [49]And proceeding into the race of virtue, he shall overcome and shall put to shame the prince of sin through the promised hope in the good news of the resurrection. [50]For through the body and blood of the Lord we shall be delivered from the torments and shall become heirs of the Kingdom. [51]For (Scripture) says: *"Glory, honor, and peace for the one who does good; but wrath, suffering, and torments for the one who does evil"* (Rom 2.10, 8). [52]Do you see how after so much scrutiny and examination he does not turn away from (showing) mercy, caring for his creatures? Rather, he brings back the straying one, lifts up the fallen, raises the stumbler, restores the broken, heals the sick, cleanses the filthy one with tears, establishes the double-minded in faith, and enlightens everyone.

[53]Now, who could ever give enough thanks to the Benefactor, who in every respect hastens with good things to give life to his creatures? [54]He sends threats like fire upon the wicked ones and sinners, the impure and the defiled, that they may turn away from evil and survive the wrath that is to come. [55]And he spreads the good news like light, that they may watchfully and alertly attain the good things and inherit the living goodness from the Creator. [56]As for those who do not turn away or repent, torments are made ready for them from the Lord, to each his own. [57]Just as he is called Compassionate because of his care, Merciful because of his grace, Longsuffering because of his forgiving, Holy because of his cleansing, and Light because of his enlightening, in like manner, he is rightly called the Righteous Judge,[28] who metes out justice[29] according to one's good or evil deeds. [58]Now, the one who does (good) deeds and is (so) inclined, will inherit the name[30] and the glory; contrarily, dishonor, the punishment for the wicked from the Righteous Judge. [59]We should understand God's judgment in the same way as when we praise and pronounce fair the earthly judges who, for the earth to have peace, condemn evildoers—the abominable and unjust—to prison, shackles, torture, or capital punishment.[31]

---

27. Cf. §81; also Disc. 9.32, where the fall of Adam and Eve is attributed to their obsession with the passions (*heštut'iwn*, which is synonymous with the word *c'ankut'iwn* used here).

28. See Ps 7.11 (7.12 LXX); 9.4 (9.5 LXX); 2 Tm 4.8.

29. Lit., "their laws."

30. Cf. §§25 and 40, on the "name" to be inherited.

31. A commonplace theodicean argument in the Fathers of the Church, taken

$_{60}$Let no one doubt knowing this: that there is definite punishment for sinners from God, who loves humankind. $_{61}$Let one (and all) remember the death that resulted from the Flood; all living souls perished in (their own) corruption, except for those in the ark, which was exhibited by God.[32] $_{62}$If you do not believe this, go to Sodom and Gomorrah, home of the five kings,[33] and you will see what catastrophe transpired there as recorded in history.[34] For *"the Lord made fire and brimstone rain down—from the Lord out of the heavens"* (Gn 19.24), and consumed both man and animal, the birds of the air and the fish of the sea, the rocks and the earth, the water and the forests.

$_{63}$If you consider this (as) remote, the divine Scriptures reveal these to us time and again: famine and the sword, slavery and untimely death, even death of animals; also plagues and aches and tormenting diseases; also strife between father and son, disobedience of children, and hatred between brothers and loved ones; and bitter plagues and death because of sin. $_{64}$Yet knowledge of truth and wisdom, and continuous care from the almighty Father and Creator and Savior King, are extended to all creatures. $_{65}$For he is the fountain of life, giver of good things, teacher and architect of things seen and unseen. $_{66}$And sages and ordinary people draw (inspiration) from him in their varied arts and inventions. $_{67}$For first they conceive in their minds the idea of the art and then translate it to an enduring, tangible reality. $_{68}$They truly receive it from the grace of the Giver, as it was in the case of Bezalel and his companions when constructing the tabernacle.[35] For the Holy Spirit made known to them the principles of the various arts. $_{69}$They became the foremost artisans because of the gifts of the Spirit, and others were trained by them, and so on till our own time.

$_{70}$Those who learn smithery or the art of goldsmiths or any other craft do consider the quality of things and the form of the objects, and are always concerned about making the most beauti-

---

from Philo of Alexandria (e.g., *On Providence* 2.82, where it appears alongside stock arguments promulgated by the Stoics).

32. See Gn 6–8; cf. 2 Pt 2.5–10.

33. See Gn 13–14.

34. See Gn 19.1–29; cf. Jude 7.

35. See esp. Ex 36.

ful weapon or ornament or any other artifact known in the world. 71So it is also with physicians who diagnose the pain by (feeling) the veins and bestow healing with medicines (obtained) by the grace of God. 72As for tailors, builders, tillers of the soil, cooks, and others who customarily cater to the needs of humans, is not their thought-engaging work—which deserves praise and compensation—by the grace of God? 73Whereas those who pursue their artistic work with indolence and disdain produce ugly and defective work like that of a non-professional, and their artwork is discredited by the experts, and the work is held in no esteem and is deemed useless; and the artists are disgraced and shamed, and are castigated and penalized, even tortured, and disrespected by everyone.

74So it is also with caution in the Christian calling and the worship of God, for with all wisdom and artfulness one should direct his manners and senses to the excellent teaching of the spiritual law and to what pleases the benevolent will of the Creator. 75(One should) think of the Lord's will day and night and remember in a real way the fear of God;[36] have the mind ready to think of every essential, good deed and do good under the guidance of the One who bestows from above; be creative in appropriating to oneself the memorable knowledge of God; 76look for the Lord's will at all times; abide always in his love and fear, for he is able to bring non-existent things into existence, to make the disrespected respectful, to absolve sin through true confession and repentance, and to guide with wisdom—in accordance with his creative justice. 77(One should) strive daily in the husbandry that pleases his almighty Lordship, with unwavering faith and impeccable life, 78in anticipation of receiving at any time the hope of life *"where moths do not destroy nor does rust corrupt, and where thieves do not vie to snatch away from divine protection"* (Mt 6.20).

79And (one should) remain inseparable from him through the sweet remembrance of his sacred love,[37] in perfect sanctity. 80Moreover, (one should) be beneficent to those far and near that they may always remain serene in the truth, in the face of hardship; 81that they may root out from their minds and senses the deluding deceptions that excite through the intruding passions and the utter

36. Echoing Ps 1.2.
37. Allusion to the *agapē* meal, an early term for the Eucharist.

iniquity of the deceitful, evil one; ₈₂that they may cleanse their hearts with remorse and repentance from guilty conscience,[38] and obtain good will toward all people; ₈₃that they may hasten to observe the commandments and be always connected to God's love, having their thoughts elevated. And may his compassion be upon us through his continuous care. ₈₄And (one should) be cautious, in his fear, and exercise discernment—being in intimate love and faith; and be vigilant and ready, abstaining from all earthly things that distract and mislead from what is quite advantageous. ₈₅(One should) not say anything that hurts or is unseemly, but speak the truth and that which is beneficial. ₈₆And (one should) pay no heed to deceptive rumors, but only to that which promotes divine things, in keeping with God's Holy Scriptures. ₈₇And (one should) not look where it is not right, into debaucheries, filthy physical pleasures. ₈₈And (one should) be mentally free from greed: indeed, generous, benevolent to all, and helpful to the spiritually and physically weak. ₈₉And (one should) not inquire into the sects or mingle with them to one's perdition.[39] ₉₀And (one should) guard against every injustice, anger, hitting, and depriving—whether out of enmity, swearing, lying, vindictiveness, bad-mouthing, cunning, or malevolence, lest the Lord be angry and destroy those who behave like this.

₉₁Those who oppose these things by upholding the virtues (will receive) respect and honor and gifts from the Lord, and will inherit eternal blessings. ₉₂For every human emotion is stirred up willingly, whether for good or for evil, since the sovereign mind exercises its will over both good and evil. ₉₃The good seeds are manifold in people, and by the invisible love of God the good roots do appear. ₉₄And those of the saints are all the more praised, consummated with the good life to come. ₉₅But the miserable and reckless life, which is from the evil seed, produces weeds.[40] This is obvious from its growth, the visible deriving from the invisible, lacking the good seed of law-abidingness. Such ones will receive their recompense from the Lord: the unquenchable fire with the worms that do not die; for they hated good and loved evil. God will justly separate the

38. Echoing Heb 10.22; cf. 9.14; 10.2.
39. Cf. Disc. 11.112.
40. Echoing "The Parable of the Weeds" (Mt 13.24–30).

good from the evil. ₉₆Whichever way one's inclination moves,[41] whether toward good or toward evil, they will be rewarded accordingly.

₉₇God's love establishes sanctity, wholesome thoughts, sound doctrine,[42] benevolence, justice, truth, brotherly love, meekness, humility, obedience, zeal to work, single-mindedness, and the rest of the advantageous virtues, whether visibly or invisibly cherished. ₉₈Compassion is (defined) by loving with good will; mercy, by kindly grace; longsuffering, by joyous willingness; tirelessness, by strength of will in prayer, by persistent fasting. ₉₉(One ought) to love these, to cherish these, to pursue these constantly; to exhibit them with utmost, intimate love that is toward the heavenly Father, the Only-begotten Son, and the Holy Spirit equal in Lordship.

₁₀₀(One ought) to hate whatever is contrary to these: wretchedness, evil desires, evil thoughts, evil deeds of lawlessness, deceptiveness that misleads, filthy waywardness, deceitful swearing with treachery, bitter conflicts, grievance that leads to anger, irritability that invites enmity, stubborn disobedience, laziness and indolence, immodesty and mockery, indecency and lawlessness, vindictiveness and envy, gluttony and drunkenness, love of glory and haughtiness, and whatever is disgraceful and utterly evil and grossly filthy and full of disrepute.

₁₀₁These are wretched lives and harmful seeds of weeds. For evil itself is not evil, nor is good itself good, since it is in the mind where good and evil are processed.[43] For it is by the love of God that goodness is established, that one loves good and hates evil. It is evil to hate good and love evil. It is good to crave for the good and to be good. It is evil to be with evil ones; and (as for) craving (evil), just the same. ₁₀₂It is good to yearn for the good, and yearning for evil is simply evil. ₁₀₃Thus, craving and yearning for either good or evil yield the result of the same. ₁₀₄So, the benevolent Lord of All sows the seeds of goodness among people, giving them the sovereign will, which they dispose toward either good or evil. ₁₀₅With val-

---

41. Lit., "the will moves with the senses."

42. Arm. ուղղափառութիւն (uṫahawatut'iwn), lit., "orthodoxy"; a *hapax* in the discourses. Cf. ուղղափառ հաւատով (uṫap'aṙ hawatov) and note at Disc. 2.58.

43. A biblical thought, contingent on knowledge and free will; see Ezek 38.10; Col 1.21.

or and piety, along with self-control, (one can) counter evil always. ₁₀₆The charioteers of utter goodness are the love of God and brotherly love,[44] for *"love does not contemplate evil"* (1 Cor 13.6). ₁₀₇Impiety and selfishness are the charioteers of evil. According to the Apostle's word, *"gratifying the cravings of the flesh and its thoughts and becoming children of wrath"* (Eph 2.3) is alienation from God. ₁₀₈He also says: *"I live, yet not I, but Christ lives in me"* (Gal 2.20). These are Christ's joy: righteousness,[45] sanctity, and truthfulness. ₁₀₉Again he says: *"I tell you with tears, the destiny of the enemies of the cross of Christ is destruction. Their mind is set on earthly things"* (Phil 3.18–19). *"They talk and do evil. They have become filled with every kind of wickedness, downright evil"* (Rom 1.29). ₁₁₀To counter evil, (one ought) to do good—thus to be worthy of crowns and glory and honor with the saints.

₁₁₁The one who says he loves God but hates his brother[46] is like one who was found and lost, was filled and emptied. We ought to pursue good things at all times and to withstand the onslaughts of evil. ₁₁₂He who yields to evil ends up doing evil; whereas he who yields to good things will receive goodness from the almighty Lord and will inherit the blessings. ₁₁₃The disrupters of good and lovers of evil will necessarily suffer with the demons in hell's unquenchable fire. ₁₁₄The word of Christ that does not lie has already passed the sentence on both: *"The righteous will go to eternal life, and sinners to eternal punishment, which is prepared for Satan and his angels"* (Mt 25.46, 41). ₁₁₅For it has been said regarding the antichrist:[47] *"The man of lawlessness, the son of perdition, the adversary, the evil one, whom Christ will kill with the breath[48] of his mouth"* (2 Thes 2.3–4, 8). ₁₁₆The same punishment will be inflicted upon those who pursue a wicked life and abominable works, ₁₁₇which the (Book of) Proverbs admonishes to mortify: the sinful members (of the body), all evil desires.[49] (Elsewhere Scripture) says: *"The man of sin, the son of perdition, and heir of eternal torture"* (2 Thes 2.3).[50] ₁₁₈But the one who pursues a saintly

44. Echoing Mt 22.37–40; cf. Dt 6.5; Lv 19.18.

45. Or, "justice."

46. Echoing 1 Jn 4.20.

47. Arm. «Ներ» (*"Neṙ"*).

48. Or, "spirit."

49. Referring to Prv 21.25 (LXX: "Desires kill the sluggard; for his hands choose not to do anything").

50. The last quotation is a likely gloss (cf. §115).

and immaculate life, in accordance with God's commandments, will be called a just, holy, and true man, perfect in every virtue in Christ; an heir of the Kingdom of Heaven and the good things that do not pass away.

119Now, always consider such exhortation and never let it escape your mind like ineffective medicine to heal the maladies of soul and body and to bestow health. To the contrary, it redirects from those things that are harmful—both seen and unseen. 120Now, be diligent in teaching this life-giving exhortation, to be heard regularly when rising up. It chips away man's iniquity, lawlessness, and filthiness; and it reestablishes those fallen in sin and always safeguards the righteous. 121As (Scripture) says: *"The one who yields fruit in due season shall be as a tree planted by the brooks of water, by spiritual exhortation; and whatever he shall do shall be prospered"* (Ps 1.3). 122And one will hear from Christ: *"Good and faithful servant, because you were faithful in little things, enter into the joy of your Lord, which has been prepared for you as your reward ... 123He who has ears to hear, let him hear"* (Mt 25.21, 23), this spiritual exhortation by the grace of God through Christ Jesus our Lord, to whom be glory always. Amen.

DISCOURSE 6

REPROOF OF MASKED THINGS THAT
EXPOSES WHAT IS CONCEALED

OR THE FATHER is not begotten of any, but the Son is begotten of the Father and not created, nor is the Holy Spirit generated, but proceeds.[1] ₂They are ever of one accord in essence with the Father, to the Father, and from the Father: ₃as flame and heat (in relation) to fire, as light and warmth (in relation) to the sun, as water and source (in relation) to a fountain, as reason and spirit (in relation) to mind.[2] ₄They are distinct in operation, yet of one accord in nature, and there is no intrusion whatsoever into their distinction.

₅These are truthful illustrations of the Trinity. ₆Essence without beginning, Life that bestows life, omnipresent Love and almighty Power: Father, Son, and Holy Spirit. ₇Three Persons yet one in nature and will: the One who creates, the One who provides, and the One who establishes.[3] ₈He has always been[4] and is God, the Existent; he has always been without beginning in his glory, and is eternal and ceaseless in his care for creatures. ₉And he has always been the Truth, and (so) he is in his immutability, and is the stability of creatures. ₁₀He has always been the inerrant and most beneficial Knowledge, and (so) he continues to be in his unboundedness and for the enlightenment of creatures. ₁₁He has always been the truly

---

1. Arm. բղխեալ (*btxeal*), Gk. *ekporeusin,* i.e., from the Father; see §23 and Disc. 1.4–5, 23; 5.3; cf. Gregory of Nazianzus, *Oratio 39: In sancta Lumina* 12 (PG 36:348B–C). Echoing Jn 15.26.

2. The same analogy as in Disc. 1.23–24.

3. Cf. Disc. 2.7: "… in God who creates, in the Lord who establishes, and in the Grace that gives life."

4. Lit., "he was," from a likely mistranslation of an unqualified past tense (thus through §19, I have rendered Arm. էր (*ēr*) as "he has always been").

unattainable Wisdom, and (so) he continues (to extend) his ineffable, providential care to all creatures. 12He has always been the Existent, life-giving Essence, who is omnipresent, enriching in counsel, and immutable in his faithfulness; and (so) he is constant in his saving grace toward humankind, close in relationship through his intimate, refreshing love. 13He has always been the almighty Power in his very being, and (so) he is for the strengthening of the weak for the spiritual warfare, be it in things visible or invisible. 14God's love has always been a living blessing and (so) it is roused unto goodness: to care for and to protect the righteous and to lead sinners to remorse. 15He has always been the luminous and glorified Holiness, and (so) he is for the enlightenment and the glorification and the renewal[5] of his creatures through grace and the luminous font. 16He has always been the One who cares with compassion,[6] and (so) he continues his unbounded benevolence in caring for his creatures—both seen and unseen, that they may reach the haven of goodness, the promised good things of the heavenly calling that is full of real blessings for life. 17He has always been gracious[7] in mercy, and (so) he is in his unbounded goodness and most generous gifts: in giving and showing evidences of his love for humankind and in calling unto dedication to the grace of adoption.[8] 18He has always been longsuffering and forgiving, and (so) he is a kind benefactor and appears not to remember evil, by his own choice; nor does he punish everyone, so that they may live by turning away from sin.[9] 19The benevolence of the Most Holy Trinity in caring for his creatures has always been abundant, never wanting, beyond measure, unlimited, ingenious in its visible and invisible ways (of responding) to their supplications and pains. 20Thus creatures stand to receive beneficial and advantageous things. And out of his utmost goodness the Existent bestows them upon the rational and intelligent beings, those who are to inherit life, to be crowned with the virtues in the Kingdom of Heaven.

5. All three nouns are infinitives.

6. Lit., "the care (or succor) of compassions."

7. Lit., "the grace."

8. Cf. §§65, 85. Allusion to Eph 1.5–6; cf. Rom 8.14–17, 23; Gal 4.1–7. See also Disc. 2.46; 3.16; 9.30; 10.48, 88 (on adoption as grace); for more, see the Subject Index.

9. Cf. Philo of Alexandria, *On Providence* 1.54, 65, on the same reason for God not punishing all living sinners (a theodicean argument).

21Those who learn the divine teaching come to hope and obedience, which is good and pleasant and perfect, for it leads to eternally abiding life that was and is and will continue to be in his infinity—of the One who by his good benevolence cares for all creatures, who lacks in nothing, who is infinite and beyond limit, is above all created beings, inscrutable in greatness and glory, who in his all-enriching and life-giving blessedness is the Giver of life and glory and light. 22He is of himself self-sufficient in everything, who justifies, illumines, and glorifies; 23who is the Father of the only-begotten Son and the Source of the Holy Spirit. 24And by his benevolent will and enriching love he makes humans heirs—with the ranks of the incorporeal ones—of the Kingdom of Heaven and the good things that are endless.

25The deluding deceitfulness through accusatory lies (crept in later), for there was no perdition in the beginning—not until the insidious efforts by the misleading evil one.[10] 26But today he cannot compel those who hate evil, who hear the preaching of good tidings and believe, who are reborn of the water and the Spirit,[11] and who do not resort to corruption and (thus) stand in need of repentance. 27There was no death when there was no sin; but now it has been eradicated, ever since the luminous resurrection of Christ, and it has been held in disdain by the saints of God.[12] 28The all-deluding deceitfulness, cunning hypocrisy, and rebelliousness did not exist in the beginning, since there were no accusations by Satan. But now he is weak and hides away from truth. 29Disbelief and the passion for evil did not exist in the beginning, for the lover of controversy, the one who wages war against God, was not yet thrown out (of heaven). He now hides away from believers and manifestations of law-abidingness and love for God. 30Disobedience and defiance did not exist in the beginning, for Satan was not yet up against God and man, nor does he now obey our Christ and leads us to do the same. 31Deceit and treachery did not exist in the beginning, for the

10. The thought, based on the biblical assumption that Satan's fall was a post-creation event, is repeated in the immediately following sections, echoing Is 14.12–15 and Ezek 28.1–19 (interpretively taken to refer to Satan's rebellion in heaven, when pride overtook him and he fell from perfection).

11. Allusion to Jn 3.5.

12. Allusion to Gn 2.17; 3.3, 19; and Rom 6–8 and 1 Cor 15 especially.

crafty, evil one was not yet (revealed); and now he rejects the truth about Christ. ₃₂Envy and irreconcilability did not exist while the evil warmonger was not as yet into his irreconcilability, and now he does not cease to envy us for the grace bestowed upon us by the pleasant will of Christ. ₃₃Hatred and anger did not exist until they sprang forth among us from the evil one; and now he is averse to the great love of the Savior, the meek lover of humankind.[13] ₃₄Arrogance and selfishness did not exist while the evil one was not proud and subjugating us; but now he hides away from the lowly One who loves us and who said: *"Learn from me, for I am meek and low-ly in heart, and you will find rest"* (Mt 11.29). ₃₅Indignation and enmity did not exist in the beginning, when compassionate mercy was active in caring. ₃₆The insatiability of gluttony and greed did not exist, nor does it exist now among the saints who exercise moderation and those who disdain the worldly things. ₃₇Excessive filthiness did not come about without cleanliness being done away with; however, the loathsome filth was eradicated when the utter holiness of God's grace shone through.

₃₈All sins and unrestrained evils, both visible and invisible, did not come into existence without being incited by Satan at their beginning. These were subsequently pushed upon us by the enemy who trapped us in them. Was it not for this reason that the life-giving Lamb was offered as sacrifice on the cross, for the remission of sins and the Father's reconciliation with his creatures?[14] He restored the believers unto life in the Holy Trinity by means of rebirth through the (baptismal) font and the saving mystery (of the Eucharist).[15] ₃₉And he toppled the impious, the proud, and the arrogant; and the meek he lifted up through the promised hope. ₄₀The encroaching sin he removed, also him who had the authority

---

13. Basil of Caesarea counsels: "Transfer your anger to him, the murderer of men, the father of lies, the worker of sin … by being grounded in the humility which the Lord taught"; *Adversus iratos* (Hom. 10.6, PG 31:370A; trans. Wagner in *Ascetical Works*, FC 9:459). Cf. Disc. 10.37; 11.64, 86; 18.32; 19.40; 23.2, on countering anger with meekness.

14. Allusion to Rom 5.10; cf. 2 Cor 5.20; Col 1.22.

15. *Pʻrkakan xorhurd* is a recurring reference to the Eucharist; see Disc. 9.49; 13.45, 66, 68; 15.59; 16.25. Further references to the Eucharist in this discourse (§§88, 99) underscore its historical orientation as *Anamnesis* (Arm. յիշատակ, *yišatak;* see note to Disc. 3.23).

of death, namely, Satan;[16] ₄₁so that those (once) seized by the latter
to do his will would (now) have life through the revealed grace and
love for humankind.

₄₂Many appeared from the very beginning as chosen witnesses for the coming of the life-giving Restorer:[17] from the righteous Abel, who was called "righteous" because of his pure and
immaculate life.[18] ₄₃Such were Enosh in hope,[19] Enoch who was
pleasing to God and was translated,[20] Noah in perfect righteousness,[21] Abraham in faith,[22] and Isaac in (foreshadowing) the good
news of God's Son;[23] Israel who saw virtue in struggle,[24] Joseph
in self-restraint,[25] Moses in legislation,[26] and David in upright and
humble kingship.[27] ₄₄So did also all the holy Prophets, the Maccabees, and the three youths in the furnace,[28] until John (the Bap-
tist),[29] who was the light of the Sun of Righteousness[30] *"who enlightens everyone coming into the world"* (Jn 1.9) with the light of the knowledge of God and wisdom and righteousness: Christ the Savior, who
came to the world to save sinners. And he enlightened the hearts
of the faithful with the benevolent will of our Creator, that we may
bear fruit in accordance with his just and righteous laws, and be
pleasing to the Lordship of the Almighty; ₄₅and may advance in

16. Allusion to 1 Cor 15.26; cf. 2 Tm 1.10.

17. Echoing Acts 3.21.

18. Allusion to Mt 23.35; cf. Heb 11.4.

19. Allusion to Gn 4.26. In Philo's etymology of the name, meaning "true
man," he adds: "since those who do not set their hope on God have no part in a
rational nature" (*That the Worse Attacks the Better* 138). See Lester L. Grabbe, *Etymology in Early Jewish Interpretation: The Hebrew Names in Philo*, Brown Judaic Studies 115
(Atlanta: Scholars Press, 1988), 155–56.

20. Allusion to Gn 5.24; cf. Heb 11.5.

21. Allusion to Gn 6.9; cf. Ezek 14.14; Heb 11.7.

22. Allusion to Gn 15.6; cf. Rom 4.3, 22; Heb 11.8, 17.

23. Allusion to the *Akedah*, Gn 22.1–19; cf. Jas 2.21.

24. Or, "wrestling"; allusion to Gn 32.22–32.

25. Or, "moderation," "temperance," etc. Possible allusion to Gn 39.1–23; see
also Heb 11.22 (on Gn 50.24–25; Ex 13.19; Jos 24.32).

26. Allusion to Dt 6.6; 32.46; cf. Jn 1.17.

27. Allusion to Ps 89.20 (88.21 LXX); cf. Acts 13.32.

28. Allusion to the apocryphal addition to Daniel, inserted between 3.23 and
3.24.

29. Echoing Mt 11.13.

30. A recurring messianic title derived from Mal 4.2.

the hope of the Kingdom, with impeccable life, to the goal of the higher calling, *"and we will be perfect as our heavenly Father is perfect"* (Mt 5.48).

46He fills all his creatures with his caring benevolence and instructs every mind to collaborate with his benevolent will: 47the One who spoke benevolently from heaven to earth, regarding repentance for sinners, to confess their sins, to have remorse for what they have committed, in order to receive the fruit worthy of repentance, which delights the hosts of angels according to the word of the Lord.[31] 48For since angels in heaven rejoice over one sinner who repents, what should be said concerning the righteous, the Apostles, the Prophets, the martyrs, the teachers, the virgin ascetics and those who are restrainedly married? those who are clean of impure inclinations that are harmful to the soul: wickedness, anger, hatred, envy, and gluttony; who cultivate piety through effort and root out their evil habits because of the admonition of the One who loved us with sacred love.

49For there was no satanic thing before evil set its enmity against the good. 50It came about after the six days during which wickedness had not as yet entered (Satan's) mind, since the Lord testifies: *"All that God had made was very good"* (Gn 1.31). As to whether (Satan) was evil by nature, there is no good testimony about it by the almighty God. 51In the Gospel there is a saying by the Lord to the disciples: *"Have I not chosen you, the Twelve? Yet one of you is a devil"* (Jn 6.70). 52The righteous Judge did not condemn him at first, when evil manifested itself or (when) the evil one set his will in motion for evil. Later on he was called Satan and banned from sacred worship. He separated himself from the life-giving love, and becoming hopeless, he cast himself into death, like the demons in the pigs in the lake who were saying: *"What is there between us and you, Son of God? Have you come to destroy us before the time, Holy One of God?"* (Mt 8.29).[32] 53They too know their and our time of judgment, and the rewarding of the lawless and the disobedient, of the unholy and the defiled, as deserved. 54There was no Satan when there was no rebellion; and now he is powerless, according to the saying of the Lord: *"The prince of this world has been judged, and he will be cast out"*

---

31. Allusion to Lk 15.10.
32. Cf. Disc. 20.79, where the verse is quoted differently.

(Jn 12.31). ₅₅There was no darkness, it did not exist; the elements were shadow, for there was no nature. ₅₆Coal is darker than shadow or anything black; this blackness existed at the (first) rising of the sun. ₅₇Shadows that are darkness, however, dissipate at the coming of light, and cannot counter it. ₅₈There was no death when there was no indebtedness to sin; nor does it exist, now that life and resurrection from the dead have been revealed. Both death and darkness departed at the rising of Light and the coming of Life.

₅₉All these principles and realities of things are from the Lord. ₆₀Consequently, all well-behaved and dutiful (persons) are crowned with the goodness of virtue, and with crowns upon their heads they enter into eternal light and life.[33] ₆₁But those who are evil and lazy, disdaining God's commandment, shall be punished in the everlasting fire of Gehenna, which is prepared for them. ₆₂For the Judge's verdict is blameless and just: since both sides, of the good and the evil ones, stand settled before justice: those (marked) for the hope of glory and those awaiting suffering and torments. ₆₃And he admonishes with both good counsel and threats of woes, so that none will be shut out of the eternal promises. ₆₄In both ways he cares with love: for those who are good, that they despair not of the hope of life; and for those who are evil, that with the fear of the Lord they turn in repentance, that they may share in the full joy with those privileged with grace. ₆₅For the grace of God will be revealed to those who love him, those who serve the Lord with fear and love, for they are welcomed with those honored and glorified, deemed worthy of adoption,[34] that they may enjoy with all the saints the good things of Christ that do not pass away. ₆₆For the benevolence of the almighty Most Holy Trinity cares for creatures with his omnipresent love, most beneficial munificence, and immutable truth, which guides in things visible and invisible and does not allow the termination of the eternally good things, which he provides for us. ₆₇For he is inviolable and incorruptible; he does not change but changes others for the better; by his wonderful nature he gives life to created beings; he brings the non-existent into existence; the despicable he makes honorable by honoring them himself and by actively transforming them for the better. And he

33. Echoing Is 51.11.
34. See note to §17.

alters those considered unfit for goodness to being fit; he changes those gone astray in double-mindedness to being faithful to him; he transforms lying and swearing falsely, those machinations of the evil one, into truthfulness.

₆₈He established a tribunal of divine counsel with the Holy Scriptures in order to enlighten everyone; to convey ingeniously, through life-giving and perfect guidance, that good portion; ₆₉to root out, through confession, the expansion of evil inclination to evil thoughts and evil deeds; ₇₀to direct the barren, idle, and despicable minds to good works; to exercise caution and discernment; ₇₁to bring the perversity of mind and body into obedience to spiritual precepts and piety; to root out and to eradicate evil habits through his fear and love; ₇₂to bring every act into the divine realm, for the benefit of the brothers; to cultivate virtue through great effort; and to demonstrate the good fruit early on and (without) delay. ₇₃Just as light does not change into darkness but lights up darkness, and life (does not change) to death but brings the lifeless into life in the Lord, so the grace of the Almighty (allows one) to leave the despicable things and to uphold the good; to appear as light to the world,[35] having the Word of Life within oneself,[36] to lead many, and to remain pure.

₇₄Together with piety, this too is to be demonstrated in the sequel of righteous orders: immaculate, holy, and truthful life attained with the help of the Creator's benevolent will; ₇₅the chasing away of worthless things and the gathering of advantageously worthwhile, beneficial things, with committed and steadfast faith. Thus should one leave a heroic and laudable name on earth, and gather eternal things in heaven, where glory and endless good things have been prepared for those who long for them.

₇₆Those who are presently being despised because of their living love and blessed hope[37] for the ineffable blessedness in the Lord, shall reign freely in the glory of the Most High and shall be elevated to (the ranks of) the elect upon the defeat of the enemy. ₇₇Those who through faith have defeated the enemy here, on a daily basis, shall rejoice over there with everlasting joy and with ineffable

---

35. Echoing Mt 5.14.
36. Allusion to Phil 2.15–16.
37. Allusion to Ti 2.13.

goodness that is in the Father, the Son, and the Holy Spirit. ₇₈Thus will all mourning be done away with, and diverse blessedness will be flowing, perpetually, for the continuous enjoyment in that eternal life which is for all of God's saints, in accordance with the blessedness of his sacred love, his inviting call to the joyous wedding.[38] ₇₉Those who have prepared themselves according to the will of the heavenly Father, will be crowned with luminous crowns to the glorious praise of God in the everlasting joys. ₈₀Here we have received the promise for the hoped-for life, and there we will be ranked with the beneficent ones—in the inheritance of the Kingdom of Heaven. ₈₁Here we have been delivered from ridicule with shame; and there from the threatening sorrows of the just judgment, from the affliction, the sorrows, and the indebtedness to bitter suffering. ₈₂And we will be greeted with a righteous name, honored with holy and true gifts, glorified with privileges and magnificent rewards; and thus we will be delivered from the threats of hell and suffering, having believed the word spoken by the Lord about sinners and the wicked. He says: *"You who are cursed, depart to the eternal, unquenchable fire, where there are weeping of eyes and gnashing of teeth, which is prepared for Satan and his satellites"* (Mt 25.41).[39] ₈₃And to the faithful he says: *"Come, you who are blessed by my Father, into the Kingdom. Because you were faithful with a few things, I will put you in charge of many things; enter into the joy of the Lord"* (Mt 25.34, 21; cf. 23), into eternal life with the holy angels; draw (near) to the King of Glory who said, *"Where I am, there shall my servant be also"* (Jn 12.26). ₈₄He will make his loved ones rejoice with living joy, each according to one's reward.

₈₅Because of their vigilance they were extolled by the Lord, to share in the inheritance of the boundless, inscrutable, omnipresent love; to share in the eternal, incomparable, unique, and immeasurable light. For they overcame[40] the earthly things and the pleasures of the body, having exercised caution and discernment vis-à-vis the common snares on earth, day and night; having asked of the Lord, without ceasing, to have a glimpse of that amazing, luminous beauty, ever remembering that warm love and the prom-

38. Allusion to the parables of "The Wedding Banquet" and "The Ten Virgins" in Mt 22.1–14; 25.1–13.

39. Cf. Mt 8.12; 13.42, 50; 22.13; 24.51; 25.30; and Lk 13.28.

40. Following the variant զարթացեալք, instead of զարթուցեալք.

ise of adoption,[41] longing earnestly for the good things that are from him, subjecting the movements of their bodies to his will. 86Strengthened by the blessed help from the Lord, they remained pure, repelling every agitation of the body; abiding in purity and sanctity within the veil, the safeguarding of the spiritual law; keen and careful about God's will. 87And rising up with clear discernment of the good news of their higher calling, being consoled by the pledge made with love,[42] they were unhindered in embracing sanctity. 88And being edified with fervent love for the fragrant life (offered) by the life-giving Word, partaking of the sacred mystery, his ineffable remembrance,[43] they looked forward to the beauty of the promised good things to come.

89Just as bees gather into their hives the best from flowers and make of it delicious sweetness, in contrast to the most bitter of tastes, 90so do those who are diligent in the life-giving counsel and draw from its beneficial wisdom; they are guided in every benevolent deed, in earnestness in faith, and in their truly holy lives, advancing with pleasing hope in the non-straying path that leads to eternal life, to the very chambers of life, to the very gate of salvation. 91With great eagerness and utter thirst they feast on the delicacies of the Benefactor's kindly care; and they always enjoy the inscrutable things in the wisdom of Christ, drawing near with ever new, holy enthusiasm. 92Having received the down-payment of the life (to come), they do not long for the endless pleasures of this world, its manifold things beggaring description, ceaselessly beguiling, moving the mind into straying, even the body—which deserves castigation with shame and ridicule—to the plagues of the passions.

93It is necessary to be vigilant on earth and to think of the things above, in earnestness for what pleases God. 94To lift up the mind unto him who is above all yet dwells within, who is the cause of our life and redemption, who has made us collaborators with his benevolent will: in finding the lost and protecting those who are good.[44]

41. See note to §17.

42. The pledge (or down payment) of the Spirit; see 2 Cor 1.22 and 5.5; cf. Eph 1.13–14; 2 Tm 1.14 (cf. Disc. 17.8; 23.119).

43. Allusion to the Eucharist; cf. "the saving mystery" (§38) and "his (Christ's) remembrances" (§99).

44. Or, "to keep the things that are good."

₉₅And to lead unto good things, to draw the distant ones closer, to acquaint strangers, to shepherd all—both near and far—with loving care for humankind, unto redemption and life. ₉₆To be ever willing to serve the brothers well, in all their needs. ₉₇To remove the passion for evil and every harmful deception. ₉₈To draw near to the Lord in every respect, with clean heart, pure life, and right faith. To love him wholeheartedly and to be constant in his holy service. To enlighten all the senses with his admonitions, as the earth is (illuminated) by the rays of the sun. ₉₉Likewise, (to observe) his remembrances;[45] to remain firm and steadfast in his caring love and teaching; to have fellowship with the saints, following his good counsel. ₁₀₀Always having the grace of the Benefactor as our helper; blessing the almighty God and Giver of good things, always, with thanks for everything; glorifying the One who made us worthy to be collaborators with his benevolent will.

₁₀₁When in difficulty, we should demonstrate the intimate calm we have in the Lord. And he will bestow his infinite grace, so that all may live and become heirs of the glory that does not pass away and to the greatness that is in Jesus Christ our Lord. ₁₀₂And we who are saved by him for virtuous deeds, cleansed from evil inclinations, and made the cause of salvation to many, will be translated from earth to the heavenly rest, to true life in the pleasant Kingdom, to be with Christ always and to enjoy his sacred blessings. ₁₀₃And just as (one's) height is sustained by the (body's) members, faith is sustained by good deeds;[46] and hope is substantiated by faith, and (by faith) all things hoped for.[47] ₁₀₄The divine love compels us to accept the grace of the Holy Spirit, to join the heavenly beings above, to become heirs of eternal life in the dwellings of the saints, to blossom in the quickening love, in the most beautiful glory, among ineffable and eternal things, and to glorify the Most Holy Trinity always—forever and ever. Amen.

45. See notes to §§38 and 88, above; cf. Disc. 23.49, "God's remembrance," and note to Disc. 3.23.
46. Allusion to Jas 2.26.
47. Allusion to Heb 11.1.

DISCOURSE 7

ON MANDATES FOR CREATED BEINGS

WHEN CREATURES grow from childhood into perfect adulthood and their wisdom increases with maturity, (then) they could satisfactorily hear the words of truth, the inerrant knowledge of which was necessarily proclaimed by the Prophets—to be spread, to be heard by people. For by faith they accept the exhortation by the Creator's inerrant wisdom and become familiar with what pleases him.[1] By following the true, spiritual law and by keeping his commandments, they come through life's perils unscathed, to advance to the better life and to be of help in the salvation of those far and near.

₂And all of this is extended to all (rational) creatures from the unreachable wisdom of the Creator, which illumines (as) with radiant beams of light. For it renews the senses (to be receptive) to spiritual exhortation, so that what pleases God would not be lost sight of; ₃and that (people) would make real progress in accumulating goodness and in bearing witness to the just and true traditions. ₄And all of this is to edify the spiritual part in us who are heirs of the Kingdom of Heaven, who are placed in this world (as a spectacle) for those seen and unseen,[2] and who should be familiar with every good ordinance and come to know the nature of created beings.

₅For God set the world as a school,[3] so that creatures would learn about the Creator's care in shaping and forming it, and about

1. On faith and hearing, see Rom 10.17; echoed here (discussed in Disc. 11.179–189, and quoted in Disc. 17.12). The role of the Prophets is restated in the next discourse (8.100).

2. Allusion to 1 Cor 4.9.

3. A *topos* in Greek philosophy; cf. the maxims attributed to Epicharmus, esp. on nature as educator (frag. 4; ed. Diels). The notion passed on to the catechetical school of Alexandria.

his providential dealing with things seen and unseen; ₆for out of nothing he created the beginnings of things, from one to a thousandfold and on to countless beings, and for one and all to attain the excellence of virtue. ₇And he set (the standard of) virtuous life at the head of all, so that he will bestow the gift of immortality at the end of the world, the inalterable and incomparable gift of the divine, eternal, and heavenly Kingdom with Christ. ₈For from the beginning the Lawgiver, the Word, first set a directive for the mind; second, (he set a directive for us) to be engaged in the husbandry of what is beneficial and to refrain from what is harmful.[4]

₉Moreover, for the study of created beings he established letters and literacy, and gave names to them, for names distinguish the letters, to separate them from one another; and letters combine as a meaningful sound, into a word. ₁₀And he made (the created beings) in two parts: (rational and irrational), that one may admonish the other; and to distinguish these two natures from one another, two distinct terms were necessarily devised. And these terms necessarily reflect the very natures of the ones designated. For (Scripture) says: "The earth was unsightly and altogether unfurnished" (Gn 1.2).[5] ₁₁And he wrought the beginning of creation by the Word. (Scripture) says: "He called the light day" (Gn 5.1), which is to reveal[6] the formation of creation, for the light is to display what the Word is to create. For the invisible and the as-yet-unformed thing was (part) of the darkness that covered the earth.[7] ₁₂As he called the light day, he began the unfolding of history, in order to start enumerating. ₁₃If there was no darkness, how would light have been called day or darkness night? ₁₄Similarly, the taste recognized by the palate is called sweet or bitter, and by (either) appellation the (particular) taste is recognized; and this has been established by the Creator's overseeing. ₁₅And light prompts people into all useful purposes, for all the inventions in the world—whether related to work or to the arts—are destined by it through vocations: be it smithery, agriculture, travel,

---

4. Allegorizing Gn 2.8–9, 15–17.

5. The quotation seems to underscore the fact that terms are descriptive of the natures of things they designate. Furthermore, this quotation is reflective of the use of the Septuagint (LXX) here.

6. Lit., "revealer."

7. Allusion to Gn 1.2b.

or any of the various profitable professions. It (that is, light or voca-
tional enlightenment) is given by God in acknowledgment of (people's) ability to exercise their free will, as from a caring father to his
children. And he designated the night for restful sleep, a consolation for labor, so that weakness may be replaced with strength; and
being renewed by rest, one may return to daytime work so that he
may profit and prosper. 16Similarly, the pleasant and sweet (flavors),
as also the bitter and sour, are designated for (use by) physicians
and others. 17Such are also the spices used professionally to spice
the various roasts, for the former are prized because of the latter,
and the latter because of the former.

18There are other appellations, like rest and labor, one comple-
menting the other; for one would enjoy his rest after profitable labor. All admixtures in creation are to be understood in this way:
19like coldness and heat, with one cooling and the other heating.
Each of these, by necessarily and beautifully blending with the other, becomes a blessing by the Creator and not a curse by being
drawn beyond its limit, for (Scripture) says: *"He set a boundary that
cannot be crossed"* (Ps 104.9 [103.9 LXX]). 20For man is inventive by
virtue of the Creator's providential care, being given a free will to
be used for his redemption and to enjoy the blessings, 21just as a son
is to enjoy the father's care not out of duty like a servant—as is the
case with the rest of creatures.

22Moreover, there are winds that dry, and there are (winds) that
dampen the earth and vegetation, and there are those that harm.
(Yet,) by God's providence, they combine (for good effect) and have
different names. 23Such is the case with health and pain; for health
promotes the husbandry of virtue with beneficial outcomes, and
pain compels one to seek healing from God and people. 24It also
brings, with patience, forgiveness of sins and rewards, as (in the
case of) Job. These also have names. 25So it is with sadness and
joy. As it is in things of this world, (the former) pertains to death
and corruption; yet with God's intervention, it offers consolation.
And joy comes with the hope for the promised good things. These
too have names. 26Likewise, fullness and shortage complement
each other, for fullness is realized vis-à-vis shortage; and shortage
points to (the need for) thorough self-restraint; and resolve in (such)

husbandry is efficacious.[8] Together, they have beneficial effects that are named as they appear. ₂₇Likewise with fear and indifference, for fear longs for indifference, and indifference for fear, which makes one cautious about the Lord's will and does not allow iniquity. ₂₈And when combined, in keeping with (God's) command, they heap up benefits in us by their respective names. ₂₉Likewise, praise and denigration, yielding to each other, remain within their bounds. But when they exceed their bounds, they cause spiritual and physical harm, as is well known to all, and we would name them accordingly. ₃₀Similarly, rewards and punishments are not the same, and there is need for both. One prompts to good deeds; the other prevents those daring to sin and compels them, with treats, to desist and to turn to goodness. ₃₁And those who do good do not forget the Benefactor and the blessed inheritance and the promised good things that will be added to those who are good, as they are so called (or named).[9]

₃₂As for those who are truly free from sin and are praised by many and repress sin among the righteous, for they desire righteousness and remember the threats made against sinners and hasten to repent with confession, they will survive the wrath that is coming upon the lawless and disobedient ones, the unholy and defiled; and being found to be righteous, they will live. ₃₃And the righteous, who have received the promise of that true adoption unto freedom,[10] will increase in righteousness, for they will be perfect like the heavenly Father,[11] after whom each of them is named.[12] ₃₄And (those who choose) homelessness—voluntary homelessness —long for riches to come flowing, for through chastity and immaculateness one arrives at the riches that do not pass away. ₃₅The truly rich in righteousness, who are called rich in their homelessness, will not be denied the eternal riches.

8. Cf. Disc. 9.33, on self-restraint as a form of husbandry.

9. The preceding argument, with the examples provided, draws on the Stoic notion of *eupatheiai*.

10. Allusion to Rom 8.14–17, 23; Gal 4.1–7; Eph 1.5–6.

11. Allusion to Mt 5.48.

12. Allusion to Rom 8.21 (cf. Mt 5.9; Lk 20.36; Jn 1.12; 11.52; i.e., "children of God"); cf. Rv 2.17 ("a new name"); 3.12 ("the name of my God"); see also below, §§38, 41.

36And weakness and strength, going hand in hand, are worthy of praise. 37For weakness teaches humility and kindness, and to wait with hope for the verdict of Christ, the righteous Judge. 38And those who are truly strong are a mighty fortress for the weak, supporters and givers of goods who will receive the real glory that does not pass away. They each will receive the name[13] and reward from the Creator.

39Both foolishness and wisdom are part[14] of earthly life. 40The foolish (ought to) respect and obey the wise, to learn good things from them; for a sovereign mind is endowed with wisdom that counsels and guides to the truth, the reception of which allows entry into the Kingdom. For God's fool is wiser than the wise of this world.[15] 41For first, God's wisdom is holy; second, it bestows peace, full of goodness and just fruit that leads to the heavenly glory, unlike that of the cunning and accursed serpent. Rather, (God's fools) are known by name and are deemed innocent.

42Success and stupidity work for their respective ends:[16] profitable success in one (case), and the end result of the compulsive passions in the other. 43In both (cases), for the work accomplished, it is essential that they receive their exact reward, which will be in accordance with the will of the provident One, who bestows the name.[17]

44Those on the side of righteousness will be truly living;[18] while the dead in sin and hopelessness (will be truly) in death, with tortures held in store for them. 45Those living in God's love, in sanctity, in the true faith, and in the firm hope,[19] have the promise of (eternal) life; there is no death to them, but life, of which the Scriptures inform. With his word Christ wakes them up from sleep at (the sound of) the archangels' trumpets.[20] 46Those who have done good, will have glory and eternal life; and those who have done evil, will have

13. Cf. §§33, 41.
14. Lit., "essential" or "necessary" (Arm. պիտոյ, *pitoy*). A likely corruption in the author's Greek source is to be suspected here, reading χρή instead of μέρη.
15. Allusion to 1 Cor 1.25.
16. Lit., "gain" or "profit."
17. Cf. §§33, 38.
18. Lit., "the life of the living."
19. Echoing 1 Cor 13.13.
20. Allusion to 1 Cor 15.52; 1 Thes 4.16.

torture and eternal death, which is endless.[21] [47]And he made man a student of all these, so that by his free will he would choose the beneficial and discern the harmful, and that he would abide by the virtues, keeping hope in the Lord; [48]so that he may receive the calling of the brotherhood that is in Jesus[22] and enjoy the good things that are from him, and that are to the benefit of both sides.[23] [49]For those who pursue righteousness will be crowned with the blessings,[24] in accordance with virtue; they will be highly praised by the Lord for their patience. Being freed from grief, they move on with certainty of freedom into the rewards of righteousness and enjoy the good things deservedly, being crowned with the blessings.

[50]God made the visible creatures, humans, with sense perception—a consolation in life. [51](He made) the heavens with clouds, dew, and luminaries so that plants and trees may yield fruit; [52]and seasonal winds and temperatures in order to nurture and protect from harm. And he waters the earth and satisfies the thirst of humans and animals, of beasts and birds, and every buzzing and creeping creature endowed with breath of life.

[53]And should men turn to mischief willingly, being wrongheaded, he would instruct with the same consoling care and punish the unrepentant with barrenness and wrath. [54]For should the same creatures who were consoled, rightfully receiving the enjoyment of good things, rebel and depart from the set boundary, the Lawgiver, equally caring, would be moved to wrath, disciplining them by it. He would bring them to their senses[25] through it all: through famine and scarcity. [55]With cold and heat he would destroy the trees and plants. He would turn the rain into hail and snow, the dew into harmful frost, health into diverse aches, joy into sadness, glory into dishonor, [56]every good success into misery, and the beneficial things to be well enjoyed into pain and deep sorrow. [57]And he would turn peace and places built joyfully, with a (false) sense of security, into confusion,[26] disappointment, and unimaginable evil,

---

21. Echoing Rom 2.6–10; cf. 2 Cor 5.10.
22. Allusion to Mt 12.50; Mk 3.35; Heb 2.11.
23. Meaning the here and the hereafter.
24. Or, "the Beatitudes"; allusion to Mt 5.6, 10.
25. Lit., "to wholesome thought."
26. Possible allusion to the Tower of Babel (Gn 11.1–9).

into confusion among families and strangers, servants and masters, and into diverse troubles, so that because of them they would have remorse.[27]

58But if they still persist in evil and do not repent with confession, the righteous Judge disciplines with greater punishments. 59Those who defile the sacred things with unholy behavior and despise the law concerning the right of the homeless and mercy to those in need,[28] and falsely hold on to the truth and ignore the tears of the oppressed, refuse to hear the cry of the detainees, and do similar evil things, 60for these (evils) the righteous Judge will deliver them to famine, to the sword, and to captivity and oblivion. 61And as the Lord commanded in the Law and the Prophets to desist from evil, yet they did not listen, as it is said in the Holy Scriptures: *"And they cried unto the Lord in their distress, but he did not hear"* (Ps 18.41 [17.42 LXX]). 62There is punishment for those who do not direct their sovereign will to the cause of fairness in justice and to console the poor and the homeless.

63But the benevolent God, in accordance with his love, who loves humankind, continues to admonish and does not turn them over to death or smite them to death, nor does he wipe out the memory of those who are defiant and senseless. 64Should they not learn, however, to give thanks to God for his gifts and obey his laws, he surrenders their glory and abundance into the hands of misery, lamentation, and deserved tears. 65The Benefactor wishes that they be admonished and be truly sanctified, so that they may be admitted into his care, always to do good before him, to stay away from disorderly and wasteful living, and not to exchange gratitude for ingratitude, and peaceful and quiet times for the troubles and scourges of perilous plagues. 66If they would exchange their disorderly life for the better one, peaceful times would return. After all, we should be collaborators with the Lord, so as not to fall under condemnation. 67The Apostle says: *"glory, honor, and peace for those who do good . . . but trouble and distress for everyone who does evil"* (Rom 2.10a, 9a). 68Now, doers of good abide gladly in his goodness, and are heirs of his consideration and care and of the good things that are

27. A common theodicean argument for the justification of the existence of evil; drawn on Stoic thought.

28. Allusion to Dt 15.7–11; 24.14–15.

in Christ. ₆₉Thus they enjoy his care on earth, in the hope of inheriting his sincere promises regarding the endless, good things for the righteous. ₇₀But the disobedient and the wasteful ones are coworkers with the Lord's threats, which transform his pleasant care into a bitter recompense of afflictions, punishments, and diverse plagues.

₇₁See, how sovereign is the individual, for he determines God's will toward himself, to do himself good. ₇₂For the Lord says through the Prophet: *"I do not wish the death of the wicked, but rather that he turn from his evil ways and live"* (Ezek 33.11). ₇₃For he is a righteous Judge, and he judges as man deserves for what he has done in his day, whether good or evil.[29] ₇₄And we have the power[30] to change our times by doing good for goodness' sake; ₇₅equally so for evil, if we are lovers of sin. ₇₆For it is up to us to turn torments to endearment and, conversely, love to anger. ₇₇Yet he does not leave us in our defiance, but forgives, so that we may have remorse[31] again and obey—in keeping with the most compassionate care of the benevolent God. ₇₈For he says: *"I have not come to call the righteous, but sinners to repentance"*; and *"a physician is not needed for the healthy, but for the sick"* (Lk 5.32, 31). ₇₉And again he says through the Prophet: *"The righteousness of the righteous will be credited to them for life, and the wickedness of the wicked will be charged against them for death—if they continue in the same"* (Ezek 18.20). ₈₀But if the righteous turns to sinning, he will surely die; and if the sinner (turns) to righteousness, he will surely live.[32]

₈₁Do you hear the Lord's just judgment of the just and of sinners? ₈₂Depending on how we exercise our will, we can turn the promised good things into threats and punishments. ₈₃We can also turn our life into death, and death into life. We can turn either unto good or unto evil as we exercise our will within the boundaries set by God,[33] ₈₄as the Prophet says: *"'If you are willing and obedient, you will eat the good things of the land; but if you are not willing to obey me, you will be devoured by the sword.' For the mouth of the Lord has spoken"* (Is 1.19–20). ₈₅And the Apostle says: *"All things are yours, whether death or*

---

29. Allusion to 2 Cor 5.10 (cf. §46).

30. Or, "authority."

31. Lit., "they may have remorse."

32. Allusion to Ezek 18.21, 24.

33. A marginal interpolation, "this is within God's power only," possibly meant to counter the preceding statement, has become part of the text at this point.

life or the world or beyond the world or height or depth. You are of Christ, and Christ is of God" (1 Cor 3.21–23).[34]

86*"All things are yours"* is said to those who in this world live in accordance with his pulsating love and will. 87For just as a censer with its fragrant incense delights those who are near—whether old or young—so the aroma of our confession of faith and of our purity rises daily before Christ. 88And when he says *"whether death,"* it is because our death for Christ's sake is a testimony to his love; for by such death we are transformed to the incorruptible, eternal life, which is in Christ Jesus.[35] 89The honorable death is not only for those who attained martyrdom in times of persecution by sword or fire or water or by some other evil means, but also for those who were baptized into Christ[36] and have put on Christ, and who have taken off the old man and his deeds and have put on the new, being renewed in the image of God, which is for righteousness and holiness and truth;[37] it is for those who have died to sin and are alive for righteousness.[38] 90*"For just as Christ was raised from the dead through the glory of the Father, we too may be transformed in the newness of life"* (Rom 6.4). 91For the one who mortifies the body and bodily thoughts, and lives in sanctity and impeccably, in accordance with the righteous law of the Gospel of Christ,[39] could say: *"I therefore live, yet not I, but Christ lives in me"* (Gal 2.20). 92For whether we manifest the virtues in this world or in the one to come, all is done through him and because of his care and for his glory, *"who fills everything in every way"* (Eph 1.23), in depth and in height.

93By "depth" we understand the weakness of the body on earth, and its rising into goodness through Christ; 94and by "height," the power of the spirit of the heavenly beings and of those who are immortal in Christ. 95(The Apostle) says: *"All that is Christ's is yours, and you are his"* (1 Cor 3.22), to the glory of the Father and of the Spirit. 96When we keep his word and abide in his love[40] and in purity of

34. Cf. Rom 8.9.
35. Allusion to Rom 6.23.
36. Allusion to Rom 6.1–7. See the twelve answers given to question(s) on why the death of the righteous is honorable in the sight of God, Disc. 12.68–78.
37. Allusion to Eph 4.22–24; cf. Rom 13.14; Gal 3.27; Col 3.9–10.
38. Allusion to Rom 6.2, 11.
39. Allusion to Gal 6.2.
40. Allusion to Jn 15.10.

life, then we no longer understand things physically but spiritually; *"for those who live by the Spirit of God are the children of God and heirs of Christ;* [97]*for if we share in his sufferings on earth, we will also share in his glory in heaven"* (Rom 8.17), which lasts forever. [98]For although we know about redemption and life, we do not quite know. [99]But God, who is all and in all,[41] beyond description, lovingly cares for his creatures and has promised to give the Kingdom and the eternally good things that are in the Father and in the Son and in the Holy Spirit. To him glory forever.

41. Allusion to 1 Cor 12.6; Eph 4.6; Col 3.11.

DISCOURSE 8

REPROOF OF HEEDLESS LIVING AND (ADMONITION UNTO) DEVOTION TO VIRTUE IN GENERAL[1]

HE CONSOLATION of the Prophets and the preaching of the Apostles lead us to an abundance of good things: that advantageous part that is in Christ. 2Moreover, they motivate us unto greater things that are gateways to every good thing and blessedness, for through them comes the good news of God's promised gifts for (more) spiritual consolation, 3as also for physical contentment: abundance of things, peace, and other essentials. 4Furthermore, that good thing (called) hope for eternal life (motivates us), and that gift (called) invisible love, that is, the treasures of knowledge and wisdom, by means of which one knows (how) to differentiate between good and evil, and which ought to be established in those of us who pursue the spiritual life. 5These are to be chosen by those committed to (prompting) one another in the virtues and to helping unbelievers forsake (their ways and) choose the good faith of knowing God. 6And the righteous should not err in (doubting) salvation by hope.[2] 7Rather, they should restrain themselves from the bitter and most evil and harmful things in life, which are gateways to anger, grief, famine, the sword, and enslavement to diverse evils. 8For he who is the Fount of every good thing and Creator of all creatures, both earthly and heavenly beings, spiritual and physical, the All-powerful, the Almighty, the Beneficent to all the living, says: *"I am the Lord your God ... You shall keep my commandments ... and you shall live"* (Lv 18.2, 5), *"for it is his will for all people to live and to come to a knowledge of the truth"* (1 Tm 2.4). 9Thus

1. Regardless of its title, the discourse in its entirety is against fornication.
2. Allusion to Rom 8.24; cf. 1 Thes 5.8; Ti 3.7.

he, who is the Giver and Sustainer of life through his resourceful benevolence, calls all to his life.

₁₀One should also love him with one's whole being, strength, and mind, and one's friend as one's self,[3] with all holiness, so that by the grace of God bestowed upon us, we may live beyond this evil world ₁₁and restrain malevolence; to anchor the unstable mind in the stability of hope,[4] both in hardship and in peace. ₁₂And we should hate recklessness, which disturbs and defiles nature, and makes one inclined to fornication and adultery.[5] ₁₃For fornication enslaves one in various excruciating and debasing harms, and draws away from faith and holy life into the lures of sin, into the filth of recklessness.

₁₄Now, let us flee from fornication, the mother of evils that leads to all evils, for it led many to destruction by water and fire and by various other catastrophes, as the Book tells.[6] ₁₅For the one who commits adultery or fornication will lose himself, for the Lord will shut out the defiled person.[7] ₁₆For all pure persons are temples of the Most Holy Trinity;[8] but fornicators and adulterers are temples of demons. ₁₇(Because of fornication) virgins are defiled and rejected by the Lord, and marriages are nullified and subjected to many evils. ₁₈Through fornication, magicians obtain help from satanic enticements, (as if) a reward[9] for defilement. ₁₉Because of fornication, evil and impure persons always cherish filthy thoughts. ₂₀Because of fornication, revenge, and rancor, men and women

3. Allusion to Mt 22.37, 39; cf. Dt 6.5.

4. Allusion to Heb 6.19.

5. These are key words in the discourse: պոռնկութիւն and շնութիւն (*pořn-kutʻiwn* and *šnutʻiwn*), esp. the former. Like its Greek equivalent, *pořnkutʻiwn* (*porneia*) has broad meanings; it is a catchword for all forms of "sexual immorality." For the sake of consistency, the word պոռնիկ (*pořnik*) is here translated "fornicator," except at §§66 and 69, where the word "prostitute" makes better sense; cf. բոզ (*boz*) at §§27 and 28, translated "harlot." The traditional distinction between "fornication" and "adultery" is that the former involves the unmarried and the latter the married.

6. Allusion especially to the flood (Gn 6.9–8.22) and the burning of Sodom and Gomorrah (Gn 19.1–29). Cf. Disc. 20.145.

7. Allusion to Rv 22.15.

8. Possible allusion to Jn 14.32 and 2 Cor 6.16, both cited in conjunction with the indwelling of the Most Holy Trinity, in Disc. 23.23–24.

9. Lit., "bribe."

are lost. 21Because of fornication, there are dissension, violation of vows, lying, and theft. 22Because of fornication, there is slothfulness in prayer and fasting, and neglect of work. 23Because of fornication, most damaging treacheries and malice towards strangers and family (members) happen to increase. 24Because of fornication, there are cunning and diverse kinds of death, both in the open and in secrecy. 25Unborn[10] babies are squeezed out of the belly and aborted prematurely; or they impair what is in the belly with drugs; and there are those who kill the newborn. 26And there are those who murder both the violator and the violated, whether in open fights or by some evil machination. 27And there are lovers who stab each other because of harlots. 28And there are harlots who take lessons in deception from magicians, for they end up killing their husbands for the sake of lovers of whom they are enamored.

29The passions wreak widespread evils among men and women, the very mention or hearing of which is detestable to those who are pure in thought and saintly. 30Those who are possessed by Satan understand that of which I speak, or mean to speak. 31For a fornicator is intoxicated with filth; as the Prophet says: *"Woe to you ... who are drunk from the passions and not from wine"* (Is 29.1, 9).[11] 32For fornication is the cause of all evils, the mother of sin, and the gate to all evils that constitute sin. 33For this reason God's wrath is kindled on earth, leading to famine, the sword, slavery, and all sorts of filth; conflict between kin and strangers, parents and children, and slaves and masters, leading to quarrels, strife, and death.

34There is greater evil in this loathsome filth than what has been said. There are those who pursue unrestrained filthiness, more than animals and beasts and creeping creatures: they defile themselves with bestiality and homosexuality. *"Having abandoned the natural role of male and female, they have become inflamed with lust for one another"* (Rom 1.27); they have fallen into unutterable filthiness that cannot be seen (even) among other breathing creatures in their loathsome filth: 35evils and excessive filth that, alas, exceed the bounds and are the fountainhead of all harmful evils. 36Early legislators had them stoned to death or burned; and of late, the Church and communities excommunicate them until they repent for days and

---

10. Lit., "half-developed."
11. Cf. Is 51.21.

nights, with weeping and sighing, in ashes and fasting, in constant prayer and labor, and brokenness of heart.[12] 37For since the Lord considers looking at a woman equal to adultery,[13] what should be said by way of punishment for more loathsome filth? 38And, by contrast, how he blesses those who are pure; for he says: *"Blessed are the pure in heart, for they shall see God in the spirit"* (Mt 5.8).

39Could one say enough about the rewards of the saints? They will see God and will enjoy the things beyond description. 40We rejoice when we see the sun after a cold night, for the warmth and light it gives, which are transient; but what about the ineffable light of its Creator, which we cannot compare (to the sun). God, the One who is incomparably good,[14] 41fills the saints with grace and makes them enjoy the immeasurable good things, eternal blessedness, and unending joy. 42There is nothing like the things that are there, the ineffable things of which we are unable to speak.[15] But to those who are pure in heart and impeccable in their body parts, Christ appears to them in an indescribable manner. 43If, however, they are impure in body and soul, it is because of the heart, from which the works of the body derive. As the Lord says: *"For out of the heart proceeds the evil of evil thoughts … and the body is defiled"* (Mt 15.19–20). 44Moreover, he says: *"If your eye or hand or any other thing causes you to stumble, cut it off and throw it away from you"* (Mt 5.29). 45This saying is not about cutting off a member (of the body); rather, it is about the excitement of the passionate desires that work to destroy the person; for fornication is the spark that ignites the unquenchable fire of sins altogether.

46When the Savior sent forth the Apostles to plant the seeds of the Word of Truth throughout the world, in the fields of believers' minds in order to set them straight by it, he commanded that first they root out the thorny plant of the passions,[16] the (evil) inclination of the body and the mind, in order to obey the Gospel; and then to plant the seeds of the invitatory good news, to call to

---

12. Cf. Disc. 19.64.

13. Allusion to Mt 5.28.

14. Allusion to Mt 19.17.

15. Allusion to 1 Cor 2.9.

16. No direct reference to this command is found in the Gospels; but see Mt 15.10–20 (cf. Mk 7.20–23).

confession and repentance, and for all to be reconciled to the Creator.[17] [47]And those who obey, following the proclamation of the
Gospel, will become worthy of his sacred beneficence, with living
hope;[18] so that we may reach the abodes of eternal life that is in
Christ Jesus.[19] [48]And at the council that considered the question
of the Jews and the Gentiles, the Apostles mandated this first and
chose to abstain from fornication, from strangled (animals), and
from blood.[20] [49]Those who do these good deeds will receive for
themselves the present and future (blessings).

[50]He endeavors to wipe out fornication first, so that the many
harmful branches that extend from it will be eradicated. Similarly (for people), to desist from (eating) dead animals, the forbidden
foods with blood, and other things which rouse the inclination to
kill. [51]So that through obedience they may turn to purity, moderation, and mindfulness; and through familiarity with the faith,
they may enter into the promised good things. [52]And to abhor all
atrocities and to keep away from the threats of eternal suffering
which is prepared by the Lord for those who have been defiled and
have become impure by fornication. [53]Since eating dead animals or
drinking blood brings such calamity and misery, how much more
is prepared by the righteous Judge for those who endanger their kin
through affliction, stress body and soul through harms, bitter suffering, and death! [54]And the Apostle says: *"Do not be deceived: neither
fornicators nor adulterers nor homosexuals*[21] *nor thieves nor murderers nor their
like will inherit the Kingdom of God"* (1 Cor 6.9), but the unquenchable
fire; as the Prophet (says): *"Their fire will not be quenched, and their worm
will not die"* (Is 66.24). [55]For (Scripture) says: *"Marriage is honorable,
and the (marriage) bed pure"* (Heb 13.4); that virginity is preferable;[22]

---

17. Echoing 2 Cor 5.20.

18. Echoing 1 Pt 1.3.

19. Echoing Jn 14.2.

20. See Acts 15.19–20.

21. The Eng. word translates two words, հգացեալք (*igac'ealk'*) and արուագէտք
(*aruagētk'*), which, as in Greek, refer to the passive and active participants in ho-
mosexual acts.

22. Allusion to 1 Cor 7.38–39; a central subject in patristic theology, where
it transcends the mere renunciation of marriage (see, e.g., Gregory of Nyssa, *De
virginitate*, PG 46:317–416).

and that God will judge the fornicator and the adulterer.[23] ₅₆And again it says: *"You are God's temple, and the Spirit of God dwells in you"* (1 Cor 3.16); ₅₇that is, you are clear of filth. ₅₈For *"Your temple is holy, remarkable in righteousness"* (Ps 65.4 [64.5 LXX]), says David. ₅₉*"And if anyone destroys God's temple, God will destroy him; for God's temple is holy, which is you"* (1 Cor 3.17) in the midst of perverse and defiled nations.

₆₀For since the earth was destroyed by the Flood because of those who were utterly corrupt,[24] why should we not be fearful—we who have the universal destruction by the Flood as evidence of wrath against sin? ₆₁Moreover, Sodom and Gomorrah were afflicted with fire and brimstone, heat in proportion to the intolerable filth with which they were caught.[25] The five kings were struck down along with their defiled households and their entire lands.[26] ₆₂These two catastrophes, because of sexual impurity[27] and defilement, were set forth as two witnesses for the fearsome Judgment, which will be held in order to punish such filthiness on the day of visitation of all nations. ₆₃The Lord says: *"For as they were in the days of Noah, marrying women and giving in marriage to men and reveling, up to the time when the flood wiped them out completely"* (Mt 24.38). Also in the days of Lot: they were reveling in lewdness and all sorts of revelry, even in inordinate passions, until the Lord called Lot out of there and burned all with fire.[28] But you are the Lord's light unto holiness. ₆₄(Scripture) says: *"Darkness (loves) the deeds of darkness that are not (done) in light"* (Jn 3.19). ₆₅When the darkness of sin is gone, the holy light appears. ₆₆It also says: *"He who draws near to a prostitute becomes one body (with her)"* (1 Cor 6.16), since the sin is committed as in one body, (also) since evil is a common thing: whether in deed, in speech, in sight, or in hearing; as in all other related evils. ₆₇But he who draws near to the Lord becomes one in spirit (with him), immersed in living holiness. ₆₈For having cleansed the members of the body, he is united with Christ in the Spirit for a life of faith and truth; and he becomes a holy member of Christ, in every virtue.

23. Possible allusion to Rv 21.8; 22.14.
24. See Gn 6.9–8.21.
25. See Gn 19.24–25.
26. See Gn 14.8–11.
27. Or, "masturbation."
28. See Gn 19.15–22.

₆₉For he is able to tell the enemy at war: *"Shall I take the members of Christ (and) make them a member of a prostitute?"* (1 Cor 6.15). (God) forbid the trading of holiness for impurity.

₇₀Many times Paul warned about the defilement of the fornicator, and counseled about *"handing over to Satan for the destruction of the flesh, so that the spirit may be saved"* (1 Cor 5.5) through genuine remorse, suppression of the flesh through persistent fasting, and moving on unto holiness through prayer; for all those whom this concerns, to abide in these things. ₇₁For diverse acts of lawlessness have been committed on earth because of fornication, for fornication has multiple evils and leads to insatiable, filthy passions. ₇₂For this reason the Apostle teaches and admonishes us with threats: to flee such filthiness and corruption, the end of which is perdition. ₇₃For he says: *"We must not indulge in fornication as some of the Jews did, and twenty-four thousands of them perished there in a single day because of fornication"* (1 Cor 10.8).[29] ₇₄It was not without justifiable reason that the wrath of omniscient God was drawn against them.

₇₅It was for this reason that through the (invading) powers he brought catastrophes against the people, for they were children of perdition because of sin, since they sinned collectively. ₇₆For the Prophet says: *"The person who sins is the one who will die"* (Ezek 18.20), even though he says (elsewhere): *"The fathers ate sour grapes, and the children's teeth are set on edge"* (Ezek 18.2).[30] ₇₇Since there are those who die in their sins without repenting, he shows that God's judgments cannot be forgotten, that there is justice in store: good news for the saints and frightful threats for the lawless; ₇₈so that the children of sinners may fear and not commit sin as their fathers did, that because of their righteousness they may survive the wrath threatening them. ₇₉*"For the son who hates the wickedness of his father and does what is right, he will surely live,"* says the Lord (Ezek 18.19). ₈₀*"And neither test the Lord nor grumble, as some of them (did) and were killed there by snakes"* (1 Cor 10.9).[31] ₈₁For the study of his teaching[32] guides in the right way, distinguishes the good from the bad, and safeguards sanctity in ac-

---

29. St. Paul referring to Nm 25.1–9.

30. Cf. Jer 31.29.

31. St. Paul referring to Nm 21.5–6.

32. Arm. վարդապետութեան (*vardapetutʻean*), in context, refers to divine precepts; cf. Disc. 5.74; 6.21; etc.

cordance with the righteous laws and the Gospel's enlightening in thought, word, and deed. ₈₂So that we may survive through the wrath coming upon the lawless and the impure, that we may stand pure before Christ and inherit the ineffable, good things.

₈₃Moreover, overseers should not hesitate to recount the threats by the Lord God. For he says through the Prophet: *"I have appointed you as a watchman … to say, 'You will surely die if you sin.'* ₈₄*If he hears you, he will live. But if he does not hear you, he will die; but you will have saved yourself.* ₈₅*But if you do not utter the threats against those who act (wickedly), should the sword or the wrath come, I will hold you accountable for their blood"* (Ezek 3.17–19, 21). ₈₆For they should be guided either by the entreaties with good news, in the hope for blessings, or by the threat of catastrophes and grief and suffering in this world and on the fearsome day set for sinners and the disobedient. ₈₇For God's commands are like messengers sent by his authority to all creatures: to heavenly beings, the hosts of angels, and to earthly beings, the genus of humankind, for our well-being, out of his loving Lordship, to rescue us from suffering and to bring us into his peace. ₈₈Let us stand firm in the true traditions, pure in life, in body and soul, before the Lord. And let us be beneficent to our friends, for their utmost well-being in life and salvation. ₈₉And let us be truly proficient in (such) husbandry, associates of God, pleasing to his benevolent will. And by the grace of the Spirit, enjoy life in this world as those freed from sin, and abound always in righteousness, utmost purity, and much patience. Thus we will be able to inherit the good things promised by the Holy Trinity.

₉₀There are also the excellent testimonies regarding his sovereign will in the teaching of the Holy Spirit that has been passed on to us in writing by the Prophets, the Apostles, and the teachers (of the Church),[33] that we may know the benevolent God who is just, caring, holy, and true; that we may abstain from the perilous, ungrateful, and incredulous life of lawlessness, and wipe out of our minds and bodies for all time the harmful wickedness.

₉₁As for the Persians and other barbarous nations who do not know the Law, according to the saying of the Apostle, *"they do by nature things required by the Law"* (Rom 2.14), and at the hands of

---

33. See note to Disc. 5.1.

judges punish the impure and the unjust. ₉₂And rulers and judges unequivocally threaten evildoers, liars, those who swear falsely, swindlers, thieves, murderers, adulterers, witches, enchanters, and others in sundry sins, ₉₃whom they imprison, hold in iron chains, torment with diverse tortures, and condemn to death so that others may fear and abstain from unbridled lawlessness. ₉₄As for those who take counsel to heart and abide by the royal law and order, and control themselves in single-mindedness and obedience, they are rewarded with honor, glory, and gifts of freedom.

₉₅The Greeks have such written statutes; they honor the beneficent and decent (people) with gifts and honors. But they inflict punishment and dire penalties on the lawless, the disobedient, the haughty, the violators, and the impure, so that they may abstain from transgression and do good (works) each day, so that the world may not fall into injustice but be preserved in peace and thrive. ₉₆Likewise, all nations that do not follow the decrees of God's just judgments have legislators and statutes to guide them through courts, so that they may not fall into anarchy and strife. ₉₇Justice is of two kinds: that which honors just people and rewards them with the promised gifts, and that which punishes the ungrateful and the unjust with threats and sundry tortures;[34] for there is no nation that lacks judiciary to dispense justice. ₉₈All these rules for the betterment of the world are established by the Lord, providentially, for the good of people, even though they neither know nor glorify nor thank God; for they chose not to know God, *"but their thinking became futile, and in their thoughtlessness they remained in darkness"* (Rom 1.21). ₉₉But by virtue of his Fatherhood and Lordship, the Creator does not overlook his creatures. He has invited and has called all into the Kingdom.

34. Based on the Aristotelian dual application of justice: distributive or constitutional (honoring citizens' merits by the *polis*) and corrective or judicial (rectifying injustices through liability), elaborated in Book V of the *Nicomachean Ethics* (1130b30–1133b28). Aristotle comments on the relationship of natural justice or law and positive justice or legislation, where Persia is cited as an example of places where natural law is as much at work with or without legislation (i.e., without law, a meaning taken by our author [or his source] with a twist, as lawlessness): "Some people think that all rules of justice are merely conventional, because whereas a law of nature is immutable and has the same validity everywhere, as fire burns both here and in Persia, rules of justice are seen to vary" (1134b25–27, trans. Rackham; see Bibliography).

$_{100}$Now all these right and just rules are witnesses to God's spiritual law proclaimed by the Prophets in the Holy Scriptures[35]—$_{101}$which leads from injustice to justice, from dishonor to glory, from transient things to things eternal, from the earthly to the heavenly, and to virtue altogether. $_{101}$And one ought to abide by all these just and sacred rules, with true faith and enthusiastic love, never straying from the will of God whether during trouble or during peace. $_{102}$To trample underfoot the fallacies of this world and to stand firm, in tranquil peace, in the hope of eternal life; that one may reach the dwellings of the saints in blessed and magnificent glory, to enjoy the ineffable goodness, the incomparable splendors in the most desirable Kingdom of the almighty Father, the benevolent Son who has given us life, and the Holy Spirit, the restorer of believers, the One Holy Trinity, to whom be glory forever. Amen.

35. Cf. the opening statement of the preceding discourse.

DISCOURSE 9

TEACHING ABOUT THE ESSENTIAL FAST
ESTABLISHED BY THE LORD

NDEED, for every order (of beings) a standard has been set by the almighty Lord and Creator, so that in the company of others, in the fear of God, we may follow virtue; that it may be achieved[1] gloriously, through faith and the grace of Christ. ₂Thus, with meritorious courage, we take the martyr's stand for the sake of the mandated husbandry, being strengthened by his sacred love, like the spiritual hosts. ₃Thereby the Lawgiver is glorified, and those who are law-abiding are crowned and led into the abodes of the Kingdom of Heaven, following the example of that omnipresent Love, into his benevolent care. ₄Thus, by emulating them in *"meditating on the law of the Lord day and night"* (Ps 1.2), we may receive the grace of righteousness and self-restraint. So that all who have pursued the excellent life may enter into the Kingdom with crowns upon their heads, into eternal and endless life; to become associates of the heavenly and immortal beings—having done before God and the incorporeal hosts according to the grace of election, which, being followed here on earth, presents us among the heavenly beings. ₅With this hope he admonishes people, in accordance with the promised good news. And the benevolent Father and the all-caring Holy Spirit make them heirs of Christ, who through his provident love does not forsake his creatures; for it is his will to make all attain life and the knowledge of truth.[2] Therefore he says: ₆*"Whoever does and teaches (these things) shall be called great in the Kingdom of Heaven"* (Mt 5.19).

₇Just as angels are ranked by the King of Kings and they abide

---

1. Lit., "crowned."
2. Allusion to 1 Tm 2.3–4.

in the same, in accordance with the benevolent will of the Giver of life and do not go beyond, so are humans commended by him to the angelic ranks. ₈Thus the Seraphim and the Cherubim have been assigned to serve the almighty Lordship, by whose benevolent care creatures are sustained continuously. ₉So have also all the wakeful ones, the hosts of spiritual or incorporeal beings. They are ministers appointed in their respective ranks, to carry out the will of the benevolent One.[3] ₁₀These are the countless armies of the (heavenly) hosts that are amenable and obedient to the will of his Lordship, demonstrating their service by ceaselessly praising the Lord. They are co-workers with the benevolent God in his beneficence and glorifiers of his greatness and divinity; and they are constantly happy in their delight in the Creator. ₁₁The one among them who rebelled with his armies and was given a bitter sentence is called Satan;[4] and demons, who are his satellites, are the ministers of evil, those who demonstrate deeds of lawlessness and oppose those who live uprightly. ₁₂Since they fell from honor, they hunt people down unto perdition, those to whom God promised to give the honor of being human. ₁₃This one acts contrary to God and is engrossed in sin, opposes humans incessantly, and is an enemy of righteousness and sanctity. He never stops his cunning, his seducing and misleading of people by diverse and sundry evils. ₁₄For this reason he is condemned, threatened with fearful torments and eternal doom; ₁₅not only he and his hosts but also those who love to do his will in thought, word, or deed. The Lord says: *"Sinners shall go to eternal torment, which is prepared for Satan and his angels"* (Mt 25.41): ₁₆those that have acted willingly and not because of compulsion.

₁₇But we have been commanded by the Lord to be mindful of his commandments, and always to stay away from (Satan's) deceptions; and in view of the promised good things, to do good before the Lord always, every hour: to abide intimately, inviolately in the husbandry that pleases God, and to exhort many to do what is good and salutary to redemption and all-pleasing sanctity. ₁₈For this reason those who are ready for just and holy deeds receive honor and glory from the benevolent God, ₁₉for they are fortified with hope against all temptations; they do not stray from the sure and

3. Allusion to Heb 1.14; cf. Ps 91.11; 103.20; Dn 7.10.
4. Allusion to Lk 10.18, quoted in the next discourse (see note to Disc. 10.131).

straight way of life; they remain steadfast in all the virtues that lead to the love of God. ₂₀For the man who on his part abides firmly in what is within his ability shall be an associate in true preaching, in accordance with that high calling; and he shall be privileged as a confidant of the Creator's will, in accordance with the gift of prophecy.[5] ₂₁And being knowledgeable in the good news of the New Testament and in the (promise of) renewal unto life eternal, and in right faith, he should dedicate himself to the priestly grace through ordination—and that by the Spirit and the overseeing love of Christ; ₂₂*"to take off the old man ... and to put on the new, who is in the image of God, holy and just"* (Eph 4.22–24); ₂₃to take off every evil, through the grace of the (baptismal) font, and to enter, through the body and blood of Christ, into the inheritance of adoption by the heavenly Father[6] and into the number of the wise virgins and all saints, *"those who have crucified their bodies along with every passion"*—as the Apostle says, ₂₄*"for we should walk in the Spirit and should not fulfill the passions of the body"* (Gal 5.24, 16);[7] ₂₅and should thus put Satan to shame, the one who had dominion.[8] ₂₆For those snared by him could live by the Creator's grace. And those who through faithful warfare become virtuous in righteousness and sanctity and truth, pure and spotless, perfect in love that is in Christ, and able to endure perils patiently, they shall attain the good things promised by Christ.[9]

₂₇But those who did not accept the righteous laws of order and piety, and whose hearts have become dark with thoughtlessness, are given over by the accuser[10] unto reckless passions, wickedness,

---

5. Preaching/teaching as a spiritual gift is part of prophesying, in keeping with 1 Cor 14.3 rightly understood. See also Am 3.7, on prophets as God's confidants (cf. Jer 23.22).

6. Cf. §§29–30. Allusion to Rom 8.14–17, 23; Gal 4.1–7; Eph 1.5–6. The linkage of adoption to baptism and the Eucharist is found also in Disc. 5.45; 13.31–35; 14.17; cf. 2.129, 133; 3.17, where it is linked to baptism only.

7. Cf. Gal 5.25 ("Since we live by the Spirit, let us also be guided by the Spirit").

8. Allusion to Rom 6.12.

9. Attainment of the Christian virtues as requisite for obtaining the promises made by Christ is often described in terms of warfare against the forces of evil. The recurrent analogy with battle in this discourse and the next, and to a lesser degree in others (see "warfare" in the Subject Index), recalls its repeated use by Theodoret of Cyrrhus in his *Historia religiosa* (PG 82:1283–1496).

10. A recurring epithet for Satan; see Jb 1.9–11; Zec 3.1; 1 Pt 5.8; Rv 12.10.

pride, and every lawlessness. God has given them over unto the tortures of eternal death. ₂₈But the Creator's care does not leave his creatures without sustenance. Rather, because of his great love for humankind, he preached conversion and repentance for the remission of all sins, ₂₉so that we may again assume tearfully the cleansing of the (baptismal) font through faithful and true confession and repentance mingled with tears,[11] ₃₀so that the compassionate One may be merciful and grant the grace of adoption.[12] ₃₁From then on, being obedient to the (Creator's) benevolent will, one may fulfill all righteousness and cast off the evil habits together with every filthy and evil desire. And being freed from the bitter debt to hell, one may become an heir to the continuous care of the benevolent love of the Holy Trinity. Being admonished in virtue and holy life, one may inherit the Kingdom.

₃₂For when the first created man and woman yielded to the utter, falsely conceived machinations of the accuser[13] and were drawn to the attractions of the passions,[14] falsely thinking about becoming gods, they were deceived and did not observe the command of their Creator. They were driven from the comfort of the Garden and obtained death for inheritance, ₃₃for they were commanded beforehand to till and maintain the Garden through self-restraint, (a form) of fasting: to eat of certain fruits but not of others.[15] ₃₄In the same manner fasting is being preached to us nowadays: on which days to observe (a fast) and on which (days) not to observe, as has been legislated by the Prophets, the Apostles, and the holy Fathers, those who are close to God.[16] ₃₅For the one who honors the sancti-

---

11. The linking of tears with the Sacrament of Baptism is not as pronounced here as in John Climacus, according to whom tears surpass baptism—in that they wash away post-baptismal sin (*Ladder* 7).

12. See note to §23.

13. See note to §27.

14. Cf. Disc. 5.48, 81; 6.29, on the passions as Satan's snare for human downfall (syn. *c'ankut'iwn*).

15. Allusion to Gn 3.1–19; cf. §89, below. A similarly analogized interpretation is found in the second oration on Easter by Gregory Nazianzen, *Oratio 45: In sanctum Pascha,* 28 (PG 36:661B–C): "We were cast out because we transgressed. We fasted because we refused to fast, being overpowered by the Tree of Knowledge" (trans. Browne and Swallow, NPNF, ser. 2, 7.433).

16. Note especially Basil's homilies on fasting and Lent, *Peri nēsteias* (*De jejunio* [Hom. 1–2], PG 31:163–84, 185–98), echoed in the rest of the discourse. Cf. the

ty and the whole righteousness of the intelligible Garden shall abide innocently in the Garden of righteousness with plants of virtue, to enjoy them by the grace of the Giver of this life, and hereafter to move on to the one that defies description. ₃₆By referring to the latter, I do not mean the intelligible Garden but the one seen by the first man, that which the flaming sword concealed from us,[17] according to God's infinite wisdom. ₃₇(The Garden) has to be understood in a twofold way: one, sense-perceptible and visible; and the other, intelligible, pertaining to the virtues.[18]

₃₈Fasting is instructive to people, ₃₉just as the tutor instructs children to abstain from harmful things and to pursue those which are beneficial—not to be occupied with detrimental things through lack of self-restraint. ₄₀For this reason fasting has been set for us (as) deterrent to laxity of self-restraint (that leads) into all sorts of harms that sinfully mitigate against the soul and the body, so that we may pursue sanctity in the fear of God, that we may move on unto the inscrutable serenity that awaits those who fast. ₄₁Let us not be like the gluttons who *"sat down to eat and drink and arose to play"* (Ex 32.6)[19] and who perished altogether by the Lord's wrath, for they did not observe his commandments but cherished vain things in their thoughts and through insatiability despised the commandments regarding fasting. ₄₂They did not keep his commandments, but became weary in their thoughts and gluttonously violated the injunction to fast; they did not abide in the covenant nor did they believe the promised gifts, but provoked God's wrath; so he inflicted punishment on them and they perished. ₄₃Whereas those who brace themselves in persistent fasting and show earnestness in patience and self-restraint and observe the commandment of the Lord, exercising self-restraint during the ordained sacred fasts, in sanctity and in every good manner, they shall have the rest that is in Christ.

₄₄For us fasts are healers. For the one who lacks in self-restraint

---

Armenian version: *Barseł Kesaracʿi, Girkʿ pahocʿ*, ed. Kim Muradyan, Ekełecʿakan matenagrutʿyun 2 (Ējmiacin: Mayr Atʿoṙ, 2008), 54–79, 80–94. Equally noteworthy are the lengthy answers on self-restraint (Arm. *žužkalutʿiwn*), followed by counsel on foods, in *LR* 16–20 (Arm. 14–16); cf. Aphrahat, *Dem.* 3.

17. Allusion to Gn 3.24.

18. Following Philo of Alexandria in providing both literal and allegorical meanings; see *Questions on Genesis* 4.51, Paradise symbolizing the immortal virtues.

19. Cited also in Basil, *De jejunio hom.* 1.5 (PG 31:169C).

heaps harm upon his soul and body, indulging in diverse foods and amassing strange and licentious thoughts and (living) an impure life; however, he is renewed upon exercising self-restraint and fasting, is cleansed from the heaps of sin, and becomes a dwelling for holiness. ₄₅Fasting comes to grant us—who exercise self-restraint—medicine for health, to melt down the heaps of filth by the warmth of the Spirit's love, and to promote virtue. ₄₆Through fragrant life it dries out the stench and removes it from our midst; it grants healing to the sick, those who are defiled by sin. ₄₇And after healing, it points out sanctity and impeccable life to the person committed to taking a martyr's stand for sanctity. ₄₈Through sanctity and immaculate chastity it lifts up the one who has harmed himself by impure passions and indiscriminate excesses. Fasting always purges gluttony and roots out evil habits. ₄₉For by the grace of Christ, sin and the prince of sin are condemned; and those who truly confess and repent receive perfect health through the saving mystery (of the Eucharist).[20] Through fasting and prayer they are fortified against harms. ₅₀They thus receive the garland of victory, which is braided with praise and esteem for those who fast. ₅₁For the benefits and the regulating effects of fasting are numerous; and those who love and always observe it receive many personal benefits.

₅₂Fasting brings perfect assurance regarding the true faith, expectation from God, and hope of healing to those who manifest flawless, unsullied, and pure love for God's beneficence. ₅₃With such means it puts an end to licentious thoughts and overindulgence of the senses; it allows the eyes to see and the ears to hear, the tongue to speak and the hands to work, and the heart to be constant. Among those who observe the holy fast persistently, through moderation in eating, it roots out every inclination to the sensual passions; and through the radiance emanating from our love for God, it wakens from forgetting good deeds. ₅₄It makes one renounce the evil yoke of sin: fornication, gluttony, arrogance, envy, anger, greed, theft, lying, swearing, speaking evil of someone, depriving, treachery, rage, enmity, vindictiveness, laziness, contempt, mockery, drunkenness, and gossip; ₅₅to retreat from such deadly infractions through right confession and to take the medicine for

20. Cf. Disc. 6.38; 13.45, 66, 68; 15.59; 16.25.

life.[21] And being healed by the Spirit's love, to take a martyr's stand in the arena of virtue, directing one's life against harmful things; 56and being single-mindedly obedient to the benevolent will (of God), to stop every eruption of evil, 57to prevent constantly the evil and bitter activity of the mind and the senses. This is the culmination and the point of fasting that lead to the threshold of life, 58when inwardly strengthened by self-restraint and patience (that result) from fasting, by exercising caution and discernment, and by being admonished unto compassion and mercy toward the needy— both far and near—in view of the glory and sublimity of the universal judgment and the resurrection of the dead.

59Fasting exposes the hidden illnesses of the body. 60Just as the medicine for bile ailment exposes the ailment and cures it when taken, so does fasting expose sin. For when foods are reduced, the body rests and is purged. 61For following the body brings about the loss of the person, but (following) the spirit (brings) eternal life in the Lord. 62Fasting strengthens spiritual life and obscures physical restiveness, for when one is strengthened, the other is weakened. 63The flying ability of vultures is decreased because of indiscriminate eating, and they are easily caught and killed by hunters; but those that eat less fly away quickly and are not caught by scheming hunters. Gluttons and those who observe the holy fast are to be perceived similarly.

64The prophet Elijah admonishes us to fast persistently, he who fasted *"forty days and forty nights"* and shunned from himself every conceivable human activity; and becoming worthy of divine revelation, *"he was taken up to heaven in a fiery chariot"* (1 Kgs [3 Kgdms LXX] 19.8;[22] 2 Kgs [4 Kgdms LXX] 2.12). 65Likewise, Moses fasted *"forty days and forty nights,"* not once but thrice,[23] in order to take care of his needs and to stop—by fasting—God's wrath against the

---

21. Referring to the Eucharist, echoing Jn 6.54. Ignatius of Antioch (d. ca. AD 110) was first to describe the Eucharist as the "medicine of immortality" and the "antidote to death" (*To the Ephesians* 20.2; trans. Glimm et al., FC 1).

22. Cf. Basil, *De jejunio hom.* 1.6 (PG 31:172B–C).

23. Twice back-to-back, without food or water; the first, immediately before he received the tablets on the mountain and the second after coming down, seeing the Israelites practicing idolatry (Dt 9.7–21, 25). The third time was prior to his receiving the tablets again (Dt 10.10; cf. Ex 24.18; 34.28). Cf. Basil, *De jejunio hom.* 1.9 (PG 31:180B).

people who, *"eating and drinking, being at play"* (Ex 32.6), worshiped the calf's head and perished. ₆₆Also John, who throughout his life demonstrated the ultimate fasting. He neither ate nor drank any food prepared of what the earth produces, but met his needs in the desert, *"eating locusts and wild honey"* (Mt 3.4; cf. Mk 1.6).[24] ₆₇And being cleansed through fasting, he became the forerunner and witnessed the ineffable events narrated in the Gospel. ₆₈Our Lord, as well, after his baptism; he pressed on and waged war against the enemy by fasting in his body, commingled with divinity.[25] He thus taught people to be armed with fasting for the war against the enemy. And taking the martyr's stand by way of fasting, and in every virtue, he received grace for triumph and did triumph over the tempter. ₆₉Thus our Lord, who on the wings of the Spirit ascended to the right hand of the Majesty on high,[26] demonstrated to us the same warfare through fasting; ₇₀that we may cast away gluttony and all sensual pleasures that constitute the burden of sin, that we may become worthy to ascend on the wings of the Spirit and see the Lord of Glory[27] and hear (the words): *"Come, you blessed of my Father, inherit my Kingdom"* (Mt 25.34).[28]

₇₁Fasting gave opportunity for sanctity to all the saints, to transcend the world and to approach the angelic beings. ₇₂For those who are purified by fasting as by fire[29] shall not be harmed by the scorching fire, like the three young men in the furnace, whom fasting did purify.[30] ₇₃For fire engulfs the flammable things, but the one purified by fasting emanates greater light and delights by enlightening. ₇₄But those who were close to the fire were burnt like chaff, for they had not attained the purity that is through fasting.

---

24. Cf. Basil, *De jejunio hom.* 1.9 (PG 31:177C).

25. Cf. ibid. Allusion to Mt 4.1–11 (cf. Lk 4.1–13), here with a Miaphysite emphasis.

26. Allusion to Rom 8.34; Eph 1.20; Col 3.1.

27. Echoing 1 Cor 2.8.

28. The institution of the forty days' fast occurs in the fifth canon of the Council of Nicaea (325).

29. Purification by fire, a theme in the rest of the discourse, is a recurring biblical image (see Ps 66.10 [65.10 LXX]; Prv 17.3; 27.71; Zec 13.9; Mal 7.3; and 1 Pt 1.7).

30. Allusion to Dn 1.3–16; 3.1–30; cf. 10.2–3. Cf. Basil, *De jejunio hom.* 1.7 (PG 31:173B).

75Since fasting is the perfecting of the righteous, be they angelic or earthly beings, how much more beneficial it is for sinners who are (caught) in diverse passions. 76For the man purified through fasting saves himself from the stains of sin, being cleansed inwardly and outwardly, as gold and silver are purified and freed of their contaminants, thus becoming a precious and useful vessel for the owner; or as iron is shaped into objects for human use by experts, through intense and purifying fire. 77For the holy Apostles and the Prophets purified themselves first, through fasting and every sacred ordinance, and then proclaimed the faith and forthright living in all sanctity.[31] 78Those who by grace believed in Christ were purified and became an abode for the Divinity.[32] 79For the saints became fountains of fire and intoxicated all with the fire of the Spirit, through the purification of fasting,[33] in order to arrive at the destination to which they were called, which is in Christ.

80Fasting is the salt that preserves soul and body from the corrupting filth of sin; that savors through purity, in keeping with the sweet will of the Holy Spirit. Salt is taken from the earth to savor other things.[34] 81Fasting leads people to repentance and sets them on the straight (path); and following the ordinance of confession and establishment in fasting, sins are forgiven. 82Those who are indifferent about drawing near to the Lord through the purity of fasting are to be considered as dumb animals. 83Those who live in hope for the promised life are wise, but those who are bound to their hopeless delusions are foolish. 84Yet fasting is essential for both: fasting savors with purity—according to the Lord's pleasure—those who are perfect in knowledge, and sets those who are ignorant on (the path of) knowing the true faith. 85Fasting keeps unshaken those who live in purity, those who are impeccable; 86and brings to life those who are dead in sin, instilling them with all righteousness. 87Just as foods are flavored with salt and tenderized with fire for human consumption, so are the intentions of mind and body flavored through fasting—by the grace of the Spirit—and

31. Possible allusion to Acts 13.1–3 (see also the next note).

32. Echoing 1 Cor 3.16; 6.19; 2 Cor 6.16.

33. Possible allusion to Acts 1.14, which describes the Apostles praying (but not fasting) before Pentecost—invoked here (see Acts 2.1–4, 13).

34. A possible gloss.

dedicated to extolling the Lord; they exude peace. ₈₈For the Holy Spirit is at enmity with insatiable gluttony, defiant audacity, and unbridled drunkenness, those who give themselves up to the will of debauchery. ₈₉As lack of self-restraint brought curse and death to Adam and Eve,³⁵ so it does to their descendants who similarly lack in self-restraint and fall into uncontrollable craving for food. ₉₀But the Savior's fasting³⁶ and self-restraint lifted the enmity from their midst and reconciled God with humanity—those who believed in the life-giving proclamation that summoned people to newness of life through the Cross and voluntary suffering.³⁷

₉₁Fasting is a mighty bulwark and an impenetrable gate that protects from the harms emanating from our cunning enemy's mind.³⁸ ₉₂Let us not be intemperate like the sons of Eli, who stirred up God's wrath against them, their father, and the people of God.³⁹ ₉₃Let us exercise self-restraint like Samuel, who was reared with fasting since childhood and became first of the Prophets.⁴⁰ ₉₄Fasting quenches the ravaging fire of passion. Just as fire is quenched when fuel runs out, so the flame of passion is quenched when gluttony and drunkenness are diminished;⁴¹ conversely, sanctity and righteousness intensify by persistence in fasting. ₉₅Fasting dries out the uncleanness of masturbation. As the moist land dries out because of drought, so is the foul person made fragrant when cleansed from the loathsome filth of masturbation.⁴² ₉₆Fasting puts a stop to the fervent passion of youth, who are tormented by the enemy's activity. ₉₇Fasting halts the indecency caused by gluttony and drunkenness in the first place, and the body is rejuvenated in purity when fasting is introduced. ₉₈Fasting dissipates the restlessness of mind and body among those smudged in the murky

---

35. Allusion to Gn 3.1–19; see above, §§ 32–33.

36. Allusion to Mt 4.1–4; cf. Lk 4.1–4.

37. Based on Pauline theology; see Rom 5.10; 2 Cor 5.18; Col 1.22.

38. Cf. Basil, *De jejunio hom.* 1.9 (PG 31:180C), where fasting is a weapon against the armies of demons.

39. See 1 Sm (1 Kgdms LXX) 2.12–17.

40. As though implied in 1 Sm (1 Kgdms LXX) 2.26; cf. Basil, *De jejunio hom.* 1.6 and 2.6 (PG 31:172A, 193B), where Hannah's fasting was rewarded with her becoming Samuel's mother (apparently interpreting 1.18).

41. Cf. §111, below.

42. Cf. §104 and Disc. 19.74.

torrents of the passions and elevates the cleansed (souls) to the intelligible and intangible land.

99Fasting is a calm harbor from the sea-waves of filth and every harm, and leads to the haven of life, lest from gluttony and drunkenness one should perish unto death in the tempestuous sea of sin. 100When fasting is introduced, it brings peace to people and rest to servants and leads all to thoughtfulness, allowing them to think of things above that are in Christ. 101Fasting is a bridle for the insolent ones who freely do injustice. 102As when the bridle is placed in the mouth of a horse and the whole body is subdued, yielding to the will of the restrainer, so it is in the spiritual warfare. 103Those whose minds are preoccupied by just and sanctified thoughts, their senses have been refined[43] by law-abiding. One who does not fast persistently, however, is easily captured at the outset of the battle.

104The given counsel forewarns us more about meat and wine. For wine makes the senses and the mind more stupid, stirs up the passions, and pushes one into wickedness, especially the youth, and they resort to masturbation, stroking their body. 105Wine is sluggishness to the heart, dumbness to the mouth, darkness to the eyes, deafness to the ears, stillness to the hands, stumbling to the feet, madness to the mind, heaviness to sleep, enmity to uprightness. 106Wine rejects fear, puts aside respect, mocks the remembrance of the commandments, renounces the ministry of sacred love, leads astray from the right faith, erases from memory the fearful judgment, and does not allow one to think of death and the eternal torments.

107By saying this I do not prevent a little wine for the sick and feeble, following the Apostle's counsel, *"for the stomach's sake and for certain illnesses"* (1 Tm 5.23) of the feeble and the elderly. 108But those who are able and young in years should be cautious when it comes to meat and wine, lest they be captured easily by the incessant enemy, being hunted down by him to do his will. 109For wine and drunkenness defile perfect and wise men; and what need is there to speak about the physically and mentally immature? 110The flame of passion tortures and burns as with fire. Yet fire burns the body only, but meat and wine (burn) the soul by their stirring the

---

43. Lit., "have been shaped."

passions. ₁₁₁As fire is curtailed by the lack of fuel, so is passion by fasting. ₁₁₂So, if the youth eat, drink, and pass time without restrictions, let none expect them to have wholesome and pure thoughts; rather, passion will boil in gluttony; it will unleash its torrents and will consume with the love of filth whatever it finds, and will lead to its own sentence of sorrow and the like. *"For their worm,"* says the Prophet, *"does not die, nor does their fire go out; and they will become a spectacle to all flesh"* (Is 66.24). ₁₁₃Gluttons and drunkards will be severely punished,[44] those who persist in the same and defile themselves with all kinds of abominations.

₁₁₄True fasting rejects every passion, spiritual and physical, and pursues all righteousness. And those who wage battle against spiritual and physical (passions) ought to exercise self-restraint in order to have their sins forgiven. ₁₁₅Moreover, they ought to continue in the efforts for piety, in Christ Jesus our Lord, to whom be glory always. Amen.

44. Possible allusion to Dt 21.18–21; cf. Prv 23.21.

DISCOURSE 10

ON THE BENEFICENCE[1] OF THE GENEROUSLY BENEVOLENT WILL (OF GOD) AND ADMONITION UNTO GOODNESS AND BEYOND, IN ACCORDANCE WITH TRUE VIRTUE PRACTICED TO THE GLORY OF THE MOST HOLY TRINITY

HAVE received grace from the benevolence of the Holy Trinity's eternal Lordship, without beginning and immutable, the originator of all creatures in heaven and on earth—all creatures there. ₂In his omnipresent caring love he makes all drink commonly from his benevolent will; enabling rational beings to become heirs of his eternal blessings, ₃for us to become perfect, holy, and impeccable by keeping his commandments. Through sincere beneficence, cordial love, and right faith we become holy abodes of the Most Holy Trinity and continue our daily husbandry, all the more for the Creator's love, for the life and salvation of friends. To be studious and obedient to his benevolent will; and to demonstrate utter goodness commensurate with the spiritual law—being edified in hope, ₄having received the seed of his living counsel and returning it as a hundred seedlings.[2] Just as we were created by him, we are likewise being cared for by his grace. ₅As the good earth receives good seed and yields manifold seedlings, so let us bring forth, in keeping with his sovereign will, manifold yields from the counsel sown in us. For the selection[3]

1. The word երախտաւորութիւն (*eraxtaworut'iwn*, "gratitude") is a *hapax* in the discourses (cf. երախտաւոր կարգս [*eraxtawor kargs*] in Disc. 7.65). A more common word, երախտիք (*eraxtik'*, "beneficence") occurs but once here (§48), and sixteen times in Disc. 11, where it is developed further as a theme. On the prevalence of the theme, see the Subject Index.

2. Echoing Mt 13.8, 23.

3. The text has ընդրութիւնք (*ĕndrut'iwnk'*) for ընտրութիւնք (*ĕntrut'iwnk'*,

of the seedlings, whether good or bad, is up to the One who sees.

₆For those who love their friends in accordance with God's love become holy seedlings: to admonish some through spiritually beneficial means and others through good counsel, and to ward off the inimical things through the Spirit's love. ₇For (Scripture) says: *"Love does not boast, it is not arrogant, it is not haughty, it does not envy, it does not think evil of a friend but good, it bears all things, it endures all things. Love never alters the good for evil"* (1 Cor 13.4–5). ₈Love is foremost to all the Apostles and Prophets; it binds us one to another and to God. ₉(Scripture) says: *"You shall love the Lord your God wholeheartedly ... and your friend as yourself"* (Mt 22.37, 39). ₁₀*"For he who abides in love abides in God"* (1 Jn 4.16); ₁₁for to love one's friend is to love God. ₁₂Those who love their God-loving friends receive personal benefits from God; ₁₃but those who are overly selfish, drawing to themselves a friend's benefits, bring about deprivation, denial, malice, deception, swearing falsely, oppression, beating, murder. ₁₄For this reason he enacted laws through the Prophets and proclaimed them through the Apostles; and he counsels through the chief-priests and heirs of the Church to espouse wholesome thoughts of righteousness, sanctity, and justice; to conduct oneself in the freedom and the relief allotted here, in the hope of the Kingdom, and in thankfulness to God, in order to save oneself and one's family and household from punishments, to be blessed by the Lord, and to receive worthily the glorious and unfading crowns from Christ in the life to come.

₁₅Moreover, God appointed kings, princes, and judges for peace and constructiveness in the world, in order to scare the wicked—adulterers, thieves, magicians, and all unjust people—with diverse torments and death, so that all evil-doers, being struck with fear, would desist from evil. ₁₆There are, however, other similar—even greater—(doers of) injustices among them: those who multiply lawlessness through bribery or some other evil, daring to inflict harm. ₁₇And for this reason they open the gates to the wrath of famine, sword, slavery, and diverse deadly dangers, and hereafter the outer darkness mixed with fire, *"where there are weeping of eyes and gnashing of teeth"* (Mt 8.12).[4]

"choosing/election"), a rare dialectical variant; cf. the infinitive ընդրել (*ĕndrel*) for *ĕntrel*, §27. See also Disc. 15.7.

4. Cf. Mt 13.42, 50; 22.13; 24.51; 25.30; and Lk 13.28.

₁₈Whereas those who are considerate and judge justly become the cause of salvation and life to many, of well-being, peace, and constructiveness here, and their heads will be crowned with glory among multitudes of righteous people. ₁₉For they are the fountains of God's justice, whence life is granted to those who do good, and plagues and death (are given) to the unjust. ₂₀The light of knowledge derived from the divine Scriptures reveals the good reward for those who do good and the plagues of wrath for the unjust. ₂₁God's justice is shown on both sides: he glorifies the just ones who in (observing) the spiritual law are well-pleasing to his Lordship and abide in truth, in sanctity, and in all righteousness; who in the last day will be gloriously crowned in the universal court, before earthly and heavenly beings, with the light that does not pass away. ₂₂There too the unjust will be condemned to punishment with reviling, those who despised his commandments and did not observe sanctity and justice, leaving themselves hopeless. For this reason they inherit eternal torments.

₂₃From one's sovereign will various behaviors proceed, and from behaviors deeds; and those deeds are called either "evil" or "good" and are recompensed accordingly. ₂₄Good will generates goodness and obedience; and from obedience (comes) submission, and from submission love, and from love beneficence (shown) in many favorable, good things. ₂₅Similarly, from scorn, laziness, and disobedience diverse troubles are generated, and ingratitude for our Creator's favors. ₂₆The sovereign will of the mind causes these developments, making perceptible the imperceptible things, whether the good or its opposite, the bad.[5] ₂₇Blessed are those who choose and do good; the iniquitous are reprimanded so that they may have remorse and repent willingly, (acting upon the volition) of their sovereign mind, that they may find mercy's grace from the benevolent Lord, who has compassion for his creatures and does not deprive them of his caring love. ₂₈He grants countless and ineffable favors to those who ask of him. He is the Giver of gifts to those *"who cry out to him day and night"* (Lk 18.7); and in accordance with the blessings of the Gospel,[6] he invites us to his Kingdom and glory, so that by

5. Cf. Disc. 7.44–49, the two-ways of the dualism associated with apocalyptic thought.

6. Or, "the Beatitudes" of the Sermon on the Mount (Mt 5.3–12), expounded

truly following the injunctions of Christ we may inherit the blessings.

₂₉The Lord says: *"Blessed are the poor in spirit, for theirs is the Kingdom of Heaven"* (Mt 5.3). They are the ones who, for the sake of the
Gospel,[7] became poor in the spirit willingly, threw away the burdensome material greatness, and with spiritual hope put on the everlasting greatness. ₃₀They fulfilled the Lord's will through purity
in mind and body, sincere faith, and love. They steered, as wise
captains, the body's ship over the world's stormy waves. Dumping
the heavy burdens of the world into the sea and taking off in the
spirit, they reached the harbor of peace. ₃₁For this reason those who
have become poor in the spirit are blessed. Having traversed with
spirit and truth all the dangers of this world, they kept themselves
from evil desires, from the love of glory and possessions. ₃₂Though
they were subject to every passion, they rid themselves from them
all for the sake of the ineffable blessedness that is reserved for those
who have hope in Christ, who for our sake became truly poor,[8]
the One who is the Lord of Glory.[9] ₃₃Those who look up to the
course of the beneficent One's voluntary poverty may thus reach
the abodes of life, the gate of salvation, the blessedness that does
not change, the fullness of sweet blessedness.[10]

₃₄*"Blessed are the meek, for they will inherit the earth"* (Mt 5.5). ₃₅By
"earth" he conveys the good news about the Church, those who
live their purposeful lives calmly, safe from a host of unsettling
temptations.[11] ₃₆Those who war against every hardship remain

---

in the sequel (§§29–73). The exposition has some common or stock elements found
also in Gregory of Nyssa's *De beatitudinibus* (PG 44:1193–1301); e.g., the "poverty"
in the first Beatitude being that "in evil" or "in vice," contrasted with the "riches
in virtue."

7. Lit., "the good news."

8. Allusion to 2 Cor 8.9.

9. Echoing 1 Cor 2.8.

10. The renunciation of property and possessions on the basis of this beatitude
is quite radical and rare. The same appeal is made by Basil (*LR* 8) on the basis of
Mt 16.24, a passage neither quoted nor alluded to in the discourses.

11. No patristic commentary known to me has this direct interpretation of "the
earth" in Matthew (cf. Disc. 17.27, on definition of "Church"). The association,
however, of "the earth" with the Church is not altogether remote when considering patristic commentaries that see the Edenic earth of Gn 2.5–6, 8–9, as an allegory on Mary and/or the Church. The promised earth is usually "the earth that is

unshaken at all times. ₃₇Those who through meekness calm down every hurtful burst of anger and rage directed at them and others:[12] whatever is full of blame, malice, prejudice, mischief, dishonor, shamefulness, and diverse troubles. ₃₈Meekness truly leads to all righteousness, chastity, sanctity, steadfast love, and true faith. ₃₉On earth (we ought) to dwell by the grace of meekness and to blossom in every virtue, being adorned with the sweet aroma of meekness, and to anticipate with hope the eternal, unchanging, immortal, and life-giving blessings.

₄₀*"Blessed are those who mourn, for they will be comforted,"* he says (Mt 5.4). ₄₁They are those who have received grace from the Spirit, which is from God: the desirable love, tearfully requested. The mourner who longs to see by grace the ineffable things that are given to the saints cannot depart from God. ₄₂By "mourners" we may also understand the remorseful: those who turn away with sincere confession from wretched lives and with tears ask daily for forgiveness of sins from the Lord of All; that they may be able to reach the abodes of life that are full of immortality, that they may inherit with the true mourners that blessedness of booming joy, which is eternal comfort.

₄₃*"Blessed are those who hunger and thirst for righteousness, for they will be filled"* (Mt 5.6). ₄₄They are those who are invited to the spiritual wedding, that they may enjoy the good things; those who greatly desire to be filled with righteousness. ₄₅Just as those who are hungry and thirsty come to satisfy their needs with desirable roasted meats and drinks, those who long for the divine delights strive duly to attain the desirable and delightful food that lasts forever, prepared blessedly for the righteous in the Kingdom, ₄₆who forever enjoy the abundant and unending good things already garnered in the storerooms of eternal life.

₄₇*"Blessed are those who weep now, for they will laugh"* (Lk 6.21). ₄₈They are those who desire to abstain from earthly pleasures, from greed,

---

above" or "the celestial regions," as in Gregory of Nyssa's *De beatitudinibus* (Hom. 2, PG 44:1208C–1217D). John Chrysostom criticizes such interpretations. For him the blessing of the meek is not merely heavenly but earthly as well; *In Matthaeum* (Hom. 9, PG 56:679–684, here 681).

12. Cf. Basil's *Adversus iratos* (Hom. 10.7; PG 31:370B–372B; trans. Wagner, *Ascetical Works,* FC 9:459–61); see also Disc. 6.33; 11.64, 86; 18.32; 19.40; 23.2.

from evil desires, and who with warm tears, self-flagellation, and many painful discomforts strive for union with God.[13] For as a result of the Benefactor's sacred, impeccable, and immaculate beneficence they wish to arrive at the Lord's joy, to enjoy the delightful rest of his sacred love, to fulfill their long desire for God. For they constantly ask with tears for the blessedness of the grace of adoption,[14] which is replete with ineffable joy to the glory of the Deity.

₄₉*"Blessed are the merciful, for they will find mercy"* (Mt 5.7). ₅₀In their acts of mercy they resemble God. They receive succoring strength from the divine strength, in that they show mercy to all by guidance, teaching, helping those in distress, satisfying the needy in their spiritual and physical needs; ₅₁that they may receive good things from God's gracious mercy here on earth and bountiful gifts to come, which are replete with every blessedness that God has prepared for the merciful.

₅₂*"Blessed are the pure in heart, for they will see God"* (Mt 5.8). ₅₃They are the ones who, by the grace of God, through faith and truth, sanctity and righteousness, have wiped away every stain of evil desires from their body and mind. ₅₄And with pure thoughts and immaculate bodies they gaze into the glory of the Lord, into the comprehensible divine light seen through the intellect as through a mirror.[15] ₅₅Had they been defiled by the corrosion of sin, by evil desires, evil thoughts, and evil deeds, without having their thoughts and senses cleansed to gaze at the divine rays that are from Christ, the Sun of Righteousness, they would not have been able to behold

13. Craving for union with God is a major mystic/ascetic endeavor. Cf. Disc. 2.37, 140, on being/becoming divine.

14. Allusion to Eph 1.5–6 (cf. Rom 8.14–17, 23; Gal 4.1–7). Cf. §§88, 154; Disc. 2.46; 3.16; 6.17; 9.30 (on adoption as grace). Prayer with tears, introduced at Disc. 5.40, 42, is a recurring subject in the remaining discourses (see the Subject Index); it reminds one of the Evagrian recommendation that one begin with tearful prayer in order to "calm the wildness within the soul" and to obtain the gift of forgiveness (*On Prayer,* 5–7). Cf. *The Book of Steps: The Syriac Liber Graduum,* trans. Robert A. Kitchen and Martien F. G. Parmentier, CSS 196 (Kalamazoo, MI: Cistercian Publications; Edinburgh: Alban, 2004), esp. its Disc. 18. For more, see Irénée Hausherr, *Penthos: The Doctrine of Compunction in the Christian East,* trans. Anselm Hufstader, CSS 53 (Kalamazoo, MI: Cistercian Publications, 1982); and *Evagrius of Pontus: The Greek Ascetic Corpus (Chapters on Prayer),* trans. Robert E. Sinkewicz, OECS (Oxford: Oxford University Press, 2003).

15. Echoing 1 Cor 13.12.

the great light of the Most Holy Trinity, who causes the comprehensible things to rise and enlightens those who are pure in heart
and immaculate in members (of the body). ₅₆For they inherit the
blessedness of immortal life that is given to those who perceive it by
faith in Christ Jesus.

₅₇*"Blessed are the peacemakers, for they will be called children of God"* (Mt
5.9). ₅₈They are those who are coworkers with the Son of God, who
made peace and reconciled the Father with the creatures. ₅₉For the
one who renounces evil throngs, agitation, anger, and evil desires,
and makes peace through love, such a person has the basis of the
rational, spiritual peace in Christ.[16] ₆₀For as the Son of God took
away the turmoil that besets people because of sin and preached
the Good News of peace, he likewise tells us to become peacemakers, so that we may become his brothers, resembling the Peacemaker. ₆₁For whoever becomes a peacemaker among the great or
the little ones for the sake of God and the salvation of people, and
removes the harmful enmity against soul and body, shall find conciliation and peace and shall inherit the name and the glory of the
Son of God, along with utmost goodness, (as) a holy, pure, and immaculate peacemaker in Christ. He shall be considered great and
honored here, and hereafter shall be elevated and glorified in the
peaceful blessedness in Christ.

₆₂*"Blessed are those who are persecuted because of righteousness, for theirs is
the Kingdom of Heaven"* (Mt 5.10). ₆₃These words point to the assembly
of witnesses and all the virtues. For those who are altogether alien
to and untouched by these earthly things and causes that affect
many, unscathed by the harmful passions, they are the ones, persecuted by the evil one, who resort to God in faith for the sake of
proclaiming the Gospel's truth. ₆₄As the Apostle says: *"Everyone who
wants to live a godly life in Christ Jesus will be persecuted, for evil men and
magicians will come forward to mislead into evil"* (2 Tm 3.12–13). ₆₅The
saints are persecuted by the evil one for the good they do for God's
(sake) and with God's (help), lest they be like the prodigal son who
was deceived by demons to depart from paternal care, to waste his
sacred gifts prodigally.[17] ₆₆Rather, they are the ones who return to

16. The synonymity of the "spiritual" (Gk. *pneumatikos*) and the "rational" (Gk.
logikos) has its basis in classical philosophy; cf. 1 Cor 14.14–15, on the association of
mind/reason and spirit.

17. Allusion to Lk 15.11–32.

the paternal care, away from the pursuit of evil-lovers, demons, and (evil) people; that by being persecuted they may attain the promised good things of the Kingdom, be crowned with that ineffable blessedness to the glory of the almighty Lord God.

67*"Blessed are you,"* he says, *"when people insult you, revile you, and falsely say all kinds of evil against you because of me. Rejoice and be glad, because great is your reward in heaven"* (Mt 5.11–12). 68Glory and honor are given to God for the good accomplished by all who take their stand as martyrs for Christ, who wage war against the enemy of truth. 69It is beneficial for all who are engaged in the conflict to wait patiently for God's will, that they may receive the promised good things now and in the hereafter.[18]

70*"For in the same way they persecuted the prophets who were before you"* (Mt 5.12), he says of those who inherited (such) a name and spirit through much patience. 71Some were unharmed like iron; some[19] were strong like a bronze wall; others were like silver, refined and purified as through the fire of trials. 72Others, still, were honored like golden utensils, or like beautiful pearls, or like precious gems used for the glory of kings. 73Likewise the saints and those who were patiently formed by trials and tribulations became the Creator's witnesses—to the glory of the immortal King.

74Just as the respective assemblies of witnesses, confessors, virgins, and the restrainedly married differ, so do the various gifts[20] deservedly distributed as determined by the Lord of All, who takes into consideration the thoughts, words, and deeds of everyone. 75Those who suffer, resisting the evil passions, and triumph—with truth and impeccable faith—over every harmful thing will receive the martyrs' crown, for they fulfill the Lord's word that says: *"Take up your cross daily and follow me"* (Lk 9.23).[21] 76For the cross mortifies the filth of the flesh and of raucous life, as the saints *"crucified their*

18. Martyrdom as part of a cosmic conflict between the forces of good and evil in Judaism and early Christianity has its roots in 2 Maccabees and Daniel; cf. Rv 6.9–11.

19. Lit., "half."

20. Echoing 1 Cor 12.4.

21. Moral achievement with reliance on God is often equated with the fidelity of a martyr, the words "endurance" and "martyrdom" becoming almost equivalents. Illustrative of this notion from Maccabean times is the title "martyr," given to St. Gregory the Illuminator and other valorous saints of the early Church.

bodies with the desires and the passions" (Gal 5.24). To this the Apostle bears witness.[22] 77As they (endured) diverse tortures, so those (martyrs endure) temptations. For like good combatants, all who (endure) severe afflictions when engaged in spiritual warfare do not suffer defeat. The granted victory is demonstrated clearly to the glory of God.

78Bishops, priests, deacons, and readers who persevere[23] in virginity are rewarded according to their abundance or deficiency in virtue. 79Also solitaries and those in holy matrimony; though they differ in their (respective) lives, yet each will (reap) the fruit of one's life, as it will surely be demonstrated on the last day, which is the resurrection from the dead. 80Also those who pretend[24] to be true; justice will be revealed with the facts. 81Also those who are not holy, those who receive bribes, those who are bloodthirsty, pleasers of men, and those who try to cover up their many stains. 82The Lord says: *"There is nothing concealed that will not be revealed, or hidden that will not be known"* (Mt 10.26). 83For the saints and the just will surely be revealed in the company of those who truly suffered scorn, enmity, and much tribulation without straying from the truth. 84They have received, even here, the blessedness of the authentic hope. Surely grief passes away, but the blessings of the promised good things remain forever. 85For here they obtained freedom, and there they will inherit the Kingdom. 86For because of their overall goodness, their good lives, they have received the pledge of blessings, which is the assurance of redemption,[25] whether in things seen or in things unseen, in what could be described or in what is beyond description. 87The Word, the Son, says to the Father: *"As you and I are one ... may those who believe in us be so (also)"* (Jn 17.11b, 21a). 88For to his own he gives the grace of adoption by the Father,[26] and he makes his holy ones his heirs.

89For he gave us light for the eyes and counsel for the mind that we may be wakeful and alert, to be led by the light of life[27] and

---

22. None other than Paul (cf. Rom 6.6; Gal 2.20; 6.14).
23. Or, "who take a martyr's stand"; cf. §75.
24. Lit., "wrongly claim."
25. See 2 Cor 1.22 and 5.5; cf. Eph 1.13–14; 2 Tm 1.14.
26. See note to §48.
27. Allusion to Jn 8.12.

spiritual counsel to every good deed and to remain holy and righteous by the attainable light. ₉₀For the spiritual counsel of the Holy Scriptures gives knowledge about true life and admonishes unto spiritual realms. ₉₁For whoever thinks of material things that are here, and dwells upon these physical things that were mentioned, corrupts both the mind and the body's senses. ₉₂But if one thinks of spiritual things, of holy things that are influenced by the Holy Spirit, and thinks of spiritual life and strives for the fullness of virtue, by the grace of the Spirit he shall enjoy what is neither describable nor heard of; for he is spiritual and intelligent,[28] and he alone would know, for they affect him.

₉₃And one should knowingly draw near to this grace, mindful of sanctity and intent on abiding in these delightful enjoyments. He should scorn the lust for beauty; with enlightened thoughts he should reject the evil onslaught of dark thoughts. ₉₄He should rise early in prayer, petitioning with warm tears and strictly fasting for strength, waiting at the gates of mercy. ₉₅He should overcome and rise above all earthly stirrings and influences, and should take a firm hold of the spiritual benefits that are pleasing to God. ₉₆He should follow the Apostle's word of counsel: *"To look up, to think of things above, where Christ is seated at the right hand of the Father."* As he says: *"For you died, and your life is hidden with Christ in God the Father"* (Col 3.1–3). ₉₇Having cast aside all earthly cares that obscure the spiritual and heavenly calling, like laborers (ready) for husbandry and soldiers armed for battle, we should steadily advance in the battle for virtue and become valiant, so that we may be able to defeat the armies of evil: the passions, arrogance, greed, and similar calamities inflicted by the evil one. ₉₈For by becoming like the faithful servant, we may enter into the joy of the Lord,[29] to receive the blessedness that is in Christ, who is the believers' Life.

₉₉For the audacious and defiant cannot approach his light, for they do not walk in the path of righteousness that leads to life, nor do they take into heart the counsel of the wise and of the divine Scriptures. Rather, they let counsel fall like the wind in a trap.

28. Equating *pneumatikos* and *logikos,* given the synonymity of *pneuma* and *logos* in classical Greek thought and—to some extent—in Paul's epistles; cf. Rom 12.1, 11; 1 Cor 2.10–16.

29. Allusion to Mt 25.21, 23.

100For this reason the Lord says: *"Do not give dogs what is sacred, nor cast the pearl to pigs"* (Mt 7.6). 101He adds: *"A good man brings good things out of the heart's good treasures, and an evil man lets out evil"* (Mt 12.3). 102For the sovereign will moves everyone's will, whether unto goodness or unto badness. 103For this reason the Apostle says: *"Renounce the wicked person after three warnings"* (Ti 3.10). 104And David does not allow the sinner to recite the Law, the person who hates counsel and casts behind him the rightful things established by God.[30] 105(The Lord) rebukes severely those who talk about the Law but do not practice it, who hear and despise.[31] 106All Scripture is for counseling and rebuking.[32] Those who preach salvation through faith garner it themselves.[33] 107Just as those who win in difficult battles rejoice much, those who win in spiritual warfare rejoice even more.

108Whether rich or poor, each has a sovereign will to incline toward either good or bad. 109The poor person is enriched with glory, which is attained through sinlessness and every virtue. 110The rich, pure and unsullied people who support those who suffer, are similarly (enriched). Poverty (cleanses) the innocent as the furnace fire purifies gold, and uplifts him to the honor of God's glory, to the greatness of heaven.[34] 111Thus those who endure poverty with patience and self-restraint, without complaining, will become great. 112Also the rich who care for and compassionately provide sustenance to the needy will inherit immortality, glory, and honor that do not pass away. 113If, however, those who suffer poverty resort to injustice and outright lawlessness, adultery, theft, wickedness, lying, and all kinds of vice, they will receive punishment on earth and endless affliction in the hereafter. 114But the rich who deprive the needy of their needs and go on living in debauchery and drunkenness, death comes to them, says the Lord, of which they are unaware: *"He will cut him out of life and will assign him a place with the unbelievers"* (Lk 12.45; cf. Mt 24.51), in the fire of hell that never goes

30. Allusion to Ps 50.16; cf. 10.5.

31. Allusion to Mt 23.3.

32. Allusion to 2 Tm 3.16. The author's devoted submission to the authority of Holy Scripture is discernible throughout the discourses. Scripture is the basis of his counsel everywhere. Cf. Disc. 12.67: "the Scriptures are our teachers."

33. Echoing Eph 2.8.

34. Echoing Mt 5.3.

out; for he was given to wickedness and did not give justly to the poor any of the wealth given him by God. ₁₁₅Both will be dealt with justly by the Judge, according to their good or evil deeds.

₁₁₆Health also has its advantages and disadvantages. Those who are physically healthy and pursue spiritual health, being diligent in piety, their labor will be rewarded with that rest that does not pass away. But the lazy (will reap) the disadvantages: the punishment of restlessness in the hereafter. ₁₁₇Likewise, those who are physically sick but spiritually healthy, being patient and thankful to God, cleansed of all sin, maintaining hope in God, and having placed their trust in him whether in death or in life, will receive God's blessing and perfect health. Pain and sadness and groaning will be dissipated. In any case, they will receive their reward as deserved.

₁₁₈Likewise, rulers who administer earthly affairs are of two kinds. There are those who are mindful of God and do not leave out his will from their mind, and who personally possess sanctity and chastity and pursue all things rightly and appropriately, doing justice to all. ₁₁₉And those in administrative duties should live amiably. (Scripture) says: *"For there is no authority except from God, and those that exist are by God"* (Rom 13.1). ₁₂₀Each will receive one's reward from the righteous Judge, both rulers and those who are ruled, for all have one Lord who is just, and he either punishes or glorifies when he comes in the glory of the Father to judge the earth. ₁₂₁Those who are righteous and are oppressed will be rewarded by the righteous Judge with many good things. ₁₂₂Whereas those who are sinful and oppress[35] will be rewarded according to their indebtedness to sin, those who despised the word of God and did not repent. For all of us earthlings will be rewarded according to our thoughts, words, and deeds. ₁₂₃For the mighty and the weak, everyone, will appear before the tribunal of Christ. Those who did good things will have eternal life in the hereafter.[36] Those who defied truth and did evil will live in endless affliction.

₁₂₄Similarly, overseers and those overseen[37] have their advan-

---

35. Read լլկեն (*llken*) for լլկին (*llkin*, "are oppressed"; *sic* in §121).

36. Following the variant reading: անդր (*andr*).

37. Arm. վերակացութիւնք և որք ընդ վերակացութեամբ են (*verakac'ut'iwnk' ew ork' ĕnd verakac'ut'eamb en*), lit., "overseeing positions and those in overseeing positions"; and in §§125 and 129 որ զվերակացութիւնն ունի / առեալ

tages and disadvantages.[38] [125]The one entrusted with oversight, who submits in obedience to God's commands in things seen and unseen, who is holy and pure, has God as his guide in upright thoughts and considers himself an adjunct of the Lord. Such a person will be led to all righteousness, to endless oversight with the Seraphim and the Cherubim and the heavenly powers in God's service.[39] [126]For the Apostles, the Prophets, and the holy priests received authority from the Lord and became guardians[40] of the truth. [127]What they bind on earth is bound in heaven, and what they pardon on earth is pardoned in heaven.[41] [128]The Savior has given this grace to all saints.[42]

[129]Should anyone entrusted with oversight glut himself[43] or be apathetic, become proud in his ruling splendor and carry out the superior's role as he wills and not according to God's will, or doubt the hope that is in Christ, he shall be thrown into tribulations and

---

զվերակացութիւն (or zverakac'ut'iwnn uni / aťeal zverakac'ut'iwn), lit., "one who holds the overseeing position" / "one entrusted with overseeing position" (or, "one entrusted with oversight"). The word վերակացութիւն (verakac'ut'iwn) is used interchangeably with առաջնորդութիւն (aťajnordut'iwn) in §129 (cf. Disc. 23.55), just as the word վերակացու (verakac'u, lit., "overseer") is used repeatedly and interchangeably with առաջնորդ (aťajnord, lit., "leader" or "guide") for the superior or abbot in Disc. 23 (28, 33, 44, 47, 50, 52, 55, 58, 64, 68, 76, 88, 91, verakac'u; 19–20, [27], 35–37, 46, [51], 56–57, 61, 115, aťajnord). The latter term is used also for God in §129 (cf. 22.26, God as verakac'u); viz., that the superior has God as his Superior. The interchangeable terminology—as the sequel seems to suggest—also reflects a period when a superior's monastic authority was considered no less than that of a bishop's pastoral authority. It is important to point out that the interchangeableness of the terms indicated here is similar to their interchangeableness in the Armenian translation of Basil's *Rules*, where both verakac'u and aťajnord invariably refer to the superior.

38. Or, "calamities."

39. Cf. Pseudo-Dionysius's parallel hierarchies: the triad of angelic hierarchies: Seraphim, Cherubim, and Thrones (*The Celestial Hierarchy* 7.1–2), and its counterpart on earth in the triad of ecclesiastical orders: Bishops (hierarchs), Presbyters, and Deacons (*The Ecclesiastical Hierarchy* 5.7). Hence the association of the *episkopos* (lit., "overseer") with "the first of those who behold God" (ibid. 5.5). See also Disc. 20.85–86, 91–93, 96, 154; 23.100.

40. Arm. վերակացուք (verakac'uk').

41. Allusion to Mt 16.19; 18.8.

42. A likely gloss. The assurance of forgiveness, as reward for confession, is given by the superior (Disc. 23.19, 93).

43. Read յղփասցի (yłp'asc'i, as in the Venice ed. of 1954 and the Ējmiacin ed. of 1894) for յզփասցի (yzp'asc'i), a misprint.

shall be cut down irreparably. ₁₃₀Such was the sad case of Satan, who, straying from the Lord, fell down from the heights and the luminous ranks, and his downfall is irreparable. ₁₃₁The Lord says: *"I saw Satan fall from heaven"* (Lk 10.18),⁴⁴ the leader of demons with his followers, who became the adversary of the saints and virtuous people, ₁₃₂those who received authority from the Lord to dilute his venom, as that of serpents and scorpions, rendering it ineffective.⁴⁵ ₁₃₃Those who follow his will and rebel against truth shall receive the same punishment. ₁₃₄For the stability of the world and the Church is through the good will of righteous rulers and holy leaders, for through them justice prevails on earth and holiness is upheld. ₁₃₅They are rewarded with good things for their good deeds. Quite opposite is the case of the evil ones who did not walk in (obedience to) God's laws. ₁₃₆Wisdom confronts both those who live godly lives and those (who live) without God. ₁₃₇The one who rules wisely and *"who meditates on the Law of the Lord day and night"* (Ps 1.2) becomes cause for the redemption of many. Such is *"the wisdom that comes from above: pure and peace-loving, full of goodness and the fruit of righteousness"* (Jas 3.17).⁴⁶

₁₃₈But the cunning person is like the accuser:⁴⁷ filled with wickedness, atrocity, envy, strife, malice, and hatred toward God;⁴⁸ one who finds and rekindles evil. Such a person shall be punished in the fire of hell, which is prepared for Satan and those entrapped by him, (caught) in his will.⁴⁹ ₁₃₉It is better for those in a ruling position to pursue the virtues than to persist in their obstructive rule. For (Scripture says): *"From one who has been given much, much will be required"* (Lk 12.48). ₁₄₀Blessed are those who are orderly in their lives, obediently abiding by the testimony of the Holy Scriptures. ₁₄₁They have given of their earnings to the needy, unhesitatingly, sufficiently, and always. They have remained genial and in impeccable purity, enticed by nothing contrary to good deeds. And being

44. Cf. Is 14.12–15, part of the oracle against the king of Babylon, whose downfall acquired a history of interpretation as Satan's falling like a star from heaven (see Rv 8.10; 9.1; 12.7–9).

45. Echoing Mk 16.18.

46. Cf. Phil 1.11.

47. A recurring epithet for Satan; see Jb 1.9–11; Zec 3.1; 1 Pt 5.8; Rv 12.10.

48. Allusion to Rom 1.29.

49. Allusion to Mt 25.41.

freed from servitude to sin, being always on the side of holiness and righteous living, they have left a praiseworthy remembrance here, and in the hereafter they will receive eternal glory and honor that do not pass away. 142For it is the will of the Benefactor that everyone should be benevolent and heir to the good things that are endless, that are hoped for.

143God is the source of all good things; he makes the believers drink of every good gift they long for with sanctity. 144And he is Life, the Giver of life that lasts forever; and he bestows life on all his creatures. 145And he is benevolent toward all, the one who from his grace grants forgiveness to those who repent from evil. 146And he is the one who enlightens every man who wishes to flee from the darkness of sin unto the holy light. 147And with his Truth he is near to those who embark with holiness on the journey toward the truly good things. 148And nothing will be withheld from them, whether from above or from within; for by his almighty power he sustains all creatures, heavenly and earthly. 149And he knows the thoughts of human beings and remembers their every deed and rewards as deserved. 150For he says: *"I myself am God, and there is no other. I put the sinner to death, and I bring the righteous to life"* (Dt 32.39), and no one could sever his creatures from him.

151There are those whom he admonishes through threatening perils, those who behave wickedly; and there are those whom he admonishes graciously unto good things—even unto the inheritance of glory, those who approach the Divinity with faith and fear and pure love. And being cleansed of sin by the grace of his benevolence, they acknowledge[50] the grantor of good things. 152Those who believe, he calls his people, for they ask[51] him for mercy and do his will. 153He calls us servants, for we cordially, with pure love and holy living, fulfill his will. 154He also calls us children, so that we enjoy the fatherly care and never through unholy living depart from adoption.[52] 155For the Lord is holy and dwells in those who are holy. For he calls the saints his brothers, saying: *"I will declare your name to my brothers; in the midst of the congregation I will praise you, Father"* (Ps 22.22 [21.23 LXX]). 156And again he says: *"When I am lifted up, I*

50. Lit., "we acknowledge."
51. Lit., "we ask."
52. See note to §48.

will draw all to myself" (Jn 12.32). ₁₅₇For the Son of God came to save the human race and to make those who believe in him rejoice; for we were made by him and were saved by him, and to him we shall go, to the One who has invited us and has called us to his Kingdom and to glory,[53] to incorruptible life, endless and unlimited. Some he himself (has called), others through the Apostles, the Prophets, and spiritual teachers, for he wishes that all may become heirs of the life that does not end, to the glory of the Most Holy Trinity—now, always, and forever and ever. Amen.

53. Echoing 1 Pt 5.10.

DISCOURSE 11

ON THE VIRTUOUS LIFE
CROWNED WITH UTMOST GOODNESS BY
THE BLESSED ONE[1]

HE HOLY TRINITY admonishes with grace to excel in every goodness, courage, and virtue; for he is the Giver, the Grantor of success to heavenly and earthly beings, the One who (chooses as his) disciples those who are intimate believers, holy and dear to him. ₂And those who have excelled, being inducted into the luminous orders, shine like lit lanterns in the world. For the Lord says: *"You are the light of the world, and your light enlightens people. For when they see your good deeds, they will glorify your Father who is in heaven"* (Mt 5.14–16). ₃And sending them like enlighteners, he tells them to go about in the world, to bear the word of life[2] for their own admonition and to benefit many. ₄Through them he spreads throughout the world the radiant beams of the word of life regarding truth and calls on believers to partake of his benevolent will—of the living glory of the Uncreated One, so that creatures may become heirs of the Creator's Kingdom and the ineffable joy of the promised good things.

₅The saints were gratified with such hope. By the will of the Creator they withstood every hardship prompted by the evil one. By the grace of Christ they thwarted the incitements of mind and

---

1. This longest discourse on the rewards of virtue deals with the benefits of faith, hope, and love (§§1–61); meekness (§§62–99); kindness, humility, and obedience (§§100–123); unity in faith and accord in living a holy life (§§124–131); compassion (§§132–139); thoughtfulness or discretion and the control of the senses (§§140–227; cf. the diatribe against the wrongful use of the senses in Disc. 20.23–55). At §132, the author employs the rather rare first-person-singular pronoun in his announcement of turning to a different subject.

2. Allusion to Phil 2.16; 1 Jn 1.1.

body, through immaculate sanctity, ceaseless prayer, warm tears, and thorough self-restraint by fasting; they restrained greed, gluttony, indecency, prodigality, defiance, and such evils. ₆They kept open the gates of mercy, the remembrance of Christ's love.[3] They were admonished in every goodness and became worthy of redemption, of the grace and gifts of the Holy Spirit, attested by utmost goodness: pure love and intimate faith when in hardship and in peace. ₇They kept their minds clear and pure, also their senses, (occupied) in all truthfulness, ₈never harboring deceit or duplicitous thoughts, unbelief, or unholy behavior, which are the causes of perdition. ₉Rather, they always cherished luminous sanctity, because of the impeccable beneficence of his sacred love; that they may blossom into a life (filled) with love for the virtues and be crowned with the eternal hope of praising God's glory. ₁₀Cleansed by the fire of the Holy Spirit, they became dwellings on earth for the Most Holy Trinity. ₁₁For sanctity is the adornment of all the virtues and the fundamentals (of faith), in things visible and invisible, spiritual and physical. ₁₂Of all things just and courageous, sanctity is always the glorious garland and crown. ₁₃Sanctity is the glory, honor, and praise to all the heavenly and earthly ranks, for it draws us to Christ our God and to the whole hosts of heaven. ₁₄Sanctity is a luminous robe and the root of goodness, for it establishes in enlightened life—in holiness—those who in truth and in unison praise God's glory: the incorporeal ranks, those who are truly united in their praise of God's glory.[4] For this reason they are the ministers of the Most Holy Lordship.

₁₅Thus were the Apostles empowered to appoint those who are saintly to the ministry of God's Church, so that they may become associates of angels, ministers of Christ's (Eucharistic) sacrifice.[5] ₁₆For as the soul abides in the body and enables it to grow in stature, so does the rational Spirit scrutinize everyone and separate

3. Arm. յիշատակ սիրոյն Քրիստոսի (*yišatak siroyn Kʻristosi*); cf. §20, "the remembrance sacrament" (*yišatak srputʻeann*), i.e., the *Anamnesis* of Christ's atoning sacrifice; see also Disc. 3.23 and note. On the implications of the Eucharist for philanthropy, see further below, §§76–77 and 127; also note to Disc. 13.45. For more, see "Eucharist" in the Subject Index.

4. Cf. Disc. 2.9.

5. Cf. Disc. 20.91, 149, 154.

those who are good from those who are evil. [17]Such is also the true faith (that leads to) knowing God; it makes one grow in the virtues that are in Christ and become mature in righteousness, equal in stature to the rest of the members of the assembly that is pleasing to God. [18]For every enlightened life abides in faith, in things both visible and invisible. For those enlightened in the knowledge of truth become strong in all aspects of Christ-centered piety. *"For all things were created by Christ, whether (things) in heaven or (things) on earth"* (Col 1.16), says the Apostle. For by the will of the Lord faith enables the discernment of the invisible vis-à-vis the visible, and the visible vis-à-vis the invisible.[6]

[19]Faith is an infinite treasure encompassing all that is good for us; and by the grace that has been revealed, the gift of salvation and eternal life (are realized) through faith.[7] We hope to enjoy every blessing; hope makes the anticipated (blessings) to bloom before our eyes—so to speak, lest we lose sight of the totality (of the objectives) that lead to the good things that do not pass away, which have been prepared for the saints. [20]For, to begin with, they are filled and adorned with love, the radiance of the remembrance sacrament[8] that guides their every member and thought in righteousness unto faith in the Most Holy Trinity, establishing them to abide lovingly by his will. [21]For a pure heart is a temple for the Holy Spirit;[9] and pure love is a dwelling for Christ, since there lies the divine will. As the Lord says, *"I and my Father will come and make our dwelling in anyone who abides in my love and obeys my words"* (Jn 14.23). [22]For through his benevolence he enables the enjoyment of the ineffable, good things [24]by those who are pure and immaculate in heart, who remain free from all harmful blemishes. [25]For those who love him are loved by him, and he rewards those who seek him. [26]But to those who do not obey his word he says: *"The very word I have spoken to you will condemn you at the last day"* (Jn 12.48).

[27]As for those who obey his word, root out of the heart the mind's evil thoughts—unbelief, double-mindedness, vice, envy, and impure passions with all their harmfulness—and let in pure,

6. Echoing Heb 11.1.
7. Echoing Eph 2.8; cf. Disc. 10.106.
8. See note to §6, above.
9. Allusion to 1 Cor 3.16–17; cf. 6.19; 2 Cor 6.16.

wholesome thoughts that are well (rooted) in Christ, ₂₈ they pursue righteousness with their senses freed from sin. Their minds remain alert, concentrating on beneficial and life-giving insights. ₂₉They do not relinquish or stop the battle at the height of the warfare, but withstand with true patience to emerge victorious in the warfare, having endured with hope, being strengthened by Christ's grace, and having arrived at Christ's haven. ₃₀They suppress the influence of evil and the inclination toward the passions. ₃₁And having received the grace of victory and praise from those above and those around,[10] they may be crowned with glory and grandeur, the life promised to the redeemed. ₃₂For the one who abides in the love that is in Christ, who saved his creatures and removed the enmity,[11] becomes a dwelling for the Lord. ₃₃Let us resemble him in greatness and win the good things and (save) our brothers; and let us exchange our goods in return for their prospects, (even) our lives to offset their death.[12] Thus we become heirs of his Lordship, living dwellings for his will, partakers of his wonderful and sacred love, and participants in his marvelous glory.

₃₄Sacred love is the mother of (spiritual) well-being and immaculate chastity; it prompts and encourages the pursuit of virtue and every good deed. ₃₅Love is the source of all good things; those who are holy drink from it. It is the pledge of all the blessings and the great gifts distributed by God. ₃₆Love is the flow of Christ's beneficence; it adorns his boundless grace; it dissipates strife and grants peace; it illumines the mind and the members (of the body). ₃₇Sacred love is an intangible, perpetual possession of the soul and the body; it is a living grace (given) by Christ, a superb blessing given for praising God's glory. ₃₈Love, with the living hope of the good news,[13] provides consolation when in trouble and grief, and dissipates every hardship that might be caused by those who wage war against virtue in general. ₃₉Sacred love from his beneficence is a messenger of peace; it repels rage, dissipates fuming, shuts out envy, and reduces evil. ₄₀Sacred love is a delightful vineyard that makes

10. Lit., "those within."

11. Echoing Rom 5.10; cf. 2 Cor 5.18–20.

12. Possibly echoing Jn 15.13 ("Greater love has no one than this: to lay down one's life for one's friends"). On fraternal love, see note to Disc. 2.46.

13. Echoing 1 Pt 1.3; Col 1.23.

the heart exult with grapes and wine, and the senses to rejoice in the will of the Lord against invading impulses of sadness. ₄₁Sacred love is a fruitful olive tree for a considerate heart, yielding oil for enlightenment in (spiritual) understanding, for the anointing and the well-being of the visible members.[14] ₄₂Sacred love is facilitator for religious orders and monitor for physical interaction; it unites and, for the common good, does not allow discord. ₄₃Sacred love is a key to the gateway of life. It dispenses life, distributes the invisible grace from God's treasury to holy individuals. It (empowers them) against hardship in life and (against) sin.

₄₄All aspects of virtue are facilitated through love: holiness, justice, (etc.). Utmost goodness is made manifest through it. It is a chaser of evil and promoter of good, strengthener of those who love God and destroyer of schemers and lovers of sin. ₄₅When sacred love is combined with faith and hope,[15] it leads to a life of piety; and this is demonstrated in the peace (that prevails) among the ranks of the enlightened. ₄₆For their virtue, God's ministers will be crowned promptly with shining crowns, and will enjoy his endless and unlimited goodness. ₄₇For those who with sacred love minister truly to the souls and bodies of everyone, becoming a blessing to those far and near, will be blessed, crowned, and honored by the Most Holy Trinity for their sacred love; they will enjoy with everlasting joy the unending and incomparable goodness.

₄₈For the one established in the true faith, which encompasses sacred love and hope, will remain unmoved. ₄₉For the grace of the Holy Spirit unites these (three) as one, strong fortress for refuge, buttressed by every virtue. ₅₀(Woe to) the one who wavers in taking refuge, that he may be kept vigilant in guarding the faith, ever steadfast in the sacred (love) and mindful of the hope, thankful to the Lord and praising him with persistent longing, conforming will, strong and yearning desire to drink from the fountain of grace at its source and to water the plant of righteousness and the seeds of piety with streaming tears in order to bear the promised fruit. ₅₁For

14. The use of olive oil for anointing suggests a non-Armenian provenience. There is no mention of *miwṙon*, the consecrated fragrant oil derived from various plants and used as Holy Chrism in the Armenian Church, in these discourses. On the baptismal allusion here, see note to Disc. 2.133.

15. Allusion to 1 Cor 13.7, 13; reverberated in §§48–55.

the spring season is time to grow spiritually, in faith and sacred love, in order to have all the virtues in bloom, as plants and shrubs shoot leaves and blossoms when freed from the constraints of winter. ₅₂Thus the warmth of sacred love, with the grace-filled tears of faith, will make the virtues shine forth by the will and grace of the Most Holy Trinity.

₅₃And in whichever direction the consensus of faith and the accord of sacred love flow, they will gather in all who are accepted in Christ. ₅₄For he is our haven and distributor of gifts, the living fountain and food for immortality,[16] who crowns all his saints with decorum and eternal life. ₅₅Each of them shows forth his valor, the finery and grandeur of his deserved glory, displaying the totality of his luminous virtues commensurate with personal goodness: having exercised caution with discernment, in opposition to all sensuality; having faith and having cherished sacred love, which rebuffs filth and physical and mental aberration; and having (stayed) pure and in sacred love toward God. ₅₆Such a person is able to differentiate between the beneficial and the utterly harmful, to direct his thoughts and perceptions toward good things, and to safeguard against deception always—through caution and discernment. ₅₇For in the fear of God, the mind concentrates on being careful about the word of God; and being guided by discernment, denounces evil and chooses the good. And it stays pure and just, wakeful and alert about things seen and unseen. ₅₈For it does not allow the cunning, evil one to penetrate the thoughts and feelings to loot the treasure of virtue, lest it be found wanting on the judgment (day) of the unwary, who did not keep watch over the treasure of virtue but allowed the eye to pay no heed to the theft of what is enormously good and is to be enjoyed in the hereafter. For this reason they are to be punished in hell, for negligence.

₅₉Now, in Christ, one should exercise watchfulness in guarding the fort and the treasure of discernment, which is a graceful adornment for the body; for through him we shall be saved from the schemes and deceptions of the accuser.[17] ₆₀And being found pleasing to his will, we will enter without stigma or shame into the

16. Echoing Jn 4.14; 6.35.

17. As often in the discourses, an epithet for Satan (Jb 1.9–11; Zec 3.1; 1 Pt 5.8; Rv 12.10).

promised good things. We will find rest in the relaxing bosom, on the comfortable lap, and in the glory of the light that does not go out. 61And, in accordance with our manifold fruits, glory and honor will be added to us. And being redeemed by Christ, we will receive the crown of glory from the almighty Father.

62I will speak about the sacredness of meekness, which is a cure for the passions of the mind and of the body.[18] 63Certainly, one who is enlightened in utter meekness and immaculate love, who by faith conforms to the delight of the Holy Spirit, to the will of the Son, and to the glory of the heavenly Father, and is revived and confirmed by his sacred love, he will endure and will be delivered from the plagues of the passions, and he will find solace when in bitter conflict. And when the winds of vice come blowing, he will remain calm in mind and body.

64Meekness is a bridle for anger, the movements of the passions, the ills of indecency and defiance, and for most anything contrary.[19] 65Meekness is pleasantness and sweetness to the palate; it reduces the fury of a mob and (the pride) of those enslaved by arrogance. 66Meekness calms down the mind's stormy waves and the body's reckless havocs. 67Meekness is the root of humility, patience, and self-restraint for those who are close to Christ. 68Meekness strengthens all the virtues; it is the foundation for every good thing discerned by us. 69Meekness is a monument of peace, and demolition and annihilation of fury, vengefulness, and envy—both seen and unseen. 70Meekness is a clear fountain, a cloud that bears gentle dew which waters the parched (earth).

71Meekness is a pedagogue, a competent counselor, a teacher (even) to the (clerical) ranks. 72Meekness is glory for the elderly, for by it they are guided to wholesome thoughts and every virtue. 73Meekness is honor for the young, for through humility and kindness they triumph over all opponents, defiant ones, and wrongdoers.

---

18. The discourse is at a turning point here, conceivably marking the beginning of an appended discourse on meekness and humility, with few notions akin to Basil's *De humilitate* (Hom. 20; PG 31:525–540; trans. Wagner, *Ascetical Works*, FC 9:475–86); cf. Aphrahat, *Dem.*, 9. Similar turning points are discernible at §§124, 132, and 140.

19. See below, §86, and Disc. 10.37; 18.32; 19.40; 23.2. Cf. Basil's *Adversus iratos* (Hom. 10; PG 31:353–372; trans. Wagner, *Ascetical Works*, FC 9:447–61).

74Meekness is a glorious crown for virgins who, with utmost gratitude and fullness of virtue, have dedicated themselves to the summons of his sacred love: 75by being wakeful, utterly undaunted in courage, having subjugated idleness and stubbornness to true faith; 76by hastening to pursue virtue earnestly through ceaseless prayer, the edifying remembrances (of Christ),[20] and cordial willingness (to serve) with humble demeanor, kind manners, and sacred love; by controlling through strict fasting the emergence of onerous and impure thoughts prompted by the evil one; by quenching the fire of desire with warm tears; 77by keeping the gate of mercy open to the needy in their need; and by eyeing with hope the good news promised to the wise virgins—78as he says: *"Come, you who are blessed by my Father; inherit the holy Kingdom"* (Mt 25.34).

79Meekness is nurture for the children of the Church;[21] and with growth, it is a prodder into discernment and truth, beginning with purity and propriety in infancy and on into luminous teachings and decency in speech and voice. Those who are thoroughly pure in life and of contrite heart will share in the glory of those above as surely as the rays of the sun light up gloriously—to the glory of God—things above and things within.

80Meekness, (like) discernment among the virtues, is an instructor to the assembly of those who are aware of the transience of earthly things and who, being delivered from harms to mind and body, cling strongly—with simplicity of heart and tireless body—to the life that does not pass away. 81For they have fulfilled all of God's commandments and have instructed others—as it is proper for the righteous to abide in purity and every virtue, and for sinners to repent with confession that they may live.

82Meekness is praiseworthy greatness to the homeless, for earthly greatness wears out and is lost in pride. But the homeless,[22] who have been made great through meekness, will live forever where no moth destroys, no corrosion decays, or thieves covet and steal.[23]

---

20. Arm. յորդորեալ յիշատակաւք (*yordoreal yišatakawkʻ*), the plural indicating the recurring Eucharistic "services" of the *Anamnesis* and its edifying implications, those cited in the following section (§77); cf. §§6, 20, 127. See also note to Disc. 13.45.

21. The youth destined for the priesthood.

22. Meaning, it seems, those who have denounced the world.

23. Allusion to Lk 12.33.

₈₃For this reason the Lord pronounces the meek "blessed"; for he says: *"Blessed are the meek, for they will inherit the land of the living"* (Mt 5.5), where the repute of death is unheard; as David says: *"I will be well pleasing before the Lord in the land of the living"* (Ps 116.9 [114.9 LXX]). ₈₄Moreover, (meekness) brings tranquility to the mind as well as to all members (of the body)—those engaged in the (spiritual) warfare. ₈₅For it instructs the poor through patience, brings the mighty to containment, and enables rule over earthly beings without turmoil and daily uproar. Modesty befits everyone, everywhere, being a tutor to the old and young.

₈₆Meekness is enlightenment to the clergy, leading the sovereign mind unto obedience; it does not allow indignation to lead unto anger and enmity, ignorance and arrogance of thought—(all) because of indignation. ₈₇Rather, being mindful of meekness as taught by Christ's Gospel, one channels the issues through such awareness. And meekness enlightens in such a way that when (others) notice your good works, (as) the Lord says, *"They will glorify your Father who is in heaven"* (Mt 5.16). ₈₈Meekness is like salt in savory foods, making them flavorful in the mouth. ₈₉For, as he says: *"Have your words seasoned with salt ... full of grace and truth"* (Mk 9.50; Jn 1.14 [17]), leveled with unpretentious teaching about the impending judgment of the righteous and the wicked, that they may bestow grace upon the hearers, so that those who hear will become wise in Christ. ₉₀Meekness is an attribute of the Lord; it made the fishermen preachers and resources of the life-giving grace of the Holy Spirit, who made believers drunk with divine knowledge.[24]

₉₁Meekness confounds bold and daring behavior, as Moses and David bear witness: one to the rebellious people, and the other to Saul.[25] ₉₂To wise hearers, meekness conveys a word of wisdom: to bear in mind true justice and to pursue what is right and all virtue. ₉₃Meekness is decorum for individuals distinguished in virtue: faith, hope, love,[26] sanctity, prayer, fasting, humility, self-restraint,

24. Allusion to Acts 2.14–15, Peter's deflecting the mocking criticism that the disciples were drunk; cf. 1 Cor 12.13–14. The metaphorical description of being filled with the Spirit as being drunk is repeated in §191.

25. Possible allusion to Nm 12.3 (Moses) and 1 Sm (1 Kgdms LXX) 16.14–23 (David).

26. Echoing 1 Cor 13.13 ("these three ...").

and all goodness. ₉₄Meekness is an attire of sanctity to those who stripped off worldly desires and, exercising discernment, lived their lives in Christ. ₉₅Meekness is a magnificent shelter and bulwark against unruly mobs; it conveys calmly the spiritual law; it is a messenger of peace to all who listen and glorify the Lord's name, who are applauded by the one who is meek and by God the lover of humankind, who have turned their lives around and will hear the Lord say: *"Come, faithful and meek servant. Because you were faithful with little, I will appoint you over much"* (Mt 25.21).

₉₆Meekness is a reflection of the glory of his Lordship, a discovery of eternal rest. The one sustained by his meekness becomes an abode²⁷ of the heavenly beings: an intimate with the holy believers in him who descended from heaven to earth, from great glory to the likeness of a servant,²⁸ so that his servants will take upon themselves his likeness in righteousness, holiness, and truth, because of his benevolent and omnipresent sacred love and the pledge he made to us,²⁹ whom he will have sitting with him at the right hand of the Father on high.³⁰ And to all who believe he promised this good news, giving reassuring hope: *"Where I am, there my servant will also be"* (Jn 12.26). ₉₇For this reason he invited all and called them into his Kingdom and glory, saying: *"Come to me through the penitential (rite of) confession, all you who toil with patient perseverance and are burdened with sin, and learn meekness (and) humility from me, and you will find rest for your souls, for the yoke of the meek who toil with hope is easy and the burden of sin is made light through humility"* (amplifying Mt 11.28–30). ₉₈The one who affirms both will abide at the right hand of God, holy and pure, having none of the misery on the left, but the righteousness that is on the right.³¹ Those who have this (righteousness) resemble Christ, the meek one, and find pasture with the lowly one. And because of his caring, sacred love, the meek and lowly in heart are crowned with blessedness by the Most Holy Trinity. They are freed from grief and eternal torment, and they will experience the joy

---

27. Arm. վանք (*vankʻ*), here and at §103, carries the early meaning of the word; cf. its usage in Disc. 23 (§§20, 39, 54, 58), in the sense of "monastery."

28. Allusion to Phil 2.7.

29. See 2 Cor 1.22 and 5.5; cf. Eph 1.13–14; 2 Tm 1.14.

30. Referring to Mt 20.23; cf. Mk 10.40.

31. Allusion to Mt 25.31–46.

that does not pass away and the incomparable good things. 99For they will rejoice with ever-growing virtue in the much-praised life. And they will be glorified and crowned, clothed with the ineffable light by Christ, with the ineffable life that does not pass away, that has been prepared for all the saints in the eternal sanctuaries.

100There is much more to kindness and humility and obedience, through wholesome thought, purity of life, and gratitude for perfect love. 101By these the bronze gates of unbelief were shattered, and the iron bars of disobedience were broken to pieces, and the invisible treasuries of the enemy were plundered by the true wisdom of Christ—due to faith in the proclamation of the Gospel.[32] Those who walk uprightly, as in the path of righteousness, have come to resemble the luminaries, which twinkle throughout the universe.[33] 102For the kindness of humility and obedience is a soothing fount of goodness, healer of bitter pains, bestowing health; it is a guide to goodness that leads to blessedness through right paths, delivering from all dreadful dangers.

103Kindness, when combined with humility, obedience, and meekness, is a catcher of good things, a gatherer of all the virtues, and an abode for the Holy Trinity. 104Kindness, when combined with humility and obedience, binds together those who persevere ascetically and does not allow separation from one another.[34] 105Kindness, humility, and obedience make strangers into family, those who

---

32. Drawing on the "Harrowing of Hell" imagery, based on Mt 27.51–53 and 1 Pt 3.19–20, and amplified in "The Descent of Christ into Hell" (chapters 17–27), utilized with the "Acts of Pilate" (chapters 1–11, with an addition in 12–16) in the apocryphal *Gospel of Nicodemus*, compiled either late in the fourth or early in the fifth century. Our author shows familiarity with "The Descent" document, as gathered from the following: "Then said Hell unto his wicked ministers: Shut ye the hard gates of brass and put on them the bars of iron and withstand stoutly, lest we that hold captivity be taken captive"; and again: "Who hath broken the gates of brass and smitten the bars of iron in sunder?" (21.1–2; trans. James). An Armenian version of the documents comprising the *Gospel of Nicodemus* seems to have been known in the fifth century; see Frederick C. Conybeare, *Acta Pilati*, in *Studia biblica et ecclesiastica* 4 (Oxford: Clarendon Press, 1896), 59–132; also Sirarpie Der Nersessian, "A Homily on the Raising of Lazarus and the Harrowing of Hell," in *Biblical and Patristic Studies in Memory of Robert Pierce Casey* (Freiburg and New York: Herder, 1963), 219–34.

33. Echoing Dn 12.3; cf. Mt 13.43.

34. On this subject, see Disc. 23.

are near to exercise thoughtfulness, the arrogant to be selfless, the feeble strong, and all the defiant ones submissive; they awaken hope in life and confidence among waverers delivered from servitude to sin. 106They are cause for all spiritual benefits, and disperser of harmful thoughts and deeds. 107They open up true confession and remorse, releasing the bonds through forgiveness of sins. 108They ward off harms and welcome unto adoption.[35] 109They distance all miseries and draw close to hope of eternal life. 110They are a feast of true preaching and a fount of nourishment, gushed forth by the Holy Spirit. 111They keep ignorance at bay; they are a treasury of wisdom and knowledge. 112They treat true friends as family and rebuke false brothers—those evil intruders.[36] 113They gather the scattered lovers of truth and disperse the wicked. 114They soothe the alienated; they bestow grace upon those who return to the rightfulness of righteousness, and organize them all in a good way. 115They comfort the bereaved and console all who are in danger.

116Kindness, humility, and obedience (reflect) serenity in (extending) his sustaining care (full) of love for humankind: 117health to those in pain and steadfast hope of things to come; 118to those adrift, a haven and support in virtue, various means toward sanctity; to those who are slow to labor in the vineyard, to receive the wages of those who were first.[37] 119Here is an open gate to life-giving accesses for those who long for the Kingdom, who are inherently good; 120the ungrateful and disobedient, the wicked and sinners, and those who do not obey his word are shut out. 121But those who humbly obey with the gentle yoke of repentance will not be denied the good things promised to those who truly confess and repent, for he *"did not come to call the righteous, but sinners"* (Mt 9.13). 122Those who live virtuously will be crowned with the living blessedness of that beneficence by the Most Holy Trinity. 123Being delivered from the bitter agony of hell, they will enjoy with everlasting, unending joy the incomparable good things in Christ, marvelous in

35. Cf. §180. See Rom 8.14–17, 23; Gal 4.1–7; Eph 1.5–6.
36. Cf. the warning in Disc. 5.89. Canon 36 of the Second Council of Dwin, convened in 555, forbids admission of sectarians into monasteries; see *Kanonagirkʿ Hayocʿ (Canon Law of the Armenians)*, ed. Vazgen Hakobyan, 2 vols. (Erevan: Haykakan SSH GA Hratarakčʿutʿyun, 1964–1971), 1:490.
37. Reference to "The Parable of the Workers in the Vineyard," Mt 20.1–16.

every aspect of blessedness. $_{124}$True unity in faith[38] and holy life—wholesome, impeccable, and immaculate—bring love's beneficence to all the members fitted into Christ's (body). $_{125}$For in it they are established in the one will of Christ and one faith.[39] Therein dwells God's prodding into growth in virtue.

$_{126}$Unity in faith and holy life are a fount of knowledge. From such emerges without reservation that which equips one for martyrdom: goodwill, discerning mind, hatred of evil, dependence on God's love, and renewal of the will, complete with repentance and heartfelt confession. $_{127}$Unity in faith and holy life combine with the Creator's grace and bind all members through his holy remembrances,[40] and at the gates of his loving mercy there is always plenty of good things for his creatures. $_{128}$Through such a gate comes the gift of unity, which liberates and affirms, and through such unity members receive one another's help for every rank's strengthening. $_{129}$And anyone who severs himself from the unity of faith and holy life not only takes leave from its blessedness but is punished. He becomes useless like an amputated member of the body or a branch cut from a tree for fire.[41]

$_{130}$Unity in faith in the Most Holy Trinity, in holy living, is a strong city, walled by heavenly power; it is a dwelling place for God's love and the heavenly hosts. To be gathered there with all the saints, jointly uttering the ineffable blessings, being immersed in the joy of the care by the sacred love, aflame with hope in God's glory, are pure favors bestowed by Jesus Christ, cherished within the unity in immaculate holiness. $_{131}$For whoever possesses such indissoluble union through the love of the Spirit, faith, and holy life, will be crowned with living blessedness by the caring Holy Trinity, being freed from the bitter torments of hell and rejoicing in the eternal, incomparable good things in the life that does not pass away.

---

38. Echoing Eph 4.13, reverberated through §131.

39. Echoing Eph 4.5 ("one Lord, one faith, one baptism," quoted in Disc. 13.57).

40. See §6 and note on the significance of the Eucharist, especially as *Anamnesis*. On the plural form, see note to §76.

41. On disciplinary measures within a monastic setting, see Disc. 23.54, 58, 62. Cf. Basil *LR* 28 and *SR* 44, 106, and 122, on the various degrees of punishment, of which separation from the community of brothers is the ultimate.

₁₃₂Now, (as) one who is grateful for the good tidings of Christ's pure, sacred, and immaculate love, I have something to say about compassion, which is bound to unity and is the mother of love and the cradle of consolation and sensibility.⁴² ₁₃₃For (compassion) is a generous gift to those near and far, a trainer to the strong and a helper to the weak, a nurturer to the household and a sustainer to aliens, an admirer of the grateful and a kind giver to the ungrateful, a lover of friends for their own good and a well-wisher to the hateful, that they may attain that sacred love.

₁₃₄Compassion is care given with sacred love, the outpouring of the self of the lover, a memorial for one's parents, and a lesson to children, concern for those who are far away and constant nurture for those who are near. ₁₃₅Compassion's roots are good things, its branches are delight, its leaves bliss, its blossom happiness, and its fruit incomparable enjoyment. ₁₃₆For through compassion the sadness caused by sin and the murkiness of boredom, which discourage the individual, even mourning, which alienates and maddens, are lifted away. ₁₃₇It dispels malevolence and promotes munificence, roots out greed and welcomes frugality, rebukes indecency and encourages holiness, reduces unbelief and lights up faith, drives out double-mindedness and introduces living hope,⁴³ alienates hatred and calms the endangered, and comforts all who are troubled.

₁₃₈Compassion knocks out pride and dissipates treachery, rebukes cunning and rejects vindictiveness and envy, haunts the disobedient and encourages the patient, strengthens those who exercise self-restraint and eradicates sexual impurity,⁴⁴ cheers the longsuffering ones and aids the meek, crowns discernment and chastity and promotes virtue, wakes up the supine and the idle and leads to rest-deserving works that are full of every goodness, having caring compassion because of the wholesome, sacred, immaculate, impeccable, and caring beneficence of his love. ₁₃₉He who takes upon himself this spiritual compassion, adding it to spiritual life, will be crowned with living blessedness by the loving care of the Most Holy Trinity, who delivers him from the bitter agony of hell

42. Note the author's turning point with the rare use of the first-person-singular pronoun, as he connects this part of the discourse to the preceding (§§124–131).

43. Echoing 1 Pt 1.3.

44. Or, "masturbation."

and rewards him with eternal, incomparable blessings to be enjoyed forever.

₁₄₀Moreover, discretion over sense-perceptible things enables one who is grounded in the faith that is in the Lord to root out by the sovereign will the harms of the senses and to admit the virtues: holiness, humility, the truth in everything.[45] ₁₄₁Such a one shuts out the intruding harms and arms himself against the evil one and destroys the enemies of righteousness. ₁₄₂And with the fire of the Spirit, with warm tears, he melts down the thick ice of winter. ₁₄₃He spreads the roots of pleasing holiness, gratifying humility, and good obedience in all truthfulness in Christ. ₁₄₄And he raises branches of agreeableness, growing in all the virtues by faith, *"like trees planted by the streams of water"* (Ps 1.3). ₁₄₅With (such) eager desire for God's grace stream the fountains of tears, by which are cleansed the visible and invisible things. And he waters with the peaceful and gentle drizzle the trees and plants that grow early and late. And he instructs all his members in the growth of righteousness, in good things and more, so that at the end he may come forth with the perfect fruit of virtue, having rooted out the alien plants, the weeds, and the rest of the evil seed sowed by the enemy in the mind and thought:[46] strife in every form of heartache, lust, audacity, insensitivity, disobedience, anger, arrogance, pride, greed, lack of discernment, negligence. ₁₄₆These are the causes of perdition, estrangement from the greater good, from the praiseworthy glory of the virtues.

₁₄₇There are other sense-perceptible means to establish what is good for single-mindedness, (such as) doing good willingly, by the gratifying, pleasant, luminous, and bountiful grace of Christ. ₁₄₈Mindful of the beneficence of his sacred love, in keeping with the pleasing will of the benevolent Lord, let us become co-workers with him in grace, to the glory and honor of the Giver of Life. ₁₄₉Let us become collaborators with his benevolent will at all times, abiding truly in the faith, steadfast (in our commitment) to his wholesome, sacred, immaculate, and impeccable beneficence.

45. From here on and through §227, the author dwells on theological valuing of the senses; cf. Disc. 20.31–55. On the spiritual "re-locating" of perception, see Harvey, *Scenting Salvation*, 156–200.

46. Allusion to "The Parable of the Weeds" (Mt 13.24–30), equally allegorized with reference to the vices (see note to Disc. 5.23).

₁₅₀The head is where all sense-perception is perceived. In Christ (as head) all members are joined and fitted together by grace (as one body), and *"it grows as God causes it to grow"* (Col 2.19).[47] ₁₅₁He distributes the grace of wisdom to each member, for essential things—both seen and unseen. ₁₅₂And from him they drink the knowledge of what is good, in order to accept what is beneficial and to reject what is harmful. ₁₅₃And from him rises the revealing light that scrutinizes everything. And all the senses are made wise as regards the joy of spiritual inclination and choosing what is good for the person. And they are guided by Wisdom to be cautious and to open the gate for the incoming grace. And having exercised discernment, and having become enlightened, one hastens fearlessly in the path of the upward call, having already gained what is beneficial for soul and body, so that he may inherit the promised blessedness.

₁₅₄And the mouth utters the sovereign Spirit's[48] true teaching regarding uprightness and pure sanctity with perfect love. ₁₅₅Through it flow all the streams of wisdom, gushing forth from the heart, to water and irrigate the parched land (of the soul) with the Word of Life, so that the plants of goodness may grow and blossom with fragrant, attractive, and delicious fruit. ₁₅₆The mouth is like a light-giving lamp of the true Word that chases darkness away and reveals shamefulness, exposing filth and uncovering strife. It should be controlled. ₁₅₇Thus through his plan, the Son of God disarmed its cunning, audacity, voraciousness, deceitful supplication, and intimidation, restraining[49] them with his truth. All other similar machinations of the evil one were exposed by the radiance of Christ's teaching, ₁₅₈that he may thus give opportunity for his witnesses[50] to become virtuous, to instruct against evil ways, to expel misleading wisdom from the mind, to confine oneself to true life, to

---

47. See also Col 1.18; 2.10; Eph 1.22; 4.15; 5.23, on Christ as "Head."

48. Cf. "the sovereign mind" in §86. As with the following senses, there is a degree of allegorization on the mouth—utilizing certain of the various meanings of *logos*, particularly the Stoic distinction between *logos prophorikos* ("speech" or articulated *logos* that courses from the mouth) and *logos endiathetos* ("reason" or "thought" processed in the mind). The author substitutes the Logos or the personified Word of God (Christ) for the latter, just as he substitutes Spirit for *nous* (or the *hēgemonikon*, "the sovereign mind").

49. Lit., "leveling."

50. Or, "martyrs" (Arm. նահատակաց, *nahatakac῾*).

be cautious of all harms, and to guide others into goodness, ₁₅₉and to cherish the memory of the sacred love like honeycomb in the roof of one's mouth, for it sweetens the bitterness of evil.[51]

₁₆₀Darkness never reaches the pupil of the one who opens his eyes to the sun's light at noon. ₁₆₁Such is also the case of the one who gazes clearly at remarkable sanctity; the delightful light is his safeguard through life that cares for him tenderly, keeping him safe from harms, pure, and blameless. ₁₆₂By virtue of its brightness one discerns (the merits) of finding the lost; it draws to the mercy of the Savior those who are near and establishes them in his care. ₁₆₃For the radiant light from preaching the Word points to hope— the living medicine—and the ineffable, unlimited remedies of the Kingdom. ₁₆₄Through true faith it leads along the way of that upward calling of the almighty Father,[52] the benevolent Son, and the life-giving Spirit, whose glory is ineffably great.

₁₆₅Now, the bands of the heavenly hosts become attendants of the Bridegroom, the Son of God, and agents for our salvation. They encourage the beloved of God who saved humans from death caused by sin. ₁₆₆*"For there will be rejoicing in heaven over those who repent and turn to God"* (Lk 15.1). ₁₆₇And those who believe in God and rejoice in him will become heirs of his Kingdom, ₁₆₈likewise those who presently, in true faith, fulfill his word and teach wholesome (doctrine) with immaculate, impeccable sanctity because of the beneficence of God's sacred love. ₁₆₉For the one who conducts his life accordingly, in all truthfulness, will be crowned with living blessedness by the Holy Trinity, will be saved from the bitter torments, and will enjoy the eternal, incomparable goodness.

₁₇₀The eye sanctified by faith beholds the glimmer of the abundant joy of the Light ₁₇₁from which is lit the light of the Sun of Righteousness[53] that enlightens all the saints,[54] that draws them close to his loving grace and dissipates the darkness of deception, and guides them unerringly to the heavenly mansions of rest,[55]

51. Likely allusion to receiving the Eucharist. Echoing Ps 119.103 (118.103 LXX).

52. Echoing Phil 3.14; cf. §217.

53. A recurring messianic title derived from Mal 4.2, here related to the primordial Light of Gn 1.3.

54. Echoing Jn 1.4, 9.

55. Echoing Jn 14.2.

to that point to which they were called, led by God's kindly light.
₁₇₂For by it they are brought to the bosom of the sacred love of
God's Son, to the embrace of the Father, and to the ineffable gifts
of the Holy Spirit. ₁₇₃For the (Holy Trinity) bestows the inheritance
upon those who on earth lived according to his will and fought
against evil with spiritual armament,[56] by doing good, according
to Christ's Gospel;[57] ₁₇₄and who partook of his suffering, sharing
his cross by voluntary death, with utmost patience, truly bound by
the indissoluble bond of sacred love, through hardship and calm.
₁₇₅Through utter self-restraint, they subdued the lures and the
strong hold of sin, keeping their eyes always fixed upon the caring
Hand that strengthens those who trust it, which is the Light for
eyes that see the intelligible as well as the visible things. ₁₇₆For they
persisted daily with entreaties to God, with contrite hearts, offering
prayers wholeheartedly, with warm tears, letting their tears stream
with longing for glimpses of the promised gifts pledged with compassion. These alleviate the pain, the catastrophes, and the harms
inflicted by oppressors, and fill remorseful (penitents) with abundant goodness, making them receptacles of the Holy Spirit, who
reveals the hidden and inscrutable things to God's beloved.[58] For
he satisfies their earnest longing with living and ineffable goodness
with its benefits. ₁₇₇And the mighty and unapproachable Light[59]
does not reject those who desire its magnificence, but fills their eye-
sight with the light of faith and always grants glimpses of the gifts
and perks up their senses. It makes those who have abstained from
worldly desires and have put on the garment of holiness to rejoice
in its undying care, those who truly, with immaculate faith in the
truth of the Holy Trinity—with the help of the Holy Spirit—have
conducted their lives in the world constructively, peacefully with
everyone, in spiritual and physical matters, until they arrive at the
tranquil haven seen intelligibly because of that wholesome, impeccable, and immaculate care—the beneficence of Christ's sacred
love. ₁₇₈He who has received this grace from God, having had a
most holy life because of the continuous care of that sacred love,

56. Echoing Eph 6.11–17.
57. Echoing Rom 12.21.
58. Allusion to Jn 16.13.
59. Allusion to 1 Tm 6.16; cf. Ps 104.2 (103.2 LXX).

will be crowned by the Most Holy Trinity. He will be delivered from the tortures of hell and will enjoy the good things with everlasting, incomparable joy.

₁₇₉And the hearing[60] (ought to be tuned) unto obedience, with unwavering faith, with wholesome and impeccably immaculate sanctity—because of the caring beneficence of his love, (befitting) those who abide by the divine injunctions of the Gospel.[61] For the inner man reflects the image of Christ our Savior in his glory: ₁₈₀having the insignia of peace on his right, the assurance[62] of adoption on his left, and the crown of glory upon his head. So too he will have the full range of sanctity, having secured his sides —by the power of Christ—with apt circumspection.[63]

₁₈₁Hearing is the venue for faith,[64] for being mindful about living a holy life that combines caution and joy. Righteousness and justice are the goal[65] for those who observe the spiritual law in blossoming holiness, having the pleasant aroma of psalms and praise rising from within. And there echo from the mouths of the saints the exaltations of the immortal King, rising like sweet incense offered by his holy servants,[66] those who in holiness praise the Most Holy Trinity. ₁₈₂There the bands of angels encamp, the vigilant ones in readiness, who are consumed with spiritual songs, all giving praise in unison.

₁₈₃Hearing, truly affirmed by faith, is acceptance of the tree of life and of atonement by faith,[67] the plant of salvation.[68] ₁₈₄Its roots spread in the hearts of those made perfect by God, who are sustained daily by grace and are covered with the dew of the Holy Spirit.[69] ₁₈₅And all creatures captured by his sacred love rejoice in

60. Or, "the ears."

61. Lit., "those who enter into the good news of divine injunctions."

62. Or, "affirmation." Arm. հաստատութիւն (hastatut'iwn); cf. Disc. 20.45: "deed of adoption." See note to §108.

63. Or, "thoughtfulness."

64. Allusion to Rom 10.17, a recurring point here; cf. Disc. 7.1; 17.12 (quoted).

65. Lit., "exits." The teleological sense is unmistakable. The paired terms and the rest of the sentence echo a number of Psalms.

66. Reading the variant, սպասաւորութիւնք (spasaworut'iwnk').

67. Reading the variant, հաւատոյն (hawatoyn).

68. The association of "the tree of life" with the Cross of Christ is commonplace in patristic commentaries on Gn 2.9.

69. "Dew" is an image for God in Hos 14.5; cf. "mist" in Sir 24.3, where it is

him; they give thanks and praise the benevolent God who made them all and keeps them contented in glorifying his holy name. ₁₈₆Hearing, truly affirmed by faith, is (like) streams from the Fountain of Life[70] that irrigate the fields of the mind and of the senses to grow virtue. ₁₈₇They flush out with good enthusiasm the burdens of hardship that have the quality of hell's fire. ₁₈₈True hearing draws all things unto itself, revivifies the familiar (virtue of) circumspection,[71] discerning both good and evil. ₁₈₉Just as speakers of a foreign language necessarily hear what is said in their (language) and not ours, so do those who have sanctified hearing: they hear everything except evil. ₁₉₀The ears of the saints hear the word from God's mouth, the word that penetrates and cuts through,[72] that sanctifies the mind and the senses and makes them obedient to the spiritual law because of the beneficence of his sacred love, wholesome and immaculate; for by the continuous care of that love, the Most Holy Trinity crowns with luminous blessedness, delivers from the bitter torments, and grants the eternal enjoyment of the incomparably good things.

₁₉₁The sense of smell, (affirmed) by faith, (ought to be) the smelling and discernment of knowledge and wisdom, in gratitude for the living, pure, immaculate, and sacred love. And truly (smelling) the spiritual aroma of knowledge makes the individual drunk with the Holy Spirit, with the spiritual law.[73] ₁₉₂The first such smell is to know the Father, to recognize the Son, and to perceive the Holy Spirit. ₁₉₃Knowing the Father is (like) a sanctuary for his praise, and those who enter it with confession (of faith) find him. ₁₉₄(Recognizing) the Son's wisdom is (like) an altar for his birth,[74] and those who touch it with confession of faith, he draws to himself. ₁₉₅And perceiving by true faith the Holy Spirit, who bestows good things to those who truly believe, leads to the light of the Deity, enlightens

---

applied to the descent of the personified divine Wisdom. On dew as symbolic of divine knowledge in Gregory of Nyssa's *In Canticum canticorum* (PG 44:756–1120), see Martin S. Laird, *Gregory of Nyssa and the Grasp of Faith: Union, Knowledge, and Divine Presence*, OECS (Oxford: Oxford University Press, 2004), esp. 140–43.

70. Allusion to Ps 36.9; Prv 10.11; 13.14; 14.27; 16.22.
71. Or, "thoughtfulness."
72. Allusion to Heb 4.12.
73. See note to §90, on the metaphor of "being drunk with the Holy Spirit."
74. Meaning the Incarnation, even the Eucharist as such.

by grace those who see, and conveys the fragrance of knowledge from above—in union with the heavenly hosts in blessing the Father, the Son, and the Holy Spirit in the highest heaven.

196The sense of smell allows those who believe in (divine) wisdom to know the almighty Father, and to recognize the Son, lover of humankind, and the Holy Spirit, giver of gifts. 197The sense of smell guides those who believe to the Kingdom of Heaven, and opens the gates of life to those who long for the Holy Trinity, who have acquired virtue, that they may be glorified with the hosts above, to bless the Father with the Seraphim and to praise the Son with the Cherubim, and to bow down to the Holy Spirit with the angels of the One Godhead. 198The sense of smell, by faith, enables one to discern between life and death, the Kingdom and hell, holiness and filth, righteousness and wickedness. 199Some sense the aroma of praise and grace, others deception and disaster. 200Some it elevates gracefully from earth to God; others it brings down and throws into the gorge of oblivion.

201The sense of smell, truly affirmed by faith, discerns between the children of light and the children of darkness,[75] understands the ends of both right direction and estrangement caused by licentiousness and ignorance. Those who are marred by the latter, given their obvious sense of smell, will be cast out of God's care, following the Lord's holy command, *"into the outer darkness, where there are weeping of eyes and gnashing of teeth"* (Mt 8.12).[76] 202But the saints, nurturing their fragrant lives with virtue until they reach the measure of maturity in Christ,[77] will inherit the delightful Kingdom. They are true to the luminous faith and (live) holy lives, having received the beneficence of his immaculate and impeccable love. 203He who possesses this refined smell of virtue, among other (requisites) for holy life, will be crowned with the living blessedness by the caring love of the Most Holy Trinity; he will be delivered from the bitter agony of hell and will enjoy with eternal and incomparable blessedness the good things that are constant and everlasting.[78]

75. Echoing Eph 5.8; 1 Thes 5.5.
76. Cf. Mt 13.42, 50; 22.13; 24.51; 25.30; and Lk 13.28.
77. Allusion to Eph 4.13; cf. Col 1.28.
78. Cf. Disc. 20.41–43, quoting 2 Cor 2.15–16. On the "fragrance" of the knowledge of Christ, see Harvey, *Scenting Salvation* (*passim*).

204And the hands, when truly set to good works by faith, because of the beneficence of his wholesome, immaculate, impeccable, and sacred love, become gardeners who are preparing for the world to come, the Kingdom of Heaven: 205by being beneficent in good works, filling the fields with seeds of hope for good fruit, extending the hand to the downtrodden, mending the broken, setting up the fallen, strengthening the weak, and satisfying the needy. One works with his hands in order to provide in accordance with the grace granted him by God,[79] wholesome and conducive to faith, 206remembering the saying of the Apostle: *"These hands supplied for me and for those who were with me"* (Acts 20.34).

207Hands equipped with holy faith are censers with fragrant incense, fired by the Holy Spirit, rising with good works for the benefit of those who are near and those far away, rising to the Most Holy, with thanksgiving to God. 208Hands, truly affirmed by faith, are tools of the mind and body, paying what is due to each, seen and unseen, working perfectly, *"to the glory of God,"* according to the Gospel (Mt 5.16). 209The light of its good news shines as the hands are outstretched, and the person who achieved victory receives the reward. 210Hands, truly affirmed by faith, are a chalice for the mystery of the cross, which plucks out the thorns from the thistle of the curse of sin and plants the tree of life, which brings forth for us the body and blood of Christ for the forgiveness of sins, through sanctity, humility, and obedience. For thus we shall enter the realm of the light of life.[80] 211Hands, truly affirmed by faith, are tillers for the truth about the Holy Spirit, who receive their wages with pride, being rewarded for their virtue. 212It is like hands steering ships on the seas of the world in order to reach the harbor of peace and find rest in Christ Jesus. 213Hands, truly affirmed by faith, are fishers, not of fish but of people.[81] The one who has received the grace of priestly ordination by the Holy Spirit catches fish with the net of the Gospel, (in keeping) with the beneficence of the sacred love, which is wholesome, immaculate, and caring. 214The one who carries out his hands' work with conviction, living a holy life, will be crowned by the Most Holy Trinity with the living blessedness of the

79. Echoing Eph 4.28.
80. Allusion to Jn 8.12; cf. Disc. 10.89.
81. Echoing Mt 4.19.

beneficent love; being freed from punishment in hell, he will enjoy the incomparable good things that do not pass away, ever.

₂₁₅And the feet, when directed by faith in the paths of holiness, in gratitude for that pure, immaculate, and sacred love, lead as anticipated, according to the Gospel, to the future mansions for the righteous who are in Christ.[82] ₂₁₆The feet, directed by faith, bring those who have lived in utmost holiness and orderly fashion to the city of the living, to the assembly of the saints.[83] ₂₁₇The feet, directed by faith, are the steeds of the sanctified will that lead to martyrdom, the upward calling.[84] ₂₁₈The feet, directed by faith in happy and holy course, prompt into spiritual rejoicing those who are invited and called, fitted with virtue, with nothing to bite their heels.[85] ₂₁₉The feet, directed by faith, bring the errant to repentance, transforming the earthly (being) to a spiritual (being), the unjust to just, the disobedient to obedient in the path of righteousness. ₂₂₀The feet, directed by faith, lead one to join those above— where the saints dwell, to trample over the power of the enemy, being fortified by virtue's protective shoes, into which the snake cannot bite, nor can it eliminate someone (walking) in God's way. ₂₂₁The feet, directed by faith, tread on fire, as did the three young men stepping in the furnace.[86] ₂₂₂Or like Peter when walking over the sea as on dry land. Had he not been drowning for lack of faith, he would not have asked Jesus for help, who restored him in his course over the waves of the sea.[87] ₂₂₃Those who present themselves in accordance with the righteous course of the Gospel, the hope of the good news,[88] will be crowned by the Most Holy Trinity and will inherit the good things that are endless.

₂₂₄Those who heed his counsel and are crowned with the anticipated hope *"will minister with fear and joyful trembling before the Lord,"* as David goes on to say: *"Follow his counsel, or the Lord will be angry and you will perish from the way when his wrath is kindled"* (Ps 2.11–12),

---

82. Allusion to Jn 14.1–3.
83. Echoing Heb 12.22.
84. Echoing Phil 3.14; cf. §164.
85. Allusion to Gn 49.17.
86. Reference to Dn 3.8–27.
87. Reference to Mt 14.28–31.
88. Allusion to Col 1.23 (cf. Disc. 15.57).

"when he comes to judge the earth according to his righteous judgment" (Ps 98.9 [97.9 LXX]). ₂₂₅The wicked and transgressors who sinned but did not repent (will go) to the undying worms and outer darkness, where there are weeping eyes and gnashing teeth, and the everlasting fire of hell is made ready for their endless torments.[89] ₂₂₆But those who sanctified themselves from all the filth of the passions and fulfilled all righteousness[90] will be honored with incomparable blessedness and will be glorified profusely by the Most Holy Trinity, ₂₂₇to whom be glory forever and ever. Amen.

89. Allusion to Mk 9.48; cf. Is 66.24.
90. Echoing Mt 3.15.

DISCOURSE 12

TEACHING ABOUT THE PROVIDENT
CREATOR'S CARE, CONDEMNATION OF DISOBEDIENCE
AND DEFIANCE, AND GUIDANCE UNTO MORALITY—THE
GOODNESS OF MORALS[1]

HE BENEFICENCES by the grace of the one benevolent Father, the care by the one life-giving Lord for the glowingly diverse creation, and the considerate gifts (given) by the one Holy Spirit are manifold, with an all-encompassing love toward all creatures in heaven and on earth. ₂Water and air, by the alteration granted by the Creator, point to (the intimacy between) what is above and what is below. The gradual growth unto perfection proceeds according to God's pleasure; and the joint intimacy between the enlightened earthly and heavenly beings proclaims their intimate collaboration in spiritual principles, uplifting (the former) to the glory and honor of the promised good things to be fulfilled for those who are to be honored with glory and grandeur, with benevolent and generous, incomparable, and life-giving gifts.[2] ₃Seeing this transformation in eminence, (earthly beings) are exhorted to greater intimacy. For this reason the invisible things are made visible through wholesome and enlightening exhortation in immaculate sanctity, (thanks to) the beneficence of (Christ's) impeccable love.[3] ₄(We humans) be-

1. Irrespective of the title, much of the discourse is about grieving over the dead, especially the unrepentant; whereas the penitent dead, as believers, need not be mourned over since they enjoy the promised blessedness they hoped for, a subject continued in the next discourse. "Defiance" is not discussed here; however, it is touched upon in the previous discourse (11.5, 64, 73, 105; for elsewhere, see the Subject Index).

2. Arm. շնորհք (šnorhk‘) also translates Gk. charismata, the "spiritual gifts."

3. Living a holy life in response to Christ's love is a recurring theme in the preceding discourse.

come bearers of the Lord's gifts, each (endowed) with a gift, ever benefiting from the One who willingly counsels us with his pleasant and benevolent (teaching), who with all the beneficence of good things appoints gardeners of his truth for all: for those seen and unseen—I mean the incorporeal powers and us, visible humans. ₅"*For in him the heavenly and earthly beings live and move*" (Acts 17.28).[4]

₆By God's benevolent will the heavenly hosts become helpers of his loved ones:[5] Apostles, Prophets, orthodox teachers (of the Church),[6] holy martyrs, priests, virgins, the just, and all who love truth—those who are virtuously martyred for the salvation of their souls and (the souls) of those near to them, who act in accordance with the Lord's spiritual principles. ₇And gradually one is nurtured unto perfection.[7] ₈Just as he himself demonstrated through his work in creation, as regards birthing. In accordance with the proper rite of matrimony (established) by God, the consenting male and female are given a child—from a fetus in the womb—for their own consolation and that of their kin, and for thanksgiving to the Giver of gifts. And much rejoicing is shown at the time of birth. With friends and relatives, the birth and the naming are celebrated. ₉The one emerging from the womb's darkness and obscurity is presented to the world as a human being. ₁₀And when the body grows to maturity through nurturing from those proficiently prepared, along with the growth of the body, the faculty of reason and thought, knowledge and wisdom is revealed in him—at the hands of instructing tutors and those who happen to be in power and authority on earth.

₁₁Before all things, to come to know God, for the Creator has to be acknowledged by his creatures—those in heaven and on earth are his creatures. They ought to be his disciples and collaborators with his will, approximating his benevolence. ₁₂To hate evil and to

4. Paul's quotation from the Cretan philosopher Epimenides (cf. Rom 11.36; 1 Cor 8.6; Col 1.16).

5. Alluding to Heb 1.13 ("Are not all angels ministering spirits sent to serve those who will inherit salvation?").

6. See note to Disc. 5.1.

7. The *NBHL* dictionary (s.v. «Յաւելուած», 2:350) draws attention to this sentence («եւ առ փոքր փոքր յաւելուածովն զալ ի կատարումն անդրեամբն»), comparing it to Basil's *Rules:* «Առ փոքր փոքր յաւելուածով կատարումն մեզ եղիցի». Cf. «Որ ըստ օրէ յաւելուած լիցի լաւութեան» (Disc. 23.45).

choose good; to be responsible for beneficial things and to eradicate injurious things. To be beneficent to those who are far away and to those who are near: neighbors and family; to wish well and to do good; and with good deeds for all, to be truly worthy (persons), just and honest, holy and truthful in life. ₁₃To appear virtuous in the eyes of the world, adorned with every virtue, in the likeness of God's image;[8] to turn the indifferent ones around to the living, immortal glory, to the hope of the resurrection, and to accepting the blessedness of his love. ₁₄For heaven and earth and the creatures there have been filled with his caring love, and they exist[9] by his providence.

₁₅And the souls of those who have died,[10] those beloved of God, wherever they are, they are recorded in his sacred love and enjoy his continuous care. ₁₆Likewise, in his care, their bodies' whereabouts are recorded, whether on land or in water, wherever they are. ₁₇For the Prophet says: *"For our God is in heaven and on earth"* (Dt 4.39), in the seas and every crevice. ₁₈Again he says: *"If I ascend into heaven, you are there; if I descend into hell, even there you are near. If I fly on the wing of the dawn and dwell by the seashore, even there your arm will lead me, and your right arm will receive me with love"* (Ps 139.8–10 [138.8–10 LXX]). ₁₉By "hell" he means the corruptible grave, which is guarded by God's care, in the hope of the resurrection. Thus they will be restored to eternal life, receiving (back) their souls. ₂₀And those who are saintly, they will be close to Christ, *"For where I am, there will my servant be"* (Jn 12.26).

₂₁He also preserves the bodies and souls of sinners, wherever they are, for the dreadful rebuke on the great Day of Judgment and the resurrection of the dead. ₂₂For they opposed his righteous laws;

---

8. Cf. Gregory of Nyssa, for whom "the goal of the virtuous life is blessedness"; he goes on to define this human blessedness as "likeness to God" (*In Ecclesiasten*, Hom. 5, PG 44:680B–696C). See also Disc. 5.45; 11.96.

9. Lit., "they live."

10. Several euphemistic synonyms are used for the departed, in this discourse and the next. I have maintained the literary or formal distinctions as follows: կատարեալք, *katarealkʻ*, "those who have died" (or "made perfect" through death, 12.15; 13.65); հանգուցեալք, *hangucʻealkʻ*, "those at rest" (12.41; 13.66, 86, 88); հրաժարեալք, *hražarealkʻ*, "the departed" (12.37–39, 58, 63–64; 13.66, 71, 72); մեռեալք, *meřealkʻ*, "the dead" (12.21, 59, 79–81, 85; 13.12, 23); ննջեցեալք, *nnjecʻealkʻ*, "those asleep" (12.65); and վախճանեալք, *vaxčanealkʻ*, "the deceased" (12.56, 65).

they loved evil and hated good, and did not keep his commandments. ₂₃But those who sought him with true love, he rewarded with gifts. *"For the Lord is righteous and his judgments are just"* (Ps 145.17 [144.17 LXX]), even though this is incomprehensible to us. ₂₄*"He makes the sun to rise on the evil and the good"* (Mt 5.45), and there are other common favors from the Lord. ₂₅But the one who does his will, abides forever. The Lord says: *"Be holy and righteous, for I am holy and righteous"* (Lv 11.45; 19.2; 20.7).[11] ₂₆Those who apply these good sayings to themselves, cleanse themselves from all desires and become attendants to true and holy life. They thus become receptacles of divine grace and dwellings of God. ₂₇Those who thus abide in his caring love are firmly established. ₂₈As he said: *"I will dwell among them and will walk among them and be their God, and they will be my people"* (2 Cor 6.16).[12] And again: *"I will be a father to them, and they will be my sons and daughters, says the Lord Almighty"* (2 Cor 6.18).[13]

₂₉Now, all creatures are sheltered within his power; however, he keeps from all harms, under the cover[14] of his loving care, his loved ones and those who do his will. ₃₀Whereas those who abhor his laws, who are given to horrible passions, outright and diverse evils, they are at a different location; they inherit the outer darkness.[15] ₃₁This outer darkness is for the evil ones, *"whose minds and senses were made dull, and were alienated from that life,"* as the Apostle says (1 Cor 3.14). ₃₂As for that place, it is the fire of hell, where there is weeping of eyes that could not see, the very same torments prepared for demons and the impure.

₃₃When earthly life ends with death, the souls go to God, who gave them, and the body turns to dust, of which it was made by the Creator.[16] ₃₄The pure and just souls are met by angels and the souls of the saints; and with psalms, blessings, and spiritual songs they are brought before God, praising the almighty power of the Lordship of the Most Holy Trinity.[17] And they return thanks for his

11. Cf. 1 Pt 1.16.
12. Cf. Lv 26.11–12.
13. Cf. Ex 4.22; Is 43.6.
14. Lit., "within the veil."
15. Allusion to Mt 8.12; cf. 13.42, 50; 22.13; 24.51; 25.30, echoed in §32.
16. Allusion to Gn 2.7; 3.19.
17. It was believed that upon death the souls of the righteous are received by angels, just as the souls of sinners are led to hell by demons (cf. Pseudo-Macarius,

benevolent beneficence that transforms earthly beings to heavenly beings, from disgrace to the honor for those invited and called into his Kingdom and glory, since he alone is worthy of glory and honor and praise.[18] 35(They come) with decorous humility, obedience to his laws, sacrificial gifts in the form of silent offerings of good deeds, (following) Christ, who offered himself with overwhelming humility for salvation[19] and (gave) hope through his priestly care: 36releasing those who are bound, forgiving debts, satisfying the needy, and doing similar acts of benevolence. (They come) with warm tears for the imminent redemption. 37Thus the departed in hope of eternal life in Christ are gone to be reconciled to the compassionate Father, the benefactor Son, and the caring Holy Spirit. And the heavenly hosts rejoice over them, as they do over sinners who truly repent with confession.[20] And their souls receive abodes, as each is worthy, to share in the rest in that place, under God's supervision.

38Those who weep and lament and despair hopelessly—like the heathen who have no hope[21]—over believers who have departed from this world cherishing hope, anger God. 39And by prolonging their mourning over the departed (person), they prevent him from having (the reward of) rest for the beneficent, good works offered to God. Moreover, they grieve the heavenly hosts and the souls of the righteous, even their own souls. 40And thus they bring punishment upon themselves, receiving sentences of condemnation because of hopelessness. 41The one who moves God's wrath and saddens the heavenly hosts and the souls of the righteous, and deprives of rest the soul of the deceased, *"shall bear the judgment, whoever he may be,"* according to the Apostle's saying (Gal 5.10). 42Now, since those who aggravate people bear the consequences, how much more those who (aggravate) God and his family, his holy angels. 43For (Scripture) says, *"God's judgments are according to truth, regarding those who do such things"* (Rom 2.2).

Spiritual Homilies, 22). An early liturgical order seems to be reflected here, as in Disc. 16.2; cf. Eph 5.19–20 and Col 3.16.

18. Echoing Rv 5.12, 13.

19. Echoing Phil 2.8.

20. Alluding to Lk 15.7, 10.

21. Allusion to 1 Thes 4.13; quoted at §65.

₄₄Human life is defined in three (phases): first, the period of gestation in the mother's belly, in the darkness and obscurity of the womb, until the time of birth; ₄₅second, the life of toil in the world, of being laden with the issues of life in the world, aided by the Creator's providential care provided from the land and the sea; ₄₆third, the land of the living, where death is unheard of, where the living blessedness is immutable—the essential brightness, the unforgettable joy ₄₇that cannot be described, since it is indescribable; for no ear has heard of it since it is incomparable to hearing and could not be grasped by thought,[22] for it is inscrutable to examiners. ₄₈Since no one could explain the formation of life in the belly, not even the visible things in general, human life, which is sustained by God's care from heaven, from the land, and from the sea, how much less the hoped-for-life that does not pass away? ₄₉The Scriptures simply invite those who believe to the promised Kingdom, and edify in hope those who are insightful. For things in heaven and on earth were fully given to nurture them with every goodness, not only for their prosperity but also because these reveal the benevolent Lord's true promises to those whom he loves.

₅₀Even those who love God are unable to describe the things to come. (To quote) from the Lord's word: *"The righteous will rise like the sun in the Kingdom of God"* (Mt 13.43). ₅₁Not only is sunlight unlike darkness; sunlight could not be compared with the light of glory with which the saints will be clothed, the light that casts no shadow, the eternal, unchanging light, full of life-giving goodness.[23] ₅₂What the sun is in the realm of the sense-perceptible, God is in the realm of the intelligible, he who gives light to all.[24]

₅₃As to those who here conduct themselves virtuously in life, following the counsel of the Lord's commandments, in hope of things to come, their good behavior will be like daylight in the world,[25] and they will not deviate from his will. Given their sense of grace,

22. Allusion to 1 Cor 2.9.

23. Cf. Disc. 2.32.

24. Cf. Plato's realm of the sense-perceptible idealized by the Sun or the son of the Good (enabler of the seen, the cause of light and sight), and that of the intelligible or the realm of the Ideas idealized by the Good (enabler of the unseen, the cause of knowledge and truth). See *Republic* 6.508a–509e. The two analogous realms are here claimed for God.

25. Echoing Mt 5.14.

they will not be scared of either pain or angels; they will not provoke God to anger, nor will they grieve the incorporeal hosts or the souls of the righteous. Those who react to every calamity mournfully and with grief, with sorrow and disquiet,[26] act outside God's will. ₅₄But those who go on virtuously through grief and sorrow, (feeling) they have not been harmed by what transpires, make God and the hosts of angels rejoice. They also gladden the souls of the righteous, as we mentioned above,[27] ₅₅which shine in the light of the promised good things, having crossed over into eternal life.

₅₆But as for sinners deceased in their wickedness and iniquity, without hope, they deserve to be mourned and cried over. ₅₇Those who have strayed from the promised good things and the everlasting joy are ushered to the unquenchable fire of hell and perpetual death, where there are weeping of eyes and gnashing of teeth always.[28]

₅₈But when those who are established in the faith and do good in life begin to mourn, (as though) without hope,[29] they may receive punishment from the Lord for their hopelessness, for they harm the souls of the departed. ₅₉These are the meritorious tears before the Lord: to hold memorial (services) for the dead by laying down one's own sins and self before God—not before the public, so that one may become a recipient of forgiveness of sins and not of punishment.[30] ₆₀And to pray with ardent tears during the day and to hold vigil at night. ₆₁(Let) those who have strayed from the heavenly light and the revealed glory of the great God mourn daily with sorrowful sobbing and steadfast fasting, with deep remorse and contrition. ₆₂Mourn with remorse and contrition for someone who because of personal sin is denied the good gifts promised by God, and pity those who have strayed from the good gifts that do not pass away. ₆₃And with fervent prayer and generous mercy, and every benevolent deed, along with (remembrance of) Christ's sacrifice for reconciliation with God,[31] be comforted about the departed into the hereafter.

26. Lit., "calm" (the opposite).
27. See §§33–37.
28. Allusion to Mt 8.12 (cf.13.42, 50; 22.13; 24.51; 25.30; and Lk 13.28).
29. Allusion to 1 Thes 4.13; quoted at §65.
30. Anticipating the next discourse.
31. Allusion to the Eucharist; see the frequent references and allusions to it in Disc. 13 (esp. 12–14, 45–48, and 66–68), including its implications for philanthropy. Elsewhere, see Disc. 11.6; 23.49.

₆₄Such are those who benefit themselves and the departed, along with their kin, and show their intimate love for the one who has departed from the world. ₆₅Regarding believers who have fallen asleep in hope, the Apostle comforts and says: *"Do not grieve like the heathen who have no hope. For as Christ arose from the dead, so will Christ raise our deceased ones and us, and will present us with all his saints at his coming"* (1 Thes 4.13–14, 17). ₆₆Hope may be illustrated by the Maccabean army, which, taking the challenge of the heathen upon itself, went to war. They gave the spoils to the priests to distribute to the poor for the remission of the sins of those who strayed from the truth.[32] ₆₇And since the Scriptures are our teachers, we receive from them the eternal hope, and we live by it in the world; and being truly established in the sacred love, we move on to the living, blessed hope that is eternal.[33]

₆₈*"Honorable before the almighty Lord is the death of the saints,"* says the Prophet (Ps 116.15 [115.6 LXX]).[34] ₆₉And how is the death of the saints honorable? Because the determined pursuit of goodness along with the rest of the virtues points to that hope in eternal life. ₇₀And how is the death of God's saints honorable? Because they have passed from this sinful life to eternal life. ₇₁And how is the death of God's saints honorable? Because they have passed from these painful sorrows to that good rest. ₇₂And how is the death of God's saints honorable? Because they have passed from the misery and gloominess of this life to the blessed life. ₇₃And how is the death of God's saints honorable? Because they were delivered from the intractable temptations of soul and body and were taken to (the place of) serenity. ₇₄And how is the death of God's saints honorable? Because they have left old age and weakness behind and have moved on to renewal. ₇₅And how is the death of God's saints honorable? Because they were taken up to the love that made them overcome all the wants of the body. ₇₆And how is the death of God's saints honorable? Because they died unto sin on earth and longed for the living hope.[35] *"For when Christ, our life, is revealed, then will the saints be*

32. Cf. the hymn on Simon Maccabaeus in 1 Mc 14.4–15; also Gregory Nazianzen, *Oratio 14: De pauperum amore* (PG 35:857–909), and *Oratio 15: In Machabaerum laudem* (PG 35:912–933).

33. Lit., "is and remains." Echoing Ti 2.13.

34. Rhetorically amplified in the sequel, §§69–78, and alluded to in §96.

35. Echoing 1 Pt 1.3.

glorified with him" (Col 3.4). ₇₇Because the saints persisted in the living virtues in the world, they now live in God's care; ₇₈*"for the souls of the righteous are in God's hand"* (Wis 3.1), in the hope that gladdens according to the true promises of God; for they will be honored in glory for their sanctity and righteousness and truthfulness in the Kingdom of Heaven by the Most Holy Trinity.

₇₉Those who while alive in this body partake of the sins of the world, its repulsive filth and iniquity, the divine Book calls them "the living dead,"³⁶ ₈₀as in the saying of the Lord (to someone): *"Let the one dead in sin bury his dead father,"* but as for him, *"to preach the Kingdom of God"* (Lk 9.60). ₈₁For those who here have lost hope and have alienated themselves from God and right living, they are truly dead. ₈₂Those who carried out the inclinations of the body and of the mind, they are like tombs rotten in sin,³⁷ (having committed) every sin indiscriminately in their own unholy and defiled bodies. They thus emit the stench of lawlessness; ₈₃as the Lord refers to the assembly of the Pharisees, who show off outwardly while *"inside they are full of wickedness, evil, and blasphemy"* (Mt 23.27). ₈₄*"Their throats are open like graves,"* says the Prophet; *"judge them, O Lord God, for they have fallen into their evil thoughts"* (Ps 5.9–10 [10–11 LXX]). ₈₅Mourn over such people who were "living dead" and died the usual death without consolation.

₈₆*"The death of the wicked is an evil"* says the Prophet (Ezek 18.23), because they are given to iniquity and unholy life. But those who hate the righteous for their wholesome counsel, will have (belated) remorse, because they will be ushered into the unquenchable fire of hell. ₈₇How is the death of the wicked an evil? Because they died in hopelessness, they sinned with no remorse; they did not repent and become reconciled with God. ₈₈How is the death of the wicked an evil? Because they ceased to be heirs of angels and became heirs of demons, and the eternal torment is prepared for them by the Lord of All. ₈₉How is the death of the wicked an evil? Because they have left this world, where they lived senselessly, without thinking of the day of departure, beyond which one cannot do good to pay for admission unto God. ₉₀How is the death of the wicked an evil? Because they will hear from the Lord of All: *"Depart from me, ac-*

---

36. Repeated in §85. Besides Lk 9.59–60, see Mt 8.21–22.
37. Echoing Mt 23.27.

cursed, to the eternal fire" (Mt 25.41), for they became willing partners of Satan and not of God, who made everything by his good will. 91How is the death of the wicked an evil? Because the gates to life through repentance are shut, and it is not possible (for them) to hear the Lord say: *"Return to me, and I will return to you"* (Mal 3.7), but rather, *"Take those who did not obey me to the outer darkness"* (Mt 22.13). 92How is the death of the wicked an evil? Because the devouring gates of hell have been opened for the manifold iniquities they have committed without remembering the eternal tortures for sinners.

93Remorse is of no avail there, because compassionate love for humankind is forbidden to those outside the nuptial chamber. 94There is not even a drop of water desired from Lazarus,[38] or (anything) to put out the burning oil of the torches or the unquenchable things;[39] nor is there any visitation. 95Rather, *"sinners will go to eternal tortures,"* the Word of God told us, whereas *"the righteous will have eternal life"* (Mt 25.46), 96those saints whose death is deemed honorable before the Lord[40] because of their holy and right lives in true faith, being illumined by the light of eternal life.[41] 97For the Word, who does not lie,[42] has established from eternity the fate of the righteous and that of sinners. *"Sinners will go to eternal tortures, and the righteous to eternal life"* (Mt 25.46). 98The (latter) will praise and glorify the One Godhead; they will be blessed and crowned with glory, honor, and privilege; they will be ushered into the inheritance that comes with adoption;[43] they will forever enjoy the endless goodness to the glory of the Most Holy Trinity, now and always, for all eternal ages. Amen.

---

38. Allusion to Lk 16.19–31.

39. Read ազշիշելիք (*anšijelik῾*) for անշրշելիք (*anšrjelik῾*, "things that cannot go [or be moved] around").

40. Allusion to Ps 116.15 (115.6 LXX), quoted and amplified above, §§68–78.

41. Allusion to Jn 8.12; cf. "light of life" in Disc. 10.89; 11.210.

42. Allusion to Ti 1.2; cf. Nm 23.19; Ps 89.35 (88.36 LXX); Heb 6.18; and Disc. 20.164.

43. See Rom 8.14–17, 23; Gal 4.1–7; Eph 1.5–6.

DISCOURSE 13

A REVIEW OF THE GOODNESS OF MEMORIAL SERVICES,[1]
DEMONSTRATING OPENLY THEIR HIDDEN BENEFITS THAT
LEAD TO VIRTUOUS DEEDS, TO THE LIVING HOPE, TO
THE ARMIES OF THE WAKEFUL BEINGS WHO HERE
ACCOMPLISHED WHAT IS PLEASING TO GOD

H, FOR THE depth of the riches of the knowledge and wisdom of God" (Rom 11.1), who in many ways leads those who hear and obey to the good pleasure of his Lordship; and who admonishes through his sacred love, through the exercise of caution and discernment, to keep his commandments—so that we may arrive at the gate of salvation, of life, into that rest which is by virtue of his providential love. So that we may inherit the glorious honor through apt righteousness, and have the true hope realized through faith;[2] ₂to wake up amid those diverse gifts when the

---

1. Pl. յիշատակք (*yišatakkʻ*, lit., "remembrances") is used thirteen times in this anticipated discourse (Disc. 12.59): in the sense of (1) remembrance of the righteous dead, §§4, 12, 14, 24–25; (2) memorial services for them, §§3, 66, 69, 70, 88; and (3) commemoration of the saints, §§51, 52, 58, 65. These "remembrances" are with Eucharistic celebration (cf. Disc. 16.24–25), itself a "remembrance" (sing., յիշատակ [*yišatak*], the *Anamnesis*, observed by those being remembered, §35), but also variously referred to as Christ's atoning "sacrifice" (պատարագ, *patarag*, §§12, 14, 46–48, 51, 66, 89; compared to Abel's, §15), the "saving mystery" or sacrament (փրկական խորհուրդ, *pʻrkakan xorhurd*, §§45, 66, 68), or "the Lord's body and blood" (մարմին և արիւն Տեառն, *marmin ew ariwn Teaŕn*, §§35, 56, 67, 68). For Eucharistic references elsewhere in the *Discourses*, see "Eucharist" in the Subject Index. On the early notion of the Eucharist as "sacrifice," see Robin Darling Young, "The Eucharist as Sacrifice According to Clement of Alexandria," in *Rediscovering the Eucharist: Ecumenical Considerations,* ed. Roch A. Kereszty (New York: Paulist Press, 2003), 63–91.

2. Hope (with faith and love) is a recurring theme in this discourse, with repeated Pauline allusions. The qualified "living hope" (as in 1 Pt 1.3; cf. Disc. 3.20; 8.47; 11.38, 137; 12.76; 15.7; 20.21, 89, 125), however, is limited to the title of the discourse.

Word of Life summons those who are worthy and just to receive the promised good things hoped for; and to fly on the wings of the Spirit to the Kingdom of Heaven. To become a means to life for many by our beautiful lives; ₃to move on, through memorial services, to the things hoped for in the hereafter; and with true faith to lay out the certainties of (eternal) life, to be coveted by many. ₄For those who came before became examples of good motivation to those who came later, and the latter are constantly renewed in virtue by their remembrance of the former. ₅By praising them and giving thanks, they glorify God, the Giver of such gifts to humankind. ₆One should be so motivated by God's love, confessing aloud the truth about God's omnipotent power, bringing good gifts of righteousness to the Lord of All, being helped by those who came before, being true to their company; ₇considering oneself inseparable from them, their hope, their intimate love, and their constant intercession with the Lord for (us to receive) the promised things; so that we may become³ true followers of those who came before, who are alive with God because of their hope.

₈There is a mutual benefit in hope: those who came before rejoice over the good works of those who came later, and the latter become established in the realized hope of the former. ₉Those of us who came later have become heirs of our predecessors' virtue; for the good works of those who came before affect the fulfillment of those who come later. ₁₀Even if one sins, yet confesses with conviction and repents with warm tears, with compassion for the homeless, and with all the good deeds that work together against sin, he leaves a good example as an inheritance to those who come later, who confess, repent, and apologize to those they have wronged. ₁₁God's compassion calls those who come later to follow the example of those who came before; so that, with the penalty for sin lifted consequent to genuine repentance, those who have abstained from all harms associated with unbelief and unholy life corrupted by the currents of evil may enter into their inheritance. And so they become healed, with their whole members sanctified and healthy.

₁₂It is customary, even in Scripture, to keep the good remembrance of the upright who came early on.⁴ It is like the bequest of

---

3. Lit., "they may become."
4. The allusion here, as the following context indicates, is to the host of biblical

the (Eucharistic) sacrifice passed down to those who came later, for the realization of the common hope, to continue with faith and right conduct the husbandry pleasing to God, who is the hope of the living and the dead. 13Many who came later offered acceptable prayers, petitions, and gifts (of righteousness)[5] to God, with respect for those who came before; who with true confession and repentance turned to God—14as the Apostle points to their distinct faith and just rewards.[6] [And with (our) remembrance, along with their intercession, to offer conciliatory, (Eucharistic) sacrifices to God, on their and our behalf.][7] 15He thus makes mention of Abel's righteous and right sacrifice,[8] himself the first of all sacrifices, mediator and intercessor for those who came later by God's[9] intimate, holy, and pleasing will: 16those who after him became virtuous, pure in thought, pleasing to God, like Enosh,[10] Enoch, and Noah, who stand as intercessors before his Lordship on behalf of those who believe in the Lord God; 17like Abraham, Isaac, and Israel, who were privileged with utmost goodness as they were chosen.[11] 18For this reason, God is not ashamed to take them as confidants,[12] and to reveal the concealed things as one would to those intimately beloved.

19From among their descendants are the Lawgiver[13] and the Prophets, the priests, and the kings, and many others. 20For Moses

---

worthies mentioned in Heb 11, beginning with Abel. In this rather complicated paragraph, "the upright who came early on" or "before" (or the first of "those who came later," i.e., after Abel) are the Patriarchs (Enosh, Enoch, Noah, Abraham, Isaac, and Israel, §§16–17); and "those who came later" are the Prophets and the rest of the saints down to the author's present ("the Lawgiver and the Prophets, the priests and the kings, and many others," §19; cf. §§9–10, 66, the "we/us" in the rhetorical narrative).

5. See above, §6.

6. See the note on §12.

7. An interruptive gloss, albeit stated accurately—given the overall context of the discourse; see note on the title of the discourse.

8. Allusion to Heb 11.4 and 12.24; cf. Gn 4.10.

9. Lit., "his."

10. Not named in Heb 11.

11. The Hebrew Patriarchs' intercession for their descendants is a recurring theme in Jewish writings of the Second Temple period; e.g., Apocalypse of Zephaniah 11.1–6; Philo of Alexandria, *On Rewards and Punishments* 166–167.

12. Allusion to Heb 11.16; cf. Gn 18.17.

13. Common epithet for Moses.

"considered it better to suffer with the people of God rather than to enjoy the fleeting pleasures" (Heb 11.25). ₂₁Thus he left the dark life of the Egyptians for the desert, becoming an alien. There he received God's command to return and lead the people to the Promised Land, with signs and wonders; and through him the covenant with the hopeful fathers was realized.[14] ₂₂For God says: *"I am the God of Abraham, the God of Isaac, and the God of Jacob"* (Ex 3.6). ₂₃God is not called the God of dead sinners, but of the living righteous;[15] for the righteous are alive unto God, for with love toward God and hope, they are always in God's presence.[16] ₂₄And we have been established in faith and in God's sacred love so that, being justified by his love, we may obtain the hope that is in the almighty Lordship. And through (our) remembrance of all the righteous, we are being constantly renewed in God's love, which was extended to us through them. ₂₅Thus the hope of all the saints is kept alive and ever burning before God, and the remembrance of the sacred love of those whose hope is in the Lord is not forgotten. ₂₆Indeed, Reuben's sin against his father removed him from his father's blessing;[17] whereas the impeccable purity of Joseph drew his father's blessing, and among the inheritance of his brothers was that of (his sons) Ephraim and Manasseh,[18] and he became the cause of life for the entire pure and holy nation.

₂₇Sennacherib's fear struck Jerusalem because of the wicked people in the days of Hezekiah. ₂₈The prayers of the king and Isaiah, however, turned the wrath against the enemies of God, and thousands (of Assyrians) were slain; the very remembrance of them

---

14. Echoing Acts 26.6–7.

15. Allusion to Mt 22.32 and parallels.

16. Echoing 2 Cor 1.10; 1 Tm 4.10; 6.17.

17. Referring to Gn 49.3–4; cf. 35.22.

18. Referring to Gn 48.5–14. Reuben's loss of the birthright, bestowed by the aged Jacob upon the younger of Joseph's two sons, Ephraim, hardly illustrates the cessation of Reuben's remembrance from among the Twelve Tribes of Israel. Joseph's remembrance was perpetuated in part by the inclusion of his two sons among the Twelve, more so after the Tribe of Levi was not granted territory but the priesthood instead (on the distribution of the land, see Jos 13–21). Since Joseph is the father of two of the Twelve Patriarchs, he is considered above his brothers. He thus joins Abraham, Isaac, and Jacob as the progenitors of the Twelve.

vanished.[19] [29]David refers to these people.[20] [30]Conversely, all the righteous will be remembered when the world is visited, from the beginning of the Holy Scriptures till the coming of Christ, who will reveal everyone's virtue; for all the saints died holding on to faith.[21]

[31]When Jesus Christ, the Sun of Righteousness and Savior of the world, our Lord, shall rise, he will fully supply what is lacking even from the outset; for he will open the gates for the gift of new life (to flow) through the enlightenment of the (baptismal) font and the right faith in the Most Holy Trinity. And (so the righteous) die the death of sin in the water of sanctification, and rise with Christ in the newness of life.[22] [32]And even when they die, they are alive in spirit, in the hope of eternal life. [33]They have taken off the old man who was indebted to the law of vengeance; for they have clothed themselves with Christ[23] and have taken on his image through adoption,[24] and have become heirs of Christ. [34]Moreover, they have strongly maintained the true faith and the right conduct until death, hoping in Christ; for their hope is in the risen Christ—in Christ *"seated at the right hand of the Majesty on high"* (Heb 1.3). And through Christ they intercede with the Father on behalf of the saints [35]who were baptized in Christ, with true faith and sacred love, through communion with the Savior's body and blood, which are a pledge for hope in the resurrection glory according to the word of the Lord: *"As often as you eat of my body and drink of my blood, you proclaim the remembrance of my death until my return to earth"* (1 Cor 11.26).[25]

[36]For he is the deliverer and justifier. It is through him that the sins of the old self are forgiven and new things begin for those who—by God—(keep) the holy and true faith in Christ Jesus, depart from every evil, and do every good deed in the hope for the life (full) of the promised good things. [37]*"For by his death, Christ broke*

---

19. Referring to 2 Kgs (4 Kgdms LXX) 18.13–19.36; cf. Is 37.1–13.
20. Likely reference to Ps 53.5 (52.6 LXX).
21. Allusion to Heb 11.13.
22. Allusion to Rom 6.4.
23. Echoing Gal 3.27; cf. Rom 13.14; Eph 4.22, 24.
24. See Rom 8.14–17, 23; Gal 4.1–7; Eph 1.5–6.
25. In this theologically loaded paragraph much hinges on the linkage of the two basic Sacraments, baptism and the Eucharist, to the notion of adoption; cf. Disc. 5.45; 9.23; 14.17.

the power of Satan, who had control over death because of sin" (Heb 2.14), that they may reign in a life of righteousness. And the resurrection hope is founded in Christ. ₃₈For (Scripture) says: *"He raised us up with him and seated us in the heavenly realm with Christ Jesus"* (Eph 2.6). ₃₉*"For with Christ they have crucified their bodies with the desires and the passions"* (Gal 5.24), so they will be glorified with him. And they rejoice in that hope.

₄₀For Christ, with his sacred love, encourages the saints through his conciliatory sacrifice, by which he saved his creatures. ₄₁Through his voluntary crucifixion he made invisible things visible, that he might reconcile the Creator to his creatures.[26] ₄₂And through his luminous teachings he established the true faith in the Most Holy Trinity. ₄₃And he takes away the grievous ailments of humans, their diverse pains, from those in the grip of suffering: by feeding the hungry multitude in the desert, by raising the dead, and by chasing away demons. ₄₄And, by rescuing humans from their grip, he lifts all the ailments of humankind through his suffering. And through diverse favors, he makes them worthy of the fatherly care and the grace of the Holy Spirit, and of the good things promised by God.

₄₅And when (the celebrant) offers the awe-inspiring, overwhelming, and saving mystery (of the Eucharist),[27] he mentions the beneficence of (God's) love for humankind;[28] and sobbing with tears, he makes petitions, asking for atonement for the dead and the living.

---

26. Allusion to Rom 5.9–11; cf. 2 Cor 5.18–20; Col 1.19–22 and esp. 2.15 ("And having disarmed the powers and authorities, he made a public spectacle of them, triumphing over them by the cross," NIV).

27. Cf. §§66 and 68, where *p'rkakan xorhurd* as reference to the Eucharist recurs; elsewhere, see Disc. 6.38; 9.49; 15.59; 16.25.

28. In "The Prayers before Communion," where the celebrant taking a fraction of the bread says "tearfully" in the first prayer: "... according to your infinite love for humankind grant that this communion be for the expiation of sins and the loosing of transgressions." So also in the "Prayer of St. John Chrysostom," which follows in *The Divine Liturgy of the Armenian Church*. This Eucharistic notion of "love" had profound implications for philanthropy in the early Church, which seems to be contemplated further, below (§66), and also in Disc. 11.6, 20, 76–77, 127; 12.63; and 23.49. For more on the philanthropic effects of this notion, see John A. McGuckin, "Embodying the New Society: The Byzantine Christian Instinct of Philanthropy," in *Philanthropy and Social Compassion in Eastern Orthodox Tradition: Papers of the Sophia Institute Academic Conference, New York, Dec. 2009*, ed. Matthew J. Pereira, SISOT 2 (New York: Theotokos Press / Sophia Institute, 2010), 50–71.

46Above all, if the one offering the (Eucharistic) sacrifice is holy, pure, and free of sin, embracing the true faith, he receives the crown of glory.[29] 47And to those for whom the sacrifice is (offered), the hoped-for atonement is granted by the benevolent Lord. 48*"For one who has a grudge against his friend, should leave his sacrifice until he is reconciled"* (Mt 5.23–24). What more need be said, by frightening threats of punishment, to the wicked who lead miserable lives, to those who offer the (Eucharistic) sacrifice in an unholy manner, and to those who receive communion unworthily?[30] 49But the Lord tells us in the Gospel: *"Much is demanded from someone to whom many gifts were given; and less from someone with less"* (Lk 12.48). 50Truth demands perfect virtue from the minister of the Sacrament, for it is life for our redemption. Let no one be found willingly under the Lord's condemnation,[31] *"for all things exist through him and for him"* (Col 1.16)—whether living or dead.

51As for the commemoration of the holy Apostles, Prophets, and martyrs, it is done with Christ's (Eucharistic) sacrifice, with thoughtful glorification of the saints' martyrdom; recounting it for the edification of those who love God and for praising the Most Holy Trinity, who gave the grace of victory to all his saints. 52The commemoration of the saints, who triumphed over tyrants and became angels, is cause for celebration among the heavenly beings.

53Now, *"the souls of the righteous are in the hands of God"* (Wis 3.1), among the ranks of incorporeal beings, a remarkable thing to the glory of God—this hope that gives joy.[32] 54And in the general resurrection, the body—in which one became pleasing to God—will be revived from the earth; and they will become like angels in heaven, as the word of the Lord says: *"At the resurrection people neither take wives nor belong to husbands; they are like the angels in heaven"* (Mt 22.30). 55Do you see? The hope of the living is to have their abode with angels and the righteous, and to rejoice together.

56But those who sin and truly confess, repenting with warm tears and every good work, they will not be deprived of the impending hope. All who truly believe in the Father, the Son, and the Holy

29. Lit., "he receives crowns of glory for himself."
30. Allusion to 1 Cor 11.27.
31. Echoing Heb 10.26–31.
32. Echoing Rom 5.2; 12.12.

Spirit, being enlightened through baptism and Christ's body and blood, are children of light and heirs of the Kingdom; fellow citizens with the saints and God's family.[33] [57]For *"There is one God, one faith, one baptism and life-giving hope"* (Eph 4.5, 4). [58]Those who commemorate the saints with faith will rejoice with hope, since they delight in their love for them and do all these good works for God's sake—with hope in Christ.[34] [59]What had remained in terms of good things for the former (saints to have accomplished), the latter fulfill;[35] for what had remained for the Prophets, the Apostles did fulfill. And what is from them (in terms of) faith and (godly) living, with rewards for each according to one's works, the teachers (of the Church)[36] have established.

[60]Crowns are given to all of them by the Lord. As the Apostle says: *"The sun has one kind of glory, and the moon another kind of glory, and the stars another kind of glory; and star differs from star in glory. So will it be with the resurrection of the dead"* (1 Cor 15.41–42). [61]Each puts on his glory from the Lord, as one deserves, from the one Godhead of glory: Father, Son, and Holy Spirit. [62]For it is one heavenly hope, a call from God.[37] The Godhead is of one nature, one essence, eternally immutable, one almighty power; inerrant knowledge, irrevocable wisdom, being without beginning, who dwells in his own true living glory and in unapproachable light.[38] [63]And his care with sacred love for his creatures overflows with ineffable, indescribable goodness. [64]And he invites all his rational and intelligent creatures to that ineffable blessedness, and calls them to his Kingdom, to the inexpressible and eternal joys of that blessedness.

[65]In commemorating the departed righteous, their martyrdom and love—as befits God's confessors, we receive many personal benefits through these saints' intercession with the Lord. [66]As for believers who have sinned, confessed, repented, partaken of the saving mystery, and have departed from the world, memorial services are held with Christ's (Eucharistic) sacrifice and with prayers,

33. Echoing Eph 2.19; Phil 3.20.
34. Echoing 1 Cor 13.13; 2 Cor 1.10; 1 Tm 4.10; 6.17.
35. Those who commemorate the saints.
36. See note to Disc. 5.1.
37. Allusion to Col 1.5–6, 23–27.
38. Allusion to 1 Tm 6.16; cf. Ps 104.2 (103.2 LXX).

with compassion for the homeless, and with other good deeds.[39] For by the benevolence of us who have come later, those who are at rest are in truth renewed[40] in eternal life.

[67]Should someone ask: If one who is near death is remorseful, confesses and weeps for the sins he has committed, promises to repent, and asks for the body and blood of Christ, with faith in the atonement, would there be hope for his salvation?

[68]Answer: (Yes), if they are near death, and were caught in a dire life because of the lures of Satan and strayed from (God's) initial, providential love, but are remorseful at the end and confess with warm tears, and wholeheartedly seek the saving mystery —believing, in hope, in Christ's love for humankind, not being hopeless regarding the promised goodness, being remorseful, and (receiving) the life-giving body and blood of Christ our Savior, who grants life to his creatures. *"For everyone who calls on the name of the Lord will live"* (Jl 2.32).[41]

[69]There is no need to talk about memorial services for those who neither repented early on nor had remorse or hope at the end, who neither made confession nor drew near to the saving mystery. Christ grieves heavily for them. [70]But for those who earlier had sinned and truly confessed and repented, there will be memorial services always, even for those who were remorseful in the hour of leaving (this world). [71]For those who remain, much consolation is offered regarding the departed from the world, (if they) free those who are bound, forgive debt(or)s, and satisfy the needy with provisions. [72]If one does good and fulfills what is commanded, his good deeds will follow him to (where his) faithful loved ones are who have departed from the world.

[73]To the truly remorseful who draw near to the Sacraments, these gifts become like purifying fire, redemptive and enlightening (to those who show) intimate faith attested by their fear of God, replete with caution and righteousness. [74]For *"the fear of the Lord is the beginning of advantageous benefits,"* according to the saying of the wise man (Prv 1.7), and all things that are impossible become possible

---

39. See note 28 to §45.
40. Lit., "renewed with the renewal."
41. Cf. Acts 2.21; Rom 10.13.

to those who fear God.[42] ₇₅As for one who is far from the fear of
the Lord, he descends into sluggishness and spitefulness regarding
God's commandment, keeps away from every good counsel and
deed, and becomes engrossed in injustice.

₇₆Through the holy angels, God will always support those who
make an effort to obey the spiritual law with fear of God, according
to the word of the Lord, which says: *"Be careful. Do not despise any
of these little ones; for their angels see daily the face of my Father, who is in
heaven"* (Mt 18.10). ₇₇For faith is strengthened through work;[43] and
prayer through love, remorse, and earnest and persistent petitions.
For one ought to abide steadfastly in the will of the Lord, in hardship and in calm, and carry the grace of victory into the battlefield
of the mind and the members of the body, by God's benevolent
care. ₇₈And to become virtuous with clean heart and sincere faith,
making the angels happy with living love and having them rejoice
always over constant good works. ₇₉For it is through them that God
provides us protection,[44] even *"the things neither seen nor heard, which
God has prepared for the care of those who love him"* (1 Cor 2.9).

₈₀Every mystery or any intimate act by heavenly, earthly, or sub-
terranean beings is weighed daily before God's almighty Lordship.
₈₁And on the side of true believers and lovers of God, the death of
Christ is presented with all his passion (as) a testimony to his sacred
love for his saints. ₈₂Around him the truly righteous, the valorous
martyrs, the justified saints, the chaste virgins, and the patient
witnesses are gathered.[45] ₈₃Surely the confessors' lives move the
compassion and mercy of the caring, sacred love. ₈₄And the acts of
the lawless and disobedient, of the wicked and sinners and all who
(follow) evil desires, along with the evil ones who confer with demons, are severely rebuked and receive their deserved punishment

42. Allusion to Lk 1.37; cf. Mt 19.26 and parallels.
43. Allusion to Jas 2.20.
44. Possible allusion to Mt 18.10; cf. Gn 48.16; Ps 34.7 (33.8 LXX); Acts 12.11,
15; Heb 10.28.
45. All adjectives in this section are renderings of nominative, abstract nouns
ending with -t'iwn, followed by genitive nouns ending with -ean. The last category,
Arm. մարտիրոսք (martiroskʻ), in the context of the persecuted Church, represents
those who endured boldly in the face of cruelty or unfair treatment—often unto
death.

in recompense from the righteous Judge, who sees and knows the intangible[46] and inner things.

₈₅Those established in the sacred love of Christ—who yielded himself to death for their sake, in order that they may be saved from bitter, seen and unseen miseries and may live—they have the saints and all the righteous (as) comrades and intercessors. ₈₆And the gates of life, of benevolence by the grace of the Holy Spirit, will be opened in the upper realms, where the assemblies of the saints are at rest. ₈₇Whereas his will is for all to live and know that they are heirs of true life; for he does not will the death of the sinner, but his return to Christ.[47]

₈₈There is so much added advantage for those who observe the memorial services for those at rest, (who do so) mindfully, in just and true and holy faith, with reverence and sacred love, in ardent hope,[48] praising God. ₈₉Thus may our (Eucharistic) sacrifice within the veil[49] be acceptable, life-giving, unto life appertaining; and may we enjoy the blessed goodness, the promised good things (provided) by his caring, sustaining love. ₉₀*"For where I am, there will my servant be,"* says the Lord (Jn 12.26). ₉₁The heavenly Father welcomes those invited into his joy, together with his only-begotten Son, the lover of humankind, and with the life-giving Holy Spirit, into the overflowing, living, sacred love, into the never-parting, eternal, incomparable, and divine goodness to be enjoyed by those who are his own. Thanks, honor, and glory be to him, now and always, forever. Amen.

46. Lit., "the things above."

47. Allusion to Ezek 18.23, 32; 33.1.

48. Echoing 1 Cor 13.13.

49. Echoing Heb 10.20. Referring to the Eucharist offered within the veil separating the nave from the sanctuary in a church.

DISCOURSE 14

ON HUMAN NATURE, WHICH IS BY GOD'S PROVIDENT[1] CARE

REAT IS the mystery of godliness[2] with true faith in the Father and in the Son and in the Holy Spirit. Presenting oneself just and holy with virtuous deeds is more luminous than the sun. For it enlightens the believers' eyes of the mind,[3] chases sin's darkness, and leads to justice and holiness. ₂(It enables one) to stay away from troublesome life and evil thoughts; to walk in the paths of the just that lead to eternal life; ₃to follow kindly the will of the benevolent Creator who brought (things) into existence from non-existence and from ignobility to honor, in two parts: weak and strong, the body and the spirit. ₄For the weak (part) perseveres in toil and trusts in the strength of the Creator, lest it stray from his benevolent helpfulness that makes one virtuous through just and holy toil. ₅Thus (the weak part) takes the reputation of valor and is crowned proudly with praise, and, hoping for the blessed life, it thrives in his abundantly sustaining care. ₆As for the strong part, the spirit, by true faith and inerrant and sure knowledge of the Holy Trinity, discerns the deluding falsehood that leads astray and is freed from servitude to sin, which caused death to enter in. And being free of sin, it becomes an heir to Christ with the weak body, and manifests its intimacy (with the body) through patient forbearance, in hope.[4] ₇And the grace of God is revealed through the strong part, according to the saying of the Apostle, who asked

1. Lit., "overseeing."
2. Echoing Col 1.27; 2.2; 4.3.
3. A commonplace metaphor in Second Temple Judaism and early Christianity, based on Ps 19.8 (18.9 LXX).
4. Allusion to Rom 8.25.

God for the removal of weakness, who strove and labored and grieved with sundry sorrows and difficulties. And he heard the Lord say: ₈"*My grace is plenty for you, for my strength is made perfect in weakness*" (2 Cor 12.9). ₉For this reason, he willingly accepted all the grief of suffering, since weakness is made perfect through strength.[5] ₁₀For the laborers (in the vineyard) are honored with rewards for their manifold labors, and the Lord glorifies them with many a rewarding gift.[6]

₁₁This is the reason why he made the creatures out of four elements, and created the visible and invisible beings in their order. He thus formed the body from dry land, from moisture, from heat, and from coldness.[7] ₁₂Out of these four elements, (the things) to be generated and (the things) for their sustenance were made, in order to manifest the caring (side) of creation: heaven (caring) through the descent of rain from clouds and through heat from the luminaries—mixed with air, in order to nourish trees and plants and every breathing creature as well as birds of the air. ₁₃The earth is sustained with water, likewise creatures that swim and all aquatic (life), through God's caring. ₁₄In the first place, he put the rational spirit in the body and mixed them. He then prepared the essentials for sustenance, to demonstrate his provident love, which is from that abundant benevolence. ₁₅He demonstrated the spirit's rational and intellectual power through the sustaining grace of the Holy Spirit:[8] (by way of) admonitions to learn from the teaching of the spiritual law.

₁₆Benefiting from this spiritual sustenance one becomes acquainted with the almighty Lordship and care of the Creator, who gave life to all from (the four elements): heaven, earth, water, and air.[9] ₁₇And through these (admonitions) he teaches and edifies in the great hope for the promised good things: the adoption into eternal inheritance. The down payment for this freedom was

5. Arm. զաւրութեամբ (*zawrut'eamb*); the instrumental, with the transposition of the nouns, alters the sense of the quotation.

6. Possible allusion to the parable of "The Laborers in the Vineyard" (Mt 20.1–16); cf. Disc. 19.81.

7. Meaning: earth, water, fire, and air; but see §16.

8. Lit., "power of sustenance through the grace of the Holy Spirit."

9. Elsewhere on the four elements, see Disc. 4.4, 11, 39, 46, and 55.

given here through the grace of the (baptismal) font and the body and blood of Christ.[10] ₁₈For the one persevering in the weak body through sundry virtues demonstrates utmost patience, in keeping with God's pleasure, doing the will of the Lord with fear and sacred love. ₁₉For (Scripture) says: *"If he is Lord, where is (your) fear of him?"* (1 Kgs [3 Kgdms LXX] 18.21);[11] and if Father, *"His will be done on earth as in heaven"* (Mt 6.10). ₂₀And setting this precept by way of given laws and established commandments, that having strived for the best degree of virtue and power, and having emerged victorious, one may be crowned by Christ the Creator.

₂₁By this fact he declared the all-bountiful grace of his benevolence. ₂₂For he collaborates with his intimate servants for the betterment of their lives.[12] And in accordance with his caring love, he makes their collective troubles pass away, and their rest eternal. ₂₃And he himself, the Lord of Glory,[13] who is the Creator and Benefactor of all powers and authorities: when he wished to reveal his invisible love for the genus of humankind—which was in misery and grief—condemned to labor,[14] he had the intelligent and rational Word, united in oneness with God by his very Spirit, mixed into a body, in accordance with the word of the Gospel, which says: *"The Word took body and dwelt among us. And we beheld his glory as the glory of the only-begotten Son from the Father, full of grace and truth"* (Jn 1.14).

₂₄For through his true grace and voluntary lowering of himself[15]—that carried all the traits of the body and soul except for sin—he pointed the way to salvation for the just, to his much-loving care, his provident[16] remedies as grace to heal the seen and unseen (ills) of the children of men. He healed the sick, forgave sins, chased away demons, and raised the dead. ₂₅And through his death he opened the gates of life and rescued souls from suffering. ₂₆And

---

10. Allusion to Rom 8.14–17, 23; Gal 4.1–7; Eph 1.5–6. The linkage of adoption to the cardinal Sacraments of baptism and the Eucharist is found also in Disc. 5.45; 9.23; cf. 13.31–35; cf. 2.129, 133; 3.17; 9.29–30, where it is linked to baptism only.

11. Cf. Dt 6.13; Ps 33.8 (32.8 LXX); 34.9 (33.10 LXX).

12. Or, "in (their) good behavior."

13. Echoing 1 Cor 2.8.

14. Allusion to Gn 3.17–19.

15. Allusion to Phil 2.6–8.

16. Lit., "overseeing" (as in the title).

he fulfilled all righteousness[17] to the glory and honor of our humanity, becoming a teacher to all creatures so that we may follow his virtue and partake of his glory, which is kept in store for those whose hope is in Christ.[18]

27For this reason the body is weak, since it receives its nourishment from the earth, from plants and trees and breathing creatures just as all irrational animals do. 28Consequently, Noah was commanded to eat the meat of breathing animals and drink wine to turn sadness into solace, since he was grieving over the whole perished world.[19] 29For because of sin we departed from the life and nourishment that were in Paradise and fell into manifold weaknesses. 30For this reason we have been exposed to death, cold and heat, and the diseases of the body. 31Conversely, from the overabundance of food and drink come vexation and death; and from scarcity, famine and thirst. 32Moreover, poisonous reptiles and bitter roots and plants could vex and kill, numb and delude.

33For this reason the body is weak; for when we hear of God's image (in us),[20] we become arrogant and puffed up, and from that puffed-up state we fall into the abyss of perdition like the one who opposed God, of whom the prophet who was in the Lord's presence said: *"He will set his throne higher than the clouds and will become like the Most High"* (Is 14.14); but lo, he was brought down to hell with all his rebellious hosts.[21] 34Whereas Christ, humbly taking this body, toppled him through humility and lifted up the humble, and rebuked his haughtiness. 35The venom of his wickedness is so great, like the venom of reptiles and the harm of bitter plants and roots. 36Physicians say that there are roots that drive demons away from humans; and this makes sense, since God's (way of) operating through a weak substance shows the strength of his presumed weakness to the adversary who is powerless regarding the saints, who have been empowered by the Lord to trample on him, as it is obvious to all believers, 37those who do his will and put their hope in his hope: *"And they will turn back and be put to shame"* (Ps 6.10 [6.11 LXX]).

---

17. Echoing Mt 3.15.
18. Echoing Eph 1.12.
19. Referring to Gn 9.3, 20–21.
20. Allusion to Gn 1.27.
21. Cf. Ezek 28.1–19.

₃₈Whereas those who bless, prostrate, and offer praise to the almighty power of the Most Holy Trinity, even with this weak body, will fulfill all virtue with holiness and will pass away from the order of this world with all truth. They spend hours, days, and years and make progress. And the progeny of virtue, having pursued a holy and just life, having become disciples of holiness and having been truly grounded in every virtue, would cross from this world to the world of the living—where, in that gratifying, eternal joy, the notoriety of death is unheard of; ₃₉where, by the power of God, they are restored in that unending, eternal joy; ₄₀where they are kindled like little suns of the unapproachable Light,[22] and are on fire with the living, sacred love, burning with excitement about the eternal joy of blessedness (bestowed) by the Most Holy Trinity. And they enjoy the unending and ineffable favors from Christ Jesus our God. With him, to the almighty Father and to the grantor Holy Spirit be glory, dominion, and honor, now and always and unto the ages of ages. Amen.

22. Allusion to Mt 13.43. This thought, that the redeemed will shine like stars in heaven, is based on Dn 12.3. On God's "unapproachable light," see 1 Tm 6.16; cf. Ps 104.2 (103.2 LXX).

DISCOURSE 15

EXPOSITION ON THE HUMAN SOUL

GOD, IN HIS great love for humankind, in his multifaceted administration, cares for his creatures as befits his beneficence. ₂He created the immortal hosts of angels, his intelligent and rational ministers, so that they may glorify his almighty Lordship and willingly assist the human race. For they are in essence spirits, sent to minister at God's command.[1] ₃For all creatures are formed and constituted by him, and are ministers and servants of the great glory of the Godhead, who invites and calls humans to his Kingdom.

₄The progeny of men, from insemination,[2] is renewed, receives its being, and grows within the determined days to the impending birth. It then grows, through nourishment and knowledge, into counsel and learning about God; into heeding true justice and directing oneself justly by the spiritual law. ₅And they come to know the Creator and the beneficence of his sacred love toward his creatures. ₆And by the knowledge of his counsel one accepts obedience to the law and chooses the good over the evil things: to refrain from the painful experiences and to cling to the righteous attainments through the Lord. ₇And one thus fulfills all the virtues chosen in accordance with the spiritual law, with the mercy of God's multifaceted care, with much patience and firm establishment in his love. And with living hope,[3] one advances to the goal to which he is called: to the heavenly grace of the most generous and benevolent

---

1. Alluding to Ps 104.4 (103.4 LXX); Heb 1.7.
2. Arm. սադմնառնութեն (*satmnaṙnut'enē*), a *hapax*, is a likely corruption of սերմնառնութեն (*sermnaṙnut'enē*).
3. Echoing 1 Pt 1.3.

Most Holy Trinity. And earthly beings complete their lives within the bounds of the earth in accordance with God's foreknowledge: some till childhood, some till infancy, some till youth, some till old age. ₈This too is managed by God's care, for they do not know the day of their death. Thus, deluded, they stray from justice. Otherwise, they would be diligent and ever ready in holy acts all the days of their lives.

₉One who dies in childhood or infancy is immune from temptations and the worries of those in the world. He becomes an example[4] to those who stir the world into all righteousness and every virtue. And being perfect in faith, love, and hope,[5] pure and innocent, they are translated into immortal life, into the incorruptible inheritance of the just. ₁₀For the souls that leave this body go on to live, each according to its merit. The souls of the virtuous rejoice there, as promised in the pronouncement of blessings,[6] which are ineffable, kept in store for the saints who lived their lives in the world in accordance with God's will, in keeping with the proclamation of the Gospel.

₁₁The Lord pronounces blessed *"those who are poor in spirit"* (Mt 5.3), those who became poor in spirit for the sake of spreading the good news, for the sake of the Kingdom of Heaven, which is in the Lord Jesus Christ. ₁₂He pronounces blessed those who are humble in heart, *"for they will find rest"* (Mt 11.28)[7] from earth in heaven, which is infinitely high, which the humble receive in Christ Jesus. ₁₃He pronounces blessed *"those who are meek"* (Mt 5.5), for they inherit the land of the living, from where pain and sorrow and sighing have been banished by the ineffable hope in Christ Jesus. ₁₄He pronounces blessed *"those who mourn"* (Mt 5.4), which is for the sake of God's love, which out of the lowliness of the heart lets tears stream with grace-filled wisdom, which belongs to those who are comforted in Christ Jesus. ₁₅He pronounces blessed *"those who are pure in heart,"* those who have been delivered and cleansed from filthy desires, *"for they will see God"* (Mt 5.8). ₁₆He pronounces blessed *"the*

---

4. Lit., "attention." Echoing Mt 18.3.
5. Echoing 1 Cor 13.13.
6. Or, "The Beatitudes"; referring to Mt 5.3–12.
7. Conflated with "The Beatitudes" and mistaken for Mt 5.4.

peacemakers" (Mt 5.9), for they resemble the Son of God, who made peace in heaven and on earth[8] for those who (once) were far away and those who were near.[9] Thus they have become (blessed).

17The souls of the righteous are happy and thrive in every blessing as they rest in Christ until the general resurrection, when our Lord will return in the glory of the Father, and the dead in Christ will rise without corruption.[10] And the righteous deeds of those individuals who are virtuous come before the Most Holy Trinity.[11] 18For faith enables familiarity with the glory of God.[12] What need is there to speak of things that are seen?[13] As for the hope that leads one to the inheritance of the good things, the things that are wished for, it has been made real.[14] 19For *"Who then hopes for or looks for what they already have inherited?"* (Rom 8.24). 20So it is with (those who follow) patience, self-control, longsuffering, meekness, obedience, guidance, purity, and truth; they are (rewarded) with every blessing, glorified, and crowned. And the heirs[15] enter into the inheritance of the Kingdom. 21There is the realization, where virtue—in general—is essential for one to enter into the enjoyment of the good things that are endless, and to rejoice with the sacred love in the eternal blessings of the Most Holy Trinity, who is ineffable, unlimited, and unbounded.

22Likewise, evil men, unholy and rebellious against the truth, who follow injustice and die in it: their acts of injustice accompany them with bitter memories of their most evil desires, with frightening threats (made) to the lawless and disobedient, the unholy and the impure, and others—whatever their sins may be. 23Woe upon woe is assured for them in the divine Holy Scriptures, and punishments by the impartial Judge. 24For their hearts were foolish about listening, and they did not hear the voice of the Lord, nor hearken to his commandments. 25For this reason God's wrath is prepared

---

8. Echoing Col 1.20.
9. Echoing Eph 2.13, 17.
10. Echoing 1 Cor 15.52.
11. Echoing Rv 14.13.
12. Echoing Rom 4.20.
13. Echoing 2 Cor 4.18; cf. Rom 8.24.
14. Lit., "it has been conceded."
15. Lit., "the heir" (singular noun).

against the wicked and sinners who personally despised God's truth, those whom he threatened beforehand.[16]

₂₆And all these threats against transgressors have a very distressing effect on the souls of sinners, with saddening places or separate and distinct locations associated with[17] each sin. ₂₇And as sinners visualize these, being aware of the verdict of the just Judgment, the unquenchable fire and the outer darkness, the weeping of eyes and the gnashing of teeth,[18] their souls become saddened and distressed by the fear of these things until the common resurrection, which is through Christ.

₂₈What if someone were to say: "That is before the general Tribunal and rewards"; and "Where is the Apostle's saying: *'That those who have (gone) before, do not receive the things of the end before us'* (1 Thes 4.15)?" ₂₉Moreover, the Prophet says: *"Do not place your hope in princes, in the children of men, for the spirit leaves them and they return to earth, and on that very day all their thoughts perish"* (Ps 146.3–4 [145.3–4 LXX]).

₃₀If the souls of the just do not rejoice without bodies, why would the Lord have to declare this good news early ˙on[19]—were it not that he makes the souls of the saints rejoice? ₃₁Beforehand he also stated the threats against the wicked and sinners. Was it not to scare them? And so they become sorrowful, distressed. ₃₂This could be understood by the following illustration: It is like a king who promises gifts to brave warriors and victors; and they know for sure that in due time they will receive the promised gifts. They surely rejoice until (such a time when) they will receive the glory and the blessed crowns. ₃₃So it is with the souls of sinners who were threatened with death because of their transgressions, like those condemned to death by kings. They are held, kept in torture, in much dread and trembling until the time they receive their reward as deserved: the scourge of eternal tortures and punishment, which they receive in body and soul. ₃₄We say the same thing the Apostle

---

16. Allusion to Rom 1.18.

17. Lit., "according to." The belief that distinct *loci* in hell are associated with specific sins (a belief amplified in Dante's *Inferno*) derives from interpretations of Mt 10.15; 11.23–24; 23.14; cf. Lk 10.13–14; 12.47–48, as do the patristic views in *Purgatorio*.

18. Allusion to Mt 8.12 (cf. 13.42, 50; 22.13; 24.51; 25.30; and Lk 13.28).

19. Allusion to Mt 10.28.

said: *"Each person receives according to what he has done"* (Rom 2.6),[20] whether good or bad, at the general resurrection. ₃₅*"Do not place hope in princes"* (Ps 146.3 [145.3 LXX]),[21] says the Prophet, for they will be removed with their arrogant authority, and their haughty intentions will be brought down. ₃₆Rather, *"place hope in God"* (Ps 146.5 [145.5 LXX]), he says, for he is immortal and has eternal authority over death and life.

₃₇There are some who say that as a fetus in the womb is devoid of sensation yet alive, silent, without talking or hearing, mobility or activity, so too—they think—is the human soul, silent and lowly.[22]

₃₈Let them know this: following insemination there is development, and one takes a fetal form, a human image. And from birth, one grows to be a youth and is nurtured in youth, growing physically and mentally beyond the womb. ₃₉And after birth, as known to the Providence of God, who joins together soul and body, one reaches maturity in body and mind, yet falls short and is subject to death as ordained by God.

₄₀This is so, because in every stage of growth, virtue, in general, is (at work) refining one unto perfection in Christ, our common Head.[23] ₄₁And with faith and love and fear (of God),[24] one proceeds in the way of those who are just, (especially) *"the leader and perfecter of virtue, Jesus Christ"* (Heb 12.2), who cares for his earthly creatures with his manifold gifts. ₄₂Thus, the reposed souls of those who are asleep (share) in the feeling and in the ineffable acclamation of the angelic songs of praise. ₄₃For the divine Scriptures say that the human soul is living and immortal.[25] ₄₄By this it is understood

---

20. Quoting Ps 62.12 (61.12 LXX); cf. Prv 24.12; also Mt 16.27; 2 Tm 2.14.

21. Cf. Ps 118.9 (117.9 LXX).

22. In negating the Origenist notion of the preexistence of souls, the author draws on mostly Hermetic views regarding the embryo (see further below, §§45–47, 55–56; cf. Disc. 20.22 and note). He also seems to follow Gregory of Nyssa, for whom the soul—never devoid of sensation—is created simultaneously with the body, infused into it at conception (*De hominis opificio*, PG 44:236B, 276B, 282B). See Giulio Maspero, "Anthropology," in *The Brill Dictionary of Gregory of Nyssa*, ed. Lucas Francisco Mateo-Seco and Giulio Maspero; trans. Seth Cherney (Leiden and Boston: Brill, 2010), 38–39; and Ilaria Ramelli, "Embryo," in ibid., 256–57.

23. Echoing Eph 4.15; cf. 5.23; 1 Cor 11.3; Col 2.10.

24. Echoing 1 Tm 6.11.

25. See, e.g., Eccl 12.7; Acts 7.59; 2 Cor 5.1–4; 12.2–3.

that they are not devoid of feeling, but that they do (feel), and they praise the Creator. ₄₅You should comprehend this by the example of the body, as when in the womb and then growing in knowledge, in mind and body, and undergoing change.

₄₆When the immortal soul, rational and intelligent, leaves the body, it is capable of comprehending God and recognizing the Lord of Glory more knowledgeably.[26] ₄₇His comprehensible vision was previously concealed as in a cloud, because of (the soul's) being in the body, even though (the body) was sacrificed[27] for good works, in keeping with the spiritual law, choosing between good and evil: despising the evil and choosing the good, following the Lord's counsel and wisdom (given) with bounteous love.[28] ₄₈There is no reason to call the human soul mortal or senseless. Rather, as the prophet Ezekiel (saw) in one location the resurrection of the dead: first, the bones, the sinews, and the body coming together as one, in all its constituents; and then, the souls were summoned from their respective places by the Holy Spirit, as by wind.[29] ₄₉*"For you send your Spirit, and you receive and renew them"* (Ps 104.30 [103.30 LXX]). Moreover, resurrections of the dead by the Lord are reported in the Gospels.[30] These are testimonies to the soul's return to the body. ₅₀The mouth speaks, eyes see, ears hear, nostrils smell, hands touch, feet walk, the heart acts with apprehension, and they give praise to God with the animating soul, which—through the Lord—activates all the senses.[31] ₅₁But when the soul leaves the body, it is called a corpse, and all the connected parts of its members become disconnected. ₅₂Similar testimonies are (borne) by the motion, apprehension, recognition, and remembrance to the self-same soul (when it returns to the body), for souls enable, edify, and animate in accordance with God's will. ₅₃But if sensation is the cause of life, where then is the animation of the soul, which has its life through God?

26. Echoing 1 Cor 2.8 as well as Hermetic teaching, as noted in the Introduction.

27. Lit., "martyred."

28. See Is 7.15–16.

29. Referring to Ezek 37.1–14.

30. Each of the Gospels relates a different resurrection miracle: the "many" who were raised at the time of Jesus's death (Mt 27.53); the daughter of Jairus (Mk 5.21–43); the youth from Nain (Lk 7.11–17); and Lazarus (Jn 11.1–44).

31. Cf. Disc. 23.52.

₅₄Such is the understanding, that all motions are by the Spirit, and souls animate the body according to God's Providence. ₅₅Just as there are testimonies to the goodness of the body's active nature, likewise there are testimonies to the goodness of the soul's nature. ₅₆The soul is called the life in the sensual, suffering, and mortal body, out of which the Creator summons it to the heavenly dwellings prepared for the incorporeal beings. ₅₇For the body returns to the ground and rests unconcernedly;[32] and the pure and good soul, in the hope of the good news,[33] rejoices with the angels in the glory of the Almighty, as though having already received the promised blessings of the Kingdom of Heaven. ₅₈For (the Apostle) says: *"The Spirit himself testifies regarding our souls that we are the children of God and co-heirs with Christ"* (Rom 8.16–17), saved from slavery to sin unto freedom, to the glory of the Son of God.[34]

₅₉For the beneficence of (God's) love toward his creatures has been made known to all believers—through the luminous font and the saving mystery of the body and blood of the One who was sacrificed on the cross and took away the sins of the world—by those who with faith draw near to our Savior. ₆₀And when he returns in glory to renew the human race—and resurrects the dead—he will newly adorn with light the living righteous and the saints who are asleep in the Lord; and he will admit them into the joy of inheriting his eternal life, which is kept in store for the saints and those whose hope is in the Lord. ₆₁The Apostle says: *"And God, himself, will become all in all"* (1 Cor 15.28), because of his living, sacred love and life-sustaining care, ₆₂which he will bestow—to the glory of his Divinity—upon those justified by the right faith,[35] who have spent their earthly lives in holy and unstained conduct, and who have earned the life that does not pass away, that is in Christ, that is celebrated in the delightful glory of the Only Begotten, ₆₃who crowns with every blessing and glorifies according to the will of the Father and the Holy Spirit forever and ever. Amen.

32. See Eccl 12.7; 9.5.
33. Allusion to Col 1.23 (cf. Disc. 11.223).
34. Echoing Rom 6.15–23.
35. Echoing Rom 3.28; Gal 2.16; 3.11, 24 (cf. Disc. 2.154).

DISCOURSE 16

ON EDIFICATION FROM THE TEACHING
ABOUT THE MARTYRS

E SHALL henceforth speak about the martyrs, for we ought to honor their remembrance and to beatify them for their true witness and love; and we shall be rewarded bountifully by their intercession. ₂We shall offer the (commemoration) service to God with psalms and blessings and spiritual songs, praising with a cleansed heart the Existent, who is without beginning, and his almighty Lordship,[1] that he may make us worthy of a share in the inheritance of the saints, in approaching the light of the glory of his Lordship. ₃And all people who gather for the commemoration of the saints should consider, in faith and love, their martyrdom collectively; ₄beseech God through their intercession and with fervent tears; and stay watchful day and night with cleansed heart, that he may keep them safe from the evil of this world, in virtue-loving life—₅like the saints themselves whose commemoration is held to the glory of God. And the Lord, the Creator God who gave them such a victory over the oppressors and enemies of the truth, shall openly reveal to all (assembled) their intimacy (with him). ₆So that we may be given grace to overcome all the odds that rise against us in conflict, both seen and unseen, and to offer the (commemoration) service to the glory of God, bowing before him.

₇This too is the will of the saints, that because of their intercession people will be prompted to (offer such) service to God, and to be rewarded for their effort accordingly by the Most Holy Trinity. ₈(Consider) Paul and Barnabas, when they performed miracles in

1. Echoing Eph 5.19–20; cf. Col 3.16. Echoes of an early liturgical order are discernible here, as in Disc. 12.34.

223

the name of the Lord Jesus Christ, healing the man crippled from birth and amazing everyone to the point where the pagan priests thought of them as gods come down in human form. 9Wherefore they were about to honor them with sacrifices as gods. 10*"Thereupon they tore their clothes and shouted, saying: 'We are humans just like you, servants of the Most-high God who made heaven and earth and all creatures in them, and in whose Name this man was healed.' 11Even with these words, they scarcely quieted the crowd"* (Acts 14.14–15, 18). They preferred to die rather than accept the honor due to God and be glorified by men.

12Satan did this very thing: he took upon himself the honor due to God. And his Creator decided to withdraw his care from him; thus, he fell from the glorious order of the angelic ranks and became darkness instead of light and an heir to punishment in Gehenna.[2] 13For the holy Apostles and Prophets and the true teachers, being servants of God, considered such a thing to be insult; for they were aware that Satan fell because of pride, arrogance, and haughtiness. The meek and the lowly rise[3] (to heaven) to take the place of those who fell.[4] 14Christ, in particular, demonstrated indescribable humility, considering his Lordship.[5] Wherefore he says: *"Learn from me, for I am meek and lowly in heart, and you will find rest for your souls"* (Mt 11.29).

2. See Is 14.12–15 on the king of Babylon; Ezek 28.1–19 on the King of Tyre, interpretively taken as Satan. Note the contrast drawn in §14, alluding to Phil 2.6–8. Among other NT passages, see Lk 10.18; 2 Pt 2.4; Jude 6; and Rv 12.7–9. However interpreted, Gn 6.1–4 marks an early phase of the mythos.

3. Lit., "The rise of the meek and the lowly ..."

4. The thought that the redeemed from the human race will replace the fallen angels recurs in Disc. 23.102, and is found also in the *Teaching* traditionally attributed to Gregory the Illuminator (§640; quoted by Yovhan Mayragomec'i [d. ca. 640] in his «Վերլուծութիւն Կաթողիկէ Եկեղեցւոյ և որ ի նմա յաւրինեալ կարգաց» [*"Verlucut'iwn Kat'otikē Eketec'woy ew or i nma yawrineal kargac',"* "Analysis of the Universal Church and of the Orders Therein," §65, in MH 4:349–54; for a translation, see Abraham Terian, "A Discourse on the Church by Yovhan Mayragomec'i," in *Armenia between Byzantium and the Orient: Celebrating the Memory of Karen Yuzbashyan (1927–2009)*, ed. Bernard Outtier et al., TSEC 16 (Leiden: Brill, 2020), 237–38. Cf. Gregory of Narek (d. 1003), Մատեան ողբերգութեան (*Matean otbergut'ean, Book of Penitential Prayers*), 34.12. The thought stems from Lk 20.36, and is part of the doctrine of restoration (Gk. *apokatastasis*) in Eastern Christianity, as in the eschatology of Origen (*De principiis* 1.8.4), Gregory of Nyssa (*De virginitate* 24), and Maximus the Confessor (*Quaestiones et dubia* 19 [CCSG 10, ed. Declerck]).

5. Allusion to Phil 2.6–8.

₁₅All the saints, by virtue of their true humility before the Lord, lead all believers upward to God, that they may become worthy of salvation and forgiveness of sins by the Lord of All, through the intercession of the saints; and never again return to the bitter sway of Satan. ₁₆Rather, to have zeal for Christ by hearing about the martyrdom of each (of the saints), their perfect and pure love, their patient hope in God; ₁₇those who (endured) through fire and cold, water and ice, ropes and whips, prisons and shackles, hunger and thirst, sword and death, threats and torments that frighten the timid and soften the brave. ₁₈None of these extreme tortures, pains and afflictions and harms to the body, was able to destroy or sever their pure love for the Most Holy Trinity.⁶ ₁₉And because of their utmost love for God, they are able to intercede boldly with God. ₂₀For they endured all these bitter afflictions by their enemies with great patience because of the beneficent, sacred love of the One who loved humankind, who invited and called them.

₂₁So, let us heed with the saints, in pure love, the One who calls. Let us seek, with fervent and ardent tears, that rest, through our labors here. Let us quench the fire of the passions with the fire of the Holy Spirit. *"Let us cleanse ourselves,"* even our senses and the invisible movements of the soul, *"from guilty conscience"* (Heb 10.22). ₂₂For by true love for God, we may be worthy to partake of the good things of the saints. ₂₃For thus we join the company of the saints, and we celebrate to the glory of the almighty God, who gave them victory over the evil oppressors. And they are glorified in heaven; whereas those (oppressors) on earth shall remain there.

₂₄Thus we put our hope and faith in the company of the saints and their intercessions. For they serve like priests before the One who sits at the right hand of God;⁷ and they offer their personal sacrifices with prayers for the reconciliation of the people, both living and dead, for sins committed willingly and unwillingly. ₂₅Moreover, because of their true faith and earnest pursuit of the virtue-loving life, their sincere and holy and upright yearnings, grace-filled love and pleadings with sobbing, they believe they will receive from the Savior of All that which they ask for,⁸ in keep-

---

6. Echoing Rom 8.35–38.
7. Echoing Heb 1.3, 13; 8.1; 10.12; 12.2.
8. Echoing Mt 21.22; cf. Mk 11.24; Jn 11.22; 14.13; 15.7, 16; 16.23.

ing with the hope of the believing people, especially (as the latter approach) through the saving mystery[9] offered with sanctity unto Christ Jesus.

26The intercession of the saints on behalf of the believing people is to be understood in this way: 27those who—through their cherished labors—sacrificed their bodies on earth as sweet aroma for the sake of God's name, present their pure spirits to God with spiritual intercession for mercy on all.[10] 28Even the relics of their bones bestow the grace of salvation to the assembly of believers, as is well known to all; for the love of God seems to dwell in their relics, and is made manifest through wonders on earth.[11]

29Now, in anticipating the things hoped for, they have the certainty and the assurance of closeness to God, the boldness to intercede—something concealed from those in the body. Yet through these things that are not concealed, through their relics, we sense the grace-imparting power of God and the invisible company, indeed the presence of the Lord. 30(Scripture) says, however, that the spirit is regarded more than the body,[12] both by God and his creatures. 31For such grace was bestowed by God upon the Apostles, the Prophets, the martyrs and all the elect—the holy ones, (when) here on earth, as also in heaven. 32We shall be pleasing to God (if we follow) the lead of their decorum and virtue-loving lives. And they, through their continuous intercession, become the cause of our salvation and life.

33So we beatify those glorified by God: those who, for their love of God, gave themselves up for torture and death and received honor and imperishable gifts from the immortal King. 34Moreover, we offer the service commemorating the death of all God's saints with glorification and bowing to the Most Holy Trinity. 35For this is the will of both the Lord and all his saints; for he is worthy of glory and honor by all saints and creatures, now and always and to the ages of ages. Amen.

---

9. Or, "sacrament" (խորհուրդ, *xorhurd*); as elsewhere, a term for the Eucharist (Disc. 6.38; 9.49; 13.45, 66, 68; 15.59). On commemorating the saints with Eucharistic celebration, see Disc. 13, *passim*.

10. Lit., "on the world."

11. Cf. Agathangelos, *Teaching*, §564; *History*, §747.

12. Among the numerous biblical passages, see esp. Rom 8.1–17; cf. Gn 2.7; Eccl 12.7; Mt 10.28; 16.26; Jas 2.26; etc.

DISCOURSE 17

ON THOUGHTFUL DISCRETION (AND THE) ADVANTAGES OF READINESS, WITH HONOR FOR THE HEEDFUL AND PUNISHMENT FOR THE HEEDLESS[1]

 WRITE endeavoring to teach you, my brothers and children whom *"I begot in Christ, through the Gospel"* (1 Cor 4.15). ₂So that those who dedicate[2] themselves to good deeds and to learning the truth, who equip themselves against harms and consider various means of doing good, ₃may exemplify the truth by doing and teaching it always. They thus stand in undisturbed conscience and without excuse before those far and near, according to the word of the Lord: *"Let your light of righteousness shine before people, that they may see your good deeds and glorify your heavenly Father"* (Mt 5.16). ₄Moreover, he declares those servants blessed, whom he blesses and glorifies by name. And he denounces with woes and curses those who cause the name of the Lord to be blasphemed.[3]

₅For those who become advocates of the truth, the Truth himself honors them with unerring knowledge. ₆And God glorifies them when he sees their efforts in piety. For what they plant and nurture, God makes grow and establishes in the life (full) of the promised good things—for their glorification and exaltation when they are resurrected from the dead on the universal Judgment (Day). ₇And they will be able to say: *"Behold, here we are and our children in the truth, whom God has given us"* (Is 8.18). ₈And being crowned with virtue,

---

1. None of the subjects in the title are mentioned in the discourse; for elsewhere, see the Subject Index. Cf. 19.34, «վասէն ի զգուշութիւն զգաստութեան շահաւոր աւգտից սիրով» ("[tears] prompt [the mind] with love for the [spiritual] benefits of thoughtful discretion").

2. Lit., "honor."

3. Echoing Rom 2.24.

they receive the promised good things pledged by Christ.[4] ₉For he says: *"Whoever does and teaches (these things), he will be called great in the Kingdom of Heaven"* (Mt 5.19). ₁₀For (Scripture) says: *"Jesus began to do and to teach until the day he was taken to heaven"* (Acts 1.1).

₁₁Those who were entrusted with overseeing the people but are slothful in providing them care in spiritual instruction and exhortation, and who do not consent to give the needy their physical needs, but eat and drink senselessly, death shall come upon them unexpectedly, on a day not anticipated. And the dividing, sharp sword of God's word[5] shall cut him asunder for having received the grace from God (in vain), and shall throw this evil one with the unbelievers *"into the outer darkness and into the fire, where there are weeping of eyes and gnashing of teeth"* (Mt 8.12).[6] ₁₂The Apostle says: *"For faith comes from hearing, and what is heard pertains to the word about Christ. And how can they believe in the one of whom they have not learned? Or how can they ask about one they do not know?"* (Rom 10.17, 14).

₁₃Moreover, the Lord of All says to the prophet Ezekiel, as one who represents all overseers: *"I have appointed you a watchman; warn yourself and the people. You should tell the wicked, 'You shall surely die.' ₁₄And if he does not show remorse and repent with confession, he shall surely die in sin, but you shall live, for you did warn beforehand. ₁₅If, however, he is remorseful and repents with confession, he shall surely live the life of the righteous and shall not die the death in sin. ₁₆But if you do not warn him, he shall die in his sin, in perdition, and I will hold you accountable for his blood"* (Ezek 3.17–18).

₁₇And Daniel demonstrated, by word and deed, just judgment to the elders who were (to be) overseers in Israel. ₁₈He was kept alive in the lions' den after he was condemned to death by his enemies, having taken revenge on them there through their death by lions.[7] ₁₉And thus the truthfulness of the righteous one and the wickedness of the evil accusers were made manifest; ₂₀thus God glorifies those who glorify him, and the true overseers as well. ₂₁The same with those who cast the three young men into the furnace to be burned

---

4. The blessings that come with the pledged Spirit, as a guarantee of redemption (cf. Disc. 6.87; 23.119); see 2 Cor 1.22 and 5.5; cf. Eph 1.13–14; 2 Tm 1.14.

5. Allusion to Heb 4.12.

6. Cf. Mt 13.42, 50; 22.13; 24.51; 25.30; and Lk 13.28.

7. Referring to Dn 6.16–24.

because of their faith in God—who were kept whole. As (Scripture) says: *"For the king's commands grew harsher, and the furnace was made extremely hot; but the fire could not reach the saints who were praising the Lord God"* (Dn 3.22). ₂₂But the fire consumed the evil ones it found. Thereafter the Creator of the creatures became known, and the king confessed his sins to God.

₂₃And they threw Jeremiah in the pit to die for reprimanding the unjust that they might repent, that they might survive the wrath that was coming upon the people.[8] ₂₄They burned his written counsel. But they received their reward for sinning: they were given to famine, to the sword, and to bondage; ₂₅and the Prophet was greatly honored by the king and the nobles, and he rewrote the prophecy and the right counsel.[9] ₂₆For (Scripture) says: *"Everyone who does the Lord's work idly is accursed"* (Jer 48.10 [31.10 LXX]).

₂₇And the Lord said this to Peter in the Gospels: *"You are rock, and on this rock I will build my church"*; that is, the faithful people of God. *"And the gates of hell shall not prevail against them"*; (namely), the saints and the righteous by true faith,[10] those who were released from earth into heaven. *"And those you bind on earth"* are the unholy and the unjust and those who believe differently;[11] *"shall be bound in heaven,"* for the ominous punishments (Mt 16.18–19). ₂₈The words spoken by the Lord to Peter are spoken to all holy overseers, those who really have the truth.[12]

₂₉Such is the distinction between the good and the unjust. There are those who became associates and spokesmen of the Word of truth because of their holiness and virtue-loving lives: warning themselves and people—the despisers and the disobedient, the unholy and the impure, and others living miserably—reasoning with all, discerning every inclination, battling the errant with the weapon of truth, with pleadings or rebukes, thereby trying to win the sinners over. ₃₀Having the winnowing fork in hand, determining—

8. Referring to Jer 38.4–13.

9. Referring to Jer 36.

10. Echoing Rom 3.28; Gal 2.16; 3.11, 24.

11. Or, "those of heterodox faith" (Arm. զայլահաւատս, *zaylahawats*), juxtaposed with those of the preceding "true faith."

12. Overseers (whether abbots or bishops) are considered successors to the Apostles (a *topos* in early Christian literature), to whom the words of Jesus were repeated (Mt 18.18).

by the Holy Spirit's wind blowing—the wheat for the barn of the saints and the chaff prepared to fuel the fire of hell, as it is told.[13] It is a selection between good and evil.

31As for those who are strangers to true supervision, God's wrath is prepared against them by the Lord, according to the word of the Apostle: *"those who hold the truth unjustly"* (Rom 1.18) and do not (act) according to the Gospel of Christ. 32It behooves high-ranking leaders to conduct themselves according to his righteous laws at all times, pleasing to God; to warn people with true doctrine, for the salvation of everyone, so that the threatening punishment at the hand of the evil angel may not reach (anyone),[14] 33as it was revealed to the Prophet, to kill the unjust and to pity none—the old and the youth, virgins and young (men), priests and the lay.[15]

34Moreover, he says: *"those who grieve and lament and mourn over the injustices done by others were ordered to be saved by the mark they received on their foreheads from the Lord, that they may live through that slaughter"* (Ezek 9.4, 6). 35The first to be slaughtered were the priests, who were (supposed) to supervise the people of God, who looked for bodily gains and were careless about the spiritual gains. For God's judgments are just. For the Lord says: *"Every scribe who has become a disciple in the Kingdom of God is like a man, owner of a house, who will bring out of his treasure the new and the old"* (Mt 13.52).

36He called the church leader "a house owner," one who has become a disciple of the true traditions. The "treasures" are the heart's wisdom, which holds positive knowledge of things "old and new," and graces those near and far with good thoughts, good deeds, and impeccable holiness. 37And the crop of evil deeds (is like) digging outside, where no remnants of good learning are left in the bad treasure, to sort the good from the bad.

38They become (living) examples of virtue's fullness, (as Scripture) says, *"when coming (and) going"* (Ps 121.8 [120.8 LXX]). For those who become disciples are instructed in the true life, which is to the glory of teachers: as they walk in the paths of the righteous, meditate on the commandments of the Lord, and lead in the luminous teaching on holy life and justice in everything. 39For all the

13. Referring to Mt 3.12; cf. Lk 3.17.
14. Cf. Disc. 2.80–90, on absolving God from evil.
15. Referring to Ezek 9.6.

heirs of the Kingdom of God are involved, becoming coworkers in (teaching) the life-giving counsel of the Gospel, without ignoring any of the true traditions. ₄₀For (Scripture) says: *"If you fall short in any one thing, you become a debtor to the whole law"* (Jas 2.10). ₄₁For those who are truly (steadfast) in the faith and cleansed from guilty conscience[16] will always be close to the body and blood of the Lord—Christ dwelling in the inner self,[17] enlightening the saints through the beneficence of his immaculate, impeccable, and sacred love, through constant spiritual and intellectual solace from the Most Holy Trinity.

₄₂The Apostle says: *"And when Christ, our life, appears, then you also will appear with him in glory"* (Col 3.4). ₄₃So that all of us who have clothed ourselves with Christ,[18] being established in the true faith and having become pleasing in our life of virtue, may draw near to the unapproachable Light[19] and become enlightened in the glory of Christ our hope,[20] in the universal court at the resurrection from the dead. ₄₄So that we may always glorify the almighty Lordship, with the angels, forever and ever. Amen.

16. Allusion to Heb 10.22; cf. 9.14; 10.2.
17. Lit., "man." Echoing 1 Cor 3.16; Eph 3.17.
18. Echoing Gal 3.27.
19. Allusion to 1 Tm 6.16; cf. Ps 104.2 (103.2 LXX).
20. Allusion to 1 Tm 1.1; cf. Ti 2.13.

DISCOURSE 18

PRAISING GOD WITH THE ASSEMBLY OF THE COURAGEOUS (AND) VIRTUOUS MARTYRS FOR (HIS) BENEVOLENCE

OUNDLESS is the care of the Benefactor and replete are the gifts of the Giver of Life, who established the heavenly hosts to the glory of his holy name. Accordingly, (he brought) humans from ignobility to praising the glory of his grace, giving them authority over all his remarkable creatures[1] and promising the ineffable blessings. ₂For the heavenly hosts and humans received the sovereign will from the Lord, so that they may participate in the Creator's benevolent will: to think always of what is good and to act intentionally according to God's will, so that they themselves may benefit from what is beneficial.

₃And he appointed two tutors: promises of good things and of threats.[2] ₄And he gave the spiritual law as teacher, the counselor for life, so that the flowers of the sovereign will may blossom[3] early on from the knowledge derived from him. ₅The one who does his best to obey, with the Lord's intimate approval, will be crowned with glory. ₆But the one who detests, disobeys, and fights the true traditions will of course be punished. ₇And the Creator's benevolent will was not against early knowledge, but willing, in keeping with his providential love, so that one may abide firmly in what is good ₈and always bear in mind the honor held out in the promises of good things to the righteous, as well as the punishment of those who detest and disobey the spiritual law. ₉For he forewarns everyone to obey his commandments—lest they be deprived of the

---

1. Allusion to Gn 2.19.
2. Cf. Disc. 2.50.
3. Read ծաղկեալ (*catkeal*) for ծածկեալ (*cackeal*, "hidden" or "concealed").

rewards. ₁₀He recommends, however, the beneficial things, without taking away the sovereign will—even though he is foreknowing, ₁₁as in the case of Isaac's children when they were in the womb of their mother: he elects, he loves Jacob, who was obviously good, and hates Esau, who appeared to be evil.[4]

₁₂Since this is so, some ask: "Why does the evil person prosper, and the good person does not always prosper?" ₁₃If this were so, then the significance of the free will would be done away with, the election of the righteous would be gone, and the courageous ones would be deprived of their crowns of glory.

₁₄For the Lord says: *"The Kingdom of Heaven is a trophy, and aggressive people grab it"* (Mt 11.12).[5] ₁₅The dead who were virtue-loving in life and had mortified sin are transformed from death to life, holiness, and righteousness, in accordance with the truth of the Gospel. ₁₆*"For sin has no dominion over them, for they are not under the Law, but under grace"* (Rom 6.14). ₁₇There are other spiritual gifts from the Lord, and different honors and glories won through virtue and courage. And there are other joys to be discovered by one who is thoughtful because of meekness, and others for those in the race for total virtue regardless of individual failures. ₁₈For all goodness, heavenly and earthly, glorious and wonderful, is theirs to enjoy from the good Giver.

₁₉Likewise, we should learn about angels and demons, the righteous and sinners. For, first, there is a sorting out between the good and the bad; then, each is rewarded as deserved by the just tribunal. ₂₀To the good, he gives honor as recompense; and to the evil, something out of his mercy—some gift out of his grace.[6] ₂₁*"For he tried them in the furnace of his law"* (Wis 3.6), and by it he either elevates or brings low; and, as deserved by the righteous and the wicked, he imparts either punishment or honor. ₂₂Because the spiritual law brings life, those who love justice do more and more good; but the indolent are awakened to (the merits of) virtue by threats of calamities. Those who desire (virtue) he brings unto glory. ₂₃Thus they are renewed unto the most excellent life, are crowned with val-

---

4. Alluding to Rom 9.13; cf. Mal 1.2; Ps 47.4 (46.5 LXX); and Gn 25.19–28.

5. The contextual gist of the quotation makes it a partial answer to the theodicean question in §12.

6. God's judgment of the wicked is seen as part of his mercy.

or—as God grants success—and share in the good news brought to the righteous.

₂₄The righteous are those who do that which is right and just, and they become heirs of the upper calling that leads to life. Crowns of glory and praise have been prepared for them by the Lord, in accordance with each of the virtues. ₂₅Many are the trials of those who persevere patiently; however, they garner many benefits from the counsel of the life-giving law of Christ.[7] In all truthfulness, they will become the heavenly Father's children of light and co-heirs with Christ, ₂₆who by his own intimate effort attained the greatness of infinite goodness and became heir to honor and glory and the Kingdom of Heaven. ₂₇For by the will and not out of necessity disobedience crept in with all the misfortunes, and planted thorns in the fields of the mind and of the members (of the body)—the accuser's[8] plants of vice and deceptive vanity in thoughtful and rational beings.[9] ₂₈For this reason, (God) assigned to his children the task of cultivating conviction by setting their minds against evil; for there are many who through patient perseverance have uprooted from the mind and body the weeds of vice, the harmful plants: deception, lying, pride, greed, and every evil yearning with all its harms—seen and unseen.

₂₉The battle of the courageous ones is waged not on just one front but on many fronts. ₃₀First, not to partake of deceptive words: sweet talk and fallacies, which stir up the mind and the members (of the body) unto harmful and impure passions. ₃₁Second, not to fall into the grip of arrogance, pride, and vainglory that condemns the body and the soul to perdition through unimaginable evils. ₃₂Third, to extinguish the workings of deceit, lying, and licentiousness; likewise, with a lowly heart, to rein in anger, insensitivity, and defiance.[10] ₃₃Fourth, (to rein in) the rising passions of sexual impurity[11] that seem to lurk with debauchery and gluttony; to be

7. Allusion to Rom 8.2; Gal 6.2.

8. Satan's epithet, the meaning of his name in Hebrew; see Jb 1.9–11; Zec 3.1; 1 Pt 5.8; Rv 12.10.

9. Allusion to "The Parable of the Weeds" (Mt 13.24–30), further allegorized in the next section.

10. Cf. Disc. 10.37; 11.64, 86; 19.40; 23.2. Echoing Basil's *Adversus iratos* (Hom. 10; PG 31:353B–372B; trans. Wagner, *Ascetical Works*, FC 9:447–61).

11. Or, "masturbation" (Arm. զիջութիւն, *gijut'wn*).

delivered from these by moderation and longing for God. Likewise, to shake off every personal indecency, conceit, and all futile things that hammer the mind and the senses; to let go of these personal things, hoping for the good. ₃₄Fifth, not to stray, wander, or drift away from the beneficent, benevolent supervision (of God). These will take one away from the blessedness and leave him in dark confusion, leaving him behind in the paths of righteousness that lead to the mansions of rest. ₃₅Sixth, swearing falsely, stealing, and depriving, which draw shame, regret, and fear of punishment, are indefensible in the Judgment—unless one is chastened[12] by these. ₃₆Seventh, one who causes grief and aggravates someone near, who plots in thought, word, and deed; unless he overcomes these through meekness, he will be cast into punishment—the eternal punishment. ₃₇Eighth, vindictiveness, envy, and hatred; if one does not forsake these evils, he will bring death to himself and others. For from those who hate, flow resentment, evil thoughts, hostility, and bitter venom. ₃₈Ninth, one (ought to) root out aggravation and laziness, which are crops of all sorts of evil, causes of unpardonable perdition, and passages to the death of soul and body. ₃₉Tenth, one who lives indiscriminately in wickedness and loathsome filthiness and all kinds of lawlessness, unless he is remorsefully chastened by fear and awe of the Lord, will be forever lost in eternal perdition.

₄₀These are the plants of vice, which the diligent gardeners uproot[13] while nurturing the good plants, irrigating them with grace-filled tears and virtue-loving lives. ₄₁The fight and the victory are left for those brave and virtuous ones who are witnesses for the Truth and living martyrs loved by the Lord. ₄₂For though they are being killed by the enemies of Truth, they are being renewed in the life that is in Christ. ₄₃They shall live, for their hope is anchored in Christ.[14] Being justified by faith[15] and found whole in virtue, always at their best by the power of the almighty Father and the help of the benevolent Son and the grace of the Most Holy Spirit,[16] the One Godhead who is the Helper of those who place their hope in him.

12. Lit., "made thoughtful," as also at §39.
13. Possible allusion to "The Parable of the Weeds" (Mt 13.24–30).
14. The notion of "living martyrs" is drawn from Rv 6.9–11.
15. Allusion to Rom 3.28; Gal 2.16; 3.11, 24.
16. A *hapax* in the discourses.

₄₄First and foremost, to affirm the true faith in the Father, the Son, and the Holy Spirit, with love and hope.[17] ₄₅For in this way the earliest saints became confessors. They came to recognize and to know that all creatures were made by him; the providence of his sacred love; and the trustworthiness of the hope placed in God, who is unseen.

₄₆Second, to be true in proclaiming the Word, in order to find those who are lost and keep those who are found. ₄₇By this they are ranked with the holy angels who are sent to serve those who will inherit salvation[18] and the blessed hope of eternal life.[19]

₄₈Third, to proceed clearheadedly in doing benevolent works and to exhort those far and near for their benefit; to irrigate the fields of the mind and the body with spiritual grace and physical needs, and thus multiply the fruit of the roots of righteousness in order to enjoy eternal life.

₄₉Fourth, for one to possess dispositions of agreeableness, obedience, and unity in conjunction with the Holy Spirit; to gather together for peace, for praising God, and for helping one another—to be of assistance without envy; and to send off for the blessed life.

₅₀Fifth, to care for everyone's needs with immaculate, pure, fervent, and spiritual love. ₅₁To lend a hand to those who are deprived and grieving, whatever their needs may be—to help them spiritually and physically; and with such beneficence to enter into the inheritance of life in Christ.

₅₂Sixth, for administrators of the true traditions—both spiritual and physical—by which one comes to believe in God, to provide in due season spiritual help and physical necessities; and thus receive the down payment of the blessed gifts of the Kingdom of the righteous.

₅₃Seventh, in all the virtues, (to maintain) purity, caution, and protection. To remain always watchful and alert for the secretly-shot arrows of the evil one, by which the sinless ones (may) die in sin. ₅₄For all who brace themselves and overcome his cunning will receive the unfading crown.

₅₅Eighth, to be humble in heart and meek in life and peaceful

17. Echoing 1 Cor 13.13.
18. Allusion to Heb 1.13–14.
19. Echoing Ti 2.13.

toward all—both far and near; to resemble Christ, the One who is meek and humble,[20] that *"by looking up to the leader of (our) faith"* (Heb 12.2) we may follow and find rest there—in his humble, meek, and peaceful love.

₅₆Ninth, to be well inclined, with moderation and modesty, toward all directive counsel that is conducive to life and redemption; to arrive at the gate of life and to enter into the place of eternal rest prepared by our Savior—in accordance with one's life (on earth).

₅₇Tenth, to participate—worthily pure—in Christ's saving sacrifice,[21] being an initiate and a confidant, given to entreating prayer and grace-filled tears, ardently fervent in spirit, full of Christ's sacred love. To draw near to God with the heavenly beings and to have one's soul and body illumined there, and to cling strongly to the eternal life. ₅₈To contemplate heavenly things always and to abhor the earthly things; to have the almighty Lordship as confidant and associate; and to keep oneself resolutely unshaken in true life and right faith. To move on, with his beneficent, sacred love, to the good things; and to admonish others in the promised good things and life (eternal).

₅₉These are the facts about the courageous and the virtuous that escort them to the heavenly stations. And they hear from the Lord of All: *"O servants, doers of good and faithful. Because you have been faithful with few things here on earth, I will appoint you over many things in the eternal life. Come, enter into the joy of your Lord, the eternal blessings which have been prepared for you"* (Mt 25.21).

₆₀Would that (one becomes) a disciple and confidant of such counsel; to take off the preoccupations of this world and to put on the luminous garb of spiritual freedom, which is woven of the incomparable light of virtue; ₆₁and to become a daily examiner of one's thoughts, words, and deeds. Should one be in violation, may he, remorseful, be directed to the best counsel of the divine Scriptures. *"For whatever you say in your hearts, you shall repent on your beds. And do offer the sacrifices of righteousness and trust in the Lord"* (Ps 4.4–5 [5–6 LXX]). ₆₂For glorious are the teachers who take up this (exhortation) and teach the same, in (the name of) the Father, the Son, and the Holy Spirit, to whom be glory now and always. Amen.

20. Allusion to Mt 11.29.
21. The Eucharist.

DISCOURSE 19

ADMONITION UNTO REPENTANCE
WITH CONFESSION

REAT ARE the rewards of the Lord's commandments and boundless is the grace of the benevolent God. *"For those whom he foreknew, he also called to the hope of eternal life, justified and glorified them"* (Rom 8.29–30). ₂Those who faithfully and reverently kept his commandments and were obedient to his all-caring, sacred love, appropriated the word of life, became fruitful, and grew in the benefits of virtue: they have their rewards assured in the life to come. ₃But the insolent and the disobedient, who abhorred the word of truth and impeded the fruit of righteousness, accepted the evil seed (sown) by the enemy and violated the true traditions and the caring love, straying from the right ways; their end is to fall into the gorge of perdition.

₄But the kind care of the benevolent God does not overlook those who turn to him. He opens mercy's gates of grace, welcomes them with compassion, with the beneficence of his sacred love, and protects those who trust in his compassion. ₅And when one truly confesses, with contrite and broken heart, becoming a remorseful mourner, the Savior visits him with compassion and mercy. ₆For he vomited the concealed bitterness of the bile and demonstrated this: *"I hated and despised sin, I loved your law"* (Ps 119.113 [118.113 LXX]), in order to be healed, cleansed, and justified. ₇And to the degree of his pain, he will receive from the Physician who loves humankind the healing medicine: that is, the righteous life to counter his sins and dire pain so that he would not fall back into the same, lest he be unable to find the Physician who loves humankind.

₈For the Word of the Lord calls those with heavy burdens to repentance with confession; those in the darkness of sin, unto the light of righteousness; those who have strayed, unto the knowledge of truth. He brings those who have departed from the paths of righteousness into the straight way, to restore them—through confession—from deadly conduct unto life, and to thwart all the guiles of Satan. ₉For the Apostle says: *"He wants everyone to live and to come to the knowledge of truth"* (1 Tm 2.4),[1] under the supervision of the omnipresent love.

₁₀For confession delights God and his priests.[2] (As) the Prophet says: *"I said: 'I will recount my sins, and you will forgive all the guilt of my sins'"* (Ps 32.5 [31.5 LXX]). ₁₁It opens up the wounds and reveals the pain; it administers with spiritual cheerfulness the healing medicine through remorse, which is repentance with tears, constant prayer, day and night, without ceasing; it exerts the body by fasting, to the point of emaciation, thus moving God to forgive sins through compassion and abundant grace. ₁₂For repentance is not defined by one thing only, but consists of many things; and the fallen and the devastated are raised to stand equally justified.[3]

₁₃When repenting, first of all, (one should) have remorse, confess one's sins, make oneself a cistern of tears with ceaseless prayer, feel constantly sad about the sins committed—earnestly and with frequent fasting and deep contrition. ₁₄Second, hate sin for all its harms and accomplices in sin, censure the mind and the senses inclined to evil—which did not observe the spiritual law committed to them by the Creator. ₁₅Third, love righteous and virtuous people and make them associates of God, in prayer and every good deed that promotes the true traditions. ₁₆Fourth, in thought and speech, stay away from transgressors, feeling shame and with a sense of humility; consider it better to suffer with the just than to be comfortable with the unjust. ₁₇Fifth, be instructed in the fear and awe of the Lord; never stop thinking about the day of death and the punishment of sinners; and mortify the members (of the body) with

1. Cf. 2 Pt 3.9.

2. The implied confession to priests has its parallel in Basil *SR* 288, and does not preclude confession to one's superior or the abbot (see Disc. 23.19–20, 64–66, 93–94; so too in Basil *LR* 25–26 and 46). Confession has an earlier history in the East, beginning with the *Didache,* which urges individual confession in the congregation (4.14 and 14.1; possibly owing to Mt 16.19 and 18.18; cf. Jn 20.21–23). An echo of this tradition could be heard in Disc. 23.19–20.

3. Lit., "in equal justice."

its desires and the passions.[4] [18]Sixth, watch day and night for personal salvation, intent on how to avoid sin and be saved from the coming wrath against the unrepentant. [19]Seventh, (one should) not forget one's failures; not be lax in pious vigils; not fall back into the previous harms, becoming unable to be healed again. [20]Eighth, being healed, made circumspect, and cleansed, (one should) be aware of one's inner and outer being and keep in mind the good things promised to the truly penitent. [21]Ninth, observe all that is commanded in accordance with the spiritual law and the Gospel of Christ; and look for the renewal through the atoning sacrifice.[5] [22]Tenth, increase doing all kinds of good deeds, noticed and unnoticed, (thus) erasing the scars of sin from soul and body; and emerge victorious in the assembly of penitents, having confidence in the atoning, life-giving Sacrament; being in communion with and becoming partakers and part of the inscrutable things. [23]Thereafter, *"set your minds on things above, where Christ is seated"* (Col 3.1–2), and the saints with him in that promised blessedness.

[24]True confessors and penitents are saved by Christ's redeeming body and blood, for he is our hope[6] and means of atonement,[7] and through him is freedom and admission into the joy and inheritance of the righteous: through the beneficence of Christ's sacred love, which justifies sinners who repent. [25]For when the sword cuts the body and injures the person, a physician is needed to treat the hurt with certain medicines in order to heal. Likewise, the plagues of the passions and impure thoughts[8] (are healed) with the remedy of repentance: the wounds are washed with warm tears and healed with impeccable purity. [26]The agony of suffering, the pain brought by impurity, the grief caused by loss, the turmoil of the soul, the absence of gain, difficult situations, dangers caused by tyrants, sudden homelessness, the loss of loved ones, the unbearable affliction by diverse miseries and the like are portals to tears. [27]Whereas the movements of the soul abducted by evil demons into outright passions cause mental torments with ominous consequences that have no place for expiation.

---

4. Allusion to Gal 5.24; cf. Disc. 5.42; 10.76; 13.39.
5. Allusion to the Eucharist, in light of the sequel (§§22, 24).
6. Allusion to 1 Tm 1.1.
7. Allusion to Rom 3.25.
8. Lit., "memories."

₂₈For this reason it is essential to entreat the Savior with tears, to save us from so many harms. ₂₉(Let us) guard against such with zeal, cut them down with the weapons of virtue, and have Jesus Christ as our protector, our helper in life. And from here (let us) go on yearning for what is good: having compassion toward those of the household of faith,[9] longing for those far away—beloved of God, thirsting earnestly for spiritual knowledge, desiring to be with the saints, having the message of peace, the modesty of humility, the consoling words of counsel that advise in virtue the hardened mind. ₃₀(Let us) assist all with loving care unto redemption, the rewards of spiritual attainment, and the enjoyment of the benefits of goodness; and (let us) be patient in hardship in order to enjoy the gifts of grace, which he (God) gives from the clear fountain of life. ₃₁For this reason, prayer and earnest, heartfelt petitions lead to the haven[10] of grace.

₃₂Constraining the mind with tears of remorse, remembrance of the promised good things, considerate entreaties, and ecstatic delight, (we ought) to let the grace-filled tears flow in order to cleanse the mind and the body, which have held the filth of the evil and impure passions. ₃₃For tears wipe away and heal the bitter plagues of sin, cast the vile (things) out of the mind and the senses; and one is brought into the Savior's provident love and is comforted with hope. ₃₄Tears move the mind in the direction of God, rouse it from the stupor of sin—as from sleep, and with love for (spiritual) benefits prompt it unto thoughtful discretion. ₃₅Tears make one drink of the spiritual drink from the fountain of abundant grace flowing unto freedom and the inheritance of the life-giving, eternal hope— through (Christ's) caring, sacred love, through the compassionate remembrance of the Benefactor's kind, directive will.

₃₆Such are the benefits of the tears of remorse that move the flow of morals toward the discovery of salvation and protection by God's will, and confine the mind within God's pleasure. ₃₇And inasmuch as there is benefit from these, there is more detriment from laziness and from disdain for tears that well up from the depths of the heart. And (the person) being prevented by slothfulness (allows) miseries brought by evil to dash in and make the mind and the members move in the direction of indiscriminate evils. And remorse and

9. Echoing Gal 6.10.
10. Lit., "harbor."

tears are prevented by laziness; and the hardened, rebellious heart disdains the extended grace and does not concern itself with it, being deprived of it. ₃₈And instead of the good, one accepts the bad: contemptuousness, haughtiness, malice, stubbornness, wickedness, snobbishness, greed, gluttony, craving, and other intrusions of evil. ₃₉The one afflicted by these could hardly be healed.

₄₀But the Word, in his love for humankind, does not leave hopeless those who are remorseful and come to obey God with fear, turning against the direction of sin: from injustice to justice, from impurity to purity, from arrogance to humility, from anger to meekness,[11] from gluttony to moderation, from idleness to hard work, from lying to being always truthful, from disobedience to obedience, from greed to contentment, from hypocrisy to single-mindedness, from tendency to swear falsely to not swearing, from rancor to benevolence, from vindictiveness to conciliation, from cruelty to kindness, from hatred to sacred love always, from impenitence to remorse with tears, from not caring to confess to conscientious confession, from hopelessness to right hope, from unbelief to being personally grounded in the right faith and to preaching the truth to others.[12]

₄₁This is a sketch of repentance in the real tradition: to do all that is righteous, seen and unseen, against all that is sinful, with intimate thoughts and remembrance of the good things promised to the truly penitent—and also of the damning threats by the Lord of All against those who do not repent. ₄₂Be on guard about these things, ever ready to do that which pleases God, with fear of the Lord, remembering the inerrant knowledge of God, the accounting to the righteous Judge on the Day of Judgment, when nothing in thought, words, and deeds will (remain) hidden.[13]

₄₃There will be separation between the virtuous and the vicious, believers and unbelievers, and rewards as deserved: ₄₄honor, exaltation, and blessings to the victorious, those who fought against sin and opponents and emerged victorious; they will be crowned with glory,

---

11. On meekness as antidote to anger, see Basil, *Adversus iratos* (Hom. 10.7; PG 31:370B–372B; trans. Wagner, *Ascetical Works*, FC 9:459–61). Cf. Disc. 10.37; 11.64, 86; 18.32; 23.2.

12. Cf. the list of vices and their antidotes in Disc. 23.2.

13. Allusion to Mt 10.26; cf. Lk 8.17; 12.2; 1 Cor 4.5.

as well as those who truly repented of their transgressions. ₄₅But the frightening threats of torments surround the unjust and the wicked, taken to be punished with torture, because they did not bow down with repentance. ₄₆As for those who prostrated and humbled themselves in accordance with the canons of repentance, he will receive them in the mansions of life, for they are worthy because of their purity, by his great mercy. ₄₇For the oppressed and the persecuted, through tears for any transgression and through good moves, have turned to the mercy of the Lord, the lover of humankind.[14]

₄₈Just like children who cannot use words to ask for needed things from their mothers' care but receive the loving care through tears, since they do not stop crying until the mothers' full attention is given, and then they stop, rejoice, and relax, so should we behave toward the compassionate Lord, who cares for us through his unseen, creative love, who sits on his throne unmade (by hand) and cares for his creatures, who made the knowledge of God known through the forefathers and showed the manner of repentance through the Prophets for those who return. ₄₉At his (first) coming he opened the gate of mercy, saying: *"I have not come to call the righteous, but sinners to repentance"* (Lk 5.32),[15] through confession, through his creative, caring love. ₅₀So that by hastening to the summons of the Gospel,[16] we may receive gifts through repentance: from him who grants atonement, who heals the unseen souls and the seen bodies.[17]

₅₁The forgiveness of believers comes first from the (baptismal) font, through the true confession of the Most Holy Trinity. ₅₂For he says to the disciples: *"Go, baptize believers in the name of the Father and the Son and the Holy Spirit, and teach them to observe all the commandments from Christ"* (Mt 28.19–20). ₅₃*"For those who were baptized into Christ have clothed themselves with Christ and have become children of light and heirs of the Kingdom through rebirth"* (Gal 3.26–27, 29). ₅₄For by grace they have become children of day, freed from the night-time birth, from the dominion of darkness, and live a luminous life on earth with the help of the Benefactor. ₅₅And through the beauty[18] of his

14. The epithet "lover of humankind" is used interchangeably for the Father (Disc. 4.35; 11.95; 23.118) and the Son (Disc. 4.90; 6.33; 11.196; 13.91; 19.7).

15. Cf. Mt 9.13; Mk 2.17.

16. Lit., "of the good news."

17. Lit., "senses."

18. Lit., "according to the arts."

grace, those far become near, strangers become family, because of faith and immaculate love. ₅₆And those who were caught in sin by Satan and consequently in the grip of death, he justifies, restores, and invites to his Kingdom and glory, which he has prepared for those who love him.[19]

₅₇Moreover, he showed sinners the gifts of repentance and made them known beforehand. ₅₈As we hear about David, who sinned, turned around, confessed, and repented.[20] He wept all night and mixed his drink with tears because of the Lord's anger. From his eyes flowed streams of tears, because he did not keep the Lord's commandment. He ruined his lustful eyes with tears and was cleansed from sin. ₅₉And in the New Testament, it is Peter who denied and did not remember the Lord's earlier saying, until he came to a realization when the cock crowed; he remembered, and, it says: *"He went outside and wept bitterly"* (Mt 26.75). ₆₀And he received forgiveness because of his warm tears, and his apostolic gift continued, as did David's prophetic (gift). ₆₁I need not cite further examples of transgressors and penitents who demonstrate true repentance, as narrated in the divine Scriptures—both Old and New.

₆₂Thus, the gate to life through repentance will not be shut till the end of the world; ₆₃so that in the font of constant tears we may wash and cleanse our constant mistakes, since we sin daily in thought, words, hearing, seeing, and every movement. Let not the daily prayers and cleansing with tears cease.

₆₄For those who have committed grave sins, such as those addressed in the canons, periods (for penance) are assigned—while they are separated from the Church, its people and altar. Commensurate with great harms, great efforts and labor are necessary.[21] ₆₅Those who have lesser transgressions, their remedy is cleansing with tears. ₆₆But if deep in the heart there is filth, contaminating the members, it is essential to have streams of tears, spiritual fire and boiling, in order to purify, melt down, and drive (the filth) away. ₆₇One who has few transgressions by straying involuntarily should be filled with remorse and have them plucked from the soul, and be cleansed thoroughly with tears.

---

19. Allusion to 1 Cor 2.9.
20. Referring to 2 Sm (2 Kgdms LXX) 11.4; 12.1–25; cf. Ps 51 (50 LXX).
21. Cf. Disc. 8.36.

₆₈One with canonical title and rank, which are from the Lord, who has serious wounds from sins committed voluntarily, bears the brunt of the threats. Much effort and warm tears and compunction of the heart, and assigned periods (for penance), commensurate with the transgressions, should be adopted by him in order to dissolve the harsh winter of the gripping sins. ₆₉For the spiritual springtime will appear with the warm southern blow of the Spirit, and more so the heavy rainfall from above, with the streams of tears. The new earth will reveal its plants and blossoms, and trees their leaves, and fruit fit for the enjoyment of kings and ordinary citizens. ₇₀Thus one will let the streams of tears flow with the warmth of the Spirit, to break the locks of sins' winter, to allow the plants of virtue to emerge and the trees of righteousness (to yield) fruit, with which heavenly and earthly beings express joy to the glory of God.

₇₁Penitents must possess such mind and morals in order to be saved from indebtedness to the plagues of hell's unquenchable fire and interminable worms.[22] ₇₂And being established through the font of tears, being clothed with the radiant beams of the sacred light and the robe of attestable virtue, they are to be crowned with the saints and rejoice in the blessings that do not end.

₇₃Repentance consists of disapproval of oneself and turning away from harmful things and the evil passions.[23] ₇₄And invoking justice against every evil, in order to have sins wiped out and for justice to thrive with sacred love and tearful prayers; drying out with fasting the murky, intemperate flow of masturbation, which corrupts the members (of the body).[24] ₇₅(Just as) water from fountains and rain showers put out the visible fire, so love toward God and warm tears put out the fire of desire and thwart the body's will to plunge into the current of sensual and filthy activities. (Therefore) do not return to the same loathsome filth, but receive cleansing with purity of thoughts; ₇₆lest the threatening punishment for impurity be meted out on that day which no one knows, at an hour which is not thought of, to inflict damaging vengeance.[25]

₇₇Rather, love the purity that is of the Lord, which dwells in

22. Echoing Is 66.24, quoted in §78; Mk 9.48.
23. Echoing Gal 5.24 (cf. vss. 16–17).
24. On this aspect of fasting, see Disc. 9.95, 104.
25. Echoing Mt 24.36; cf. Mk 13.32.

the saints. 78He says of the impure: *"Their worms will not die, and the fire will not be quenched; and they will be made a display to all mortals"* (Is 66.24).[26] 79And every hazard of sin (ought) to be shed from the mind and the body, to the point where one could say, according to the Gospel of Life:[27] *"The prince of this sin-loving world is coming, and he will not find a particle of sin in me"* (Jn 14.30), since Christ renews us again through true confession and tears, through repentance, followed by compassion (shown) for the homeless and a life regulated by every virtue, pleasing to God. 80And (we ought) to become gardeners in the vineyard of truth, from our start in the faith and through right living; to live thus on earth and become virtuous. 81And when departing from this world, one takes with him all righteousness: the innocence of infancy, the impeccability of childhood, the chastity of youth, the purity of old age, capping every stage (of life) with consummate virtue. And the Lord of All rewards laborers of all ages who have faithfully worked in the vineyard.[28] 82Be helpful in one's upward calling, *"where Christ is seated at the right hand of God"* (Col 3.1),[29] in *"Jerusalem which is above, the mother of us all"* (Gal 4.26), where also our early, good treasure of virtue is stored,[30] where our hope is anchored; the unending blessedness, the eternal beauty, the everlasting joy, the abundant goodness to be enjoyed with Christ. 83(There will be) joint rejoicing for the heavenly and earthly beings, blessedness in the glory of Christ, because of the favors of that sacred love—84of the One who presented us for adoption by the Father,[31] delivered us to the care of the Holy Spirit, and made us heirs of his Kingdom; 85who justified us here and will glorify us there in his divine banquet, by crowning our heads. That we may continuously rejoice in the unending favors of the Most Holy Trinity, 86to whom glory, dominion, and honor are befitting forever and ever. Amen.

26. Cf. Mk 9.48.

27. Cf. Disc. 2.129.

28. Allusion to "The Parable of the Workers in the Vineyard" (Mt 20.1–16); cf. Disc. 14.10.

29. Cf. Ps 110.1; Mk 16.19; Mt 26.64; Acts 2.33; 5.31; Rom 8.34; Heb 1.3; 12.2.

30. Echoing Mt 6.20; cf. 19.21; Lk 12.33; 18.22.

31. Allusion to Rom 8.14–17, 23; Gal 4.1–7; Eph 1.5–6.

DISCOURSE 20

GUIDANCE THROUGH ESSENTIAL
COUNSEL: FUNDAMENTALS OF KNOWLEDGE
AND UNDERSTANDING

HAT KIND OF thanksgiving, praise, and glory could one give to the almighty Lordship for the most generous benevolence? He does not withhold his caring love, but provides for his creatures and distributes his grace in streams. ₂First, the Lord appointed rulers on earth, who are subject to the heavenly Rulership, so that we may recognize the care of his creative love and learn his commandment *"to fulfill all righteousness"* (Mt 3.15), and receive the good reward at the time of visitation; then, over time, strive for the incorruptible life.

₃Just as the forefather's life was ordered by the Lord, in sinlessness, (he shows) the same sacred love to us: ₄*"Just as Christ loved us and offered himself (as) a fragrant sacrifice"* (Eph 5.2). ₅But we provoked the Creator's wrath, for we did not keep his commandments. ₆He did not show his caring love (only) to those who are grateful but (also) to those who are ungrateful, as it befits God.[1] ₇For the good things God has shown us are not as we deserve; rather, he resorted to mercy, with the triumph of his immaculately sacred and creative love. ₈Nor does he seek reciprocity from us for his beneficence.[2] Rather, he wills that we live with love for justice and become heirs of the Kingdom of Heaven.

₉For he is our hope, our life, and our fount of goodness.[3] ₁₀The fount does not seek water, nor the sun (seek) light. Such is God: he bestows good things and does not receive anything (in return) for

1. Allusion to Mt 5.45.
2. See §11, below.
3. Echoing 1 Tm 1.1.

his great benevolence and replete fullness—[11]only for (people) to be beneficent to one another; he considers that (as) done to him.[4] And he reciprocates on earth and in heaven with things that abide. [12]For doing good deeds to one another, he reciprocates by sending seen and unseen things. [13]As the blood of Abel—who was killed by Cain, punished by the Lord—cried out to God,[5] likewise good crying moves God unto good, benevolent care. [14](As for) those who do not seek revenge against those who deprive, he will avenge (their suffering) according to the just Judgment.[6] For the recompense is commensurate with what is deserved: for both good and evil deeds.

[15]To resemble God is this: to be beneficent to the ungrateful, to seek the lost, and to keep by one's own labor and effort the one found, [16]to resemble the Son of God who gave himself to death for our sake—who through his voluntary suffering delivered us from servitude to sin and invited us to the good life and its good things, who made us worthy to receive the Holy Spirit. [17]And he promised the almighty Father's incomparable blessings, so that we may always express blessing to the One Trinity who keeps the gate to salvation unto life always open for those who believe, and who helps all who call on him. [18]And by becoming disciples of the sovereign Word,[7] we become collaborators with his benevolent will, to think and do what is good, and to be well-pleasing to the Creator by caring for those near and far. [19]So that they may receive the good things, in accordance with the purity of his sacred love: to make progress in what is good, and with the fullness of virtue fight against sin; and wholeheartedly relying on the care of his love for humankind, to root out every weed of lawlessness from the mind and the senses, together with every reckless and evil disposition.[8] [20]To chase away from their midst pride, greed, cunning, anger, vengeance, treachery, lying, swearing falsely, envy, and gluttony along with drunkenness.[9]

---

4. Allusion to Mt 25.40.

5. Referring to Gn 4.1–14.

6. Echoing Rom 12.19; cf. Heb 10.30.

7. Rendering of Gk. *hēgemonikon logon;* cf. Disc. 11.154.

8. Allegorizing on "The Parable of the Weeds" in Mt 13.24–30. See below, §69 and note to Disc. 5.23.

9. Lit., "drunkards."

₂₁To chase away with threats of eternal suffering the harms and similar miseries of these sins, and to plant in mind and life the good plants with appropriate virtue, impeccable holiness, and true faith, being encouraged by God with hope,[10] with promises of good things. Having here received the down payment of freedom and being invited to the prepared Kingdom of Heaven, to the living hope,[11] to the goodness of eternal blessings that could neither be comprehended by the mind nor described with words—the blessings that are there.

₂₂Just as infants in their mothers' wombs, held in bloody water, buried in darkness, do not know the beauty of the earth; the brightness of the sun, the moon, the stars; the cycles of time and of months; the fruitfulness of trees and plants; the enjoyment of birds and animals, whether cattle or wild beasts, whether fit for food or to be domesticated, those on land and those swimming in water, which are caught in traps set by hunters; other enjoyments and attractions that await: of gold, silver, precious gems used as adornment by people and to the glory of kings, over which those who love the world rejoice; so, just as infants do not know this life, which is unlike life in the womb, we too do not comprehend the life to come.[12] Even this light and life do not compare with that life and the light of the almighty Lordship's glory: *"What no eye has seen and no ear has heard, and what has not fallen into the human heart—the things God has prepared for those who love him"* (1 Cor 2.9), the eternal blessings in Christ Jesus.

₂₃Also, neither the troubles nor the heartaches, nor the suffering,

---

10. Echoing 2 Thes 2.16.

11. Echoing 1 Pt 1.3; cf. §§89, 125.

12. "Just as infants in their mothers' wombs ... we too do not comprehend the life to come." This entire section is dependent on the fragmentary Hermetic *Definitions* (*DH* frag. vi.2–3; vii.3), whether in Greek or in its sixth-century Armenian translation; see Joseph Paramelle and Jean-Pierre Mahé, "Nouveaux parallèles grecs aux *Définitions* hermétiques arméniennes," *Revue des études arméniennes* 22 (1990–91): 115–34, here 117 n. 7a, 120–23. Cf. Disc. 2.40: "Just as infants in their mothers' wombs do not know how they are about to grow and see and enjoy God's creation, so we are unable to comprehend"; Disc. 15.37: "There are some who say that as a fetus in the womb is devoid of sensation yet alive, silent, without talking or hearing, mobility or activity, so too—they think—is the human soul, silent and lowly." On the implications for the date of the *Discourses*, see the "Introduction."

nor the tortures with fire and water, like those of Sodom and the Flood,[13] could be compared with the unquenchable fire and the eternal tortures prepared for the wicked and sinners. 24For by his all-wise will God created the mind and the senses as instruments for a life given to sanctity, justice, and every beneficence, to enrich itself and others by gaining good things, and to make the Lord happy by having the mouth preach the true faith and purity of life. 25For one has to keep oneself, and everyone who is willing, constant in wholesome thoughts, vigilant, attentive, obedient to the spiritual law with fear and perfect love—hating evil and loving what is good, what is full of kind and pleasing goodness. And (thus) praise and thanksgiving will be raised to God, preparing (the way) for the blessedness of the Kingdom of Heaven. 26For they were pleasing to God in hardship and in calm, and remained connected with his love through their true faith, being lovers of peace and good will toward all, departing from every evil thing—seen and unseen wrongdoing. 27For God says: *"I am he who hates injustice and loves justice"* (Is 61.8). 28Thus the beloved of God and the household of faith are revealed, for we always have the same love for sanctity and justice, always. 29Moreover, we have hatred for displeasing passions and all sins. 30For it is written, saying: *"I hated and demeaned sin, but loved your Law"* (Ps 119.113 [118.113 LXX]).

31Such are the mouthpieces[14] for God, who are full of life-giving, sustaining counsel, counsel for life, gushing forth as from a fountain. 32*"For everyone who calls on the name of the Lord will live"* (Rom 10.13), those who lay their hopes on Christ Jesus. 33Whereas those who speak slanderously for the perdition of many, through cunning, licentiousness, fallacies, and diverse harms, who lead astray the ignorant from the true traditions, invite God's vengeance according to his just judgment because of the perdition of the unjust—who become heirs of the unquenchable fire and the eternal torments.

34And the eyes, which see justly through the guidance of the intellect, become rightly cautious of the harms. God ordered them to watch over all the members (of the body, to keep them) pure,

---

13. Echoing Lk 17.26–29 (cf. Gn 7.11; 8.2; 19.24–25). The author returns to these examples further below, §§108–114; cf. §145.

14. Lit., "mouths."

holy, and immaculate.[15] ₃₅For *"the eye is the lamp of the body,"* says the Lord (Mt 6.22). ₃₆One with enlightened eyes, who does not have any part in the darkness of sin but stands enlightened in the light of God, has the whole body enlightened. ₃₇But as for those in darkness, (away) from the beams of light, in the filthiness of the passions and every worldly deception of the most evil kind that is seen, that distracts from the true sight as though blurring the eyes from sin, not allowing (to see) the essentials but the darkness of evil, they will inherit the outer darkness, where there are weeping of eyes and blindness in hell's unquenchable fire.[16] ₃₈Recompense is for both: those who love to see the truth and those who passionately see evil.

₃₉And the ears, which open the gates to hear the true preaching and lead the mind and the senses to accept the life-giving Word and the whole truth—seen and unseen—of God's commandments, through these same ears enter the words of the good news, saying: *"Come, enter into the joy of the Lord and enjoy the ineffable and eternal good things, you who appeared to be faithful in little on earth"* (Mt 25.23). ₄₀But those who shut their ears to the truth of the Gospel and allow the entrance of the words about perdition and the all-deluding harms, and make their minds nests of vipers and asps,[17] who will not take the medicine for life and sensibility from the dispenser of the medicine of the divine words, they will hear the sorrowful news and the terribly frightening chastisement from the Lord: *"Depart from me, accursed, to the eternal fire which is prepared for Satan and his angels on the day of visitation"* (Mt 25.41).

₄₁And the nostrils are for the sense of smell which discerns the sweet aroma, the fragrant grace of the saints' souls, which are cleansed of every corruption of physical filth—according to the Apostle: *"We are to God the pleasing aroma of Christ among those who are being saved and among those who are perishing. To the one we are an aroma that brings death from death; to the other, from life to life. And who is equal to such (a task)?"* (2 Cor 2.15–16) ₄₂They discern the good from the bad, the impeccability of the faith and life of those who enjoy the sweet favors. ₄₃But those who fail to discern the smell of impurity and

15. Lit., "God ordered the pure, holy, and immaculate watchfulness over all the members."

16. Echoing Mt 8.12 (cf. 22.13; 25.30).

17. Allusion to Ps 58.4 (57.5 LXX).

wickedness and worldly passions—which are full of stench and ma-
levolent and indiscriminate movements, who reject the fragrance
full of grace, they will receive the disgusting smell of the plague of
sleepless worms and the scorch of the fire, and will be shut in the
intolerable tortures of the piercing and the tearing and wearing of
soul and body.[18]

44And hands in the care of (divine) supervision labor constantly
to promote prosperity, being of help to the fallen and the needy,
assisting in every necessity, never slowing in God's work. As the
Lord grants them success, they definitely attain the needs of the individual and of those near and far. 45These hands receive from the
Lord the verdict of freedom, the deed of adoption,[19] the unfading
crown gloriously made with esteem by God's hands. 46But hands
that constantly reach for one's obscene and shameful passions or
collaborate with lovers of filthiness, and steal, torture, afflict, or
kill, these hands will be bound with fiery shackles and sentenced to
the eternal torments of the unquenchable fire, and will be blotted
out from the book of life, the register of Christ.[20]

47And feet that have become steeds for constructiveness and
peace, holy life, true preaching, and spiritual help to those far and
near, pleasing to the Lord's will—feet that (did not) disdain the
hard labor for the gathering summoned above, these feet will ascend to the gates of life and will enter the abodes of the nuptial joy,
the orderly decorum at the right hand, that great joy that does not
pass away. 48But feet that strayed from the path of righteousness,
running in vain, drifting into evil, onto a harmful course: into impurity, robbery, iniquity, defiance, going in every unjust way that
leads to eternal perdition; such feet—having departed from life itself—are sent into the abyss of hell, where there is neither end nor
relief nor release from the shackles of torture.

49As for the intelligent mind that dwells in the brain, which is
in the head, which is the crown above all the members and the
headquarters of the senses, it is the guide of the movements, the su-

18. Cf. the equally spiritualized and lengthier interpretation of the sensual experience of smell in Disc. 11.191–203, and note at the end of the passage.

19. Arm. մուրհակ որդեգրութեան (murhak ordegrut'ean); cf. Disc. 11.180: "assurance of adoption." On divine adoption, see Rom 8.14–17, 23; Gal 4.1–7; Eph 1.5–6.

20. Alluding to Rv 3.5 (cf. 20.12, 15; 21.27).

perintendent and teacher and commander of all the members. ₅₀It directs the feeble members, restores the errant ones, makes wise the ignorant, satisfies the needy, attains salvation by all clever means for oneself and others, and becomes home for spiritual treasures of wisdom for those near and far. This is granted by the Holy Spirit, who is the fount of all goodness and wisdom, from whom rises the light of knowledge that enlightens everybody through the proclamation of Christ's Gospel of good conditions and fills every member with blessedness according to the truth of his benevolent will, for one to receive the crown of the Kingdom, which is in Christ. ₅₁But minds that stray from the wisdom of Truth and fall into the filth of the passions and every perilous injustice, not thinking of sin, and bring death instead of life to themselves and many (others), they will bear severe punishment. (Scripture) says: *"Sinners will perish from the earth, in hell"* (Ps 37.38 [36.38 LXX]); and *"The wicked will no longer find rest from excruciating tortures"* (Is 57.20). ₅₂Such are those who fall into peril: they will perish in an evil (way) and will have utter darkness with excruciating and bitter tortures. They will not see light, and no one will comfort them in their tortures.

₅₃Also consider the heart, which is the recipient of the movements of the soul. *"Establish a clean heart in me and renew a steadfast spirit within me"* (Ps 51.10 [50.12 LXX]). ₅₄One who rejoices in the hope of being restored unto desire for the virtuous life and directs all the members from evil to good, thinking wholesomely, will receive the promissory down payment of that liberating hope, and will enter to inherit the Kingdom of Heaven. ₅₅But one who from the heart generates clusters of vice, those of the most hideous kind, as the Lord says: *"Out of the heart come adultery, arrogance, anger, and all other evils"* (Mk 7.21–22),[21] such a person will be left out of the Benefactor's care, in the outer darkness and eternal perdition, in so many dreadful tortures that I cannot cite.

₅₆The cleansing of the innards of the body in general should also be considered. As the Apostle says: *"The inner man is renewed day by day"* (2 Cor 4.16). ₅₇Temporary, minor troubles bring about considerable good for the individual, through pain and even—for some—plagues afflicting the innards of the body respectively: namely, the

21. Cf. Mt 15.19.

liver, the lungs, the spleen, the intestines, and the kidneys, which, as ordained from the beginning, (could afflict) those who have done no wrong. ₅₈One who obviously has done considerable harm to his body and invisible soul, to all the innards of the body, could still become a host to pure thoughts. ₅₉For the Apostle says: *"The members that are less presentable have more modesty"* (1 Cor 12.23), that is, (one becomes) utterly pure and immaculate in sanctity, being mortified through persistent modesty; and, with grace-filled tears, the fire of the passions becomes quenched through the fire of the Spirit.

₆₀All the members, the innards of the body, and the soul must be subjected to the will of the mind; for we were justified through the luminous font and were reborn by the grace of Christ, ₆₁who freed us from servitude to sin for the freedom (he set) through his redemption.[22] He put on the same body and soul and mixed them with his Divinity because of his immeasurable love. And he bore all of the human traits except for sin. And he admonishes us to consider his course of conduct, to become like those corporeal beings who lived up to the truth. *"For if indeed we share in his sufferings, we may also share in his glory"* (Rom 8.17) because of his love.

₆₂And we have been commanded to love him, as he loved us[23] *"and gave himself (as) a ransom for all"* (1 Tm 2.6).[24] ₆₃*"All the Law and the Prophets hang on these two commandments"* (Mt 22.40), says the Lord: to love God and to love one's friend.[25] ₆₄For he who loves God is distant from every injustice—seen and unseen—and is close to every justice and holiness. For being empowered by divine love, he eclipses the untrue loves that enslave the mind and the senses. ₆₅So is the one who loves his friend as with Christ's sacred love, which flowed generously toward people: ₆₆these are pleasing to God, the Apostle says: *"Having the same love, being one in spirit and likeminded . . . ₆₇fleeing from selfish ambition, in humility valuing friends above ourselves"* (Phil 2.2–3). ₆₈For by being spiritual and holy toward God and true toward friends, we become heirs of the heavenly beings. ₆₉For Christ sowed the good seed, and Satan, the enemy of truth, the weeds of injustice, which Christ orders us to root out over time and

22. Or, "renewal" (cf. Gk. *sōtēria*). Echoing Gal 5.1.
23. Referring to Jn 15.12.
24. Cf. Gal 1.4; Eph 5.2; Ti 2.14.
25. Referring to Mt 22.37–39.

to throw in the fire for fuel; and to grow the good seed that yields hundredfold, and to sow the various seeds that yield more or less.[26]

₇₀And, at first, Satan was not created as an enemy, but became an adversary of good by his own sovereign will. For in Hebrew terms (his name) means "adversary."[27] ₇₁As we hear from the Lord to Peter: *"Get behind me, Satan! For you do not have in mind the concerns of God, but of humans"* (Mt 16.23), ₇₂for he was not aware of the saving suffering and (tried) to prevent it by opposing. ₇₃Everyone who opposes good is called "Satan"!

₇₄All creatures were made good by the Benefactor, and became demons in their perverse minds. ₇₅As for Satan, he fell from glory because of his personal pride.[28] Likewise, people who are similarly infected by Satan's deceptions: he had promised them divine honor[29] so that, like him, they will become enemies of God. ₇₆As for Gabriel, he was an archangel, also the bearer of good news to the Virgin, announcing, *"Rejoice, you who are highly favored!"* (Lk 1.28) and the redemption of the human race, ₇₇which is through the Incarnation of the Son of God, by whom the whole world was saved from sin: those who were defeated by Satan and received death, ₇₈whom Christ brought to life, reconciling the Creator to his creatures.[30] And he invited the believers in the Most Holy Trinity, those who love virtuous life, into the Kingdom of Heaven. ₇₉Even the demons confessed the Son of God: *"We know who you are—the Son of God, who has come to the world! And do you torture us before the time?"* (Mt 8.29).[31]

₈₀If he were evil and a liar by nature, would not (Scripture) have rightly said that demons were in existence or that they will come into existence? No one is evil by nature. Rather, for his will and deeds he is called by that true name, ("Satan,") and will be recompensed for his evil will. ₈₁For this reason, those who teach evil and those who learn it will be recompensed in the unquenchable

26. Conflating elements from "The Parable of the Sower" (Mt 13.3–23, esp. vss. 8, 23) and "The Parable of the Weeds" (Mt 13.24–30, esp. vss. 25, 30).

27. An etymology based on Heb. *śatan;* cf. Ps 38.20 (37.21 LXX); 71.13 (70.13 LXX); 109.4, 20, 29 (108.4, 20, 29 LXX); Zec 3.1.

28. Allusion to Is 14.12–15; cf. Ezek 28.1–19.

29. Referring to Gn 3.4.

30. Echoing Rom 5.10; 2 Cor 5.18; Col 1.22.

31. Cf. Mk 1.24 and Lk 4.34, for the first part: "I know who you are—the Holy One of God!" The verse is quoted differently in Disc. 6.52.

fire. ₈₂One who seduces into evil and teaches it, is Satan; and those who are neither seduced into evil nor learn it, are (true) men. ₈₃For the thief and his accomplice receive the same punishment; likewise, those who collaborate with evildoers: in vengeance they will be afflicted with them.[32] ₈₄For the Lord says: *"Sinners will go to the eternal fire prepared for Satan and his angels"* (Mt 25.41), who are the seducers.[33]

₈₅Let us not consider the holy priests and the honorable ecclesiastics—who are co-workers for the Gospel, ministers of the Sacraments, and in accord with the angelic hierarchy[34]—(as) unimportant (persons), but rather ordained by God for the salvation of God's faithful people. ₈₆For he appointed the leaders of the Church (as) preachers, in place of the Apostles, and said: *"Anyone who welcomes you welcomes me, and anyone who dishonors you dishonors me"* (Mt 10.40). Furthermore, he says: *"Whatever you bind on earth will be bound in heaven; and whatever you loose on earth will be loosed in heaven"* (Mt 18.18). ₈₇For the authority that is from God is powerful to forgive sins, to bring healing to the sick, and to drive out demons from people.[35] ₈₈For whom God ordains does God's work by the grace of Christ. ₈₉And the extended beneficence is a gift by which the hopeless ones are brought to living hope and redemption through the Gospel.[36] Those destined to death and all sinners are drawn by true teaching to confession and repentance, in accordance with the spiritual law; and by the redemptive (power) of the Gospel, to the glory and praise of the Most Holy Trinity. ₉₀The Prophet says: *"For the messenger of the Lord is almighty; and the law shall proceed from his mouth"* (Mal 2.7). ₉₁For those holy leaders (of the Church) who make disciples of the Truth by teaching the word, they will receive the glorious blessings and crowns from the almighty Lord, with the archangels and all the saints.[37]

₉₂There is a relationship between angels and humans, heaven

32. Echoing Rom 1.32.

33. See Disc. 23.101 and note.

34. Evoking the Pseudo-Dionysian parallel ecclesiastic and angelic hierarchies, on which see note to Disc. 10.125; cf. §§91–93 below, from which §96 seems to have been detached because of likely redaction—with reference to apostates and renegades.

35. Echoing the commissioning in Mt 10.8.

36. Echoing 1 Pt 1.3; cf. §§ 21, 125.

37. A repeated thought here (see below, §§149, 154), as elsewhere (Disc. 11.15).

and earth. ₉₃Now, (there are) archangels and angels, and holy leaders (of the Church) and all the elect who are God's beloved. ₉₄Now, one among the hosts of heaven, one of the archangels in opposition to goodness, was called Satan; and his hosts, demons: those who consented to his will and rebelled against the good ranks. ₉₅Likewise here. Men, indeed many people, are misled by heretics and are lost in lawless lives—even those who are called leaders (of the Church). They fell into the trap because of pride and became the cause of the loss of many, *"being hunted down by Satan into (doing) his will"* (2 Tm 2.26), much to their detriment. ₉₆For the overseers of truth—Apostles, Prophets, and saintly priests—are in concord with the holy hosts of heaven for the enlightenment of both those in heaven and those on earth. ₉₇And from among us are those who have rebelled and apostatized against the Word, by whom we were made disciples of the Truth.[38] They were estranged and became backsliders, like pagan priests and sorcerers and such evil ones.

₉₈Yet God's works and creatures are good; the unjust are evil by their own free will, whether demons or people. ₉₉Just as a palace[39] is ordinarily fit for a king, so is a prison for prisoners. ₁₀₀The good part is for the enjoyment and most beautiful adornment of those who are intimate (with God) and who think well of good deeds. ₁₀₁But the awful part and the rebuke and the diverse torments are for the unjust and the defiled, who were indiscriminately (practicing) injustice. ₁₀₂For hell is called prison, where fornicators and sorcerers and murderers and all the unjust are held for torture.[40] Those are the ones who despised the word of the Lord and did not follow justice.

₁₀₃Does Satan have authority over hell when it is clear that God, in accordance with his righteous law, is Satan's avenger? [41] ₁₀₄May it never be understood in this way! It was for him and his associates that hell was prepared by the Lord, not for people. ₁₀₅Those who delight in thinking and doing evil shall suffer the unending death with them. ₁₀₆God's law and justice were made manifest to his crea-

38. Echoing 1 Jn 2.19. In all likelihood, the clergy apostates included those who have repudiated their monastic vow; see Disc. 23.42–44, 61–63 and notes.

39. Lit., "temple."

40. Echoing Rv 22.15.

41. The author returns to this question at §115.

tures,[42] for needed rain and beneficial dew reveal God's care for the needs of his creatures. [107]Whereas thunders, hail, and flashes forecast his frightening wrath: the chastening threats to the wicked and sinners that will be revealed at the end.

[108]For the universal Flood was from the Lord because of the impure and the defiled, to wipe out the lawless ones, a punishment from heaven and earth.[43] Yet, in his most caring mercy, he saved the just ones and other beings through the ark, leaving seed for the world.

[109]And he killed the Sodomites with fire and brimstone,[44] for they were defiled by the fire of the passions and abominable sexual impurity.[45] Yet he rescued the righteous Lot from the fatal plagues. [110]The earth, water, rocks, trees, and plants, with all the inhabitants, were put to the torching flames. [111]Through these the most severe deaths were shown by God, the righteous Judge, to the wicked and sinners, and the redemption of the just by his caring love. [112]And even nowadays[46] in Sodom and Gomorrah, the punishment by God's wrath is seen on earth, water, rocks, and trees. [113]For by seeing that catastrophe nowadays, those who *"broadcast and display their sins like the Sodomites,"* as the Prophet says (Is 3.9), shall fear the impending wrath. [114]These and other (catastrophes) happen nowadays because of sin: famine, the sword, bondage, premature death, diverse pains, illnesses, and dangers, to admonish and to chasten; so that they may repent and survive the wrath coming from heaven.

[115]Now, let those who say that Satan is the lord of these chastening punishments and not the almighty God, be ashamed. [116]For from whom the legislation is, to him belong the decrees for catastrophes and for mercy, in accordance with his profound wisdom and administration. [117]For he is the forge of every mind. To all who are intimate with him, given the testimony (borne) by their love

42. Allusion to Rom 1.20.
43. See Gn 7.11; 8.2.
44. See Gn 19.24–25.
45. Or, "masturbation."
46. Lit., "now"; here and in the next two sections. It is unclear whether the author is referring to contemporary eyewitness accounts by travelers or he is simply drawing a general comparison between catastrophic consequences because of sin.

and fear, he shows his generous beneficence—provided by his benevolent will. ₁₁₈For God always reveals the beneficence of his sacred love, the administration of his grace to those who are obedient and have wholesome thoughts. For them, as for intimate children, he has prepared an inheritance and life with every goodness.

₁₁₉But (as) for those who show disdain for his laws and disobedience toward his will, and go astray and indiscriminately do filthy things and every awful sin, *"because of these things the wrath of God comes on the children of displeasure,"* says the Apostle (Eph 5.6). ₁₂₀For he will show his just judgments to the upright and to sinners. There is just judgment on earth; and as for the hereafter, there are blessings and torments.

₁₂₁For the plagues, which will be visited upon the world, understandably are because of sin; therefore, (people) should remorsefully exercise thoughtfulness and repent in order to be saved. ₁₂₂To such the Lord speaks through the Prophet, saying: *"Priests, comfort my people, for their suffering has been completed. Their sins will be forgiven, for they have received from the Lord's hand double recompense for their sins"* (Is 40.1–2). ₁₂₃For the plagues, which will be coming with catastrophes from the Lord, affect (also) those who repent for forgiveness of sins. ₁₂₄For the Lord says: *"I am he who puts to death and brings to life. I strike and I heal, and no one can deliver you out of my hand"* (Dt 32.39). ₁₂₅Every expectation by creatures draws them to the true, living hope,[47] lest they go astray after false opinions and the delusive, deceitful words of licentious people and sectarians, different from what we learned from the divines: the true traditions of the Holy Scriptures and the right fundamentals (of the faith). Let us lift up our minds daily to eternal blessings, decidedly away from vain opinions.

₁₂₆For this reason, under the sovereign will, the mind and the senses are full of every benefit of wisdom, leading a virtue-loving life, seen and unseen. ₁₂₇*"For in him we live and move"* (Acts 17.28), and in him we keep proceeding to the impending good things of the pledged and true promises. ₁₂₈For he is our Creator and we his creatures; for we call him "Our Father" as we do his will;[48] and he says: *"'You are my children. I will accept you with love, and I will be your*

---

47. Echoing 1 Pt 1.3; cf. §§21, 89.
48. Echoing "The Lord's Prayer" (Mt 6.9–13), referred to in §130.

God and you will be my people,' says the Lord Almighty" (2 Cor 6.16, 18).[49]
129Moreover, the Prophet says: *"Come, my children, and listen to me; and
I will teach you the fear of the Lord"* (Ps 34.11 [33.12 LXX]). 130And the
Son of God granted us to call his natural Father our Father and
God;[50] and he was not (slow) to consider us ignoble ones part of his
brotherhood and heirs of the Kingdom.[51] 131And the Father above
speaks of his love for the Son, who did his will and everything the
Father had said. 132And it is said of the Holy Spirit: *"When he comes,
he will teach you all things"* (Jn 14.36) (about) the will of the Father and
the Son regarding salvation. 133For those who have been saved by
the Father, the Son, and the Holy Spirit will receive grace and will
pursue the virtues.

134But one has to marvel at this: that the names of the Creator
are related to creatures: "Father" to fathers, "Son" to sons, and
"Holy Spirit" to the human spirit. By these we comprehend the
providence of his sacred love with which we have been privileged.
135And when we disregard such great beneficence and advantage
given us by his sacred love, would God be unjust if he directed
his wrath against those who truly disdain[52] his loving benevolence
and fail to remember[53] the abundant gifts of his sacred love *"which
he poured generously upon us"* (Ti 3.6)? 136According to Moses, the man
of God, there is this judgment: if a forceful man defiles a weak
woman against her will, being feeble vis-à-vis his strength, the man
shall be put to death, but the woman shall live according to the just
judgment.[54] 137For the Lord says through the Prophet: *"The person
of the father is mine, and the person of the son is mine; the person who sins,
the same shall die"* (Ezek 18.4). 138For the person sins of his own will.
139He also says of the righteous: *"The one who follows righteousness will
surely live ... the one with lawlessness will surely die"* (Ezek 18.19–20).[55]
140For the Lord is righteous and his judgments are just, for the upright and sinners.[56]

---

49. Cf. Lv 26.12; Jer 32.38; Ezek 37.27; Rv 21.3.
50. Referring to Mt 6.9.
51. Alluding to Mt 12.50; Mk 3.35; Heb 2.11.
52. Lit., "disdaining they disdain" (Semitism).
53. Lit., "leave out of the mind the remembrance of ..."
54. Referring to Dt 22.25–27.
55. Cf. Ezek 33.12–16.
56. Echoing Ps 145.17 (144.17 LXX); Zep 3.5; cf. 2 Tm 4.8.

141Through our sovereign will, by good deeds, we could turn God's will to our benefit; or to punishment for evil deeds. 142For it is up to our will either to enjoy the good things or to reject them. 143For he does not will the death of the sinner; but rather, for him to turn away from the evil way and live through repentance.[57] For the Lord says: *"I am merciful, and I will not take vengeance on those who turn to the right way"* (Jer 3.12). 144For he, lover of humankind, does not overlook someone worthy of compassion, mercy, or forgiveness, but like a physician, he heals the inner parts and the external members; and he amputates the incurable (part) which infects the rest.[58] 145But those who do not turn away from their corrupt lives are reminded of the loss by the Flood and the suffering and death of the Sodomites by fire—who were judged here and will be judged there according to the word of the Lord in the Gospels.[59]

146Those who are remorseful and repent are like the Ninevites. They turn the threatening wrath and the impending punishments from the Lord to mercy, according to the prophecy of Jonah.[60] 147But those who harden their hearts like Pharaoh—who perished with his own while the people of God lived—will receive the same plagues that were inflicted upon those who did not obey the Lord's command to them by Moses and Aaron.[61]

148For God is One, Creator of heaven and earth, who created the angels and humans with sovereign will, by which both angels and humans determine their detachment from misleading evil thoughts. 149The Lord has glory and crowns prepared for the holy among the corporeal and incorporeal beings; 150the righteous Judge has punishment and suffering and hell for the incorporeal, evil demons and for the wicked and defiled among the corporeal beings, as deserved by each. 151For demons have a role in the evil deeds called by their name; and evil men, sorcerers and the defiled, come forth from among these evil ones and are in unison with the evil demons.

57. Allusion to Ezek 18.23, 32.

58. A *topos* in ancient moral literature; cf. Disc. 11.129 and 23.54, where the same medical analogy is used.

59. Referring to Lk 17.26–29; see note to §23, above. Cf. Disc. 8.14.

60. Read Յովնանու (*Yovnanu*) instead of Յովհանու (*Yovhanu; Yovhannu* in the 1894 Ējmiacin edition).

61. Referring to the plagues in Ex 7.14–11.9.

₁₅₂Anyone who wishes to flee from these adversaries and to become an angel ought to love God and do what pleases him with all his heart and being and strength, and (what pleases) one's friends, with sacred love in (deeds) seen and unseen; be grateful for all favors from those far and near; be holy, immaculate, pure, healthy, single-minded, agreeable, compliant, obedient, peacemaking,[62] true, abstaining from every evil thing; love what is good and hate what is evil; and possess a good reputation for good deeds— in order to be in glory. ₁₅₃As for one who withdraws from what is good and becomes in semblance like Satan: opponent of good, disobeyer, lover of sin, lover of the passions, proud, arrogant, cunning, crafty, liar, libeler, contentious, lover of evil and not of good, departing from truthfulness, and possessing evil reputation for evil deeds: wrath and endless suffering (he will have) in recompense—for rewards and punishments are as deserved.

₁₅₄Now, the sovereign will is (granted) to thoughtful and rational beings for honor and glory so that the benevolent God may be glorified. Crowns of angelic order will be made for those (who set their) sovereign will on virtue-loving lives; and they will receive gifts from the Lord for persevering and holy lives: apostleship, prophesying, and priesthood.[63] ₁₅₅We who in every way are established in the truth will inherit the prepared Kingdom. ₁₅₆Since the Kingdom belongs to God, we have been granted, through the abundant love of him who loved us and showed us beneficence,[64] to come into the Kingdom by way of right faith and true life. ₁₅₇Those whose lives are impure and supine regarding the virtues, who are deluded and lovers of sin, *"they fall short of the glory of God"* (Rom 3.23); they are ruined, humiliated, fallen from grace into shame, and scorned by all.

₁₅₈For this reason our God and Lord established the Kingdom for the righteous and dire punishment for sinners, so that all—the righteous and the wicked—will come to know the straightforward Judgment. ₁₅₉And let no one be astonished when he forgives. (Scripture) says: *"For God's kindness brings about repentance"* (Rom 2.4).

62. Lit., "peacemaker."

63. Alluding, in part, to the spiritual gifts, the *charismata* of 1 Cor 12.27–31; Eph 4.7–14; cf. Disc. 4.72; 5.15. On angelic honor, see Disc. 5.19–23.

64. Echoing Rom 8.37; 2 Thes 2.16.

₁₆₀And if they have no remorse, they will be judged without mercy on the day when the wrath is revealed. ₁₆₁And sinners will behold the glory of the righteous; they will melt away, vanish in eternal sadness and shame. On earth they considered themselves to be greater than the righteous; their pride prevented them from seeing who the righteous and who sinners are. ₁₆₂After the recompense, however, the glory of the righteous and the eternal shame of sinners will be revealed.

₁₆₃This is clear: with God there is no exalting of dynastic prestige[65] except for the good dynasty of virtue—₁₆₄even though in Armenia and Persia none (was) greater than the Arsacid Dynasty that had descended here, from Abraham,[66] as also the kings of all nations on earth; this according to the word of the Lord of All, which does not lie.[67] ₁₆₅But if (dynasts) do not show good discernment,[68] they will receive more punishment from the Lord. ₁₆₆Even their servants who are pleasing to God will be glorified as kings by the Lord; whereas they will be punished as debtors to sin in the just tribunal—₁₆₇unless kings, princes, and judges think justly, weigh justly, in accordance with God's justice, and judge justly, taking into consideration the spiritual and the physical aspects, (as) overseers of orphans and widows, guardians of all who have been dispossessed, and helpers to all who are vulnerable. For such (dynasts) are the foundations of goodness, who keep the world well established by their creative ingenuity—within the resourceful love of the Creator of All, ₁₆₈by whom the good for this world continues, to the praise of God's glorious grace and to the praise of the almighty Lordship of the Father and the Son and the Holy Spirit; to whom honor, dominion, and glory are befitting now and always, eternally. Amen.

65. Lit., "there is no glorification of dynastic glory."
66. On this nostalgic yet tempered affection for the past, see "Introduction": the discussion on the date and provenance of the document, pp. 41-51.
67. Referring to Gn 17.6. Cf. Disc. 12.97, on the truthfulness of the divine word, "which does not lie" (echoing Nm 23.19; Ps 89.35 [88.36 LXX]; Heb 6.18; Ti 1.2).
68. Or, "But if they do not judge well"; the text has: *Ayl etʿē očʿ zgastanaycʿen i bari.*

DISCOURSE 21

A FEW WORDS ON THE GIFT OF WISDOM BESTOWED
BY THE HOLY SPIRIT[1]

HE OVERSEEING care of the Creator is measureless; so is his enlightenment of the creatures he created. ₂God demands more good fruits from those to whom he has given much; and from those who were given less, (he expects) the gain they have made, the profit derived. ₃As one learns from the parable of the talents,[2] (even) the one with less has gained. God gave discerning minds to angels and humans so that they will become agents of the Benefactor and preachers of his grace, cultivators of his beneficence among all creatures with free will and the grace of choice. ₄For there are advantages to wisdom, power, and greatness, in heaven and on earth.

₅This goodness of God's foreknowledge extends to us. For he who has received much, loves more, and renders more good things to God.[3] And he who has less, given his ability and modest gain, counts on fairness in God's deep knowledge. ₆Moreover, those who have a difficult life, they have more—(not) less—discernment of evil. ₇And those who repent are not ignored by his loving kindness, even though they were agents of the evil one in their submissive minds. This shows his benevolent care. ₈Let no one think that grace is bestowed with bias toward deserving creatures.

₉He also visits the undeserving, even though they do not realize it. For their sovereign minds have been made dark, and they do not see their Light. ₁₀For the thoughts of the earthbound flow to

---

1. The Spirit is not mentioned in the discourse; in fact, not until the concluding line, with the Trinitarian formula, of Disc. 22.

2. Allusion to "The Parable of the Talents" in Mt 25.14–30.

3. Echoing Lk 7.47.

waste, unable to see the causes; they drift into harmful concerns, and find nothing good but evil. ₁₁For this reason they are prevented from grace, since they are unwilling to be open to sacred love and be inclined toward the virtues, his generous beneficence for the sustenance of all, with much patience and real trust, that they may become true agents in life and bring glory to themselves and to others. ₁₂And if it were only for the righteous to have their minds set in many ways on wisdom, (then) it would seem that (only) the righteous make progress in virtue. But all know that the righteous are motivated by the fear of the Lord, and the sinners are made sluggards because they do not fear (the Lord). ₁₃For this reason they sin and are drawn into darkness in their mind; they are blinded by the sin of thoughtlessness. ₁₄*"Although they considered themselves to be wise,"* thoughtful in their own eyes, yet *"the way of peace they did not know"* (Rom 1.22; 3.17); for the fear of the Lord is not before their eyes. ₁₅For this reason they were corrupted and defiled, and did not proceed in the straight way.

₁₆But those who love God are guided into all righteousness,[4] goodness, and more; so that they may remain inseparable from *"the wisdom that comes from above, pure, peace-loving, and full of good fruit"* (Jas 3.17), ₁₇*"being enlightened, certain in behavior, bearing in mind what is right and just, and always giving guidance in fairness"* (Prv 1.3). ₁₈*"I speak wisdom to the mature"* (1 Cor 2.6), to those who know how to distinguish between the eternal and the transient things, not the wisdom of this world that is coming to nothing, but the righteousness of God: true faith, sacred love, purity and humility, meekness and truth, and being adorned with every virtue—with the fear of God. And to be cautious about the all-deluding fallacies and to ascertain with discerning wisdom pure thoughts, words, and deeds. ₁₉For Wisdom's gate to life is open, even though there are many adversaries conspiring with the accuser[5] to hunt down humans for perdition. ₂₀But God does not forsake those who have placed their hope in him, who pray to him day and night and ask for mercy and victory over all harms caused by demons; so that God may be glorified now and always and through the ages, forever. Amen.

---

4. Echoing Mt 3.15.
5. A recurring epithet for Satan; see Jb 1.9–11; Zec 3.1; 1 Pt 5.8; Rv 12.10.

DISCOURSE 22

ON THE UNCHANGEABLE ESSENCE
OF GOD'S BEING[1]

HOSE WHO ascribe weakness to divine power stand outside the true faith. ₂For they say that sometimes (God) is able and sometimes unable. ₃Thoughtless fellows! If God is weak, who then could strengthen? ₄Let this teaching of the evil teacher be refuted, for God is able and perfect; he never lacks in perfection and power. Rather, he fills and strengthens all, yet he is not filled and strengthened by another.

₅For this reason creation is always ascribed to God, who chose angels and—from among humans—the Apostles, Prophets, and saints to be witnesses to the truth of divine knowledge and (God's) justice-loving and holy works. These were done with power, signs, and wonders, so that God may be glorified through them. ₆And the Creator does not receive help from his creatures, whether heavenly or earthly. Rather, he is their helper and strength. ₇As God told the Prophet: *"I have known you before you were formed in the womb. I have ordained you a prophet by grace"* (Jer 1.5). ₈Thus, through his foreknowledge, he invites and calls, justifies and glorifies with love.

₉All creatures stand in need of help from the Creator, and not the Creator from the creatures. ₁₀For God is immutable, but creatures are subject to change: as from childhood to youth, from youth to old age, and from old age to corruptibility; or as from spring to summer, from summer to fall, and from fall to winter, which hinders the growth of all animals, plants, and trees. ₁₁Even the sun changes from time to time, as God has determined the length and shortness of days. ₁₂(Scripture) says: *"Its rising is from the ends of the*

---

1. The word ինքնութիւն (*ink'nut'iwn*), here translated "essence," does not occur in the discourse; it occurs but once elsewhere, in Disc. 1.1.

earth, as also its setting; and none can hide from the heat of its light" (Ps 19.6 [18.7 LXX]). And so it serves the creatures at the Creator's command. ₁₃The moon serves likewise, indicating changes of time as it waxes and wanes. Hence we recognize the waning of earthly beings and their renewal at the resurrection. ₁₄Moreover, stars serve sailors at night, and, by their various movements, (other) corporeal creatures—certainly not how the heathen blabber about them, in their interpretations of chance and births.[2]

₁₅For God is the Creator who fashioned everything and set boundaries that cannot be crossed.[3] ₁₆All creatures were made by him, and by the caring power of his Wisdom they were assembled. ₁₇And the knowledge for inventing, the necessary arts, the systems of making things, and the measures have come from his supervision and care. ₁₈None of those who receive inventiveness and power from him is mightier than he. ₁₉For he is the source of every goodness, who fills the earth and (satisfies) its creatures—₂₀he, who made everything out of nothing and who is capable of destroying things as he wishes. ₂₁Knowledge, intelligence, wisdom, and power have their origin in him. ₂₂As creatures could see, he has power to raise water to heaven, even above it,[4] and to (establish) seas, rivers, mountains, and creatures on earth. ₂₃And he needs neither pillars nor helpers for the foundations of heaven and earth. Rather, they are sustained by his power, and without him they will collapse.[5]

₂₄Now, what is the punishment for those who blaspheme against God? ₂₅By him the weak are strengthened; by him the righteous are counseled and triumph over despotic opponents. They come forward to keep his commandments and become wise in good things. ₂₆Who is the overseer and helper of those in danger? When in trouble, who provides a way out of temptation if not God?[6]

₂₇Let us then inquire about the evil tongues, who say that God needs the help of the heavenly hosts or of the righteous on earth. ₂₈He does not receive help from them. Rather, *"they serve those who*

---

2. See Philo of Alexandria, *On Providence* 1.77–88, against astral fatalism.
3. Allusion to Ps 104.9 (103.9 LXX).
4. Allusion to Gn 1.7.
5. Lit., "they will not be corrupted."
6. Allusion to 1 Cor 10.13.

will inherit salvation" (Heb 1.14) by the will of the Creator. ₂₉Even
the heavenly hosts were created by him from nothing, and by his
grace were the saints elected from among humans. ₃₀He established
the sovereign will among intelligent and rational beings. Moreover,
he exalts, together with those in heaven, those who exercise sound
judgment on earth, who keep his commandments, and who will
become his heirs. ₃₁And God will be revealed as all in all.[7] ₃₂*"For
by the word of the Lord were the heaven and the earth established, and by the
breath of his mouth all his hosts"* (Ps 33.6 [32.6 LXX]).

₃₃For this reason the three young men in the furnace[8] summon all creatures to praise constantly the almighty and all-giving
Lordship. ₃₄For they said: *"Bless the Lord, all works of the Lord"* (Dn
3.57 LXX = Song of the Three Young Men 35). Bless the Creator
of heaven and earth and all creatures in them, seen and unseen.[9]
₃₅Intelligent and rational beings, day and night, light and darkness,
sea and dry land, aquatics and aerials, beasts and domestic animals, reptiles and birds, clouds and rain, dew and snow, cold and
heat, air and earth, trees and plants, mountains and hills, fields
and deep ravines, dragons and whales, fire and fresh water,[10] they
all sing praises to his name—blessing and honor to the Most Holy
Name.[11] ₃₆And he pronounces Israel blessed above all others,[12] for
from their midst the Patriarchs, the Prophets, the Apostles, and
others were elected. By grace they appeared as servants of the Most
High God and priests of the Lord, righteous people and souls, holy
and lowly in heart.[13] God's blessings are realized in them, for they
are not considered just another nation. But that all, through them,
may come to know that they are creatures of the Creator of all, that
they are called to sing spiritual songs of praise.

₃₇These spiritual songs[14] have been passed on to us, so that by
these songs of praise,[15] composed thoughtfully, for the feasts, for

---

7. Allusion to 1 Cor 15.28.
8. Reference to Dn 3.8–30.
9. Summing up all the refrains in Dn 3.57–90 (LXX), further summed up in §35.
10. Lit., "spring and river water."
11. See Ps 148.7–12; Is 43.20.
12. Echoing Dt 7.14.
13. Echoing Ps 73.1 (72.1 LXX).
14. Lit., "This spiritual song."
15. Referring to the biblical Psalms.

Christ's Incarnation with regard to our redemption, for the commemoration of the holy martyrs, for calls to repentance with remorse, and for the deceased, we may bless, praise, and magnify the Most Holy Trinity, who created all creatures and gave us comfort and good hope in his glory. 38For they were created for good works and to abide by the will of the One who is without beginning, omniscient, eternal, and fount of all goodness—inner and heavenly. 39For through his wise counsel and knowledge he sustains all who were created, as their natural constitution requires and whatever may depend on it. 40Who created things out of nothing and made his holy and righteous ones prominent and glorified, and invited them to his Kingdom and glory, to the immutable blessings, the endless joy, and the pure and incorruptible life—41from which all sadness and sorrow are banished and to which the unapproachable Light[16] is ever near, to the glory and praise and blessing of the Most Holy Trinity: to the Father, the Son, and the Holy Spirit, forever and ever. Amen.

16. Allusion to 1 Tm 6.16; cf. Ps 104.2 (103.2 LXX).

DISCOURSE 23

COUNSEL TO ASCETICS AND
GENERAL DIRECTIVES THAT
PROMOTE VIRTUE

LL WHO HAVE renounced the world and have dedicated themselves to God in obedience to the true traditions of the holy Fathers, to lead a life of ascetic virginity for the sake of the promised good things, abide cautiously in thoughts, words, and deeds *"so as not to be bitten by the treacherous serpent"* (Nm 21.6) and be led astray from following God with holy and righteous and virtue-loving lives.[1]

₂They abide single-mindedly by every spiritual counsel: (to counter) anger with meekness at all times;[2] insensitivity with sen-

---

1. As noted in the "Introduction," some of the counsel that follows has parallels in Basil of Caesarea's ascetical discourses and monastic rules, especially *The Long Rules* (*Regulae fusius tractatae,* PG 31:889–1052; trans. Wagner, *Ascetical Works,* FC 9:223–337, abbr. *LR;* to be distinguished from *The Short Rules,* abbr. *SR*). Like the *Long Rules,* the discourse favors cenobitic life over solitary life (cf. *LR* 7 and 24). Although the dependence on the *Rules* is evident, there is no indication of direct borrowing except for a single instance of clear reliance on its sixth-century Armenian translation (see note to §67). By the same token, the asceticism presented in the discourse is not thoroughly "Basilian," for here, as in the preceding discourses, a degree of the early Syrian ascetic tradition is reflected; and some allowance must be made for local practices. The cenobitic community depicted here shows ascetic solitaries and monastics enriching one another spiritually, under the leadership of a superior with absolute authority. This points to a period in the history of monasticism when both entities had ceased practicing public service as their ultimate calling (on which see Harvey, *Asceticism and Society in Crisis,* 13–21, 43–56, 94–107), and certainly a time of increasing restrictions following the Messalian controversy (on which see Daniel Caner, *Wandering, Begging Monks: Spiritual Authority and the Promotion of Monasticism in Late Antiquity,* TCH 33 [Berkeley: University of California Press, 2002], esp. 83–125, 235–41).

2. On meekness as antidote to anger, see the concluding paragraph of Basil's

sitivity; animosity with commendation; disobedience with obedience; defiance with compliance; impatience with patience; vengefulness with forbearance; covetousness with admiration;[3] bitterness
with kindness; viciousness with benevolence; idleness with indus-
triousness;[4] insinuation with candor; superfluity with modesty;
teasing and joking with tears; hatred with the possession of pure
love; hopelessness with hopefulness; sadness with joy; temptations
with longsuffering; greed with moderation;[5] love of possessions
with disdain [for things];[6] love of honor with selflessness; unbelief with true faith; and any of the machinations of the evil one
who wages war against the truth, through sight or hearing or smell
or taste or tongue or hands or feet or heart—which is the store-
room of thoughts, both good and its opposite, evil.[7] ₃These are
the foremost harmful things to eradicate through virtuous living,
in accordance with the fundamental counsel previously iterated to
counter the evils that constantly rise up to wage war against the
ascetics.[8] ₄This is a great battle, and greater the victory,[9] annihi-
lating the opposition that hopes to triumph over novices through
enticements.[10]

₅As for you, O soul, who were dedicated to God, do not take
him (the evil one) as your counselor, but *"fight the good fight"* (1 Tm

Adversus iratos (Hom. 10.7; PG 31:370B–372B; trans. Wagner, *Ascetical Works*, FC
9:459–61). Cf. Disc. 10.37; 11.64, 86; 18.32; 19.40.

3. Lit., "non-envy."

4. Lit., "love for labor."

5. Arm. չափաւորութիւն (*č'ap'aworut'iwn*), a *hapax* in the discourses (usually,
պարկեշտութիւն, *parkeštut'iwn*, as in §§13, 88; or, զգաստութիւն, *zgastut'wn*, in the
sense of "circumspection," as in §§33, 46, 69, 75, 82, 88, 120).

6. Indicative of property renunciation; cf. Disc. 10.29–33 and Basil *LR* 8, as
well as his homily on detachment from worldly goods, *Quod rebus mundanis adhaeren-
dum non sit* (Hom. 21; trans. Wagner, *Ascetical Works*, FC 9:487–512).

7. Cf. the list of vices and their antidotes in Disc. 19.40. For a similar counsel,
see Basil *LR* 51.

8. Allusion to the preceding discourses. The view of asceticism as battle against
the forces of evil is repeated in §§10–11 and 16; for elsewhere in the discourses
see "Warfare" in the Subject Index. The recurrent analogy with battle recalls its
repeated use by Theodoret of Cyrrhus in his *Historia religiosa* (PG 82:1283–1496).

9. Echoing Eph 6.12.

10. Our document is not clear on rules of admission to the monastic community; however, much of what follows seems to be counsel to novices—if not also much
of the preceding discourses.

6.12) and adhere firmly to these counsels, always remembering the Champion of the holy ascetics that knead and wrap both soul and body together. ₆Pursue asceticism[11] attentively, conscientiously, and worthily, in accordance with the Gospel of Christ.[12] ₇Take off all worldly desires and *"put on the new man"* (Eph 4.24),[13] adorning yourself with good works inside and out, becoming holy and impeccable, perfect in righteousness, and being cleansed from all earthly desires.

₈First, one must establish firmly within oneself, with pure heart and genuine faith, the basic principle of fearing God; be ready and worthy of one's commitment to his calling; be pure and thoroughly spotless, well-pleasing to God; ₉remain firm, immovable, and unshaken in mind and every member (of the body) within the gathering of one's ascetic order; ₁₀fight the spiritual fight against the daily enemy who wages an internal war against the senses and thoughts; and (win) the victory with help from above; be led in spiritual wisdom, in all righteousness; and defeat those who battle against the morals of the (holy) orders and piety—₁₁*"For the weapon of those who strive*[14] *is not physical but, on the contrary, spiritual, divine, to chase away the evil one"* (2 Cor 10.4); ₁₂imbue purity in every member (of the body) in place of impurity; and altogether wipe away impure thoughts with wholesome thoughts: ₁₃gluttony with moderation; drunkenness with perseverance; overindulgence with modesty; general laziness with every effort; ₁₄vacillation with resolve; lethargy with diligence; arrogance with humility; pride with selflessness; vainglory with lowliness; lying with forthrightness; swearing falsely with truthfulness; cunning with perfect love.[15]

11. Arm. կրաւնաւորիլ (*krawnaworil*). The verb is a *hapax* in the discourses; however, its noun forms occur in §§106 and 108 only (see note to §106).

12. Echoing the basics of early monasticism, i.e., living the teaching of the Gospel in a life of *imitatio Christi*, fulfilling the Gospel measure of poverty seen in the *kenosis* (the "emptying" of one's self) of the Incarnation (Phil 2.1–11); cf. §94.

13. Cf. Rom 13.14; Gal 3.27; Col 3.9–10.

14. Or, "of the ascetics" (Arm. ճգնաւորաց, *čgnaworac‘*), gen. pl., not found in the Arm. biblical text of this verse). The word *čgnawor*, recurring in various forms throughout the discourse (in the title and in §§3, 5, 9, 18, 25, 91, 98, 99, 102, 105), lit., "one who strives or perseveres," thus becomes the usual word for "ascetic" or "one who perseveres in the austere or ascetic life."

15. Echoing and expanding upon the opposites of the Seven Deadly Sins:

₁₅And you should remain cautiously firm in prayer and fasting, with warm tears, pure love, grace-filled hope and tender compassion, according to God's will. ₁₆You should constantly try to advance in the course of piety, with awe and fear; to increase in good works without losing merited virtue, both seen and unseen; and to thwart by overall progress the profound malevolence of the evil one. ₁₇Through the principles of justice and the soundness of purity you should totally cast away boastfulness as well as the inclination to evil and easily creeping sins. ₁₈With the impeccable beneficence of God's sacred love, you should persevere in ascetic husbandry, according to his kind and loving beneficence, in obedience to God and those who have a love relationship with him.

₁₉For one should truly keep the communal fellowship,[16] united in peace, unwavering in thoughts, in full harmony and obedience to the brotherhood as well as trusting the superior,[17] through whom

---

Humility against pride, *Kindness* against envy, *Abstinence* against gluttony, *Chastity* against lust, *Patience* against anger, *Liberality* against greed, and *Diligence* against sloth.

16. Arm. միաբանութիւն (*miabanut'iwnn*), word used also for a monastic (cenobitic) community or brotherhood, rendered "(the) communal fellowship" throughout (§§32, 42–44, 62₂, 113, 116); cf. the synonymous եղբայրութեանն (*ełbayrut'eann*), rendered "(of the) brotherhood" in the next line and elsewhere (§§20, 32, 35, 39, 42, 44, 46, 52, 54–55, 57, 59, 51, 67, 82, 86, 94, 113, 115). Note esp. զմիաբանութիւն եղբայրութեանն (*zmiabanut'iwn ełbayrut'eann*, "the communal fellowship of the brotherhood") in §§32, 42, 44, 113. As noted earlier, the discourse is blatantly partial to cenobitical life and critical of solitaries; cf. Basil *LR* 7, 24.

17. Or, "abbot"; Arm. առաջնորդ (*aṙajnord;* cf. Gk. *hegumenos*, Syr. *riš dayrā*), rendered "superior" throughout the discourse (§§19, 20, 35–37, 46, 51, 56–57, 61, 115, all in singular; in §§27 and 51 the plural *aṙajnordk'* is used with reference to Heb 13.17 and, as elsewhere in the discourses, pointing to spiritual leaders in general; see "Leaders" in the Subject Index); cf. առաջնորդութիւն (*aṙajnordut'iwn*), "(superior's) oversight," in §55 and Disc. 10.129. Elsewhere the word վերակացու (*verakac'u*) is used interchangeably and just as frequently, similarly rendered "superior" throughout (§§28, 33, 44, 47, 50, 52, 55, 58, 64, 68, 76, 88, 91, all in singular also, and plural in other discourses, referring to spiritual leaders or ecclesiarchs in general; see "Overseers" in the Subject Index); cf. վերակացութիւն (*verakac'ut'iwn*), "(superior's) oversight," in Disc. 10.124–125 and 129, where in the last instance it is likewise used interchangeably with առաջնորդութիւն (*aṙajnordut'iwn*). It is important to point out that the interchangeableness of the terms indicated here is similar to their interchangeableness in the Armenian translation of Basil's *Rules*, where both *aṙajnord* and *verakac'u* invariably refer to the superior. A third term, with contextual distinction, is տեսուչ (*tesuč';* cf. Gk. *epitērētēs*, Syr. *rabbaitā*), rendered

his confession (of sin) was truly presented to God, through whom he also receives the reward of repentance from sinning in thoughts, words, or deeds. ₂₀Forgiveness is obtained from the Savior, through the testimony of the superior and the brotherhood, those who live steadfastly, firmly established in the same monastery.[18] ₂₁And they are not double-minded; *"for the double-minded person is like one driven by the wind and tossed by the waves of the sea. Such a person should not expect to receive anything good from the Lord"* (Jas 1.6–8). ₂₂Rather, one should live out the virtues with true faith, pure life, and awe of God, being strengthened by the Holy Spirit, and with great forbearance, as the Apostle admonishes: *"In troubles, in hardships, in distresses, in beatings, in imprisonments, in riots, in labor, in vigils, in fasting, in purity, in kindness, being molded by the goodness of the Holy Spirit"* (2 Cor 6.4–6).

₂₃The Lord says: *"Anyone who loves me will keep my commandments, which the Holy Spirit made known; then I with my Father will come and will make our abode with him"* (Jn 14.23).[19] ₂₄How great and glorious and affable are those who become temples for the Most Holy Trinity. For the almighty Lord says: *"I will dwell with them and will sanctify them, and I will be their God and they will be my people"* (2 Cor 6.16).[20]

₂₅Now, since ascetics have such good news, let us fulfill sanctity with the fear of God, by being obedient beneath his extremely light yoke, which is heavy for those who love the world but light for

---

"superintendent" (§§74, 78; cf. Disc. 3.18), used for one responsible for some practical aspect of monastic life. In the literature of the period, առաջնորդ (*aṙajnord*) and վերակացու (*verakac'u*) are used for church leaders in general; synonymous with եպիսկոպոս (*episkopos*), a term used in these discourses specifically for bishops (§§55, 58, and Disc. 10.78). On obedience to the superior, see further, §§28, 35–36, 51, 71, 93–94. Monastic life was centered around obedience and its attendant humility, patterned after Christ's example. Only through the enabling "fatherhood" of the presiding superior could such discipline be made possible in communal life. Cf. Basil *LR* 25–28, 41, 47–48.

18. For more on the role of the abbot in attesting to and passing on divine forgiveness following confession, see §§65, 93–94. The Arm. word վանք (*vank'*), is used in its strictly monastic sense throughout this discourse (see §§39, 54, 58), unlike its generic meaning of "dwelling" or "abode" (see Disc. 11.96, 103). The use of the word is limited to the sections referenced here.

19. Cf. §116. On the centrality of this verse in Christian mysticism, see note at Disc. 2.23.

20. Cf. Lv 26.12; Jer 32.38; Ezek 37.27. None has "I will sanctify them." See also Disc. 8.16, on the indwelling "Most Holy Trinity."

virtuous people whom he calls with sweet voice, saying: *"Come to me, all you who are weary and burdened, and I will give you rest. Take my yoke upon you and learn from me meekness, humility, obedience, and all righteousness, and you will find rest for your souls. For my yoke is easy (leading) unto hope, and my burden is light (leading) unto greater reward in return"* (Mt 11.28–30).

₂₆Let every dire difficulty be restrained with active goodness,[21] with peaceful liberty and impeccable sanctity, that one may enter the haven of tranquility for soul and body and be delivered from every painful rage of the evil passions. ₂₇*"Listen to the counsel of (your) leaders[22] and submit to their orders"* (Heb 13.17); and let the latter not be indifferent to the people who have taken a vow,[23] for they will account for them on the day of visitation.

₂₈Let the love of truth be in everyone; no one accusing, no one cunning, no one disobedient to the orders of the superior,[24] no one complaining about work or other things, no one creating confusion or sowing animosity. ₂₉*"The one who is throwing you into confusion, whoever that may be, will have to pay the penalty"* (Gal 5.10), says the Apostle. ₃₀Rather, follow peace and pure love, and become children of God and co-heirs with Christ, *"who made peace … in heaven and on earth"* (Col 1.20). ₃₁Obey and be pleasing to one another in the fear of the Lord. ₃₂Keep the communal fellowship of the brotherhood[25] intact through the (mutually) pleasing pure love that binds one to another and does not allow disjointing or separation from one another for (any) reason, by someone seeking vengeance and not the unity of love.[26]

21. Echoing Rom 12.21.

22. Arm. (*ar̄ajnordacʻ*, gen. pl.); cf. §51, where the same verse is alluded to, and Disc. 10.134; 17.32, 36; 20.86, 91, 93, 95, where the plural *ar̄ajnordkʻ* seems to refer to spiritual leaders in general. The singular form is used strictly for the monastic superior in this discourse (see note to §19).

23. Arm. ժողովրդեան ուխտին (*žořovrdean uxtin*) here seems to be the same as ամենայն ուխտին (*amenayn uxtin*) of §61, referring to the brotherhood or the "covenanters," those who have taken a monastic vow, as in §§51, 54, 61–63; cf. the collective ուխտ (*uxt*) in §86.

24. On Arm. վերակացու (*verakacʻu*), used synonymously with առաջնորդ (*ar̄ajnord*), and on obedience to the superior, see note to §19.

25. Or, "of the cenobitic brotherhood"; Arm. զմիաբանութիւն եղբայրութեանն (*zmiabanutʻiwn ełbayrutʻeann*), similarly in §§42–44.

26. Cf. §§44, 57, 71, 86. For earlier stresses on fraternal love and care, see Disc. 2.46; 5.106; 6.72, 96; 11.33.

₃₃As for the superior, let him be circumspect toward those who are near and welcoming to those who are far; to admonish his brothers with deep knowledge, in a timely manner, to the degree of their receptivity, from the goodness of his heart; ₃₄to counsel the novices[27] in the awe and fear of the Lord and in obedience to the brothers; ₃₅and for all to agree with the will of the brotherhood's superior. Let nothing be done apart from his will. ₃₆And should someone contemplate something or say or do (anything) apart from his will, he should be obliged to repent; for the one who offends the superior offends God.[28] For the Lord did say: *"Whoever disrespects you disrespects me, and whoever welcomes you welcomes me, and whoever accepts your word accepts mine"* (Lk 10.16).

₃₇Rather, with humility and willing obedience subject yourselves to the common good, in compliance with God's command and allegiance to the superior (appointed) by God. ₃₈*"For those who are (in authority),"* (Scripture) says, *"have been appointed by God; and those who rebel against them bring judgment on themselves, whoever they may be"* (Rom 13.1–2). ₃₉Comply to stay in one monastery and with one brotherhood to the glory of the Most Holy Trinity, *"being one in spirit and of one mind, with nothing out of selfish ambition or vain conceit,"* as the Apostle admonishes. *"Rather, in humility value one another above yourselves"* (Phil 2.2–3).[29] ₄₀Such are those who always have the oil of pure love with them and *"with their lit lamps . . . enter the nuptial chamber"* (Mt 25.4, 10), ₄₁whom the almighty Father welcomes with good news into the heavenly Groom's unending joy.

₄₂But those who decide to depart from the communal fellowship of the brotherhood[30] are like the foolish virgins who do not have the oil of love, for whom the bridal chamber is shut because of their unlit wedding torches.[31] ₄₃They are those who hear the voice of the

---

27. Arm. կր<տ>սերն (*kr<t>sern*); նրամատ (*noramut*) in §4.

28. The absolute authority of the superior contrasts sharply with the Basilian counsel, where the superior stands to be corrected by eminent brothers (*LR* 27). Obedience to eminent brothers is generally expected of novices.

29. Cf. Basil *LR* 35.

30. Or, "of the cenobitic brotherhood," as in §32 (see note there) and further below, §§43–44.

31. Reference to "The Parable of the Ten Virgins" (Mt 25.1–13), uniquely applied to the monastic community with a rebuke to those who separate themselves from it. See further below, §§54, 58, 62.

Groom: *"Because you did not show love to your brothers and broke the bond of the communal fellowship, 'depart into the outer darkness'"* (Mt 25.30, 41, 45).[32] 44Whereas those who keep whole the communal fellowship, with spiritual love for the brotherhood and single-mindeness toward the superior, are blessed; and every good characteristic and manifestations of virtue are stamped upon them.

45Let each brother steer his brother into good works, good zeal, love for God, urging him to progress with all faithfulness in every work, to give praise to the Lord, and to increase day-to-day in goodness and usefulness. 46Workers should be circumspect and careful in what they are entrusted with, that it may be done with utmost trustworthiness—pleasing God, the superior, and the brotherhood.

47Furthermore, the Midday Office[33] should by no means be neglected except when, with the permission of the superior, one is occupied with something necessary for the congregation;[34] but let him offer his prayer there.[35] 48And everywhere the Divine Office[36] should be conducted fervently, without neglecting any: when

32. The author draws from all three parables of Mt 25 in this mix of terms and concepts. Cf. Mt 8.12; 22.13.

33. Arm. հասարակաց պաշտաման (*hasarakac῾ paštawnn*), corresponding to the *Sext*, the noontime prayer of the Daily Office (on which see below).

34. Arm. եկեղեցւոյն (*eketec῾woyn*), "for the *ecclesia.*"

35. Cf. §75, on not neglecting prayer on account of attending to guests. On this common situation, no less the problem of neglecting work on account of prayer, see Basil *LR* 37–38 (Arm. Q-33–34). On relating the latter problem to the "heresy" of *argia* or idleness in Messalian monasticism, see the discussion in Caner, *Wandering, Begging Monks,* 104–6. As Caner observes, Basil does not mention the Messalians anywhere in his writings.

36. Arm. պաշտաման աղաւթիցն (*paštawn atawt῾ic῾n*), the communal prayers of the canonical hours, known also as the Divine Office, observed in Christian monasticism. The section is but a scanty summary of the latter half of Basil's counsel in *LR* 37 (Arm. Q33), where no less than eight specific times for prayer are mentioned, each with biblical justification, as obligatory for the monk under all circumstances: *Prime*, the morning prayer at the first hour of the day; *Terce*, at the third hour; *Sext*, at the sixth hour or noon; *Nones*, at the ninth hour or afternoon; *Vespers*, the service of evening prayer; *Compline*, the prayer before retiring for the night; *Nocturns*, the night service; *Lauds*, the daybreak prayer. On the *ordo*, see Robert F. Taft, *The Liturgy of the Hours in East and West: The Origins of the Divine Office and its Meaning for Today,* 2nd rev. ed. (Collegeville, MN: Liturgical Press, 1993); M. Daniel Findikyan, *Commentary on the Armenian Daily Office by Bishop Step῾anos Siwnec῾i*

resting at home, when on the road, when working, when lying down, and when rising. ₄₉And one ought not forget[37] the remembrances of God;[38] rather, to do his will with all diligence of holiness and righteousness. And in one's mind, to linger daily around the gates of God's mercy, with constant petitions, fervent in spirit, and always with warm tears, so that one's prayers may be worthy of acceptance. And may they be granted by almighty God, who wills salvation for all and (for all) to be found worthy of the Kingdom in Christ Jesus.

₅₀And may all be agreeable, with sincere love, toward the superior. And let no one ask him for work according to one's wishes, but rather, that which he (the superior) believes to be for the common good, for physical necessities, and for spiritual gain.[39] ₅₁So that all may be able to say: "Following his example, we were dedicated to God. Forsaking every will of body and mind, we have given ourselves to the service of God first and then the leaders, in obedience to God's command that has been passed down to us through the holy Fathers."[40]

₅₂For as the members of the body constitute one body, joined together and efficient, while each has its own inherent function: eyes see, ears hear, nostrils smell, the tongue speaks and the mouth eats, hands work, feet walk, the mind comprehends and by it the senses are activated for spiritual and physical work,[41] so are the people of God: being joined together in love and made one in God's

---

(d. 735): Critical Edition and Translation with Textual and Liturgical Analysis, OCA 270 (Rome: Pontificio Istituto Orientale, 2004).

37. Lit., "not to leave out of mind."

38. Arm. զիշատակն Աստուծոյ (zyišataksn Astucoy) is an allusion to the Eucharistic Anamnesis, based on Jesus's words in Lk 22.19; cf. Disc. 6.88 սուրբ խորհրդոյն յիշատակաւք անճառիչ՛ն (surb xorhrdoyn yišatakawkʻ ančařičʻn) and 99 յիշատակք նորա (yišatakkʻ nora); 11.6 յիշատակաւ սիրոյն Քրիստոսի (yišatakaw siroyn Kʻristosi), 20 յիշատակաւ սրբութեանն (yišatakaw srbutʻeann), 76 յորդորեալ յիշատակաւք (yordoreal yišatakawkʻ), and 127 սուրբ յիշատակաց նորա (surb yišatakacʻ nora). On the Eucharist's implications for philanthropy, see note to Disc. 13.45.

39. Cf. Basil LR 41: "Whoever chooses a task conformed to his personal wish brings accusation against himself" (trans. Wagner, FC 9:314); SR 123, 142.

40. Cf. Heb 13.17 (quoted in §27, where similarly ařajnordkʻ [pl.] is used). The quoted lines seem to echo the monastic vow taken by the brothers. Cf. §62 and note, below.

41. Cf. Disc. 15.50.

will and in the superior's sovereign mind as he regularly oversees the brotherhood, and the rest in compliance (to him), each according to his function. ₅₃Those members who seem to be weaker are essential to the others in their respective roles.[42] ₅₄Moreover, it is inconceivable for the healthy members to be amputated, but (it is conceivable) that the incurably diseased be severed—the cankerous ones that are beyond cure. It is also inconceivable to rejoin members separated from the others. Similarly, the one who severs himself from the unity of the brotherhood and separates himself from the monastery is incurable; since he repudiates the vow and the love and the pact (made) before God and becomes liable to eternal tortures.[43]

₅₅But if, by the will of the superior and of the whole brotherhood, one is compelled into the office of a bishop or that of a superior to (lead) others,[44] or into the priesthood, those who rank equal in the Lord, and he is not inclined to accept it, ₅₆let him—if such a person is to be found—with much supplication and contrition yield to the compelling by the superior and the brothers, (to work) for the salvation of others so that the name of our Lord God be not blasphemed.[45] ₅₇Let him, however, not be cut off from the brotherhood's sincere, pure love and the superior's favor. Let (all) care for one another's spiritual fulfillment.

₅₈Moreover, every orthodox episcopal synod that affirmed the orthodox faith[46] and set canons for the Church also set the following with an anathema, saying: "Let no brother be allowed to leave the monastery to go wherever he pleases without the will of the superior of the brotherhood. Should anyone dare to do this, let him

42. Allusion to 1 Cor 12.21.

43. Ultimate punishment for disobedience included severance from the monastic community; see further below, §§58, 62, and notes at Disc. 11.129 and 20.144, where the same medical analogy of amputation is used, as in Basil *LR* 28; cf. *SR* 44 and 122, which mention deprivation of blessing, of food, and of fellowship or association with the brotherhood, or whatever punishment the superior rules, according to *SR* 106.

44. Lit., "into leadership of others."

45. Echoing Rom 2.24; cf. Is 52.5 (LXX); Ezek 36.20, 22.

46. Or, "the right faith," as I have rendered *uttap'at hawatsn* elsewhere (see note to Disc. 2.58). Here I have departed from that earlier consistency because of the immediately preceding use of the same adjective.

be bound by the anathemas of the Fathers."[47] ₅₉For God's Apostle says: *"Each is to remain in the order to which he was called"* (I Cor 7.20).[48] ₆₀For all were called to one hope in Christ,[49] that they may be reconstituted into one honorable body, glorified through his sacred body and blood.

₆₁If one has reason for seclusion, let him not conceal it from the superior and the brotherhood, because the testimony of many is believable before God and the entire company of those who have taken a vow.[50] ₆₂Since those who held the Law of Moses in disdain were put to death without mercy by (the testimony of) three witnesses,[51] how much more deserving of punishment shall we consider those who have made a pact through the body and blood (of Christ)[52] to be in communal fellowship with a vow, who have early on renounced association with the world in order to observe the traditions of communal fellowship until death?[53] ₆₃We also know

47. Cf. the fourth canon of Chalcedon. The similarities notwithstanding, the cited canon is not a direct borrowing. For similarities to the monastic rules of Rabbula, bishop of Edessa (411/12–435/36) and others, see Caner, *Wandering, Begging Monks*, 210–11. This traditional rule, basic to all early monastic establishments, is attributed to multiple conciliar authorities (note the opening of the paragraph) and Paul (note the epistolary quotation that follows); still, it could not be identified verbatim with any known canon. Except for the preceding (§§55–57), allowing a monk to leave in order to serve as superior, bishop, or priest elsewhere, travel is not permitted. Cf. Basil *LR* 44: "Who should be permitted to go on journeys and how they ought to be interrogated upon their return."

48. Cf. 1 Cor 7.24.

49. Allusion to Eph 4.4.

50. The following immediate context places these lines in the sphere of obedience: seclusion with the superior's permission; cf. Basil *SR* 120. In the rules attributed to Rabbula of Edessa, seclusion within the monastic complex was allowed to a monk only rarely, restricted to the most worthy; see Vööbus, *History of Asceticism*, 2:275; idem, ed., *Syriac and Arabic Documents Regarding Legislation Relative to Syrian Asceticism*, Papers of the Estonian Theological Society in Exile 11 (Stockholm: PETSE, 1960), 24–33; also McCullough, *A Short History of Syriac Christianity*, 74; and Harvey, *Asceticism and Society in Crisis*, 20.

51. Allusion to Dt 17.6; 19.15.

52. Allusion to Heb 10.29.

53. Cf. Heb 10.30. On the dire consequences of repudiating monastic vows, see Basil *LR* 14 and *Q*36; *Letters* 44 and 45, "To a Fallen Monk." Commenting on the Basilian view, Morison observes: "Disobedience is not merely an offence against the discipline of the community, but a sign of grave moral defects. Insubordination and defiance are the proofs of a multitude of sins, of tainted faith, of doubtful hope,

what the Lord has said regarding punishment (in both) the Old and the New (Testaments): *"Vengeance is mine, I will repay, says the Lord"* (Dt 32.35; Rom 12.19).

₆₄The superior should make efforts to be cognizant of giving counsel to all, both quietly and openly, that he may direct the errant ones into the paths of righteousness and true traditions. ₆₅He should not be indifferent towards anyone's confessions and should direct all spiritually and physically,[54] *"so that he may present perfect before Christ's tribunal all who believe in him"* (Col 1.28). ₆₆*"For he who does and teaches (these) is great before God"* (Mt 5.19).

₆₇The steward should consider himself as God's attendant, serving believers in God's traditions with fear and awe. And he should take care of the vessels, lest he lose any because of indolence, or discard some because of disdain,[55] or, being indifferent about the traditions, become often wasteful, not pleasing God and coming under the Lord's judgment, which takes into account every thought and deed. For everything is a gift from God for the needs of the brotherhood.[56] ₆₈He should not be slow in work, nor distribute unequally,

---

of proud and overweening conduct" (*St. Basil and His Rule: A Study in Early Monasticism,* 57). The seriousness of the vow, of which §51 appears to be a part, is here underscored by its solemnization through the celebration of the Eucharist. Indeed, a formal vow is part of the monachal initiation rite found in the more broad-ranging manuscripts of the Armenian *euchologion,* the *Mec Maštoc'*, titled after the compiler's name (Catholicos Maštoc' [in office for a year, 897] and founder of a monastery at Sevan in accordance with Basil's *Rules,* this according to Step'anos Asołik [d. ca. 1015], *History,* 3.2–5 [MH 15:741–742]). The rite is followed by an exhortation to the superior as part of his installation. The latter text is comprised of excerpts from Basil's *Sermo asceticus* and *LR* 25, including Rom 13.1–2 from the first and Ezek 3.20 and 1 Thes 2.8 from the second (PG 31:884B–C, 984C, 985B–C). The exhortation is followed by the brothers partaking of the Eucharist administered at the hands of the superior (Eng. trans. in Conybeare, *Rituale Armenorum,* 140–60, esp. 146 and 159–60; cf. Wagner, trans., *Ascetical Works,* FC 9:218–19, 287–88).

54. Cf. §§19–20 and 93–94, on confession to the superior; and Disc. 19.10, on confession to priests. For the requirement of confession to the superior, see Basil *LR* 25–26 and 46; and *SR* 288, for that to priests. To receive confession and grant absolution, the superior and/or other high-ranking monks must have received sacerdotal ordination. A monk with added priestly roles was known as վանաց երեց (*vanac' erec'*), lit., "monastic priest," a designation not found in the *Discourses.*

55. On the use and care of implements, see below, §73; cf. Basil *LR* 41; *SR* 143, 144.

56. Verbatim drawing on Arm. Q125 (= *SR* 144); see Uluhogian, ed. and trans., *Basilio di Cesarea: Il Libro delle Domande,* t. 19, 177; cf. t. 20, viii–ix (for more, see the discussion on authorship and date, pp. 41–51 in the "Introduction" to this volume).

but keep God before his eyes in everything. He should truly serve with the fear of God, with the superior's approval. ₆₉He should be alert and circumspect, always willing to serve, providing the necessary sustenance according to one's needs: ₇₀to the elderly, the sick, the weak, the sojourners, the laborers, and to those who are vulnerable; attending to their needs as deserved, spiritually, as it were to God. ₇₁Let it not be with partiality or fury, lest one be deprived of his reward. Let it be done as with motherly care for everyone, that one may receive his reward from the almighty Father: "*Come, blessed of my Father, inherit the Kingdom ... for in serving my brothers you have done it to me*" (Mt 25.34, 40).[57] ₇₂I shall not mention the punishment, the inextinguishable fire, for those who do not act accordingly.

₇₃Let those doing weekly assignments be careful with their implements, and let them do their work devoutly.

₇₄The superintendents[58] of guests should not ignore the needy. They should cheerfully attend to the guest's every need, without grumbling about the matter; rather, to direct everyone with love and calm in both word and deed. ₇₅And they should not absolve themselves from fasting and praying because of the guest, lest they be deprived of God's rewards. Rather, let all workers be sober[59] during the prayer hour, lest they fall under judgment with the slothful.[60] ₇₆And let everything be done according to the superior's will, with his consent, for his saying should be received by all, at all times, as the Lord's will. ₇₇And whatever is served by them (the superintendents of guests) should be made entirely known to him, as it is proper.[61]

₇₈Superintendents of the tillers' oxen, the herders' sheep, the (cattle) herds for milking, and the burden-bearing animals, should

---

57. Cf. Basil *LR* 34, on love and care for the brothers, where the same Matthaean verses are similarly applied. Elsewhere in this discourse, see §§32, 44, 57, 86; cf. Disc. 2.46; 5.106; 6.72, 96; 11.33.

58. Arm. տեսուչք (*tesučʻkʻ*), as in §78, are administrative assistants to the "superior" (cf. Basil *LR* 35, 45, 48, 53) and are to be distinguished from վերակացու (*verakacʻu*) or առաջնորդ (*aṙajnord*), both terms rendered "superior" throughout the discourse (see notes to §§19 and 28).

59. Or, "circumspect."

60. See §47, against neglecting prayer on account of work, and note there on the "heresy" of *argia* or idleness in Messalian monasticism. Cf. §120, on the Eucharist as a means to renew a sense of moderation or sobriety.

61. On hospitality to guests, see the more elaborate directive in Basil *LR* 20.

be attentive in caring for all; faithfully to show profitable results in all truthfulness, as God's laborers and wise, successful gardeners, gathering in the storerooms so that there will be plenty to give to any who have needs.[62] [79]They should bring the fruits of their labor to the house of the Lord God,[63] and they will be rewarded, each according to his gain by the Creator, *"who sees in secret and rewards openly"* (Mt 6.4)[64] with unending gifts on the day of visitation: *"The one who was faithful with few things shall enjoy many things"* (Mt 25.21, 23).

[80]Likewise, those entrusted with footwear: they should provide shoes to everyone, without antagonism or bias, and whatever else is needed as footwear. [81]Let all show meekness, both those who are in need and those who provide with love and contrite heart what is needed, that they may inherit the blessings.[65]

[82]Likewise, all those entrusted with the work of caring for the needs of the brotherhood: they should carry out everything with fear and circumspection, without treachery, [83]keeping God always before their eyes and not departing from the truth in any way, as God's true gardeners, in all things without treachery. [84]Again, let the fear of the Lord be the constant principle to all managers and laborers, and let them fearfully manage the work for the gain of spiritual progress, faithful in the work of husbandry, with bold urgency; [85]not as men-pleasers but as to God, who examines the heart and the inner organs, remembering the motives, words, and deeds of every individual.[66] [86]Those who are faithful in every spiritual and physical grace, in accordance with God's commandment, and (strive) for the edification of the brotherhood, in accord with their vow, shall inherit eternal life. [87]Whereas those inclined to controversy, heartlessness, negligence, departing from truth into discord and envy, defiance, complaining, gossip, use of slanderous words, God's wrath will always remain upon them—the fearsome and untried fire that consumes the wicked but illumines the saints with infinite light.

62. Cf. Basil *LR* 37, on the importance of manual labor.

63. Echoing Ex 23.19; 34.26.

64. Cf. Mt 6.6, 18.

65. The making of articles is here limited to the needs of the brotherhood, not for trade as prescribed in the expanded or "long" rules of Basil, where mention is made of weaving clothes and making shoes among other goods "for common use in daily life" (*LR* 38; cf. 39, on the sale of monastic produce).

66. Allusion to 1 Thes 2.4; cf. Gal 1.10.

₈₈The superior should be an affable father, congenial and benevolent, exemplifying all the morals of the (holy) orders and piety: prayer and fasting, humility and meekness, guidance and truth, steadfastness and tears, peace and calm, love and longsuffering, fairness and justice, diligence and self-restraint, moderation and discernment, purity and immaculateness. One who is not a libeler but excellent in every way, upholding (God's) righteous laws for all, trusted to instruct the people of God in wisdom and knowledge, ever improving himself in sanctity and (showing) the love of God through virtuous living and abhorring the love of the world. ₈₉He should surely exhibit God's sacred love to all, in every respect. ₉₀*"Anyone who loves me will obey my commandments, and anyone who does not love me will not obey my commandments"* (Jn 14.23–24).[67]

₉₁Just as the superior is called spiritual father, those born of him are spiritual children in the order of ascetics, who have greater status than physical children; (a birth that is) similar to baptism in every respect.[68] ₉₂Thus they become children of light and children of righteousness,[69] renouncing worldly preoccupations that cloud the mind, darken the senses, and beget children of darkness, heirs of hell.

₉₃And it behooves spiritual children to live spiritual lives, in perfect obedience to the spiritual fatherhood; to present through him confession to God, without any lie in the confession, ₉₄in order to obtain easily a remedy for every detrimental mistake.[70] Furthermore, of every order obedience and submission (are expected), as of one who receives an order from the heavenly Father to carry out a command. These are the characteristics of the common brotherhood, in spirit and truth.[71] *"Think and do as Christ Jesus ... who became obedient to the Father to death, even the death on a cross"* (Phil 2.5, 8).[72] ₉₅Moreover, *"He does not consider it a shame to call them his broth-*

---

67. On the superior's qualifications, see the "Ascetical Discourses" of Basil, trans. Wagner, *Ascetical Works*, FC 9:210–11, 218; cf. *LR* 43.

68. Cf. Disc. 2.133; 6.36, owing to Jn 3.3–8.

69. Echoing Jn 12.36; Eph 5.8–9.

70. Cf. §§19–20 and 65.

71. Allusion to Jn 4.23–24. On the pivotal place of obedience in asceticism, see note to §28.

72. On the centrality of these verses in ascetic life, see Sebastian P. Brock, "Radical Renunciation: The Ideal of *msarrqûtâ*," in *To Train His Soul in Books: Syriac*

ers," who were called and invited to the divine fellowship of ascetic life, *"saying, I will proclaim your name to my brothers; in the midst of the congregation I will praise you"* (Heb 2.11–12).[73]

96Also, with such a compliant mindset and pure love one counters all harmful things that defile the earth, and follows those above—the heavenly and immortal ones—for whom virginity is a (prized) possession, along with impeccable life and daily praise of the Most Holy Trinity. 97For the pure, unblemished, and impeccable virginity has affinity with the assembly of the heavenly hosts above, who likewise praise God. 98For the life of the ascetics resembles that of the heavenly ones, after whom they receive their characteristic ranks in every respect. 99For on earth the armies of true ascetics, in pure love and unblemished senses, being arrayed in angelic order, possess the decorum[74] of the heavenly armies. 100Now, chiefs and heads of the incorporeal ones who in their respective ranks serve God, one another, and the human race, have their will—like all others—determined by the Lord, according to his providence: to each their rule, honor, and ministry. 101As for the one who—from among the rulers above—rebelled with his armies that were cast down from that bliss, they became our adversaries and were named Satan and Demons, names that indicate their opposition to good works, their delight in every sin, both he and his evil armies.[75]

Asceticism in Early Christianity, ed. Robin Darling Young and Monica Blanchard, CUA Studies in Early Christianity (Washington, DC: The Catholic University of America Press, 2011), 122–33. Brock points to how the term, built on the "emptying" of Christ in Phil 2.1–11, is later applied to ascetics' renunciation of possessions, to stripping away of their passions, and ultimately to their liberation of body, soul, and spirit from the world—demonstrating their spiritual maturity. Note the opening lines of the discourse and §§5–7.

73. Cf. Ps 22.22 (21.23 LXX).

74. Or, "modesty."

75. See notes at Disc. 2.123 and 16.12, on the fall of Satan and his angels; cf. Disc. 6.25–41 and 20.70–84, on misuse of free will as the cause of their fall and on their being the primary cause of all human ills and misconduct (the traditional etymology of the name Satan is found also in Disc. 20.70). These notions rest on Gn 6.1–4 (cf. Jb 1.6; 2.1; 38.7) and the history of its interpretation as of 1 Enoch 6–19 (cf. Jude 6; 1 Pt 3.19–20; 2 Pt 2.4), especially by the Apologists of the second century (Justin Martyr, *Apologiae* 1.5; 2.5, 7; Athenagoras, *Legatio pro Christianis* 24; Irenaeus, *Adversus haereses* 3.23, 4.40.1, 16.2; *Epideixis tou apostolikou kērygmatos* 16) and

[102]It is clear that the armies of ascetics, having assumed the angelic ranks on earth, are elevated to the same angelic ranks in lieu of the fallen angels.[76] [103]The Prophet speaks of them, saying: *"To them I will give a notable place better than to my sons and daughters; and I will give them an everlasting name that its glory will not decrease"* (Is 56.5). [104]The armies of holy assemblies receive this good news—those who are united with the Deity in pure love and virtue-loving life. Those bound to such a heavenly hope cannot be brought down by the deceit of the Adversary, this daily enemy of righteousness who schemes against the pious ascetics. [105]He is the one who attracts and distracts from the true traditions. Some he severs from the brothers through vainglory—under the pretense of charity—and through frivolous misleading into sin; others by injecting the harms of wickedness into their thoughts and senses.

[106]Ascetics[77] ought to have such hope as to be engaged in the husbandry of a moral life, with much diligence and sanctity—both visibly and invisibly, so that they will not be denied the prize for virtue: angelic rank and glory, bestowed on them by the Creator. [107]They ought to compensate from above for what they lack in inner virtue; to rise up from their earthly crawl and have fellowship with that good citizenry, who offer praise with one accord, with unutterable blessing to the Most Holy Trinity.

[108]As for those justified by true faith[78] and impeccable in ascetic

---

Tertullian, *Apologeticus* 22; *De idololatria* 9; *De virginibus velandis* 7; *De cultu feminarum* 1.2. Cf. Eusebius of Caesarea, *Praeparatio evangelica* 5.5, 7.8, and Cyril of Jerusalem, *Catecheses* 2.8; and among Jewish authors, Philo, *De gigantibus* 6–7, and Josephus, *Antiquitates judaicae* 1.3.1. For a discussion, see Jeffrey Burton Russell, *Satan: The Early Christian Tradition* (Ithaca and London: Cornell University Press, 1981).

76. The belief that redeemed humans will take the place of fallen angels appears earlier (see note to Disc. 16.13; akin to the common notion that angels and humans are rational creatures endowed with intellect and free will, and that it is possible for humans to become more like angels, see §§99, 106, 111, 120).

77. Arm. կրաւնաւորաց (*krawnaworac'*); cf. կրաւնաւորեայք (*krawnaworealk'*) and կրաւնաւորաց (*krawnaworac'*) in §108, noun forms limited to these sections and not used elsewhere in the discourses; cf. the verb կրաւնաւորիլ (*krawnaworil*) in §6. Here they are used synonymously with ճգնաւորք / ճգնաւորաց (*čgnawork' / čgnaworac'*), the usual word for ascetics throughout the discourses (underscoring the sense of "perseverance" in their calling). The synonymous usage of the terms is anticipated in §104, where the text has ճգնաւորաց կրաւնից (*čgnaworac' krawnic'*).

78. Allusion to Rom 3.28; Gal 2.16; 3.11, 24. See note to Disc. 2.154.

life and pure love, theirs is the new earth in the renewal of life for God's delight and the new heaven, *"which eye has not seen and ear has not heard, and which have not entered the heart of man, that God has prepared"* (1 Cor 2.9)[79] for the holy virgins and truth-loving ascetics.[80]

109Bearing in mind the hope from above, the good-loving, compassionate, and thoughtful fathers become like the heavenly Father,[81] who cares for all creatures through his providential love, spiritually and physically, through seen and unseen means of sustenance, through Spirit-filled[82] love and the most-venerable manifestation of Christ Jesus. 110And the well-pleasing, holiness- and truth-loving children overcome all difficulties, seen and unseen, 111and adhere strongly to the angelic life with a pure heart, spotless body, wholesome thought, true faith, right reason, and obedience to the Father of spirits[83] and Superintendent of bodies. 112Those who are bound together in a well-pleasing, worshipful spirit, with the certainty of spiritual, intimate belonging, in their exceptional union are like interdependent members within a body.

113*"Since we are one body in Christ"* (Rom 12.5), let us hold firmly onto the confession of hope that cannot be swayed.[84] Let us be perfect in this very faith, bound together in one spirit, fittingly joined,[85] firmly attached to this very faith by an inseparable relationship. Let this strong, communal fellowship of the brotherhood not be broken with pretentiousness of morality. 114For this singular tradition from the Lord, who is the Head of our perfection, has been unmistakably entrusted to us through the Apostles: it says, *"By this you will become known by everyone that you are my disciples, if you have inseparable love for one another"* (Jn 13.35).[86] 115Conversely, if anyone considers attaining virtue on his own, even if he were to achieve it to the uttermost, yet without the will of the superior and the broth-

---

79. Cf. Is 64.4; 65.17.

80. Arm. սրբոց կուսանաց և ճշմարտասէր կրաւնաւորաց (*srboc῾ kusanac῾ ew čšmartasēr krawnaworac῾*).

81. Echoing Lk 6.36.

82. Lit., "spirit-mixed."

83. Allusion to Heb 12.9.

84. Allusion to Heb 10.23.

85. Allusion to Eph 4.16.

86. On the centrality of this Johannine passage and its immediate context for monasticism, see Basil *SR* 98.

erhood, it is unacceptable to God and is considered sinful.[87] ₁₁₆But
to those who hold fast to the true tradition, *"I will give them a place in
my house"* (Jn 14.2) to dwell together both spiritually and physically. And they will not be separated from one another; rather, with
pure love they remain together in communal fellowship; for this is
the mother of all good things. ₁₁₇For this reason I often repeat the
words of love, for this is good and acceptable to God, indeed his
very command.[88]

₁₁₈Let no one waver in thought and stumble bodily; but let him
abide in the best practices with single-minded will and mindfulness
of the adoption from above by the heavenly Father, who loves humankind.[89] ₁₁₉Let (all) cherish the pledge of the Spirit,[90] study the
constitution of things, and distinguish between those that (truly)
exist and those that are visible,[91] and abhor the earthly by desiring
the heavenly. ₁₂₀And leaving worldly preoccupations, let us draw
near to the angelic life without looking for earthly things, but from
now on being receptive to the light, which through the body and
blood of the Lord regenerates circumspection in us by daily partaking (of the Eucharist), worthily,[92] in keeping with Christ's truly
cleansing and life-giving redemption, which was granted to those
who love God—the saints invited to the divine realm. ₁₂₁And at his
second coming may he grant the unending favors that are in the
Father and the Son and the Holy Spirit, to whom be glory forever
and ever. Amen.

87. On the disadvantages of solitary life, see Basil *LR* 6; on the advantages, Q7.

88. Cf. Jn 13.35; 14.23–24 (quoted above, §§23, 90, 114). There is reason to believe that the statement is invariably related to the title given to this collection of
discourses.

89. Allusion to Rom 8.14–17, 23; Gal 4.1–7; Eph 1.5–6. For the recurring theme
of adoption, see the Subject Index.

90. Allusion to 2 Cor 1.22 and 5.5; cf. Eph 1.13–14; 2 Tm 1.14 (see Disc. 6.87;
17.8).

91. Echoing the Platonic notion of the "ideas" and preference for the immaterial.

92. Allusion to 1 Cor 11.27–29. "Self-control" is among recurring lessons of
"moderation" drawn from the Eucharist, in patristic commentaries on the Bread
of Life; see esp. Cyril of Alexandria's *Commentarius in Johannem* (4.2 on Jn 6.48–58;
PG 73:560C–585A). Arm. զգաստութիւն (*zgastut'iwn*), as in Gk. *sōphrosynē*, also de-
notes "sobriety"; cf. §75, on sobriety during prayer.

APPENDICES

APPENDIX I

A PRAYER FOR WHEN ONE IS
CAUGHT IN A SNARE

Said by St. Gregory the Illuminator[1]

₁Your love for humankind is beyond measure, my Lord Jesus Christ. Why do you forsake me? Should it be for sin, you alone are sinless and your name presents you as unvengeful and the lover of humankind. ₂Have mercy on me, for you alone are the lover of humankind. ₃Make me, who have fallen into sin, live. ₄Pull me out of the mire of my wickedness, that I may not sink forever. ₅Save me from my enemy, for he roars like a lion eager to devour me. ₆Now, my Lord, send your lightning and strike down his power. Let him fear you and hide away from your presence, for he is weak and has no power to be in your presence, nor (in the presence) of those who love you. ₇May he be terrified upon seeing the power of your Cross, and may he be chased away—being put to shame by those who pray to you. ₈Now, Lord, grant me life that I may live, for I have placed my trust in you. Pull me out of my predicament lest the seducer lead me astray, for he wages battle against me with hidden machinations. ₉Since you are Lord over thoughts and you search the hearts and the innermost parts, cleanse my heart and mind from distressing and filthy thoughts, lest I be lost in eternal damnation. ₁₀O you Almighty, my God, have mercy on me. Grant my sinful soul the grace of tears that my manifold sins may be washed away, that I may survive the merciless angels who cast the wick-

---

1. As with the attribution of the *Discourses*, there is good reason to suspect its authorial authenticity. On linguistic grounds, it cannot belong to the author of the *Discourses* either. It is provided here simply because it appears at the end of both the manuscripts and the published editions. Text in MH 1.137.

ed into the fire of hell. 11Would that I had cried daily, pleading
with you, God, that I may not be found unworthy in the hour of
your coming. 12Let me not hear the fearsome voice (saying), "Get
lost, cultivator of wickedness; I do not know where you are from."
13Uplifted God, the only sinless One, grant me—a sinner—your
manifold mercy on that day so that my hidden wickedness be not
revealed before the watching angels, archangels, and the righteous
saints. 14Make me, the guilty one, live by the grace of your mercy.
Receive me into the comfort of Paradise, (to be) with the righteous
who are perfect. Accept the prayer of your sinful servant through
the intercession of the saints, those who pleased you, Jesus Christ,
our Lord, who are blessed with the Father and your Holy Spirit,
forever and ever. Amen.

APPENDIX II

THE ARMENIAN TITLES OF
THE DISCOURSES[1]

(1) Յաղագս Ամենասուրբ Երրորդութեան.

(2) Ի Սուրբ Երրորդութեանն առանձնաւորութիւնն.

(3) Մխիթք Հաւատոյ.

(4) Յանդիմանութիւն մոլար մտաց և ընծայութիւն աստուածպաշտութեան.

(5) Հաստատութիւն ճշմարտութեան և առաջնորդութիւն կենարար խրատուց.

(6) Յանդիմանութիւն ծածկութից իրաց որ զաներևոյթան յերևելիս ածէ.

(7) Վասն յօրինուածոց արարածոց.

(8) Յանդիմանութիւն դժնդակ վարուց և ընծայութիւն առաքինութեան հանդիսից.

(9) Վարդապետութիւն կատարեալ ի Տէր ամենարուեստ պահոց.

(10) Երախտաւորութիւն անզեղջ բարերար կամացն և յորդորումն ի լաւն և յառաւելն ըստ ճշմարիտ առաքինութեանն ի փառս Ամենասուրբ Երրորդութեանն ճառեալ.

(11) Վասն վարուց առաքինութեան որ հանդիսիւք լաւութեան պսակեալ երանին.

(12) Վարդապետութիւն բարերար Արարչին խնամոց և կշտամբութիւն անհնազանդութեան և ստահակութեան և առաջնորդութիւն բարութեան բարեացն լաւութեան.

(13) Հանդէս վասն լաւութեան յիշատակաց ի պէտս օգտից զաներևոյթան յերևելիս ցուցանելով ի գործ առաքինութեան

1. Cf. the titles in manuscript M1337, 5r–126v, a miscellany of the year 1706 (*General Catalogue of Armenian Manuscripts of the Mashtots Matenadaran*, 4:956–58).

փոխիլ ի յոյսն կենդանի ի բանակս զուարթնոցն որ աստ կատարեցին զճաճոյսն Աստուծոյ.

(14) Յաղագս մարդկութեան որ յԱստուծոյ խնամք տեսչութեան <կան>.

(15) Վասն հոգւոց մարդկութեան բացայայտութիւն.

(16) Վասն մարտիրոսացն վարդապետութիւն ուսմանց.

(17) Զզուշութիւն զզաստութեան շահաւոր պատրաստութեան ընդ մտերիմսն և ընդ դժնդակ<ս>ն պատիւ և պատիժս.

(18) Գովութիւնք Աստուծոյ երախտեացն հանդիսիւք մարտիրոսաց քաջաց առաքինեաց.

(19) Յորդորումն ապաշխարութեան խոստովանեալ.

(20) Առաջնորդութիւն ամենարուեստ խրատու, հանգամանք զիտութեան և իմաստից.

(21) Վասն տրոց իմաստութեան որ ի Հոգւոյն Սրբոյ պարգևեցաւ՝ սուղ ինչ բանս.

(22) Վասն անփոփոխ ինքնութեան էութեանն Աստուծոյ.

(23) Խրատք ճգնաւորաց և ցոյցք հանդիսից որ<ք> յառաքինութիւն յորդորեն.

APPENDIX III

DEPENDENCY ON HERMETIC TEXTS

As noted in the Introduction, Jean-Pierre Mahé and Joseph Paramelle were first to notice a certain dependency by the author of the *Discourses* on the sixth-century Armenian translation of Hermetic texts, that is, of the fragmentary *Definitions* (especially *DH* frag. vi.2–3; vii.3), in Disc. 20.22.[1] Similar echoes are found in three other discourses: 2.40; 12.9, 44–46; 15.37–56. These are worth quoting in Armenian, beginning with the two Hermetic fragments.

DH frag. vi.2–3

Որպէս յորովայնէ ելեր՝ այսէս և ի մարմնոյս ելցես ...

Որպէս յորովայնէ մանուկն կատարեալ ի դուրս գայ, այսպէս և անձն կատարեալ ի մարմնոյ անտի ի դուրս գայ: Քանզի որպէս անկատար մարմին յորովայնէ ելեալ աննունդ և աննաճ է՝ սոյնպէս և անձն ի մարմնոյ ելեալ անկատար մարմին է. զի կատարելութիւն անձին զիտութիւն էւկացն:

Just as (you) emerged from the womb, you shall likewise emerge from this body ...

Just as the whole child emerges from the womb, so shall the whole soul emerge from the body. For as the immature body emerging from the womb is unnourished and unnurtured, so too the soul emerging from

---

1. "Nouveaux parallèles grecs aux *Définitions* hermétiques arméniennes," *Revue des études arméniennes* 22 (1990–1991): 115–34, especially 117 n. 7a, 120–23; cf. Mahé, *Hermès en Haute-Égypte,* 2:376–80. Also by the same authors: "Extraits hermétiques inédits dans un manuscrit d'Oxford," *Revue des études grecques* 104 (1991): 109–39. On the sixth-century date of the Armenian translation, see Mahé, *Hermès en Haute-Égypte,* 2 vols. (Québec: Presses de l'Université Laval, 1978–1982), especially 2:327–28.

the body is an immature body, for the perfection of the soul (is in) the knowledge of beings.

DH frag. vii.3

Ի թիւղ ի լոյս եղանէ մարմին յորովայնէ և անձն ի խաւար ի լոյս մտանէ ի մարմինն:

From the obscurity of the womb the body emerges into light, and the soul from darkness into the body of light.

Disc. 2.40

Որպէս տղայք յորովայնի մարցն ոչ գիտեն յորպիսի հասակս փոփոխելոց են և տեսանել զարարածս Աստուծոյ և վայելել, սոյնպէս և ոչ մեզ է իմանալ:

Just as infants in their mothers' wombs do not know how they are about to grow and see and enjoy God's creation, so we are unable to comprehend.

Disc. 12.9, 44–46

Որ ի մթին և յաղջամղջին յորովայնէ յառաջ եկեալ մարդ կերպարանեալ ցուցանի յերկրի (9):

Եւ զի երրորդ մարդկային կեանք բացայայտին, առաջին է յորովայնի մաւրն սաղմն առեալ և աճեալ, ի մթին և յաղջամղջին արգանդին զկեանս տնաւրինեալ մինչև ի ժամանակ ծննդեանն: Եւ երկրորդ՝ կեանք երկրագործ. որ յաշխարհիս քաղաքավարի ըստ աշխարհիս բերմանց, նախախնամութեամբ Արարչին դարմանեալ յերկրէ և ի ծովէ: Իսկ երրորդ՝ կենդանեաց աշխարհն. ուր ոչ լլի համբաւ մահու. որ ոչ փոփոխի կենդանի երանութիւնն (44–46):

The one emerging from the womb's darkness and obscurity is presented to the world as a human being (9).

Human life is defined in three (phases): first, the period of gestation in the mother's belly, in the darkness and obscurity of the womb, until the time of birth; 45second, the life of toil in the world, of being laden with the issues of life in the world, aided by the Creator's providential care provided from the land and the sea; 46third, the land of the living, where death is unheard of, where the living blessedness is immutable (44–46).

Disc. 15.37–38, 45–46

Են ոմանք որ ասեն՝ եթէ որպէս մանուկն յորովայնի անզգայ և կենդանի՝ լռեալ և դադարեալ կայ ի խաւսելոյ և ի լսելոյ, ի գնալոյ և ի գործելոյ, այսպէս համարին զոգին մարդկան լռեալ և ցածուցեալ:

Զայս գիտասցեն, զի ի սաղմնառութեէն անտի յառաջագայի և լինի մանուկ յաւրինուածովք ըստ կերպարանին մարդ, և աճումն առնու տղայն ի ծնունդ և ի սնունդ տղայութեանն՝ աճմանն մարմնոյ և մտաց յորովայնին (37–38):

Ապա եթէ ըստ մարմնոյ աւրինակի իմասցիս, որպէս յորովայնի, և յետ այնորիկ գայ ի գիտելութիւն մտաց և մարմնոյ և փոփոխի:

Այլ հոգի անմահ բանաւոր և մտաւոր՝ յորժամ ելանէ ի մարմնոյս, յառաւել գիտութեան իմաստից է իմանալ (45–46):

There are some who say that as a fetus in the womb is devoid of sensation yet alive, silent, without talking or hearing, mobility, or activity, so too—they think—is the human soul, silent and lowly.

Let them know this: following insemination there is development, and one takes a fetal form, a human image. And from birth, one grows to be a youth and is nurtured in youth, growing physically and mentally beyond the womb (37–38).

You should comprehend this by the example of the body, as when in the womb and then growing in knowledge, in mind and body, and undergoing change.

When the immortal soul, rational and intelligent, leaves the body, it is capable of comprehending more knowledgeably (45–46).

Disc. 20.22

Զի որպէս մանկունք որ յորովայնի մարցն լինին յապաճոյժ, և ի խաւարի թաղեալ, և ոչ գիտեն զերկրիս վայելչութիւն... արդ որպէս ոչ գիտել մանկանցն զայս կեանս և ոչ նման է յորովայնի կենացն, սոյնպէս և ոչ մեզ իմանալ զհանդերձեալ կեանսն:

Just as infants in their mothers' wombs, held in bloody water, buried in darkness, do not know the beauty of the earth ... so, just as infants do not know this life, which is unlike life in the womb, we too do not comprehend the life to come.

APPENDIX IV

SOME PHILOLOGICAL OBSERVATIONS

The *Yačaxapatum* is replete with grammatical irregularities that often create awkwardness in syntax, including disagreement between subject and verb, and noun and adjective. There are even odd choices of terms from among synonyms. On syntactical grounds, it cannot be assigned among works of fifth-century Armenian church fathers whose familiarity with classical literary culture, especially classical rhetoric, has long been established. Their original compositions contain prose rhythms, which they at times employed with stylistic differences between sermons and other prose works, as seen especially in works attributed to Ełišē. The virtual absence of such rhythms in the *Yačaxapatum,* coupled with its grammatical irregularities, suggests a later period for its composition with some poorly translated, elusive sources.[1]

The scriptural citations alone, whether cast as quotations or simply as allusions, indicate a removal in time from the period in which the Bible was translated. From the scores of such instances, on which dissertation(s) could be written, only one example will suffice—without getting into observations on the evolution of the "classical language" since the fifth century. Whereas the "biblical language" of the "Golden Age" uses imperatives like «եղերուք նմանողք Աստուծոյ ...» (Eph 5.1), in the quotation the author has «Նմանեցէք Աստուծոյ ...» (Disc. 2.127).

---

1. The enormous number of grammatical irregularities and the overly free rendition of biblical citations could well be the result of twice-translated sources: first from Greek into Syriac, and then from Syriac into Armenian. While questioning the "Golden Age," and even the Armenian authorship of the *Discourses* on the basis of grammatical anomalies and literary style, Durian went on to date the work to the end of the fifth century, *Patmut῾iwn Hay Matenagrut῾ean,* 414–26.

Adjectival modifiers generally follow the noun in Syriac noun phrases, an order that creates an occasional inverse or mirror-image ordering in Armenian translation. From among the countless examples of this sort of ordering, here are but a few, beginning with all the references to "Holy Scripture" (the first in the paired or clustered examples below is generally the proper form in Classical Armenian):

Սուրբ Գրովք	6.68 (cf. Սուրբ Գիրս 4.86; 13.30)
Գրովք Սրբովք	2.12; 3.2; 8.100
Սուրբ Գրոց	2.51; 4.55; 5.86; 10.90, 140; 20.125
Գրոց Սրբոց	2.19, 31; 7.61; 15.23

Inconsistencies persist even when a second modifier is used properly, as in յաստուածեղէն Գրոց Սրբոց 15.23 (cf. աստուածային Գիրք 5.63; 10.20; 12.79; 15.43; 18.61) and Սուրբ Գրոց Աստուծոյ 5.86.

Other examples, including the use of some abstract nouns as adjectives:

ըստ արդար աւրինացն	20.103
ըստ արդարութեան աւրինացն	2.85, 123, 146; 4.53; 5.47; 6.44; 7.91; 17.32
ըստ աւրինացն արդարութեան	5.23; 8.81; 12.22; 23.88
ճշմարիտ հաւատք	2.68; 4.29; 5.40; 9.101; 11.164, 168, 195, 213; 12.96; 13.3, 34, 35, 42, 81, 88; 14.1, 6; 17.27; 18.44; 20.21; 21.11, 18; 23.108
հաւատք ճշմարիտ	11.17; 13.36
հաւատք ճշմարտութեան	2.145; 3.19; 4.27; 7.45; 9.52; 11.75
ճշմարտութիւն հաւատոյ	3.1; 9.84; 20.24; 22.1
ճշմարտեալ հաւատով	11.183, 186, 198, 201, 204, 208, 210, 211; 13.46; 16.25; 17.41, 43; 18.43; 19.55; 20.26; 23.22

անկեղծաւոր հաւատք	2.6; 23.8
անխարդախ հաւատք	11.179
ճշմարիտ աւանդս	4.33; 17.39; 23.105 (cf. ստոյգ աւանդս 19.41)
ճշմարիտ աւանդութիւնս	23.116
ճշմարտութեան աւանդս	2.119; 7.3; 8.88; 18.52; 19.3, 13; 20.33, 125; 23.64
լուսաւոր պսակ	6.79
պսակ անեղծութեան	2.121; 18.54
(փառս) անեղծութեան	11.4
պսակս անեղծս	10.14
զպսակն անապական	20.45

The following examples employ various qualifiers of "life"
(whether good or bad):

ամբիծ / անբիծ վարք	6.98; 20.24; 23.22
վարուցն ամբծութիւն	20.42
ապականեալ վարք	20.145
անապականութեան վարք	20.2
առաքինասէր վարք	11.9; 12.53; 16.4, 32; 17.29, 43; 18.40; 19.79; 20.54, 78, 126, 154; 23.1, 3, 104 (never առաքինի վարք)
առաքինութեան վարք	4.67
վարք առաքինութեան	7.7; 11. title, 122; 12.53
արդար վարք	6.42; 12.12; 14.38 (cf. արդարասէր և սուրբ վարք 22.5)
արդարութեան վարք	9.11; 10.141; 19.7; 23.1
դժնդակ վարք	5.23, 95, 101, 116; 7.1, 66; 8 title, 7, 90; 11.43; 12.79, 86; 13.48, 68; 16.15; 21.6
դժնդակութեան վարք	17.29
ճշմարիտ վարք	6.74; 11.158; 12.12; 17.38; 18.58
կեանք ճշմարտութեան	11.4

ուղիղ վարք	9.19, 77; 12.12, 81, 96; 13.12, 34; 19.80
ուղղութեան վարք	9.55
սուրբ վարք	2.144; 5.34; 6.90; 8.13; 9.31; 10.153–154; 11.79, 124, 126–127, 129–130, 139, 202, 214, 216; 12.12, 26, 96; 20.47, 61, 154
զվարս սուրբս	5.118
սրբութեան վարք	10.65; 17.38; 23.1
անսուրբ վարք	12.86; 13.11; 11.216
վարք անսուրբբ	20.157
անսրբութեան վարք	11.8
բարի վարք	7.1; 14.22
բարեպաշտութեան վարք	11.45
լաւութեան վարք	9.4
ստուգութեան վարք	13.3
որ ամենաշահ կենաւք հանդարտութեամբ են	
վարք	10.35
վարք անաւրէնութեան	20.95
վարք անիրաւութեան	10.27

Much more could be said about the awkwardness of the text. Dangling modifiers are ubiquitous, leaving little doubt about the author's dependence on sources that needed translation when utilized by him. The following examples suggest reliance on a Eucharistic text, when compared to relatively simpler expressions such as եւ ի մատուցանել զահաւոր և զսարսափելի զփրկական զխորհուրդն (13.45):

Կենդանարար ամենագիւտ ամենաշա՛ խրատիւք յանփոփոխ
հաւատարմութեան իւրոյ էութեանն էր, և է յաւէ<ր>ժ
փրկական շնորհաւքն յազգս մարդկան առ մերձաւորութիւն
հաղորդութեան կենդանական սիրովն (6.12)

զՔրիստոս պատարագեալ զսարսափելի խոնարհութիւնն
վասն նորա փրկութեան և յուսոյն թականայական
խորհրդածութեամբ (12.35)

The following examples are limited to Disc. 11 (the variants
ամբիծ / անբիծ are in the text):

11.9	ամբիծ երախտեաւք սիրոյն սրբութեան
11.100	ողջախոհութեամբ և անարատ վարուց և անբիծ սիրոյ երախտեաւք
11.124	առողջ ամբիծ անարատ ունի զերախտիս սիրոյն
11.132	առողջութեան, անարատ սուրբ ամբիծ երախտաւոր սիրոյ
11.138	զխնամս գթութեան առողջ սուրբ անարատ անբիծ երախտեաւք խնամով սիրոյն
11.148	յիշատակաւք երախտեաց սիրոյն սրբութեան
11.149	առողջ սուրբ անարատ անբիծ երախտեաւքն
11.154	առողջութեան անարատ սրբութեան անբիծ սիրով
11.168	առողջութեամբ, անարատ սրբութեամբ, ամբիծ երախտեաւք սուրբ սիրոյն Աստուծոյ
11.177	առողջ անբիծ անարատ խնամաւք սուրբ սիրոյ երախտեաւքն Քրիստոսի
11.178	սուրբ վարուց կենդանի խնամաւք սուրբ սիրոյն
11.190	առողջութեան անարատ և սուրբ երախտաւոր սիրոյն որ կենդանի խնամաւք սիրոյն
11.191	առողջ անարատ ամբիծ երախտեաւք սուրբ սիրովն
11.202	անարատ և ամբիծ երախտեաւք սիրոյն
11.204	առողջ անարատ անբիծ երախտեաւք սուրբ սիրոյն
11.213	առողջ և անարատ անբիծ երախտեաւք խնամակալ սուրբ սիրոյն
11.215	անարատ և ամբիծ երախտեաւք սուրբ սիրոյն

On the lesser side of compositional inconsistencies, note these
examples within close textual proximity:

արասցուք զկամս նորա	10.152
կատարեսցուք զկամս նորա	10.153
անապաշխարիցն	19.18
անապաշխարողացն	19.41

INDICES

INDEX OF PROPER NAMES

References are to sections of the numbered Discourses.

SUBJECT INDEX

References are to sections of the numbered Discourses.

actions / deeds (*gorckʿ*): evil, 5.100;
6.69; 7.89; 8.64, 66, 71, 85; 9.11;
10.23, 55; 13.84; 15.22; 17.37; 20.14,
80, 141, 151, 153; good, 2.52; 4.88;
5.14, 20, 21, 26, 58, 75; 6.72; 7.30,
49; 9.18, 53; 10.23, 50, 89, 115,
135, 141; 11.2, 34; 12.12, 35–36, 63;
13.36, 66, 72, 75; 15.8, 17; 17.2; 18.2;
19.15, 22; 20.12, 14, 100, 141, 152;
of God, 1.21; 3.2; 5.13; judged by
God, 5.37, 57; 10.74, 115, 122, 149;
13.80; 19.42; 20.14, 141, 153; 23.67,
85; *coni.* thoughts and words, 8.81;
9.15; 10.74, 115; 11.106; 17.17; 18.36,
61; 19.42; 21.18; 23.1, 19, 67, 74, 85;
virtuous, 13 title; 14.1; willed, 10.23

adoption (*ordegrutʿiwn*), 2.46, 129, 133;
3.16–17; 5.4, 45; 6.65, 85; 7.33; 9.23,
30; 10.48, 88, 154; 11.108, 180; 12.98;
13.33; 14.17; 19.84; 20.45; 23.18; deed
of, 11.180; 20.45; grace of, 2.46; 3.16;
6.17; 9.30; 10.48, 88; inheritance of,
9.23; 12.98; 14.17; promise of, 6.85;
7.33; and the sacraments, 2.129,
133; 3.17; 5.45; 9.23, 29–30; 13.31–35;
14.17. *See also* anointing; Baptism;
children of God; font

adultery, -er (*šun, šnal, šnutʿiwn*), 8.12,
15–16, 37, 54–55, 91; 10.15, 113;
20.55. *See also* fornication; sexual
impurity

angels (*hreštakkʿ*), 4.5; 6.47–48; 8.87;
9.10; 12.42, 53–54, 88; 15.2; 17.44;
18.1; 22.29; administrators of sacraments are like angels, 11.15; 20.85;
22.5; becoming like angels, 2.22–23,
139; 5.14, 19–24; 9.7; 10.125; 11.13,
197; 13.52–55; 16.13; 18.47; 20.94, 96,
152–54; 23.97, 99, 102, 106, 111, 120;
fallen, 2.82, 125; 5.114; 9.11–15; 14.33;
16.12; 17.32; 20.40, 84, 94; grieved by
mourners over the departed faithful, 12.39, 41–42, 53; as heavenly
or spiritual hosts, 2.29, 90, 92, 123,
139; 4.5; 5.4, 14, 16, 18; 9.2, 4, 9–10;
11.13, 130, 165, 195, 197; 12.6, 37, 39;
13.53; 18.1–2; 22.27, 29, 32; 23.97,
100; their help not needed by God,
22.27; messengers, 8.87; 11.39, 95;
20.90; ministers to people, 4.32, 36;
11.130, 165; 12.4, 6; 13.76, 78–79; 15.2;
18.47; 22.28; 23.100; ranks of, 3.9;
5.19; 9.7–9; 23.100; rational beings
with free will, 1.10; 2.12, 31, 48, 146,
149; 3.29, 33; 4.5, 14; 18.2; 20.148;
21.3; with the redeemed in heaven,
2.29–30; 4.32, 36; 6.83; 11.182, 195,
197; 12.34, 37; 15.42, 57; 20.85; 22.31;
unable to describe God's greatness, 2.92; unable to praise God
worthily, 2.94; as wakeful ones, 3.9;
5.14; 9.9; 13 title. *See also* archangels;
Cherubim and Seraphim

anger (*barkutʿiwn*), 5.90, 100; 7.76; 8.7;
9.54; 10.59; 11.39, 145; 20.20, 55;
countered with meekness, 6.33;
10.37; 11.64, 86; 18.32; 19.40; 23.2;
God's wrath, 1.16; 2.63, 82–83,

INDEX OF HOLY SCRIPTURE

References, limited to citations in the text, are to sections of the numbered Discourses.

Apocrypha